The Buckleys

A FAMILY EXAMINED

by Charles Lam Markmann

7844

WILLIAM MORROW & COMPANY, INC.
NEW YORK   1973

Printed in the United States of America

Markmann, Charles Lam.
    The Buckleys: a family examined.

    Bibliography: p.
    1. Buckley, William Frank, 1925-   2. Buckley, James
Lane, 1923-   3. Buckley family. I. Title.
E748.B8835M37   929'.2'0973   72-13137
ISBN 0-688-00152-1

We find it difficult to blow our own trumpet, to pose as charismatic leaders, to feel that self-assurance that permits others to believe in their indispensability to the world at large. We are, therefore, happier as advocates of someone else (a sibling will do); of, particularly, an intellectual or moral idea. . . .

If there is a "Buckley mystique," it is embedded there in the abiding recognition of our moral and intellectual deficiencies measured against the goal of perfection. We learned from our parents to prefer the good man to the brilliant man. It is a sacred humanity in people we respect. Our compassion is earned in the equality of the human condition. People are surprised to realize that we, princelings of Dame Fortune as they may feel us to be, tread the same hard interior landscape.

And it may be this that comes through, that fascinates, because we do not presume, "Come, let *us* lead you," but, instead, petition, "Come, our philosophy is your way, the human way, and it is you who will and must lead yourselves. . . ."

> —F. REID BUCKLEY, in
> "The Buckley Mystique,"
> *The New York Times*, 12 November 1970

Beware of the man who takes pride in his humility.
> —ISRAEL BAAL SHEM TOV
> (1699–1761), FOUNDER
> OF HASSIDISM

By Way of Explanation
and Acknowledgment

AMERICANS' NEED for a dynasty has long been plain. Having almost
grown out of its adulation of stark-naked plutocracy, the United
States was ready for the Kennedys, and they were no less girded
up to meet its need, but circumstances have aborted the fruit of
that union. Even before the bereavements, however, the Buckleys'
candidacy was lustily developing, and now it glows forth una-
bashed: moreover, all the evidence indicates that its acceptance by
the convenience-culture is anything but unlikely.

The Buckleys and their circle are the acknowledged and practical leaders of the growing American conservatism. They are the
rallying center for every kind of Rightist, from Archduke Otto
von Habsburg and Russell Kirk, with his multiple international
academic prestige, to the middle-class Jewish hooligans of Forest
Hills, New York, who burn construction offices in order to keep
out housing for the black and poor; and Buckley followers do not
by any means exclude admirers of George Wallace and members
of that John Birch Society that William F. Buckley Jr. has so
equivocally denounced. For years, too, his closest collaborators
have been men who spent the first halves of their lives as activists
in the totalitarianisms of the Left in preparation for their own
peculiar pilgrims' progress.

The Buckleys of the present generation, like the Kennedys, constitute a large Irish Catholic family in its first season of unearned
wealth and position. In each family the father was self-made, a
powerful arriviste in the business world with a determination to
establish his family at the highest social level and with an unshakable conviction of the unique rightness of his way of life. In each
family a younger son became the standard-bearer designated by a

buccaneer father who into and after the Second World War was closely linked with extreme isolationists and cold-warriors; and in each family that son gained national prominence remarkably early and (whatever his mask) took himself remarkably seriously with the utmost conviction of his mission. In each family the paladin's siblings are for the most part lesser fry solidly aligned behind him. In each family the pretty half-truth is too often the Law, the Prophets, and the Evangel. In each family the existing order is beyond question.

It is these fundamental characteristics that link the Kennedys and the Buckleys—these and a decided gift for panache and tinsel. The differences between the families are of another kind and may indeed be such as to make a Buckley dynasty much more plausible and attractive to the majority of Americans, and perhaps considerably more dangerous to the majority and the minority alike. The founding Kennedy was interested in money, power, and recognition merely as ends in themselves in a world made up of his betters; the founding Buckley was interested in those same three things as means, and at least equally concerned with intellectual, moral, and spiritual perfection as he conceived it his and his family's duty to preserve these qualities in a world made up largely of the lesser.

This basic element of goals, of motivations, is what apparently is universally overlooked by those who specialise in comparing and contrasting Buckleys and Kennedys. It is impossible, if one may borrow a metaphor from the literature of psychoanalysis, to conceive of any of the Buckleys as a man driven by the demons of a Don Juan. Nothing in their private or public *personae* conduces to the belief that what they do is done in order to gain reassurance of identity: they are clearly working for a cause in which—however dangerously for the society—they whole-heartedly and confidently believe. None of them bears any resemblance to the characteristic Kennedy striver—at least equally menacing to the society—ravaged incessantly by the need to prove his ability to repeat conquests (as if the body politic were an infinity of women to be perennially seduced) and painfully incapable of any vision or commitment beyond this egolatry.

The more outrageous the views that may emerge from this book, the more certainly they are the responsibility of the author alone.

But it would have been impossible even to attempt the work had it not been for the generous cooperation of friends and enemies of the Buckleys and, not least, of some of the Buckleys themselves who opened their gates to the declared enemy. To assess gradations of gratitude, however, would be impossible, and thanks would appear to be best extended by alphabetical precedence. If there seem to be enormities of omission, they derive from the author's unwillingness to afford a tribune to the self-serving and the professionally envious, and indeed from his refusal to waste time on anyone who is not, in the French phrase, a serious person. The exclusion of virtually all the *camelots de feu le roi*—who trafficked and traffic still in all the *camelote* that was Camelot—is obviously, therefore, intended.

Thanks go then to:

Louis Ames, Corporation for Public Broadcasting

The Rev. George R. Bach, Belchertown, Mass.

Roger Nash Baldwin, New York

Mr. and Mrs. Frank Bentley, Corrales, N.M.

Frances Bronson, Executive Secretary, *National Review*

F. Reid Buckley, Madrid

The Hon. James L. Buckley, New York, Sharon, Conn., and Washington, D.C.

John W. Buckley, Lakeville, Conn.

Priscilla L. Buckley, Managing Editor, *National Review*

William F. Buckley Jr., New York and Stamford, Conn.

James Burnham, *National Review*

Ellen Carney, *Firing Line*

Boyd D. Cathey, Mecosta, Mich.

The Rev. William Sloane Coffin Jr., Yale University

Mr. and Mrs. Peter Coley, Madison, Conn.

Prof. and Mrs. William B. Coley, Middletown, Conn.

Kevin Corrigan, New York and Riverside, Conn.

Francis Donahue, *Yale Daily News*

Agatha S. Dowd, Director of Research, *National Review*

W. H. von Dreele, New York

L. Clayton DuBois, Washington, D.C.

Harry Elmlark, President and Editor, Washington Star Syndicate

Prof. Thomas I. Emerson, Yale Law School

Jean Evans, Curtis Brown Ltd.

Mrs. DeLancey Ferguson, Falls Village, Conn.

Prof. Irving Ferman, Howard University School of Law, Washington, D.C.

Joseph Fischle Jr., Corrales, N.M.

Neal B. Freeman, Executive Editor, King Features Syndicate

William Gavin, former Assistant Director, United States Information Agency

Ira Glasser, Executive Director, New York Civil Liberties Union

Maurice Goldbloom, New York

The Hon. Charles E. Goodell, New York

Mrs. Frances Goudy, Special Collections Librarian, Vassar College

Jeff Greenfield, New York

Dr. Milton O. Gustafson, Acting Chief, Diplomatic Branch, Civil Archives Division, General Services Administration

Michael Harrington, former co-chairman, Socialist Party

James V. Healion, Bureau Chief, United Press International, Hartford, Conn.

Karl Hess, Institute for Policy Studies

The Editors of Jarrow Press

John L. Jones, Executive Director, American Conservative Union

Daniel F. Joy, former Director of Public Relations, Young Americans for Freedom

Murray Kempton, New York

Peter Kihss, *The New York Times*

Dr. Russell Kirk, Mecosta, Mich.

Prof. George F. Kneller, University of California, Los Angeles

Irene Corbally Kuhn, New York

Dr. Ralph A. Lewin, Scripps Institution of Oceanography, La Jolla, Calif.

J. Daniel Mahoney, New York

Serphin R. Maltese, Executive Director, Conservative Party of New York State

Eric McCrossen, chief editorial writer, Albuquerque *Tribune* and *Journal*

Wesley McCune, Director, Group Research, Inc., Washington, D.C.

John McMillion, business manager, Albuquerque *Tribune* and *Journal*

James McQuinn, Project Coordinator, Southern Educational Communications Association, Columbia, S.C.

The late Frank S. Meyer, *National Review*

Aryeh Neier, Executive Director, American Civil Liberties Union

Christopher Olson, West Albuquerque, N.M.

Robert Osborn, Salisbury, Conn.

Prof. Rollin G. Osterweis, Yale University

Judson Philips (Hugh Pentecost), Sharon, Conn.

Richard Reed, Alhambra, Ill.

Alan Reitman, Associate Executive Director, American Civil Liberties Union

William F. Rickenbacker, Editor, *Rickenbacker Report*

Mrs. Carol Rhoades Robinson, Sharon, Conn.

Prof. Fred Rodell, Yale Law School

Prof. Murray N. Rothbard, New York

Michael Rufolo, *The News*

William A. Rusher, Publisher, *National Review*

Leonard Saffir, Press Secretary to Senator James Buckley

Mrs. Gladys Segal, Group Research, Inc., Washington, D.C.

Prof. Richard Sewall, Yale University

Stephen Shaffer, Albuquerque, N.M.

Artie Shaw, New York

Ernestine Smith, Group Research, Inc., Washington, D.C.

William D. Smith, *The New York Times*

Dr. Benjamin Spock, New York

Mr. and Mrs. George Norton Stone, Lakeville, Conn.

Dr. Michael O. Stone, University of New Mexico, Albuquerque

John Stratton III, Assistant Director, Yale University News Bureau

Mary Sullivan, Yale University News Bureau

Paul Sweeney, Assistant Producer, *Firing Line*

Randal Cornell Teague, Executive Director, Young Americans for Freedom

Ralph de Toledano, Washington, D.C.

Lois Wallace, William Morris Agency

Tom Wallace, Editor-in-Chief, adult books, Holt, Rinehart & Winston

James Wechsler, Editorial Page Editor, *New York Post*

Prof. Paul Weiss, Catholic University of America, Washington, D.C.

James R. Welsh, Sharon, Conn.

Sylvia Westerman, *Face The Nation*, Washington, D.C.

Garry Wills, Baltimore, Md.
Henry S. Wright, Springfield, N.J.
Robert H. Yoakum, Lakeville, Conn.
William Zinsser, Yale Alumni Publications, Inc., New Haven

A special debt is owed to the handful of research workers
without whom the endless but essential drudgery incident to such
a book could never have been accomplished: Myrna Fishman,
Brooklyn; Patricia Flanagan, Middletown, Conn.; Michael H. P.
Flynn Jr., Middletown, Conn.; Carole J. Gottschalk, New York;
Diana Greenly, Newbury, Berks., England; Betty Burger Jones,
New York and Flint, Mich.; Francine Krisel, New York, and
Chris Robbins, Middletown, Conn.

Nor can I omit to acknowledge the secretarial assistance of
Lisa Bentz, New York; Mary L. Britton, Lakeville, Conn.; Ellen
Charak, New York; Diane Steelman, New York; and, most especially, Donna M. Sliby, New York and Paris, and Cecilia Somer-
ville, New York.

I am most appreciative of the perceptive editing of James Landis
of William Morrow & Co., and of Rachel Whitebook.

My debt to Oscar Collier and James F. Seligmann is *sui generis*.

The Buckleys

I

"Conservatives do not deny the existence of undiscovered truths, but they make a critical assumption, which is that those truths that have *already* been apprehended are more important to cultivate than those undisclosed ones close to the liberal grasp only in the sense that the fruit was close to Tantalus, yet around whose existence virtually the whole of modern academic theory revolves. Conservatism is the tacit acknowledgment that all that is finally important in human experience is behind us; that the crucial explorations have been undertaken, and that it is given to man to know what are the great truths that emerged from them. Whatever is to come cannot outweigh the importance to man of what has gone before."

The man who wrote that paragraph, italics and all, is the leader of a band that has taken it upon itself to change the course of the United States by, in the first instance, pointing a gun at the President. The man who wrote that paragraph spent nine years and a great deal of his own money to save a stranger whom he believed innocent and who had been sentenced to the electric chair. The man who wrote that paragraph accomplished more for himself and his cause by losing his campaign for the Mayoralty of New York than he might ever have gained by winning election. He has been called "Rapier on the Right" (by *The Wall Street Journal*) and "The Show-Biz Conservative" (by *Life*).

His elder brother was elected Senator from New York on the Conservative Party ticket—a fourth party. His eldest brother is the head of an international nexus of closely held companies engaged in oil, gas, mineral, and some manufacturing ventures in a dozen countries. Two of his sisters tried to drive the "liberals" and the "Reds" out of the most august of the women's colleges; one of those sisters publicly assaulted a leader of women's liberation on the ground that she had insulted God and his mother.

The author of the paragraph is William F. Buckley Jr., whose father inculcated in him the conservative creed as well as the Catholic faith, and left him the financial means to work for the redemption of his country. In addition to doctrine and money, his mother and father endowed him and his nine brothers and sisters with genuine education, not merely schooling; deep culture, refined taste, exquisite manners, lively curiosity, and an independence of spirit to match their independence of fortune. All the Buckleys were imbued as well with a fierce, almost fanatical family loyalty that has made them an unbroken phalanx against all comers. Brought up to believe that the secularists, Socialists, and Communists and their dupes were taking over the country, the Buckleys regard themselves as appointed to save it and to lead the forces of light in restoring the old, good order.

Their whole creed, and that of the considerable movement that has come to acknowledge them, and especially William Jr., as its chiefs, is epitomised in the quotation from his *UP From Liberalism* with which this book begins. It is their stated objective to turn back time and culture and to re-establish an aristocracy of which, it goes without saying, they are already the cornerstone. To this end the most active of them, William Jr.—Bill—has published a full dozen of books, carried on a syndicated newspaper column for eleven years, conducted a network television debate program for seven years, written innumerable magazine articles, made thirty lectures on conservatism every year, and, for eighteen years, published a thin fortnightly, *National Review*, that has acquired a political influence out of all proportion to its small and unprofitable circulation. As a reporter in a paper opposed to all that the Buckleys represent has observed, Bill Buckley "is 'Mr. Conservative' to millions."

Since 1970 he has not stood alone in this rôle. When, to the amazement of all the "experts" on all sides, James Buckley was elected to the Senate on an unequivocally conservative, if not reactionary, platform from that same New York State that only a few years previously, in the befuddlement of drawing-room-liberal circus antics, had elected Robert Kennedy to the same seat, American conservatism could no longer be written off as a fluke or a freak. By that time President Nixon had appointed the Buckleys' close friend, Frank Shakespeare, to be director of the United States Information Agency, and Shakespeare had successfully urged the President to appoint Bill Buckley to the agency's Advisory Commission. Bill Buckley had for ten years had access to Nixon, and he continued to use that access until his discontent with the President's conduct led him first to head a public "suspension of support" for Nixon and then, in mid-March of 1972, even when Nixon, in his fright, had begun again to try to curry favor with the Right Wing to which he largely owed his election, to slap the President's face by refusing reappointment to the USIA Advisory Commission and to augment his public criticisms of the Administration's policies both foreign and domestic.

All the Buckleys, including the quiet ones and the youngest brother, Reid—who lives in Spain, writes bad novels and indifferent screenplays, and, like Bill, makes an annual lecture tour to spread the gospel of conservatism to the universities—are dedicated advocates of holy war against Communism. Bill Buckley has for years been urging the bombing of Chinese factories and military intervention in Eastern Europe; he has denounced the preservation of radicals' and dissenters' civil liberties in this country. In the latter matter he has had the full support of his brother in the Senate. They are firm champions of increased powers for the police and diminishing concern for arrested persons. They insist that they are not racists, but they and the rest of the conservative movement that they lead turn up invariably on the side of the most vehement segregationists; and to William Jr. in November of 1971 the Chinese were "a race of madmen who in a single century have slaughtered many times the number of men who gave their lives for their faith during the first two millennia of Christendom." The Buckleys declare their love of human life, so that abortion is anathema to them, and they simply do not understand what it is to be poor or why the poor do not stop being poor. They fearlessly call on the nations under Communist rule to rise in revolt, reminding them that it is nobler for them to be dead than to be Red, and they are enraged by young—or less young—Americans who risk their bodies and their freedom to endeavor to stop the massacres perpetrated in Vietnam by an American imperialism that the Buckleys refuse to recognise even if the nation's biggest banks have for years been the most intimate of the camp followers in Vietnam. The Buckleys are proud of their Catholicism and their devoutness, and they denounce clergy of

whatever rank, up to and including the papacy, for social, political, or economic utterances at variance with the most Calvinistic
of Manchester liberalisms and the most un-Christian of self-aggran-
disements and -enrichments.

The Buckleys have never been quite so extravagantly praised
by their admirers as they have been flayed by their enemies, and
the identities of some of these are distinctly a credit to the Buckleys. Gore Vidal, who is so often their mirror image, has called
them "the sick Kennedys" simply because they are numerous,
rich, Catholic, and of Irish extraction—and *not* hypocrites. Vidal
has not been, it is true, deceived by the decency—it is real, but
it is very strictly confined—that is so impressive in all the Buckleys
and yet cannot or does not inhibit the lowest blows, the most
unkind stabs, the most unjust personal attacks; but no one has
publicised the innumerable acts of kindness and generosity, many
of which are not well known even within the Buckley family.
To return to their enemies, it is to the credit of the Buckleys
that they have never had or wanted the esteem of, say, a junior
Schlesinger. On the other hand, they have lent their own prestige
and authority to such egregious *canaille* as Joseph McCarthy, his
epigone, Roy Cohn, Richard Nixon, Spiro Agnew, John Mitchell,
the late Thomas Dodd, and that ultimate vulgarian, Al Capp.

These men are all heroes to the lower middle class, too—and
that is the overwhelming majority of Americans. It is there, far
more than in the upper middle class, that the aristocratic Buckleys
have created a loyal following. To the less sophisticated, these
rich and well-spoken men who share their basic ideas of good
and evil, of God and Stalin, represent the ideal lords for the ideal
lieges, in both their private and their public comportment. More
than anything else, they relieve the strivers of the burden of
identity, which the Buckleys most gracefully assume for them.
Those who hunger for a demigod to follow, who for all their generations in America as free citizens of a supposedly classless democracy retain the feudal impulses that are by no means confined to
the South, find it natural and reassuring to be recruited into the
Buckleys' host, the legion of what is good and familiar. Both these
masters and these servants are to be taken with the utmost seriousness if only, as Michael Harrington, the former co-chairman
of the Socialist Party, emphasised recently, "because of the obvious trend in New York State, and certainly among Irish Catholic
workers, who've been moving to the Right for thirty, forty years.

. . . The Conservative Party [which was founded with Buckley brains and Buckley money and Buckley manpower] is a very serious development that could be a portent of significant changes in American political life. And the Buckleys obviously are the first family of this not inconsiderable phenomenon."

I said that the Buckleys' greatest appeal is to the lower middle class. This is not to pretend that they do not exercise a strong attraction elsewhere: particularly in certain segments of the academic community and among the young. Their own youthful conservative militancy, many Buckleys have said, was in a sense their way of rebellion—not against family and tradition but against the nonconforming conformism they found round them in their colleges. Their creation, Young Americans for Freedom, has struck roots all across the country among a new generation of young people who rebel at the cult of the scruffy and of the cop-out, who are greedy to accumulate the possessions and the supposed status that so many of their contemporaries have grown up enough to look at askance. One has only to teach, for instance, in any public college to recognise how unready for revolution, how ripe for counter-revolution, are most of the sons and daughters of the no longer silent majority—and it is the majority. As James Burnham of Buckley's *National Review*, once an authoritative figure in the Trotskyist movement, rightly points out, organised conservatism in the United States is still in the minority, but inarticulate conservative sentiment is the prevailing mode.

As usual, what has been happening in Europe has laggardly crossed the Atlantic. For ten years the swing back to the Right has been growing in Europe, which never got much, if any, beyond a tenuous center—in Christian Democratic Germany and Italy, in Gaullist and post-Gaullist France. Corrupted by the American economic and cultural invasion, the Right in those countries has, like so many converts, outdone its American exemplars (the current government of Germany by a party that nostalgically calls itself Social Democratic is no contradiction of the thesis) and is falling back into its pre-war forms. The Buckleys deny any contact with the new German Right led until recently by Adolf von Thadden and other former Nazis and dependent for its votes primarily on people who had not been born when, as we like to delude ourselves, Naziism "fell," or with the *Movimento sociale italiano* under Marchese Valerio Borghese and Giorgio Almirante, again reliant on brand-new voters who must have learned through some Lysenko-like process the *squadrista* terrorism and the Mussolinian histrionics whose originator was shot before they were begot. But *Nationaldemokratische Partei Deutschlands*, MSI, or Young Americans for Freedom and Conservative Party, they all have the same programs, the same ideals and the same methods: "law and order," repression of dissent, selective franchise, rule by oligarchy, minimal government intervention in the economy, maximal government intervention in private morality, state support for religion, exclusion of the alien, "anti-Communism," and preparation for war against "the Communists." It is not coincidence that Bill Buckley has close friends in the most conservative circles in Britain and that one extreme Right-Wing British journalist with impeccable connections and sound knowledge of the United States believes that the Buckleys can go as high as they wish in American politics.

But it is not personal ambition or vanity that makes them dangerous: on the contrary. Bill Buckley does not want public office; James Buckley is more often than not uncomfortable in it. What is hardest for their compatriots to conceive is that they do not really want anything for themselves: they actually serve an ideal without ulterior motive. Nothing is more dangerous than a fundamentally honest champion of a cause that he values above himself. The Buckleys have nothing of the desire for eminence of a von Thadden or a Borghese or an Almirante—or a Nixon or a Kennedy: therefore Buckleys will not trim and trade in all the shabby dickering that is the price of successful personal politicking. The politician on the make is not much of a menace: one way or another, he can always be bought off or fooled or flattered, or frightened, or stampeded, as recent history amply attests. But the man with a cause knows he has the true faith for all men, and only death will stop his work for that cause, regardless what surrogates he may send into battle or establish in power: all that matters to him is the principle and its prevailing.

This is a fascinating phenomenon in a country where a man of honor is as rare as a unicorn. Two of them in the same generation of the same family constitute almost a divine portent. Some rural wiseacres—head-scratching newspaper editors among the mesas, perhaps—may be too smart to be taken in by such clever fellers, but they will very likely still be scratching their heads and admiring their own smartness when the clever fellers have taken in all the rest of the country.

Now, after the spring of 1972, when James Buckley was genuinely resisting the growing movement to nominate him in place of Spiro Agnew as the Republican Vice Presidential candidate for 1972 and when the enlarging ranks of Young Americans for Freedom, acclaiming Bill Buckley as the man they would most like to grow up to be, were talking more and more seriously of James as President of the United States within a decade, the Buckleys have mounting support also in the colleges and universities. Real scholars like Russell Kirk are their untiring advocates; worn-out 1930's "liberals" and once more-or-less radicals like Sidney Hook collaborate with them in the Lord's work; young scholars with impressive credentials, like Peter Witonski of Harvard, preach the good tidings of conservatism. Reactionaries frightened by the paranoias of the John Birch Society turn gratefully to the reasonable Rightism of the Buckleys and *National Review*. Solid, uncomplicated Middle Americans everywhere read Bill Buckley three times a week in four hundred newspapers, or watch him every week for an hour on well over a hundred television stations; thousands crowd to hear him lecture in the flesh, and as many more fill whatever auditorium James Buckley can be persuaded to visit for a speech. In newspapers throughout the country every broadcast of Bill's *Firing Line* is exhaustively reported and commented on, usually with admiration. His only child, Christopher Taylor Buckley, a Yale sophomore, was chairman of Youth Against McGovern in the autumn of 1972 (the absence of Nixon's name from the organisational title is not oversight).

Why are the Buckleys so attractive? For one thing, because they are honest Right-Wingers and make no pretenses otherwise. For another, because they preach and, at least seemingly, practice that planless free enterprise that is the American cliché. Furthermore, they are so much more plausible than their striving opponents of the center and the "Left": the Buckleys are relaxed, with that tranquillity that comes of being born into wealth, a homogeneous family, superior intelligence, and The One True Faith That Is Salvation; they know they are right, know it in their blood, and so they rarely need to emphasise or strain in defense of what they and most of the rest of the nation already accept, whereas the "liberals" and the "radicals" must exert every effort to convert, to persuade, to convince. And, too, the Buckleys are always so obviously having fun doing what they do—there is never anything of that faintly unpleasant Messiah touch of self-righteousness that no Kennedy could ever shed. The Buckleys, moreover, know their business, which is conservatism, and that is a quality that Americans have always respected; whereas, as the man in the street always felt uneasily, the Kennedys had continually been so preoccupied with their own advancement that in all the non-personal issues and problems on which they attempted to touch they were always, it was glaringly obvious, the rankest *dilettanti*, whether they were playing at civil rights with other people's blood and bodies or promulgating New Frontier Culture Conveyors.

The two Buckley brothers who represent the family to the nation are ideally complementary. James is indeed what he seems to be: natural, warm, bright, sincere, essentially shy, genuinely modest. Bill is brash, slightly less learned than he may appear, tricky, skill-fully savage, capable of great tenderness, a lover of language and music and color and form and mountains and the sea, a scintillat-ing performer with that precise blend of the aristocratic and the faintly vulgar that virtually no one can resist. People who would be slightly afraid to vote for anyone so brilliant and elusive are nonetheless won by him, and easily persuaded to vote for the man who, he tells them, epitomises the ideals by which and for which they and their progenitors have lived, the ideals that are all Ameri-cans' ideals. Thoughtful high-school boys often try to emulate him; girls are much taken with him. He provides the color and, with his international ties, the glamour; Jim is the solid, dependable plugger who spends hours watching birds and figuring things out and then goes unspectacularly but effectively to work to protect our neighborhoods and our schools and our environment, who at the end of a hard week far from the Washington cocktail circuit flew home (until his family moved south) to a country week-end with his wife and six children, none of whom is likely ever to permit the exploitation that made the Potemkin village of Camelot, and who was back on the job early Monday morning.

And the job he is trying to do is one that Middle America wants done. The twenty-odd years of harping on the Red Menace may bore more than amuse by now, in some circles; but it admirably answers Middle America's need for a scapegoat and a devil. In polysyllables or in monosyllables, with knife in the groin or simple good-faith reasoning and appeals to what we all believe, it is more than comforting to observe St. George in duplicate doing battle against the Red dragons.

Bill is the philosophical St. George. When he offers conservatives that same frighteningly pessimistic philosophy—all the truths that matter have been learned, there is nothing left to discover—that was Edmund Burke's justification for the status quo two hundred years ago and Plato's two thousand years ago, his acolytes are grateful for the absolute that he has given them (for relativism, he preaches, is a snare of Lucifer and his card-carrying helots) and do not analyse it to its conclusion: it is a doctrine of deadness and despair. They see it only as security: but death too is security. This is the absolute that the Buckleys would offer the American people, and that in all probability the majority of that people will with pitiful eagerness embrace. That is why the Buckleys, who are so often—though not this time—right as well as Right, are so dangerous.

II

"I wrote somewhere—I forget where," William F. Buckley Jr.
said toward the end of 1971, "that I simply wasn't aware that we
were somewhere along the line taxonomised as Irish Catholics until
somebody told me, and that was fifteen years after I graduated
from college."

One's initial disbelief persists when one reflects that all his
father's grandparents came from Counties Cork and Limerick. The
skepticism is shaken, however, when one reflects that Sartre once
defined a Jew as anyone whom others regard as a Jew, while
Malamud (quoted by Buckley) preferred to define him as one
who considers himself a Jew. There is also the kind of mind to
which a man with a black parent is a *nigger*. The alien component
is usually important only to those for whom it has a pejorative
use. Verbal pyrotechnic aside, then, one's surprise abates when
one reflects further how very little it takes to make one an alien
in the eyes of a society, regardless of one's own view.

F. Reid Buckley, the youngest of William Frank Buckley Sr.'s
four sons, told the story of the family's American beginnings in
the chapter he contributed to the memorial volume that the family
published privately after William Sr.'s death. The first Buckley
to cross the Atlantic westward was an Irish Protestant who had
married a Catholic and who found it advisable to leave with her
after he had split another Protestant's skull with a plowshare in a
dispute over an Orangemen's parade route. The proto-Buckley
went to Quebec and then to Ontario, where, though he remained
a Protestant, his children were brought up as Catholics. One of
them, John, moved to Texas, where he maintained his father's tradition of strong action in support of strong views, became a county

sheriff, and fathered six sons and two daughters. The fourth son
was William Sr., who was born in 1881 and who was twenty-three
when his father died.

The family was then living in the town of San Diego, in the
southwest Texas cow country. Ninety per cent of the population
of two thousand was of Mexican or Spanish origin, and Buckley
grew up totally bilingual. Before he went to the University of
Texas in Austin he taught in the local elementary school, and at
the university he taught Spanish while he was an undergraduate
(as William Jr. was later to do at Yale). His mother had indoctrinated him thoroughly with patriotism and religion; he had begun
serving the altar very early and continued to do so for fifteen
years, even during university vacations. He worked to meet most
of his university expenses; after his father's death he recognised
that he could not continue his studies unless his eighteen-year-old
sister, Priscilla, went to work. She became a translator and later a
teacher, sacrificing any personal ambitions to the support and education of her brothers and sister.

In college and law school Buckley was apparently highly regarded by fellow-students and faculty members, and his friendship
was often prized. Walter S. Pope, one of the contributors to the
family's memoir, comments—approvingly—that his friend never,
to Pope's knowledge, had a date with a girl but spent all his leisure
with his semi-invalid mother and his male friends. His Catholicism
was intense; his admiring old friend recalls the baseball game between the University of Texas and St. Edward's College at which
the priest who was umpiring made a decision that angered a hereti-
cal student into shouting: "That damn priest is lying," whereupon
Buckley knocked him down.

But it was his eldest child, Aloïse Buckley Heath, now dead,
who wrote proudly of the time when her father, still a student, was
pressed for funds and entered an essay competition for a hundred-
dollar prize offered by an insurance company. He won; but by so
doing he was disqualified from future competition. The next year,
however, he again needed money; and the contest was held again.
Buckley wrote another essay, submitted it under a friend's name,
and won again; he paid his friend ten per cent of the prize for his
collusion.

Appointed translator in the Texas General Land Office while
still a student, Buckley resigned when, having earned his law degree, he decided to practice in Mexico. Subsequently two of his

brothers, Claude and Edmund, took over the practice when he concluded, as he wrote to Pope in 1914, after six years, that "the practice of law is the most trying thing in the world." Will Buckley was a man of considerable courage, and what might be called an admirable gambler: when he perceived a potential in a situation he would very deliberately plunge regardless of the inadequacy of his resources, borrowing in a manner that to most business men and certainly to most lawyers must have seemed reckless. No doubt it sometimes was; his children have written that "Father's broke again" was not an uncommon announcement in his various well-staffed homes and on the family's various *grand-luxe* travels. *Broke*, of course, is a relative adjective.

It was oil that first lured Buckley away from law in Mexico, where he had worked so hard in his first big year that he had had to spend the entire ensuing summer under medical care in the United States—a curious aspect of the cult of success that appears always to have been peculiarly American. His letter recites the fact almost as if it were an achievement; and anyone who grew up among Americans of similar ethos will recall how many of them have often recounted similar anecdotes with comparable complacency. Thus, at this debatable cost, Buckley had accumulated a small but respectable fortune in Mexico before he was thirty-five.

Men who worked with him in those years—Mexican associates and subordinates—have testified to his love for their country, his respect for its sovereignty, his friendship and esteem for its people. Yet on 6 December 1919—two years before his expulsion from Mexico—Buckley told a subcommittee of the Senate Foreign Relations Committee: "The truth is that it does not matter what a great majority of the Mexican people think; the mass of the people have not the ability to think clearly; and have not the knowledge on which to base convictions, or the public spirit to act on them." And again, describing for the same hearing a Pan-American conference summoned by the United States in 1914, when, as he said, it was "supporting bandits in Mexico," Buckley declared: "The Latin American representatives in this case showed the weakness that men of their race usually show in a crisis."

Buckleyan political orientations first appeared in connection with the Mexican revolutions that resulted in the presidency of Gen. Alvaro Obregón. Will Buckley was on eminently sound ground in denouncing President Wilson for his efforts to help the Mexicans arrive at the self-determination that would please Wilson and his circle—a typical manifestation of what the late H. L. Mencken has called the international Calvinism of the United States. But Buckley as a private person was hardly less guilty: he exerted all his influence, his friendships, and his economic power to defeat the Mexican revolution—he was especially outraged, as he informed the Senate subcommittee and his friends, by its resolution to break the grip of the church, though that was not how he put it—and in November of 1921 he was expelled from Mexico by Presidential order. The ground alleged was counter-revolutionary conspiracy, a melodramatic charge in which there may have been some truth.

A man who never concealed his views, Buckley had for years been sending reports to American officials in which he was as openly disparaging of the Mexican revolution as he was in conversation with Mexicans. Obviously his religious, economic, and political alignments would have accounted at once for his ideological opposition to what he regarded as atheism and socialism; in addition he was angered by the endemic corruption that existed everywhere and that thrived in particular on the greed of foreign—which essentially meant American—business and industry. Buckley was especially angered by the willingness (and perhaps the resources) of the large oil companies to buy what was so universally for sale; as far as can be determined he never took a mortgage on any revolutionary's allegiances.

As long as Woodrow Wilson was President of the United States, Buckley could not command much of a hearing in his own country, though there is no question that his reports from Mexico, where he was living and conducting his oil business, as well as ventures in real-estate development, were voluminous, detailed and circumstantially not inaccurate. He had served as counsel to the pre-revolutionary oligarchic Mexican government at the Niagara conference of the A.B.C. powers—Argentina, Brazil, and Chile—that mediated between the United States and Mexico after the United States' naval bombardment of the port of Vera Cruz in April, 1914. Victoriano Huerta, the repressive President backed by Buckley's friends, the *científicos*—the educated upper class that owned and operated the country—had defied Wilson's command that he hold free elections; he was being armed by Germany, and Wilson was therefore arming the so-called constitutionalists who opposed Huerta; in addition Wilson seized the port in order to prevent the German munitions from reaching Huerta, and to punish him for having arrested United States Marines who had landed at Tampico.

The military governorship of Vera Cruz was then offered to
Buckley, whose refusal of it was a point of pride for the rest of
his life.

Regardless who was in power, Buckley, like all the other foreigners resolved to make their fortunes in Mexico, continued to do
business, and indeed to prosper. He lacked the means and hence the
power of the giant companies, and he was always their adversary,
though he could do business with them when it was to his advantage—in Mexico, in Venezuela, and elsewhere later. He was possibly no better and certainly no worse than everyone else in an
industry never known for Christian forbearance, and the practices
recognised in it were applied by him, as by others, in their ancil-
lary activities. One of these, for Buckley, was large-scale real-
estate development, and his daughter Priscilla, now managing editor
of *National Review*, has described one such venture in her contribution to the memorial volume (the copyright to which, by the
way, is vested in her). Her father transformed a large sandbar in
the Pánuco River into what was named Buckley Island, complete
with streets, sewers, and lights. He was ready to sell building lots
when his local lawyer, in collusion with a judge, perpetrated a
forgery that ostensibly invalidated Buckley's title. He sent for a
Texas gunman and "a dozen of the toughest fellows he knew" and
posted them to the island with shotguns, at twenty-five American
dollars a day, to prevent his former lawyer from selling the lots.
This was so effective that the judge in question came to heel and
"we fixed it up": the validity of Buckley's deeds was formally
reconfirmed.

(Douglas Reed, an early business associate, gives a rather different version in his chapter in the memorial volume. According
to him, squatters invaded the real-estate development, and "Buckley
convinced the authorities that the neighborhood sportsmen sorely
needed a rifle range on the property for practicing their marks-
manship." Thus "persuaded of the basic human right which they
had challenged," the squatters withdrew.)

On the land between his own mainland house and the river a
squatter built a shack without the formality of permission. Buckley,
according to his daughter, said to Ramón, his servant ("the world's
laziest man but he would work feverishly if he ever had the
opportunity to earn a dishonest dollar"), that every stick of the
shack would belong to Ramón—"I don't care *what* happens to
it"—if it were gone by the next morning. When, subsequently,

the squatter came with the police to complain, Buckley resolved the whole question, for which he had been called away from a dinner party, with the observation that he knew nothing of any house built on his land without his permission. On the other hand, when he was under surveillance by the Mexican military authorities, he displayed exemplary consideration to his tails, seeing to it that they were provided with drink, transport, and his detailed timetable and itinerary—a gesture that one can only commend.

His testimony before the Senate subcommittee in 1919, which was highly tendentious, increased the antagonism toward him that existed in most sections of Mexican opinion. He had opposed American intervention on behalf of the revolutionists who wanted to throw out Huerta's dictatorship, but he had testified in favor of unarmed intervention on behalf of what he called "the decent people of that country," the majority of whom, he maintained, had been expelled from Mexico "with the tacit consent of the American government." But he was vehemently opposed to the use of force by the United States, even to overthrow the enemies of the church and the foreign property-holder. Yet he never denied his involvement in the *opera buffa* failure of a counter-revolutionary movement led by a Gen. Manuel Pelaez, whose ammunition train, sponsored by Buckley, got lost as its Washington representative, an old intimate of Buckley, was announcing himself to the State Department in Washington as the Pelaez "government's" representative.

Once the Republicans had taken over again in the United States, under Warren G. Harding, Buckley campaigned vigorously against recognition of Obregón's government in Mexico and formed The American Association of Mexico early in 1921, with offices in New York and Washington. He himself was commuting fairly regularly between the two countries, and maintaining a residence with his bride in Bronxville. His Association denounced Obregón as the associate, if not the accomplice, of "dangerous bolshevists" and his Cabinet as the fief of radicals. In 1919 he had told the subcommittee: "I think we should settle this matter with Mexico without reference to Latin America or to what Latin Americans or anybody else thinks; I think we should settle it in the right way without reference to anybody else." Of the conference at which he had represented the "decent people," he said that all such meetings were useless: "Latin America respects us more when we attend to our own business and do not call Latin Americans in for consultation. Our relations with Mexico are our own business and nobody else's." *Autres temps, autres noms de pays. . . .* This opponent of armed intervention had concluded by stating that "nothing would have raised our prestige so in Latin America as the dispatching of an army across the border the first time an American was touched and the execution of all those who had injured him." To his credit, Buckley was more than willing that every word of his testimony be published: "I would not give testimony for consideration only in executive session."

The memorial volume, however, is less expansive. "Witness," a chapter of more than eighty pages, consists entirely of excerpts from the transcript; but almost twenty pages are omitted, and one wonders whether the only reason is that of space: much of what is left out, it is true, is dull, but much more is interesting and some is fascinating. For example, pages 839–40 of the original official transcript, after a tribute to Edward L. Doheny, an American oil man who was to figure prominently in the Teapot Dome corruption, tell more about the General Pelaez to whom the family's book referred so amusingly but cursorily. The questioner was Francis J. Kearful, counsel to the subcommittee.

MR. KEARFUL: What do you know about the practice of the oil companies in paying tribute to Manuel Pelaez?

MR. BUCKLEY: The oil companies are paying a monthly tribute to Pelaez, but the charges made against them to the effect that they are deliberately financing Pelaez are untrue. They are paying Pelaez, not because they want to, but because Pelaez compels them to. Pelaez has given them protection, the protection that they could not get from the constituted government, but nevertheless, they are so short-sighted that he has had to force them to give him the money to support his troops; the only thing that has stood in the way of actual confiscation of the oil fields is the fact that Pelaez has had possession of those fields for the greater part of the time.

MR. KEARFUL: Are you personally acquainted with Pelaez?

MR. BUCKLEY: Yes, I know him well.

MR. KEARFUL: What character of man is he?

MR. BUCKLEY: Pelaez is a splendid type of Mexican. He and his two brothers are men of independent means, were born and reared in the territory now constituting the oil fields; they have always been leaders in that section and law-abiding citizens. They took little part in politics and were ready to submit, and did submit, to the new regime upon the flight of Huerta, but the Carrancistas* were not content with this submission; the Pelaez brothers had property and stock and money and the Carrancistas proceeded to take over their stock and hold them up for forced loans. After depriving them of all the money they had, the Carrancistas kept demanding more, and finally Manuel Pelaez had the alternative of leaving the country or revolting, and he preferred the latter.

MR. KEARFUL: What is the attitude of Pelaez toward Americans?

MR. BUCKLEY: The evidence of everybody in that country, the evidence of the oil companies, the reports of the American consuls and special investigators of the American Government, all show that Pelaez has been uniformly friendly toward Americans. The State Department is in possession of a mass of evidence to this effect. Ninety per cent of the robberies and murders of Americans that have been committed in the oil fields have occurred in the territory controlled by Carrancistas, and most of them have been perpetrated by Carrancistas. Pelaez has given Americans and their properties, and Mexicans and their property, every protection. During the war, when Carranza was pro-German and was trying to drive Pelaez out of the fields with arms and ammunition obtained in the United States with the consent of the American Government, Pelaez was pro-ally, was protecting the oil fields for the Americans and the Allies and was driving out of these fields all German spies that were reported to him by either the oil companies or the American consuls.

MR. KEARFUL: How is Pelaez regarded by the Mexican people in that locality?

MR. BUCKLEY: He is looked upon by the Mexican people in that section of the country as their only hope, the man who has saved them from the confiscation of their properties. The fact that he has remained there for four years, with scarcely

---

* The followers of Venustiano Carranza, who in the Mexican civil wars succeeded Huerta as President and whose recognition by Washington Buckley opposed.—C.L.M.

any resources and no arms or ammunition outside of what
he could capture or buy from the Carrancistas is evidence
of the support of the people.

On the other hand, the memorial volume does not omit this
interchange:

MR. KEARFUL: What class of people were his [Obregón's] forces
    composed of?
MR. BUCKLEY: Almost entirely of Yaqui Indians.

The confusion of class with race was not an isolated instance,
either at that time or in that person. Indeed, it lends substance to
the argument that the Buckleys are not primarily racists as such.

In any event, the point of view enunciated by Buckley before
the subcommittee and constantly reiterated in The American Association's irregular *Bulletins* consistently exacerbated the feelings
of Mexicans in government who detested all Americans anyway.
They detested equally the Association's program, which was aimed
at undoing all the confiscatory legislation, restoring the special
privileges of United States citizens, and eliminating the "humiliat-
ing provision of the Constitution of 1917 that forbids an American
clergyman of any denomination to exercise his sacred office in
Mexico." In the perspective of time it is difficult indeed not to be
neutral against both sides in this quarrel. There seems to be no
evidence that Buckley engaged again in such overt activities as
those involving Pelaez, and the order of expulsion would appear to
have immediately followed his refusal to pay the bribe of fifty
thousand pesos demanded for the revalidation of his Tampico
land contracts (though, according to his tale to his children, he did
succeed in arranging matters).

Buckley was further told that he would be allowed to leave
privately, without a guard, and after a grace period for the liquida-
tion of his affairs. Obregón asserted that such a departure would
be "best for the safety of Mr. Buckley," who replied properly that,
if this were the sole consideration involved, he would risk his
safety and remain. Having thus called the bluff, he was formally
expelled under a safe-conduct dated 27 November 1921, and he
thereupon applied to the State Department in Washington, by
letter of 20 January 1922, in which he "invoke[d] the protection
and redress to which I may be entitled." The letter, on eleven
single-spaced legal-size pages, rehearsed, not untendentiously, the
history of relations between Mexico and the United States as well

as between Mexico and William F. Buckley Sr., and it was accompanied by numerous appropriate exhibits, including support for him from anti-American Mexicans. It concluded by asking that there be no suggestion that he seek his remedy in the Mexican courts against an action by the Mexican government, in part because of his certainty of defeat, as a result of which "the stigma of having appealed to my government without success would attach to me in Mexico." What Buckley sought, indeed, one would find it difficult to challenge if one accepted the premises of his action:

"If this case should merit the consideration of my Government, I would request, not that the Obregón Government be asked to permit me to return to Mexico, but that the request be made that the Mexican authorities give assurance that upon my return I be allowed to attend to my business in that country without molestation. If the request should not be so based upon my rights as an American citizen, I should regret figuring in this incident at all."

The State Department found no ground to act on his behalf. Neither he nor the Department alluded to the fact that, from the end of the 1914 A.B.C. conference to the termination of William Jennings Bryan's tenure as Wilson's Secretary of State, Buckley had served as the Secretary's closest adviser for Mexican affairs. In 1924 Plutarco Elías Calles, who had succeeded his friend Obregón as President of Mexico, invited Buckley to return—according to Douglas Reed's chapter in the memorial volume, after Buckley had told *The New York Times* (again, unexceptionably) that he agreed with Calles that the American oil companies were hypocrites in their simultaneous professions of friendship to the government in Mexico City and demands for armed intervention in Washington. Buckley did return, on a number of occasions, and even lived in Mexico for a time with some of his children, but he had long been looking elsewhere for a place in which he could do business as he wished. His first company, however, the Pantepec Oil Co. of Mexico, had been founded there before his expulsion.

Pantepec of Mexico was the foundation stone for the fortune that was to be built up elsewhere. When Will Buckley died in 1958, Reed estimates, "the net worth of the companies under Buckley management" was approximately one hundred ten million dollars, though this figure is rudely challenged by Ferdinand Lundberg in *The Rich and the Super-Rich* and urbanely minimised by some Buckleys.

III

In 1917, when he was thirty-six years old and she was twenty-two, Buckley met Aloïse Steiner of New Orleans, the daughter of an old though hardly wealthy Southern family. A week later he asked her to marry him, and, after discreet investigation through priestly connections, her family approved. The archetype of the well-born Southern lady—with all the virtues as well as the disabilities of such an upbringing—she went back to Mexico with him. Their first child, also named Aloïse, was born in 1918 (she died early in 1967).

A small, delicately made woman whose pictures attest to her beauty, Mrs. Buckley devoted herself from the first to husband and family. She was to have nine more children: John, born in 1920; Priscilla, born in 1921; James, born in 1923; Jane, born in 1924; William Jr., born in 1925; Patricia, born in 1927; Reid, born in 1930; Maureen, born in 1933 (she died in 1964, of a cerebral hemorrhage, like her eldest sister), and Carol, born in 1938. Always averse to public attention, Mrs. Buckley was almost never mentioned in any accounts of her husband's activities; but those who have known the family over the years testify to the influence of her gentleness and her gentility on him and on their children. Widowed since 1958, she spends most of her time at the estate that her husband bought in 1938 in Camden, South Carolina, traveling for the summers, with a small staff of servants who have been with her for decades, to the family's first big property in Sharon, Connecticut, in the foothills of the Berkshires.

Buckley moved his wife and children out of Mexico before his own expulsion and the attendant financial losses, and from Bronxville he took them in 1922 to Sharon, where he bought an eighteenth-century house that was subsequently to be enlarged and modified. It is called Great Elm. He launched a new career from a base in New York, but its foundation was still oil and the hope of oil, and he was almost as often away from his base as at it. That he was devoted to his children even in absentia is manifest from the attention that he gave to their education, not only in person when he was in residence, but also through the various governesses and tutors whom he provided, the schools that he so carefully chose, and the emphasis he always very properly placed on the humanities in the children's most malleable years. He believed too in early political indoctrination—religious training was of course important in a household in which both parents were devout Catholics—and at least some of his children apparently carried on the tradition when they became parents: his daughter Aloïse wrote of her four-year-old's admiration for Barry Goldwater because (the child believed) he had killed John Kennedy, and of her six-year-old's preparations to resist with his iron leg-brace the Communists who were skulking just outside the country's miserably defended borders. (This was the child who was told by his mother that the neighbor who planned to vote for Johnson against Goldwater would not go to hell because hers was a sin of ignorance, whereas such a choice made by Aloïse would be a far greater sin inasmuch as she knew better.)

From the start the Buckleys were sure of themselves, at least toward the outer world. "I don't think the family as a whole suffered from the usual problems of having too much money—that is, a tendency to treat people as commodities," William B. Coley, who grew up next door to the Buckleys in Sharon, said. "Their sense of constituting a more or less complete society in and of themselves gave them an assurance in dealing with outsiders. I felt they did consider themselves superior to other people—more talented, more intelligent—and they undoubtedly were. Money may have contributed to this state of affairs, but money itself was not the issue. Perhaps there is a connection between thinking that theirs is the True Church and that other people either willfully turn from the light or are too stupid to recognise it—perhaps that and their sense of being a privileged family made for an ineradicable separateness, an apartness.

"Let me explain what I mean by 'privileged' in this connection. It is not simply a matter of having more money and the things money can buy. It begins at the theological or religious level, comes down through the intellectual level, and only becomes visible, so to speak, on the material level. The integrity of all three levels is what gives a special force to the sense of privilege. Some of us have it on one or another level. The Buckleys conveyed the impression that they had it on all three.

"Also, I suppose the Buckley family sees itself vis-à-vis those of us who are not members as the True Church vis-à-vis the heretics. The treatment that a believer in the True Church gives to an unbeliever has theological justification: affection that recognizes the differences and inferiorities; a kind of condescension."

Coley and his brother, Peter, who were friends and playmates of the young Buckleys, recall that there was never anything but the utmost affection and mutual respect between the Buckley children and the many servants from governesses to farmhands. The elder Buckleys taught their children early not to question the authority vested in the parental vicars, and not to take advantage of their own privileges. The sense of responsibility to one's dependents that was one of the virtues of the feudal world was and is strong among the Buckleys, to whom lack of consideration toward a subordinate would rank as a cardinal infraction of human decency.

There is no fundamental contradiction between this and an innate conviction of election. The twelve tribes of Biblical Israel could as well have been the ten tribes of mid-century Buckley, who exemplify the phenomenon that, while the Jews are arrogant because their deity chose them above all others six thousand years ago, the Catholics owe their *superbia* to their ability, four thousand years later, to persuade him of their greater eligibility.

In the Buckley family this superiority was nurtured on more than mere certainty. Will certainly and Aloïse probably were perfectionists, though their methods differed; but they shared the belief that their children bore the responsibilities of the aristocracy, in both the private and the public worlds: election might be conferred, but it must constantly be merited. Many of the ten children have written at varying length about the education—in the broadest sense of the word—that was laid out for them: thorough grounding in the humanities, fluency in languages, familiarity with history, more than formal acquaintance with the arts, proper respect for the rights of others, the origins and evolution of societies and of the physical world, all imparted not only by excellent schools and governesses, but also by special resident summer tutors from those schools, a veritable miniature zoo of great diversity, and, above all, the constant encouragement of intellectual competition within the family. All this was interwoven with extensive foreign travel—in Latin America, Europe, and Britain—and, for some of the children, reasonably long periods of attendance at boarding schools abroad, which must have contributed materially to the cosmopolitanism of their very real culture. It has been said, and probably accurately, that no Buckley is ever rude by accident—a quality that can command only admiration.

Since young Coleys and young male Buckleys were quite frequently in and out of each other's houses in the years of childhood and adolescence before the Second World War and the separations, physical and other, that it entailed, William Coley absorbed much of the ambience in which his friends were being brought up. Discussing the question why the Kennedys went one way and the Buckleys another, Coley observed: "One plausible answer is that, although both families wanted money and power, Joe Kennedy seems not to have wanted much else, perhaps did not 'know' there was anything else. But Will Buckley Senior seems to have found out early in life that money and power, while very enjoyable, were means, not ends. And of course he had a very wholesome respect for the uses of language."

There were two dinner tables in the Buckley house: the elder children (and their guests) dined with the parents and Mademoiselle, while the younger were in a nursery dining room with their Spanish-speaking nurses. (Some of the children spoke Spanish or French before they knew English.) Coley recalls that Will Buckley's relation with his children on such occasions tended toward the formal: it was their mother who seemed to be the source of warmth; and Reid Buckley has written that "Father was as much a figure of awe as of fun."

"At table," Coley remembers, "their father made them defend their intellectual and political positions. He would catechise them, so to speak, on the various things they had learned. The dinner table was his place for checking them out, a place where he could keep in touch with them and where, if someone had something bright to say, it could be offered up for the family—and perhaps the guests—to pick apart. There was an element of 'performance' attached to meals at the Buckleys'. You had to be on your mettle. I remember a meal or two where he asked me the kinds of questions he asked his children. This was always very chilling.

"The active participants, as I recall, were the younger Aloïse, Patricia, and Billy, and, more modulatedly, Priscilla. Jimmy was usually rather quiet, and I don't remember John's being there when I was. If some people at the table did not speak, Will sometimes specifically asked them to. I don't think Aloïse Senior disapproved of this device, but, as I recall, she took no part. Rather, she was solicitous of the guests who might be thrown to the lions. In my infrequent rôle as catechumen, I felt her to be, quietly, on my side. She was a serious, strong contributor to family solidarity, but in more emotional ways, more quietly, more informally.

"People who were not members of the family tended to think Aloïse Senior was the human, the humane—perhaps both—parent. She would likely be the one to inquire if you were having a good time or if you were bored by the conversation or troubled by the absolutism of the politics. A most attractive person. She smoothed Will's roughnesses when necessary and tranquilized the guests when that was necessary. I seem to want to attribute the family's interest in esthetics to her, though Will Senior certainly approved. She humanized, she softened, made the family appear more pleasant, more elegant.

"Though I doubt that their contemporaries in Sharon differed all that much from the Buckley politics, many of them would probably have conceded that it was Aloïse Senior who had the graces and made it possible to overlook the arriviste qualities that some affected to see in Will. One must remember that in those days, at least, Sharon was a place with a good many 'Anglo-Saxon attitudes.' And, when Will came out so strongly against aid to Britain, that tore it for many people, even people his age.

"I guess I related much better to her than to him, though of course I saw more of her and in more contexts. To me Will Senior was a forbidding, somewhat cold figure. His relation to his children was certainly more formal than that of my father to me and my brothers, more patriarchal."

One Sharon resident whose divergences of view from the Buckleys had nothing to do with her affection and respect for them is Mrs. Carol Rhoades Robinson. The elder Buckleys were her parents' close friends, and Mrs. Robinson, whose generation falls midway between Mrs. Buckley's and her children's, is a close friend of Mrs. Buckley. "We never discussed politics or religion," Mrs. Robinson said, "and we are perhaps the best of friends. I respect the Buckleys' beliefs and I believe they respect mine." Much the same is to be heard from people of assorted ages, far to the left of Mrs. Robinson, who find genuine friendship with various Buckleys quite enjoyable by virtue of analogous tacit accords.

"The most descriptive thing I can say about Mrs. Buckley," Mrs. Robinson, who is not a Catholic, said, "is that her life is completely —without thrusting it on you—wholly guided by faith. And her faith is so great that she can meet any problem, she can cope with any sort of situation. But this strength of hers is an inner strength and it's wholly based on faith. Her faith is unique, especially to a non-Catholic, because it is so strong, and so gentle as far as other people are concerned." George Norton Stone, who teaches at Hotchkiss School in Lakeville, near Sharon, and his wife made almost the identical observation, adding that Mrs. Buckley's wholeness of belief is shared by virtually all her children.

What binds the Buckley children, in Mrs. Robinson's view, is "their respect and admiration for each other," which is "based on each one's recognition of the others' particular gifts. It's a fundamental admiration of each other's ability, and each one helps the other, so that they are not only dependent on each other in a sense but they contribute to each other." Aloïse has written that "Buckleys tolerate disparagement of Buckleys only from Buckleys —and only from Buckleys within the same degree of consanguinity."

"The children," Mrs. Robinson added, "were brought up on a really strong intellectual basis by their father. He respected the authority he had, and he used it wisely. He also developed in each one of them whatever he or she could do best, and it was stressed." One of the striking aspects of the ten children is the apparently unquestioning acceptance of parental dogma from the very first: not one of the ten, it would seem, ever seriously challenged anything that came from authority unless it be that prevailing "liberal" philosophy that the father regarded as a usurper. Mrs. Robinson believes that the young Buckleys embraced the whole of the parental doctrine "because it was made sufficiently exciting. Mr. Buckley was a very creative man himself in his approach to things. There were certain small rebellions, undoubtedly, but where they perhaps differed Mr. Buckley would say: 'Go right ahead—develop it.' Mr. Buckley gave to his children what he thought was the special privilege of intellectual freedom, and that's what made them not rebel. What he gave them in any way—whether it was intellectual freedom, music lessons, dancing lessons, riding lessons

—that particular thing was a privilege. It was a gift. But it was a gift that they were grateful to have and it was something to make the most of."

Not everyone in Sharon was so immediately friendly to the Buckleys as the elder Coleys and the Rhoadeses. Sharon is the sort of frontier-of-New England community in which one is an outsider longer perhaps than anywhere else except Old England or Switzerland. And Connecticut, as a perennial Democratic member of its legislature has pointed out, is in every sense the Mississippi of the North: the dwindling old genuine aristocracy in the Berkshire foothills, the New York-veneered carpetbaggers in Fairfield County and along the Sound, the "nigras" in their place (which includes a few token posts in the state's community-college system for those who know their place), and the middle-class and lower-middle-class redneck horde of Snopeses that fills the towns and the farms (the Minutemen and the Ku Klux Klan are strong and active) and really runs the state. (Most recently it has succeeded in abolishing the requirement of a high-school diploma for aspirants to the state police.)

Though the Buckleys always welcomed everyone in Sharon, especially the young, to use their swimming pools and tennis courts, and the hospitality was always accepted—it extended to their music rooms, their large music library, their riding stables—without any feeling of condescension on either side, except perhaps some unconscious patronizing of those who had not the faith or were of lesser intelligence, according to several sources, "they were not liked by large segments of the town. This is the kind of thing that the older people who knew the senior Buckleys would tell a reporter. Partly—and not to the credit of the town—it was because the Buckleys were Irish Catholic arrivistes in the eyes of some of these people, who paid much more attention to that than to the fact that Mr. Buckley may have had enormous talent. It was not a merit- or talent-oriented society. Some were still in the money business, but all had less money, and it had been made a long time ago. And there was anti-Irish and anti-Catholic bias, especially toward people who made no secret of either origin."

"Besides," I was told by another source, "Mr. Buckley tolerated fools very unwillingly, and there were a lot of foolish people there. The town's reaction to the Buckleys was stuffy and snobbish; on the other hand, if ingratiating themselves with the town was what the Buckleys wanted (though it's hard to think it was), they didn't go about it terribly well. Will and Aloïse did see something of a number of local families, though they were always busy with their own house guests—they were not ostracised, it wasn't as simple as that. They were tolerated rather coolly and then mildly talked about; but it wasn't a systematic vilification of the Buckleys.

"They were never really inside, partly because they lived part of the year in Camden, part in New York. The tenor of their life was quite different from that of the rest. But they didn't flaunt their money. The Buckleys were in a town the power structure of which—if there is such a thing there—is Protestant and . . . well, it was like the Hamptons on Long Island up to the mid-thirties, as far as Irish Catholics were concerned. Sharon is a town that submerges its money, like Boston. Well, the Buckleys didn't flaunt it, but on the other hand they all had cars when they were eighteen, and they didn't stint on the equipment end of things."

The years immediately preceding the Second World War brought the nearest approach to a division between the Sharon area and the Buckleys. The predominant sentiment was pro-British and anti-German as well as anti-Nazi, and it was fortified by the presence of such academic intellectuals as various Van Dorens and other Columbia professors, as well as some from Yale, in Cornwall and other nearby towns. Like then Ambassador Joseph P. Kennedy, Col. Robert McCormick, Capt. Joseph Medill Patterson, and many other rich men, Will Buckley was a fervent isolationist and backer of America First, though unlike these others he would have nothing to do with its chronic vulgarities. Like them, too, though not nearly to the same degree, he was anti-Semitic (as, undoubtedly, were his anti-Nazi Protestant neighbors, and with equal politeness): "There is no question," Senator James Buckley admits, "that my father was anti-Semitic in the same way as other men of his age and background." The fact is hardly scarifying, and it is noted here if at all only to dispose of it. No form of bias is pretty, more especially when it manifests itself in those who have themselves suffered from it; but there is a difference of kind as well as of degree between choosing one's company, however bigotedly, and exterminating those whom one refuses to invite.

Franklin Roosevelt's transfer of destroyers to Britain by way of inaugurating Lend-Lease in 1940 occasioned the first open discord between the town and the Buckleys. A town meeting was held, under the auspices of the local branch of the Committee to Defend America by Aiding the Allies, in support not only of Lend-Lease but also of further action in the direction of intervention; the Buckleys organised counter-demonstrations at which the older children distributed violently anti-British propaganda whose anonymity evoked such denunciation that their father was compelled to acknowledge authorship. Several Buckleys, including even the mother, wrote angry letters to *The Lakeville Journal*, then as now the weekly paper that is the region's only journalistic organ. It must be conceded that, when Will Buckley attacked the morality of St. Franklin's devious procedures and declared that, "if we want war with Germany, the honest and courageous course is to declare war on that country," he was on incontestable ground. But he proceeded at once to cut it out from under himself by his unwarranted personal attacks on the courage and sincerity of those who disagreed with him. When the United States entered the war, however, no eligible Buckley resisted military service, and much of the propaganda stopped.

By this time Will Buckley had bought the old South Carolina estate that he named Kamschatka, and after the war he spent much of his leisure there, especially in winter, when his wife was always there with varying numbers of children. Thus the family's contacts with Sharon tended to diminish, though it was still the summer residence; and, as some of the children married, they bought and built there until the original estate expanded so that John Buckley observed ironically in the summer of 1971, when telephoning driving directions, that "you'll understand why we hesitate to call it the compound." In one of its buildings John has established a branch office of the family-held Catawba Corp.—its other offices are in Hartford, Denver, and New York; his own residence has for some years been in Lakeville, a few miles northeast of Sharon. His father, after his stroke in 1955, spent more and more time in Camden, where he built an office on the estate grounds; and, when he died in 1958 in New York, he, like the French governess who had for so long worked for the Buckleys, was buried in the Quaker cemetery in Camden.

Nineteen months earlier he had made his last characteristic gesture. Increasingly alarmed by the "blight of Liberalism and Communism they will encounter in almost all elementary schools," he proposed to open on his Sharon estate a private school for children four to fourteen, and he sent out a circular to this effect to some three hundred families in the Sharon-Lakeville-Salisbury area. Detailing his classic academic program—according to *Time*, he once rented a house in Paris and, for his own children, established a music teacher on the first floor, an English tutor on the second, a Latin tutor on the third, and a French tutor on the fourth—he assured the community that there would be nothing "progressive" about his school, which would include religious instruction according to each student's faith. The children would be taught to admire Cleveland and Theodore Roosevelt as the paradigms of what Presidents should be, to "oppose all participation in war unless the vital interest of the United States is affected," and to follow the big-stick philosophy rather than the course taken by "Franklin Roosevelt, Truman, and Eisenhower, which has won the contempt and derision of the world." So it had, though for reasons other and better than his.

His widow, of whom their youngest daughter, Carol, told a writer for *McCall's* that "Mother has always been ten degrees to the right of Father, Bill, and Jim, if that's possible," thinks of herself as essentially a Southerner and spends the greater part of the year at Kamschatka, which, like Great Elm, has excellent facilities for music. Like her son William Jr., Mrs. Buckley loves Bach and Mozart, and mother and son enjoy playing them in piano duet. One of her reasons for preferring the South is the aloofness of northwestern Connecticut. Describing the family's return in 1933 after four years in Europe, she told L. Clayton DuBois, the author of an excellent sketch of the family in *The New York Times Magazine*: "In Sharon, our neighbors walked by me on the street and said: 'Good morning,' just as though we'd never been gone. In Camden, our neighbors came by, sent flowers, invited us over and welcomed us home." And DuBois adds: "Aloofness is something she would never have tolerated in her children. It helps explain why guests of the Buckleys, sometimes expecting snobbishness or worse, tend to come away mumbling dazedly about southern hospitality."

A Sharon neighbor, Van Zandt Wheeler, who contributed a brief chapter to the tribute to the father, wrote: "Will was the founder and architect of the Buckley family as it exists today." Irene Corbally Kuhn, the veteran newspaper woman who has known the Buckleys intimately for twenty years, ever since her work attracted Will Buckley's interest because of her strong conservatism, complemented rather than confuted this appraisal when she spoke to me about Aloïse Steiner Buckley. "It's a very unusual family in its closeness, and a warm and natural and utterly sincere family," Mrs. Kuhn emphasised. "Today you don't think of this kind of thing any more—closeness of the family where the grand-children are as close as the children. This, I think, is largely due to Mrs. Buckley. In her own quiet way she gathers them in. For instance, the grandchildren all write to her and ask her advice and talk to her frequently, confiding in her as they would not in their mothers—the ones in college and the little ones, all the way up and down the line."

One has never read any attacks on Mrs. Buckley: I have not heard even the cruelest enemies of the family criticise her: on the contrary, those who have met her (a privilege the lack of which is a loss to this book and to its author) have all been overwhelmed by her. In an interview in *The State* of Columbia, South Carolina, published in April, 1971, she stands clearly as that much abused entity, a lady, who is also a woman who has had what she has the grace to consider the good luck of a predominantly happy life.

IV

WHEN WILLIAM BUCKLEY SR.'S WILL was proved, each of his children—none had yet died—received seventeen dollars. Obviously, he had managed earlier to convey virtually all his assets to them, to his wife, and to trusts.

The basic wealth lies in Catawba Corp., which is headed by his eldest son, John, and in which, until his election to the Senate, James was extremely active at home and abroad. The company was divided into ten shares or blocks, one for each child (and his heirs), and there are no outside stockholders. Nominally, Catawba is a consulting firm; it oversees a world-wide duchy—perhaps a grand duchy; certainly not an empire or even a kingdom—of speculative ventures in gas, oil, and minerals, title to which is vested in publicly held corporations in this and other countries. Several of these were listed on the American Stock Exchange (formerly the New York Curb Exchange) until they were removed at various times in the 1960s—two by order of the Exchange and the four others voluntarily, because of a dispute over Exchange regulations, according to John Buckley. Thereupon— and in three instances before removal notice—they moved to a new exchange, the National, founded by Edward McCormick, who had been dismissed as head of the American Exchange and had founded the National in 1963, the year in which the Buckley companies began to leave the American.

The National Exchange is extremely reticent: it will not specify its criteria for accepting applications for listing, nor those for delisting companies previously accepted. Its average daily volume is a few hundred thousand shares, some of which (including those of some Buckley companies) are quoted in sixteenths of a dollar.

Forty-one of its two hundred twenty-five member firms are also members of the New York Stock Exchange. Knowledgeable financial observers describe the National Exchange as "a sort of fringe situation" for people who are willing to take unusually big chances. It is not, however, the major trading place for shares in the Buckley companies, which, it is said, do not relish even this minimal kind of exposure and which are dealt in principally over the counter.

Pantepec, Buckley's first company, founded in Mexico and transferred to Venezuela in 1924, is now Pantepec International, a Delaware corporation with its principal office in Hartford, Connecticut. But the vicissitudes of this progression, and the other events that paced it, are not without interest.

Unlike most foreigners arriving in Venezuela with a view to making a fortune out of it, Buckley did not immediately crave an audience with the incumbent dictator, Gen. Juan Vicente Gomez. But Gomez had heard about Buckley's Mexican career and requested (in effect commanded) that Buckley call on him. In the words of Buckley's close associate, George S. Montgomery Jr. of Coudert Brothers, the international law firm so closely identified with the Right, "a healthy relationship took hold, based on mutual respect that lasted until the President's death." According to Montgomery's chapter in *W.F.B.—An Appreciation*, this "proved a considerable asset" as Buckley went about assembling his oil concessions and in later years when they were frequently menaced. Much of the initial work was financed by the Venezuelan government, which had ultimately to be reimbursed. The first step was the financing of the Pantepec Oil Co. of Venezuela. The name, Montgomery explained, was that of a river in Mexico on whose bank Buckley had once found refuge from hostile revolutionists.

One of the earliest collaborators named by Montgomery—who did not meet Buckley until 1927—was a Virginia financier, Fergus Reid, for whom Buckley was to name his youngest son. Another was Joseph H. Himes of Washington, an important financial and political figure. A third was an investment broker, E. A. Pierce, the founder of the firm that ultimately became Merrill Lynch, Pierce, Fenner & Smith. Together they evolved a modus operandi that involved agreements with such large corporations as the Union Oil Co. of California—and, later, even bigger industry giants—under which the latter undertook to explore and develop Pantepec's concessions, the acreage of which was vast. Buckley was well aware of the very high odds against success in any wild-cat drilling, and indeed he assumed that there would be, as indeed there was, no exception for his properties. As the stock-market craze mounted, he raised new capital not by diluting his company with a fresh stock issue but by borrowing a million dollars from a French bank; at the same time he persuaded Union to divert some of the money earmarked for Venezuelan exploration into the purchase of properties in the United States. It was this foresight, Montgomery said, that saved Pantepec from extinction during the depression.

The depression was eased for some of Buckley's employees by the acts of generosity that have distinguished two generations of the family—always anonymous to all but the recipient and thus unknown even to close relatives. It is idle to speculate on motivations or to try to psychoanalyse in the void, and no analogies can be drawn with Rockefeller's dimes (which were his press agent's stunt) or with his foundations. It is fact that this family of ruthless exponents of free enterprise and rugged individualism, those two clichés of their formative period, frequently exercised a humanity that was notably lacking in Buckley philosophy. Even today the sons are sometimes informed, by a beneficiary, of some gift or annuity given by their father of which they had never known, and occasionally to people of whom they had never heard.

During the 1930's Buckley managed to make Pantepec solvent and to obtain a contract with a subsidiary of Standard Oil of New Jersey that labored for years before it made the first oil find on a Pantepec property. In later years some of the Buckley companies have been accused of exploring for oil and gas in much the manner of the job applicant whose opening remark is in essence: "You don't want to hire me, do you?" In 1935 Pantepec stock was selling for less than a dollar a share; it was four years later, on the eve of the Second World War, that the first commercial well on its property was brought in. In the interim, though the high incidence of failures on his three million acres had earned Buckley the name of Dry-Hole Bill, there were involved capital-raising operations, battles for control as Wall Street professionals thought they perceived long-term opportunities, and substantial support by such major banks as Chase National. More large oil companies were brought into cooperation, and after the war Pantepec prevailed on the Compagnie Française de Pétroles to make a tremendous investment in exploitation of Pantepec properties, as well as a large cash payment. "Owing to a miscalculation as to the oil resources in one of the fields," as Montgomery phrased it, this program could not be carried out, and the CFG won a huge judgment against Pantepec.

Though Reid, Himes, and Pierce virtually always enjoyed a unanimity of view with Buckley, there were other large stockholders who did not, and in 1948 Buckley began a complicated series of maneuvers involving spin-offs, new ventures, and further foreign expansion. The first of the new companies was called Pancoastal Oil, and two shares of it were given to every Pantepec holder. Pancoastal traded out its own stock in 1949 for large exploratory territories in Saskatchewan and Alberta, Canada; in 1951, under another split, it acquired the Florida and Venezuela assets previously owned by Pantepec, as well as new acquisitions in Ecuador. All these were then conveyed to a new firm called Canada Southern Oils, Ltd., all the stock of which belonged to the Pancoastal holders.

The Saskatchewan field came in just as a Toronto investment house launched a ten-million-dollar debenture issue for Buckley. The money thus brought in was used for further extensive land purchases. Subsequently it became advisable to divide the Canadian company into three: one to search for gas and produce it, one to exploit oil properties, and one to remain principally exploratory. This decision was made in 1954, not long before a severe recession struck the Canadian petroleum industry, but Buckley's companies survived and the debentures were converted into shares in Canada Southern Petroleum, Ltd.; Canso Oil Producers, Ltd., and Canso Natural Gas, Ltd. By now Buckley had learned to set up his companies with voting trusts in order, to quote Montgomery again, "to obstruct irresponsible outsiders with designs on them." He had been one of the few men in the oil industry to reject the view that demand for petroleum products would collapse after the war: he was, his associates have said, an incisive and incessant student of every relevant factor and he refused to be influenced by emotion or sentiment.

Having further formed, for his Western Hemisphere operations, Coastal Caribbean Oils, Ltd., Buckley ranged eastward in 1953 with Pan-Israel Oil Co. and Israel-Mediterranean Petroleum, Inc. In 1956 he went into the Orient—the Philippines, specifically—with San José Petroleum, Inc. A year later the Middle East companies initiated explorations on behalf of the American Grecian Oil Co. on the Greek island of Zakynthos, which was believed to be the world's oldest oil field. By the time of Buckley's death there were holdings also in Guatemala and Australia. Subsequently the two Canso companies were merged into United Canso Oil & Gas, Ltd., and the two Israel companies were absorbed into the Magellan Petroleum Corp., which has since expanded its activities far beyond the Levant.

After the war Buckley was joined in the management of the companies by his two eldest sons, John and James. John, who had served four years in Army Intelligence, had planned at first to go to law school; James did do so, and worked afterward for a while with the New Haven firm of Wiggin & Dana, in the hope of acquiring enough practical experience to set up for himself as a country lawyer because of his love for the rural life and his distaste for cities; but he found the law less to his liking than he had expected, and his father found himself short-handed, so James was drafted into the family business and remained in it until he entered the Senate in 1971. Some who know the family best insist that, though John is the titular head of the clan and its interests, it is James who, "in the background, holds the whole thing together and had more to do with the family business than anybody else."

Both men certainly emulated their father's firmness. One cannot know whether they would also be capable of such a magnificent gesture as that described in the memorial volume by Douglas Reed, a South African industrialist who was long close to the elder Buckley and who writes sometimes for *National Review*. Just before the depression, Reed reported, Buckley had obtained two and a half million dollars for Pantepec from a French financier. When the crash came, the Frenchman's wife begged Buckley to turn back the money, and he destroyed the check although Pantepec was virtually broke and his own assets were chiefly shares in it. The sons and their associates have certainly continued their father's policy that led to the spin-off from Pantepec in the thirties: the rejection of dividends in favor of plowing back funds into new projects. Reed credits Buckley with two major contributions to the survival and growth of his companies: diversification and expansion of companies working with a naturally diminishing resource, and capital appreciation rather than dividends in a time of increasing—Reed's word is "punitive"—income taxes. Reed is worth quoting here: "W.F.B., as was to be expected, believed he knew what was best for stockholders; to him it seemed obvious that the stockholder should prefer a capital-gain run for his money to sitting waiting for dividends, ever more heavily taxed, from the same source, ever depleshing [sic]."

It is Reed who contributed what was to be made known of Buckley's misadventures in Venezuela after the Second World War. Gomez having proved to be neither immortal nor immovable, Romulo Betancourt became his more or less revolutionary successor and at once made gigantic increases in oil workers' wages—which were not exactly high—and oil companies' taxes and royalty payments—which also were not exactly high. As Reed tells it, Buckley was caught once more between "a revolutionary regime" and "a home government and big oil companies which both had acquired the habit of capitulation." Once again Buckley's exhortations were ignored by government and industry: the government recognised Betancourt and the oil companies did business with him. Buckley went into his courts and lost, after the State Department, citing its own "expert," had advised him that Betancourt was the only alternative to Communist rule in Venezuela. Again one must quote Reed: "This expert, a Mr. Lawrence Duggan, was later named as a Communist agent by Elizabeth Bentley and Whittaker Chambers and met his death in a mysterious episode of defenestration."

A form filed with the Securities and Exchange Commission by Pancoastal records that, "in order to avail itself of the services of qualified technical and administrative personnel, the Corporation pursuant to the authorization of its Board of Directors has retained the services of The Catawba Corporation." It goes on to explain that Catawba was organised in April, 1948, "for the purpose of rendering financial, technical and other services to corporations primarily engaged in the exploration for, and the production of, petroleum in foreign countries." Catawba, it adds, "employs eleven professional and administrative personnel on its staff." In addition, it has retainer arrangements with consultant experts in appropriate domains. The description of Catawba's relation to Pancoastal is (to use a favorite word of William F. Buckley Jr.) paradigmatic, since Catawba performs the same services for other Buckley companies (Reed again: "Its [Catawba's] members effectively control all the companies through strong stock positions in them"):

"The Catawba Corporation maintains cognizance of conditions under which the Corporation operates, particular attention being paid to its obligations with respect to operating associates, personnel requirements, security holders, financial organization and foreign

and domestic governmental regulatory bodies and political representatives. Catawba handles, on behalf of the Corporation, such
public relations as may be required and assists the Corporation in
the acquisition, and exploration and operation of its properties
and shares."

Evidently no great public-relations requirement was envisaged,
since Catawba is not listed under its own name in the New York
telephone directory; nor is John Buckley, its president. (During
the great burgeoning of the expensive "look-at-my-name-and-face-
in-the-papers" syndrome that has so long characterised what is
called *society* in this country, a practitioner offered to keep the
Buckleys thus vulgarised for only three hundred dollars a week,
and Will Buckley retorted: "I'll pay you that to keep us completely
unpublicised.") The office is housed in a splendid old brownstone
in the Murray Hill section, which bears no identifying mark
(though a decal of an American flag is accurately centered in one
of the double entrance doors) and which has suffered an absolute
minimum of alteration from its original interior and exterior appearance. Though its simple furnishings are in full harmony with its
design, one feels a sense of desecration that so beautiful a residence
is now no more than an office. One of the rare public mentions of
Catawba—though not of its address—occurred in the Sunday business and financial section of *The New York Times* in the form of
a pleasant, bland sketch of its president, who can be a very pleasant
gentleman but is not in the least bland.

Reed credits him with a major rôle, "with the elders of the
group and Dean Reasoner," in all the big financial dealings between
1950 and 1956, and with responsibility for the Canadian and
Latin American ventures in particular. He lived four years in
Venezuela. James, according to Reed, was the chief negotiator
with foreign governments and firms, and James has confirmed this.
He scored great successes in Italy and Israel, but his failure in
Libya is to be attributed solely to that nation's boycott of firms
and individuals doing business with Israel. Benjamin W. Heath,
who married the Buckleys' eldest daughter during the war and
joined Catawba after his discharge from the Air Force—he was
trained as an engineer—handles its extremely inconspicuous public
relations. Reasoner, a Washington lawyer widely regarded as
brilliant, is also a principal negotiator and served as preceptor, so
to speak, to the younger Buckleys. Montgomery, who has been so
extensively quoted here, was Buckley Sr.'s closest associate, accord-

ing to Reed, and no major decision was ever made without his complete participation. Hence he was in full accord with Buckley's preference for doing business in "politically stable" areas—though it may be inquired whether the appraisal of stability, which seems often to have been equated with oligarchy and/or dictatorship, was always shrewd or realistic. Reed concedes that Israel in 1948 did not look very stable, but he surmises that Buckley chose to go in simply because the big companies were afraid to do so. Politically they guessed wrong, though geologically they would appear to have been on sounder ground: Buckley's loss was four million dollars.

There has been one real sensation surrounding a Buckley company, though from all available evidence it was not the Buckleys or their associates but that paragon of journalists, the late Walter Winchell, who was responsible (if that adjective may be coupled with his name). One Sunday night in 1955, when he was still broadcasting, he embarked on one of his characteristic staccato pretenses at news, summarising well-publicised economic reports, and then said: "Here is another piece of big advance news. Pantepec Oil—Pan-te-pec Oil—P-a-n-t-e-p-e-c Oil, on the Small Board. Pantepec Oil has newly discovered substantial oil reserves in the El Roble field in Venezuela. Pantepec Oil will hold a meeting on January thirteenth to increase its common stock to be used for stock dividends." This was and is a usual device, favored not only by Buckleys. But Pantepec had announced the find two months earlier, and *The New York Times*'s financial page had covered the stock dividend the day before the broadcast, pointing out, as Winchell could hardly have been expected to understand, that this was not quite the best news for stockholders expecting income. But the broadcast came at the end of one of the most spectacular weeks of recovery in years in the stock market, and the reactions of lay buyers of securities are primitive in direct ratio to their ignorance of the facts of what they are doing.

Consequently, when the American Exchange opened on Monday morning, Pantepec started off with orders to buy 357,500 shares— the largest block of any single stock ever transferred at one swoop on any exchange in the country. It had closed the previous Friday at 6¾, and David Sidney Jackson, the specialist handling the stock on the floor, had sell orders for only 234,500 and would have to make up the balance with five hundred shares of his own and 122,500 sold short. He opened the stock at 8⅞, and thus, according to testimony later given to a Senate committee by Edward McCormick, then president of the American Exchange, saved Winchell's victims hundreds of thousands of dollars. The stock never reached that opening price again in the week of speculative activity in it that followed, and the specialist had hours of anxiety before he could make up his short interest; but in the end he came out fifty thousand dollars ahead as well as clear in conscience.

There was never any evidence linking the Buckleys or their associates to Winchell's broadcast; and not everything that man said was planted by press agents or people's enemies: he had an active pleasure in simply playing God. It is conceivable that, once the Pantepec escapade began, Buckleys, like others, made or hoped to make or lost money on it; no one knows. But it did the company no good, and the taint of association, by an interesting irony, spread to some of the other Buckley corporations. Some students of the financial markets profess to believe that the episode played a part in the removal of the companies from the American Exchange much later, in 1963 and 1968.

The first delisting was that of Pantepec, on 10 March 1963. The reason given by the American Exchange was the company's three-year record of losses; there was also the narrow geographical distribution of its ownership. This was true also of the other Buckley companies subsequently delisted: the exchange requires that listed companies' ownership be distributed throughout the country, and the Buckley firms' shareholders are almost wholly East Coast residents. Buckley puts their total number at about a hundred thousand, and, he says, sixty per cent live in the Greater New York area: this, he explained, is why there is no telephone-book listing for Catawba: if there was activity "either way" in the stocks of Catawba's client companies, the phones would be busy all day long. His own account of the delistings, while it differs circumstantially in some minor respects from the exchange's, seems perfectly plausible:

"The exchange has certain requirements for continued listing, which by and large are logical and reasonable: they concern minimum number of shareholders, geographical distribution, etc. The most onerous requirement in our case was that there had to be earnings in at least one of the three years immediately past. We did not qualify on that basis. Nevertheless my understanding is that there is a discretionary power in the Board of Governors to waive that requirement if they so desire. Finally, in an access of messianic zeal, they decided that it would be desirable to have all the stocks sell at five dollars or more. Most of ours did not. So they suggested to us that we have reverse splits.* We found that condition, by God, intolerable, and we refused to put up with it. Two of our companies were delisted by them: Coastal Caribbean and, I think, Magellan. With United Canso, Canada Southern Petroleum, Pantepec, and Pancoastal we refused to submit to this requirement of a ten-for-one—in one case twenty-for-one—reverse split. If you want to buy a dollar stock, hoping maybe it will go to three bucks, you look for a dollar stock: you're not going to buy a ten-dollar stock hoping it will go to thirty."

In any event, Pantepec did not appear on the National Exchange until September, 1965. But Coastal Caribbean, which was delisted on the same day, began to be traded on the National Exchange four months later. Three other companies were delisted in June of 1968 —Pancoastal and Magellan on 17 June and United Canso Oil & Gas, Ltd., the next day. As early as 21 April, however, Magellan was being traded on the National, where United Canso appeared on 4 June and Pancoastal on 9 June. The dates would indicate ratification by the exchange after action by the companies.

The assets of these various firms include a number of subsidiaries in this and other countries through which a policy of diversification is being steadily developed. One such is Colorado Western Land & Cattle Co., which in turn owns part of the Wilhelm Co., a livestock-feeding and meat-processing enterprise in Colorado. Another is Magellan Petroleum of Australia, Ltd., a holding company with various subsidiaries through one of which Pancoastal has acquired American marketing rights to a steam-driven automobile engine being perfected by Pritchard Steam Power (Pty.), Ltd., of Australia. This does not mean neglect of oil, gas, and minerals, including uranium, exploration for which goes forward, directly or indirectly, in the Arctic, off the Florida coast, in various Canadian provinces, in several regions of Australia and New Zealand, in the Fiji Islands, in the Philippines, in Venezuela, and in South Africa.

The closing prices of the companies traded on the National Exchange at the end of 1971 ranged from $4\frac{1}{16}$ for Canso to $\frac{11}{16}$ for Pancoastal and $\frac{3}{8}$ for Coastal Caribbean. Canso had the fewest outstanding shares—5,660,838—and Coastal Caribbean the most—

---

* The term is the financial community's. What it means, of course, is consolidations.—C.L.M.

9,220,795. Each pays for Catawba's services on a fee basis plus an overriding royalty of one sixty-fourth. Working capital tends to be small and distributed over several million shares: for example, Coastal Caribbean had capital of $3,659,859 as of October, 1971, or approximately forty cents a share, which is more or less what it was selling at, while United Canso at the end of 1970 had a working capital of $3,562,538, the equivalent of about sixty-five cents a share, when it was selling for several times that. According to some investors who have ventured into one or another of these companies after close observation, the prices of the shares have consistently moved up with reports of oil strikes on the companies' concessions or in the vicinity, and then have subsided again.

This was the case too during Will Buckley's lifetime. He was a plunger: "If an idea is good, if you see or think of something you really want," he told John, who quotes the counsel in his chapter of the memorial tribute, "you should grab it and then think of the money." (An interesting precept from one who opposed the deficit financing of the New Deal, or borrowing to feed the hungry who had been improvident enough to become unemployed when depression struck.) John Buckley asserted that often his father would save his stockholders by pumping family money into the companies.

John attributed the errors to what he called his father's two weaknesses: inability to judge character (the son does not appear to share the trait) and a *faible* for believing what he wanted to hear, which, of course, was what a good many people thereupon told him. One is also made to reflect, however, by another of John's comments: "Wells would be drilled, and they would be dry. The stock would drop and the stockholders' letters would be increasingly abusive. Then a discovery would be made and the stock would go up. The company looked as if it might become self-supporting. Father was getting bored."

Things are not quite the same today. "Anything that affects my livelihood takes precedence," John told me with a laugh; but it was not a laugh of embarrassment. He and Heath are listed as voting trustees, officers, and/or directors of all the companies. So is William Shields, a lawyer who retired relatively young from Coudert Brothers. Reasoner appears often; so do a number of others. Alan S. Anderson is a retired oil securities analyst from a major brokerage house; Marion Brown is a retired statistician for Standard Oil of Indiana; Dorothy Bush, whose husband, John, is a member of the Interstate Commerce Commission, was in the

V

"The most important thing to do in the Buckley tribe is to be loyal. All the rest, intellectual competitiveness and so forth—I think they really felt that this was only part of the family game plan. Actually there was one unwritten but compelling law: ideological and family loyalty. In other words, you didn't really have to be that damn clever: what you had to have was family solidarity."

"All Buckleys always have to win."

Both quotations come from northwestern Connecticut, from people who have known the Buckleys well since the mid-1920's. One of them was a founding member of the Black Widow Spider Club of Sharon, no member of which was old enough to smoke without throwing up. But not even James Buckley's membership in this *"Our Gang*–Mark Twain kind of thing" could make the other members really like his brother Bill.

"Even as a young boy Jimmy was immensely likable to us," my Black Widow (male) continued. "He was lovable, humorous, made real friends of snakes, wild foxes, pigeons, any animal. Bill Buckley, on the other hand, was definitely not one of the gang. He stayed within the Buckley clan, which was like a town within the town. Kids were more than welcome on Buckley turf, but somehow it meant being really absorbed. To resist this and still use their swiming pool and tennis courts made us feel guilty.

"Even when Bill was very young, there was something about him—his British governess, that's where he belonged—with his nanny and his sisters. Somehow he didn't belong with us kids in the hayloft of the neighborhood barn where our club met. But he wasn't the kind of little spoiled brat with a nanny that you wanted to beat up. He had a tongue and a wit that could cut, even then, and we just wanted to walk away from it."

But was it not true that Reid, the youngest brother, had been a rebel when he was young? "Not so," Peter Coley, his closest childhood chum in Sharon, declares. "He was the most faithful advocate of them all. He worshiped Bill and used to emulate him. He still does. He is a staunch advocate of the Buckley philosophy in everything political or social and always was. But there's something different about Reid. You have that feeling that there's another personality trying to get out but it can't.

"When he was a kid, he had a hell of a temper and occasionally a Buckley would be in the path of his croquet mallet or a flying fist. But he outgrew the temper and became a highly productive Buckley at Yale. There he pretty much followed in his brother's footsteps, but he was a potential goof-off and more of a fun-lover than Bill.

"Once I heard a telephone conversation between Reid and Bill at Yale when Bill was head of the *Yale Daily News*. Reid was going virtually without sleep while trying to stay on the freshman debating team and in the Political Union and still 'heel' the *Daily News*—in itself a twenty-four-hour-a-day job when you're trying to be Number One. Naturally his grades were suffering. Bill called to hand him one more propaganda assignment—a speaking engagement out of town, I think it was. I was sitting in Reid's room with his roommates while Reid was trying to turn down Bill's request. Out of the phone in an electric crackle, as if suddenly it were being amplified, came '*You've got to drive yourself.*' It was like a pronouncement from God and the Devil at the same time. It was all over after a 'Yes, Bill' from Reid.

"At the time, our freshman English class was reading Conrad's *Heart of Darkness* and I remember thinking how striking was the similarity between Bill's voice and the way I imagined that of Kurtz, the missionary turned tribal god in Conrad's darkest Africa. In the book Kurtz's last words came out of a phone-like, dying mouth: 'Exterminate the brutes!'

"Somehow the Buckley cloak of missionary zeal has never fit Reid very well. It was like a Brooks Brothers suit always looking like a Brooks costume. Clearly, the guy would give you the shirt off his back, and yet there he was zealously propounding survival-of-the-fittest social theories.

"Reid a rebel? No. A lovable and loyal friend? Yes. But if you'd woken him in the middle of the night, he would have mouthed all the Bill Buckley expressions of Marie Antoinette philosophy that the whole family has. Even if you woke him up with a Gestapo flashlight."

"Actually, when you're kids, you know each other pretty well," another childhood neighbor recalled. "The Buckleys' wealth might have been very imposing, their multi-columned mansion and the number of help they had running around in huge lawnmowers, and pools and tennis courts—but they themselves, as individuals, with all their tutors, there were glaring flaws. They didn't really impose: we thought we were better than they were. Imagine, at six, eight, ten, twelve—I'm talking about myself and the other Huck Finn types that were hunting and fishing and stuff. We really didn't feel we were inferior. We knew there were flaws in them that we kind of felt uneasy about. It was phony, and it wasn't just the English tutors and the Spanish nana and the Mademoiselle and the crazy portraits on the wall, each one done by some crazy Russian who came in and took a year for each.

"The old man had a grandiose idea. He was going to produce this dynasty: it was almost like the military—to produce a cadre of people loyal to him, and the way to do it was to breed them. He was going to train them with all his propaganda experts. It's the Old South, and the servants, and loyalty. If I'd been a member of the Buckley family, I'd have felt a sense of togetherness that I never felt in my own family. We were always so brutally honest with one another.

"We had none of this fake brotherly-love shit. We raked each other over pretty well in public—not just acrimoniously: all in the name of being open. The Buckleys, even though they might be privately pissed off at one of them, closed ranks like crazy. No sign that anyone was pissed off at anyone else. At the same time there was always a high premium on acerbic wit in that family. Anybody who could really get the knife to somebody—that was eighty-five points right there. Carol was too young for all this: when the action was going on, she was the baby."

Carol, who is now Mrs. Ray Learsy, corroborated that statement when she talked to Susan Sheehan of *McCall's* in 1971. When she was born in 1938, her father was fifty-seven—old enough to be her grandfather; her eldest sibling, Aloïse, was twenty, and her youngest, Maureen, was five; Reid, the next youngest, was eight. A woman friend of her own age said in 1971: "Carol's best friend in the family, the one she's closest to, is Jimmy Heath, the eldest of Aloïse's ten children, who's only a couple of years younger than she. He turned his back on a lot of things—wanted to go into the theater, and then he found he could make it running an apartment house on the East Side. Carol had the capacity to break away, but she's back in the fold."

It must have been a most difficult fold from which to make a lasting escape, if the family's own accounts of it are to be believed; and there is every reason to suppose that, even with the idyllic aura appropriate to the circumstances, the reminiscences that have been published are essentially true. Yet they are not incompatible with outsiders' unsentimental appraisals. Whatever the atmosphere when Will Buckley was at home with his family—and he was often absent on long business trips—and whatever the warmth of their mother's love, the children were largely in the hands of governesses, tutors, and schools. When the Buckleys lived in Europe for four years, for example, the children were sent to various boarding schools, not always Catholic (though William Jr. studied at Beaumont in England, the Catholic Eton, to which Coco Chanel sent her sister's son at about the same period); when they were in the United States, they were enrolled in various nearby boarding schools of the quality of Millbrook in New York State or (for the girls) the Ethel Walker School in Farmington, near Hartford.

Some of them were red-haired when they were small, and occasionally evidenced the hot temper that is supposed to be the corollary. One was William Jr. "In spite of family loyalty," William Coley said, "I saw Jim and Bill in a physical fight. Bill had a very short fuse. His edginess is very real."

In the family's own accounts, Bill emerged very early as the outstanding figure. It was he who at the age of six wrote an indignant demand for payment of British war debts to the King of England, as his father recounted in a speech intended for delivery at Bill's wedding. At Beaumont, two days after his arrival at the age of ten, he called on the president of the school with a catalogue of its failings. A visiting friend of his sister Jane was dressed down with a pomposity remarkable in a person of any age. Impressed at the age of twelve to deliver to the post office the isolationist newspaper that his elder brothers and sisters had begun to publish in 1938, he at once asserted himself as the final arbiter of its policies. When Patricia, who was also red-haired, was dispatched to Ethel Walker, he inspected and condemned the shortness of the other girls' dresses. At Millbrook, he invited himself to a faculty meeting in order to protest the deprivation of his right of free speech and to bring to his mentors the illuminations of the theological and secular doctrines that had been imparted to him at Great Elm. Some years later, on his transfer to a military base in Texas, he afforded—or sought to afford—the benefit of his views on organisation to the commanding officer, but the draft document was intercepted.

Of the other children, only Reid, who is four years his junior, received comparable attention in the volume of tributes to their father. Reid, who spoke Spanish long before he learned English, in his early years saw his father so rarely that he spoke of him as "*el Señor*, who comes once in a while and eats and sleeps here. They also call him *papá*." As a child Reid loved to perform, whether for the family or for a London crowd waiting to see the King and Queen pass with the President of France. Old friends of the family say that from childhood on he has been closest to Bill, whom he emulates to the best of his ability. His arrogance at fifteen, when an accountant for his bank, in the usual routine, asked him to confirm his balance, was formidable, to judge from the letter quoted in *W.F.B.—An Appreciation*. One can discern no tendency to discourage this or his propensity to dazzle the servants, the siblings, and the guests. But he was too late to attain to the title that the family had already conferred on Bill (whom his father often called Billy): The Young Mahster. And, though their father referred to Reid as the family intellectual and was extremely proud of Reid's literary aspirations and actual output, it was his namesake whom he sought to groom for a public career —not surprisingly, given Billy's obvious predilections and forcefulness. At fifteen Billy was told in a letter from his father: "Your Mother and I like very much your attitude of having strong convictions and of not being too bashful to express them. . . . [But] you would have to learn to be more moderate in the expression of your views and try to express them in a way that would give as little offense as possible to your friends."

The other children were unquestionably loved quite as much but excited less individual comment, though John at fourteen was reminded of the necessity of keeping one's promises, however trivial ("cc. Miss Aloïse Buckley"), and Jimmy at about the same age was commended for the gravity with which he took his financial obligations. When Will Buckley was not at home—and

often when he was—he communicated extensively with his children by memorandum, brief or elaborate. Almost always a copy
of every memorandum went to every child, unless one or two in
particular were under severe castigation in the document. Everyone was always kept informed of Billy's progress in school. All
were repeatedly exhorted not to smoke (though for the most part
in vain) and to use their legs and feet for locomotion. There was
often a good deal of humor in these memoranda, though of the
rather heavy-handed kind that seems to have afflicted that generation of cultivated American fathers, regardless of ambiences of
religion or region, when dealing with their growing children. The
values that were emphasised—also repeatedly—were equally widely held (and not all to be discarded then or since—one of the most
radical and brilliant Left anarchists in America would be delighted
to see the genuine courtesy in which he, like the Buckleys, was
brought up prevail among our fellow-radicals, or even manifest
a sign of life among the "liberals"). One is thankful not to have
been exposed, as the Buckleys were by paternal fiat, to the compulsory mastery of such accomplishments as playing banjos and
marimbas or wood-carving, but there is much to be said for at
least encouraging one's children to make the acquaintance of the
natural world and to acquire such skills as carpentry and cooking,
stenography and typing, though tap-dancing might be made an
option.

On the other hand, the paternal memoranda dealt often with
books that had impressed Will, whether novels or serious non-
fiction (and sometimes with articles in *Reader's Digest*), and that
he thought his children should read—usually for some uplifting
reason as much as for esthetic value. From various parts of the
world they received advice also on the care of their own children
(*in esse* or *in futuro*), their handwriting, their speech; but as his
own children grew his tone often changed. "The absurdities of
adolescence," Aloïse Heath wrote, "were far less amusing to him
than those of children, and what amusement they did provoke in
him was apt to be tinged with exasperation." Almost regardless
of his children's ages—and this was again characteristic of a generation and a class of fathers—he *knew* what was best for them
and attempted to secure their acquiescence by appearing to take
it for granted in his letters on the subject, whether it be the choice
of a profession or of a place of residence for a grown woman with

a handful of children. He relied more on reason with his sons than with his daughters, Mrs. Heath wrote.

From the letter that she quotes extensively it is evident that the elder Buckley profoundly influenced his namesake's career. Billy was urged to supply the country's lack of "a politician who has an education, and I don't know of *one*." Writing after the publication of his son's first book, *God and Man at Yale*, Buckley Sr. urged him to spend two years at Oxford or Cambridge under outstanding scholars because "the English have an innate mastery of politics and government which is not reflected in their stupid incursion into Socialism." Alternatively, he suggested that his son join his brothers in the family business: "In my opinion, you would make a great executive . . . and I believe this is a field that would fascinate you. You would get primarily the pleasure coming from adventure (and gambling), and in addition the multiple interests of dealing with governments and bankers and oil companies." But the name of William F. Buckley Jr. appears on no published list of officers or directors of the family's firms. And Maureen, whom her father urged to become a lawyer, persisted in her determination to have a career in publishing until the pressure of multiple motherhood compelled her to abandon it.

Besides their father's frequent memoranda, the Buckleys had also a sporadic family newspaper, *Grelmschatka*, which was often several years late in its reportage. Its title represented a telescoping of the names of the family's two estates, Great Elm and Kamschatka, and its style was a cross between the heaviness of the memoranda and the archness that has come to afflict almost all the writing Buckleys: Aloïse Heath, Priscilla, Bill, Reid—even John, whose writing is largely confined to letters to his critics, either personally or through the editorial page of *The Lakeville Journal*. *Grelmschatka* made six appearances between 1947 and 1958; the first four issues and the last were edited by Priscilla, who by the time *National Review* was founded was a veteran of the Paris bureau of United Press and of the European desk of the Central Intelligence Agency, and the fifth was produced by Aloïse and Patricia, who by then was Mrs. L. Brent Bozell and who, like Aloïse her sister and Aloïse her mother, was to be the mother of ten children. It consisted of family news—which, given the size of the family and the intervals between issues, was voluminous—told largely in italics, and at times it would be difficult to distinguish between *Grelmschatka* and that other family publication, *National Review*.

The tone of *Grelmschatka*, if not of *National Review*, was softer than that of the letters that the Buckleys began to send to *The Lakeville Journal* before the United States entered the Second World War. Will Buckley had published an open letter to the community in opposition to aid to the Allies, and it had evoked a spirited reply from Robert Osborn, the author and artist, who was living in Salisbury and teaching art and Greek philosophy at Hotchkiss, and who accused the elder Buckley of giving in to fear. These two letters appeared in September, 1940, and were followed by one in which John Buckley, then twenty, almost drowned Osborn in a torrent of rhetoric denouncing his "maudlin emotionalism" in supporting a war "which is as yet neither justi-fiable nor imminent." Osborn, John said, ought to join the Ca-nadian Army with other interventionists if "[you] have allowed yourselves to be frightened into a blind, unreasoning panic of one man thousands of miles away. . . . My father . . . although he despises Hitler," had not been affected by "the prevalent fear of him . . . to the extent that he can no longer think straight."

The controversy subsided then (though Mrs. Buckley wrote in defense of Anne Morrow Lindbergh's book *The Wave of the Future* and those who admired it: "There are still a few of us who know the real meaning of 'patriotism and spirituality' "), but in the following October it flared again after civil-defense prepara-tions had begun and Sharon had been visited by various military men who had explained the mechanics of the problem. Billy, not yet sixteen—he had just won the yacht club's Community Service trophy by scoring thirteen wins for the season in a craft called *Sweet Isolation*—and Aloïse, who was twenty-three, fused their passions in a letter denouncing *The Journal*'s book reviewer, known only as M. F., for having praised the intelligence of the visiting officers. "Since M.F. is a member of various interventionist committees," the apprentice polemicists wrote, "we know that he is gullible."

A resident named Ward Hutchinson replied promptly with a rebuke to "opinionated youth . . . born with a silver spoon in the mouth." He added that the young Buckleys' "attitude (like their clever and rather priggishly sarcastic style) is extremely English—in a depressing way. . . . [Those who love the British] hope that this sort of Englishness is now in the melting pot." To which the young collaborators responded that Hutchinson must be, "like M. F., though perhaps not too old to fight, certainly too old to have to fight."

This letter appeared in October of 1941. One forbears to cite the apposite French platitude.

Rhetoric, however, was not always the limit of response by young Buckleys to the world round them. In the late thirties Sharon—certified by the Garden Club of Connecticut as the state's second most beautiful town, after Litchfield: and it would be fascinating to know how one could have chosen finally between them —was defaced by a singularly vulgar Coca-Cola sign, which the young Buckleys offered to tear down when they heard their father excoriate it and its owner. This his principles would not permit him to countenance, though he did tell his children that, if the town rose against the excrescence, his sentiments would be with his fellow-citizens. One December night in 1939 some of the Buckleys, below voting age, whited out the offending billboard, which the owner promptly replaced.

This experiment in direct action was not repeated until 1944, when, in pursuance of a feud with the daughters of the local Episcopalian rector (who have since become well-known television actresses), three Buckley girls—Priscilla, Jane, and Patricia— and two out-of-town guests went into Christ Episcopal Church on a May Saturday and, *inter alia,* smeared honey and feathers over the pews and inserted obscene pictures in the prayer books. Brought to book by the state police, each of the Buckley girls was fined a hundred dollars. Described by the family as a "prank," the incident was brought up twenty-five years later against William F. Buckley Jr. by Gore Vidal in a magazine article that became one of the grounds for a successful libel action.

Through all the years of growing up, to judge from various family and individual reminiscences, there were quite as many instances of strife among the brothers and sisters as their number would lead one to expect. But even in their earliest days the Buckleys presented to the rest of the world a front as seamless as a concrete slab, and the kind of unquestioning support of all for each that was to mark their activities until very recently—when the change was not manifested by any visible crack, though the inner unity had been broken—was evident almost from the first.

Nor, aside from the differences with the townspeople over the war, and the three girls' invasion of Christ Episcopal Church, is there any evidence of clashes with the outside world. The family almost never lost a servant: even the Buckleys' detractors freely concede that their servants have always adored them, and *noblesse oblige* was apparently second nature. The Frenchwoman who became Aloïse's governess in 1922—Jeanne Bouchex, a native of Evian-les-Bains, only three years younger than Will Sr.—assumed successively the charge of the nine subsequent children and remained with the family until her death at Kamschatka in 1949 at the age of sixty-five. She too was drawn into the magic circle of unity, Aloïse Heath's little essay on her death reveals: whatever Mademoiselle's strictness of the moment, whatever her disciplinary measures in hot pursuit, her final record always showed perfection for all her charges.

The Coley brothers recall their childhood friends the Buckleys as already under training for the rôles that their father had laid down for them: John and James to be the managing directors of the family fortune, Billy to be the ambassador (or, perhaps, the evangelist) to the heathen and the peasantry, Reid to be the intellectual and writer (the sisters, of course, would be primarily wives and mothers—except Maureen, as noted). Almost as soon as they had learned English and reading, they had begun their indoctrination in patriotism, Catholicism, and capitalism, in the absolute rightness of the established order and its various hierarchies. Thus buttressed ideologically, armed and armored intellectually by the best tutors and schools and the suppleness that came from almost daily jousting that further tempered natural endowment of superior quality, secure in the fealty of those lieges, the servants, and in the all but fanatical solidarity of family, no Buckley could have thought of himself and his ideas as other than perfect, standards for all the lesser breeds to emulate. For some of them this knowledge was enough in itself; for others it was what was to send them forth into—and against—a world too benighted to know its salvation and too stubborn to be brought to the light.

VI

FROM THE FIRST, the Buckleys, unlike the Kennedys, treated public office with the contempt it deserves: again unlike the Kennedys, the Buckleys were subtle enough to know where the real power lies, and to want it less for the glorification of a name or the reassurance of an ego than for the furtherance of real beliefs. What Kennedy would ever have refused any expression, any gesture that might have been expected to gain him popularity or votes? What Kennedy has ever admitted that it was his goal to preserve and reinforce the nexus of basic injustices, inequities, and moral outrages on which alone (one is constrained to believe) every society, and certainly this one, can be erected and carried forward? The opportunist is almost never really a threat because he will never take an authentic position. What makes the Buckleys most dangerous—even beyond what they believe—is their incapacity, despite innumerable despicable condescensions to the ignobilities of quotidian contest in any public arena, to pretend to any goals other than their real ones, to any creed other than their undisguised closed élitism; and, even worse, the deadly fascination that any honest man exercises even on those who have never seen one before.

The first to emerge from the nest into the exotic world of the university were Aloïse, John, and James. Before the war she entered Smith and they matriculated at Yale, against whose "liberal" and "Leftish" bedizenments they had been amply warned and prepared, and they graduated into the specious national unity that was invoked after Pearl Harbor. A classmate of James was John Lindsay, later Mayor of New York and Bill's butt. The two sons went into the armed forces; the daughter soon married and be-

came a mother, ignoring public life and public questions. But by
the time Patricia and Billy entered college—she Vassar, he Yale—
imposed "togetherness" had already begun to dissipate and patriotism, as conceived in the Buckleys' philosophy, demanded not
forbearance but—*avant la lettre*—activism. They, if not the world,
knew by now the almost immeasurable enormity of the liberal
and Communist peril, and they—particularly Billy—clearly saw
their duty to contend against it. Through most of her Vassar
career, however, Patricia did not thrust herself into any prominence; but her brother had been a Yale freshman barely two
months when, with a colleague named Carl Wohlenberg, he addressed a long, very self-assured letter to the *Yale Daily News* on
the subject of the compulsory freshman physics course. The letter
was, of course, hostile: the course was denounced as much too
advanced for freshmen, and one is in no position to assess the validity of the criticism. It was November, 1946; Buckley had
served several years in the army, and its bureaucracies had not
made him more patient.

Meanwhile Buckley had decided to "heel" for the paper—the
oldest college daily in the country: it was founded in January,
1878—and to try out for the freshman debating team. Here he met
L. Brent Bozell Jr., a red-haired scholarship student from Omaha
who in those days was a World Federalist: in fact, in the next
semester Bozell was president of the Yale chapter of United World
Federalists, still unaware that he was to be made into a Catholic, a
conservative, and (almost) a Buckley: in 1949 he married Patricia
Buckley. But Bozell and Buckley were at once recognised as outstanding debaters: highly intelligent, extremely well grounded,
superbly alert and almost magically sensitive to an opponent's
vulnerabilities.

Buckley was also ready to show Yale where it ought to go: to
the Right. Every year the university conducted a kind of United
Fund drive, the purposes of which were announced in advance.
In 1946-47 contributions went well beyond the goal, and the
Budget Drive Committee decided, with the approval of eighty-
five per cent of the students, to allocate the surplus to a scholarship fund for Negroes (one did not then say "blacks," except in
derogation). On 14 February 1947 the *Daily News* published a
long letter from W. F. Buckley Jr. challenging the decision and
the subsequent measures proposed to appease those students who
disapproved. These included a plebiscite on the question and, if

the decision were again approved, the return of contributions to the disgruntled, who would have to request it. Buckley contended that it was the duty of the fund's sponsors to canvass each contributor for his approval or disapproval and to refund all or part of his gift if he disapproved. He argued that the scholarship proposal was illegal unless approved unanimously by those who had given money, and that in any event no new purpose could properly be set ex post facto. At no time did he specifically attack the concept of scholarships for Negroes. But he had grown up in a family environment in which integration was believed to be contrary to "the natural order of things"; and twenty-five years later he was still to be impaling the "cannibals" and "semi-savages" of Africa on his verbal skewers.

The rich man's son who was challenging the allocation of charitable contributions to scholarships for Negroes was, however, going through Yale on funds supplied under the GI Bill of Rights, to which his legal claim was unchallengeable. But as long as he had been literate he had been denouncing the "socialism" of precisely this kind of legislation and championing the virtues of self-reliance and independence. A genuine moralist, he had already—as in the case of the scholarships—formed the habit of weighing every issue on principle: an admirable approach, provided . . .

But even a quarter-century later he was still able to defend what to a less subtle mind might have seemed a rather coarse abandonment of principle. "I have no difficulty at all," he told me, "in reaching the conclusion that, if the majority votes in such a way as the minority disagrees with, the minority has no philosophical difficulties in accepting whatever are the incidental benefits of that system. As a matter of fact, my brother Jimmy, who was in law school at the time, turned down a hundred-dollar veterans' bonus that was voted then, and I remember telling him at the time that I simply thought this philosophically exhibitionistic. It's one thing to vote against the bonus, another to say *Because I'm against it, or because I'm against social security, I'm not going to accept the benefits.* It's simply a form of trying to recapture something that you are perfectly well entitled to say is your due according to the system." In the matter of this morality of convenience a Buckley becomes indistinguishable from a Kennedy—or from that Ortegan *Massenmensch* whom Buckley so vigorously contemns.

Virtually every major position held by Buckley and supported by his associates today was first taken and enunciated during his years at Yale, often in terms that have altered hardly at all with time. But in those days students were not taken seriously by anyone in this country—not that so many Americans take them seriously today—and in particular the few articulate, cultivated voices of the Right were genially scorned by those who thought of themselves as liberals and also as the new majority.

While Bill Buckley was shaping his positions and sharpening his rhetoric, James was progressing inconspicuously through Yale Law School. During his undergraduate time, before his war service in the navy, he had been a quiet student, making firm friends in spite of his native shyness (which has not left him even now that he has become a Senator by force of persuading some millions of strangers to vote for him); he had been a member of the board of editors of the *Daily News*, but he had never made or sought to make the kind of reputation that his brother Bill quickly established. John, who had preceded both of them at Yale, had passed through most inconspicuously, attending to his work and doing well, but taking little if any part in the life of the college or in public matters. Reid, who entered Yale two years after Bill, was to repeat him as much as circumstances and his own capacities would permit.

Probably the greatest single influence that Bill Buckley encountered at Yale—and his allegiance to it has never wavered—was that of a professor of political science who was completing his journey into salvation from the snares of the Left and to whom, in the view of other members of the Yale faculty, the ostensible student became the guru. Willmoore Kendall, in Buckley's words, had arrived at Yale "as somebody who had been a liberal, or, as you prefer, a man of the Left. He recoiled very sharply against Henry Wallace and against the Soviet Union during the diplomacy immediately after the war. He was then left rather shaken, and, when we ran into each other, if I contributed anything at all, it was simply a settled position which, when he explored it, he tended to find rather comfortable. But, for instance, at the time I wrote *God and Man at Yale*, he was absolutely impatient—not absolutely but largely impatient with free-market economics. He came around to free-market economics. But during that period I would say that it was nothing to do with me except that in a sense I was a conduit to people and to a literature which he found compatible with a series of positions which were forming, exactly the same,

I think, as—with interesting philosophical differences—was true of James Burnham, and true of Max Eastman too."

Kendall was seventeen years older than his student/guru; Burnham (who gives a rather different account: for example, the disclosure of Kendall's long closeness to the Trotskyist position) and Max Eastman, much more eminent men of the Left whom Buckley met later, were Kendall's seniors: Eastman, in fact, was only two years younger than Will Buckley. Yet all of them—strong personalities in themselves, almost always certain of the correctness of their positions—certainly seem to have fled sooner or later into the same opposite adoration of authority, and to have accepted the leadership of this very much younger man, before whose intellect Burnham and Eastman, at least, had no occasion to defer. One must add that, for himself and Eastman, Burnham challenges this interpretation as to both authority and leadership. Buckley, Burnham says, sought him out.

Burnham at thirty-five, when Buckley was fifteen, was a professor of philosophy at New York University; he had just resigned from a breakaway faction of the Trotskyist movement, the Workers Party, which had split off in rejection of the concept of allegiance to the Soviet Union and its revolution, and he was shedding all his previous political training and writing *The Managerial Revolution*, which so accurately forecast what has proved to be the dreadful technocratisation of American life. As a leading Trotskyist theoretician he had been unafraid to polemicise even with that magnificent mind that was Trotsky and that he still respects. He had known Kendall in pro-Trotskyist circles—though Kendall had never joined any Left party—and it was through Kendall (whose intellect and style Burnham also esteems) that he came to know Buckley in 1950. It is his opinion that Buckley and Kendall exercised reciprocal influences on each other rather than that either was the disciple of the other.

Eastman, who died in 1969, had been a leading radical during the First World War, when he was a Socialist and the editor of *The Masses*, which was suppressed for its opposition to the war. He had then founded another radical publication, *The Liberator;* later he had spent considerable time in Russia and had returned in disillusion, which grew with time until it sent him as far Right as the *Reader's Digest*, of which he became a contributing editor. But he had shone on the Left not only as a political publicist but also as a literary critic of considerable quality, as well as a poet.

Eastman, it is true, after he had become an early collaborator with *National Review* at the highest level, was ultimately impelled to break with Buckley and his circle because Eastman could not stomach a loyalty oath to some supernatural divinity as a condition precedent to certification as a thorough conservative. Burnham, who objects to such rigidity, which he says has by now greatly diminished, never felt it necessary to break and is Buckley's alter ego in *National Review;* Kendall, by all accounts—he died in 1967 —was far too abrasive to be long endured at close quarters by even his ideological twins—too abrasive and too independent. Yet Buckley still speaks of him with a warmth of loyalty and admiration that cannot be discounted, and his influence on Buckley's style—intellectual and rhetorical, especially in its more baroque obscurities—is unmistakable. For a period Kendall was one of the senior editors of *National Review,* and his complex nature burgeoned there until his inability to agree long with almost anyone and the zest of his pogroms against various other chieftains of conservatism sent him once more into the wilderness (the name of which was Dallas).

Men who were teaching at Yale in the late 1940's remember that both Kendall and Buckley had very few friends in the university—Kendall far fewer than Buckley. One finds it difficult, however, to believe that in Buckley's case his politics had much to do with his relative isolation (just as one finds it hard to believe that Yale was the hotbed of moral obloquy that he said it was): he was both too bright and too much a snob to have attracted many of his fellow students, most of whose interests he did not share. When he was president of Torch, an honor society, he initiated and vigorously prosecuted a more or less successful campaign, supported by the other members, to reduce substantially the emphasis placed on athletics and to increase the attention given to intellectual pursuits outside the classroom and the library. The unpopularity that resulted among what he now calls "the Stakhanovite athletic types" did not perturb him. His friendships were not always circumscribed by ideologies, and he was often the guest of the widowed Mrs. William Sloane Coffin Sr., whose son was at Yale with Buckley and is now its chaplain as well as a founding member of Resist, and of Professor Paul Weiss, the distinguished philosopher and author, and his late wife, Victoria—people who esteemed his mind, liked many aspects of his personality, and deplored his beliefs. "You could send us all to the gas chamber without a blink of the eye, couldn't you?" Mrs. Weiss remarked one evening at a dinner party at the Coffins'; there is no record of a denial. Yet Buckley refused to accept membership in Yale's most exclusive club, Skull and Bones (whose "tapping" procedure he had publicly attacked because of the humiliation it caused those who were publicly left untapped), unless it also elected his roommate, Thomas H. Guinzburg, who is now president of The Viking Press, occasionally a Buckley publisher. This was rather bold, given the fact that the club had only recently begun to accommodate itself to Catholics; but Buckley prevailed, and so Guinzburg was perhaps the third Jew in its history. Will Buckley's anti-Semitism was no part of his children's patrimony, though it is sardonically amusing to hear Bill speak of Russian Jews almost as peevishly as if he were a German Jew.

There are other Yale connections from that period whose affection for Buckley is still strong. Dr. George F. Kneller, who is a professor of education at the University of California, Los Angeles, was his friend at Yale and thinks of him as "the most intelligent commentator on the public scene today," who "has developed the use of logic and language further than anyone I know," and "is one of the most remarkable men in America today." On the other hand, Dr. Ralph A. Lewin, an oceanographer at the Scripps Institution of Oceanography at La Jolla, who took his doctorate at Yale in 1950, remembers Buckley "as a pink-faced young man who turned up at debates, etc., usually accompanied by a bevy of pink-faced sisters. . . . He was on a debating team which vied with a visiting group from Oxford one year, and he made up in *ad hominem* attacks (somewhat ungracious, in view of the courtesies one should extend to visitors) what he lacked in logic." But Lewin is wrong in thinking the Oxford team won; it was defeated. It was upholding the nationalisation of basic industries.

Rollin G. Osterweis, who teaches history at Yale and coaches the debating team, knew both Bill and Reid well and considers them and their brother-in-law Brent Bozell outstanding among all his debaters. Bill Buckley, Osterweis said, explained that he had had no debating experience in school and was applying for the debating team on his father's advice; Bozell "was a rather green, callow kid from Omaha who'd won an American Legion oratorical contest, which was no training for audience debating." Nonetheless Bozell and Bill Buckley gave Osterweis the most successful freshman debating team that he has ever had; having been a guest at Great Elm meals where the full manifest of the Buckley family was in attendance, Osterweis attested to the values of that informal day-to-day debating platform, where every meal, he said, was a performance to delight the amateur of debates. A passionately neutral man—"hell is for people like you, who never take positions," he has been told by both Coffin and Buckley, each of whom accuses him of aiding the other's cause by his refusal to embrace or anathematise—Osterweis is equally passionate in his affection for the Buckleys despite his reluctant admission in conversation that he cannot share most of their views. Yet he will concede that, as a student at Yale, Bill was extremely sarcastic and ironic in his humor and could be very cruel; he adds (and the tense could probably be present): "I saw no humor in Bozell at all."

Buckley, Osterweis said, "had a messianic kind of spirit. He was always running campaigns." Osterweis professes also to observe in the Buckley family a survival of the Southern romantic tradition —immediately apparent in hospitality and social behavior, which he had opportunities to observe because of the loyalty with which Buckleys attended debates in which Bill and later Reid took part, and which brought him into personal touch with them—and one cannot help wondering whether too there was not from Bill Buckley's earliest public advocacies and crusades something of the *noblesse oblige* of the aristocrat (self-made or other) and the fascination of the losing and lost cause.

And most of his causes at Yale, if not elsewhere, were lost ones. It is true that he did mount a successful drive to move athletics down toward its rightful place, and he did lay the groundwork for the inception of a course that Osterweis began to teach the year after Buckley was graduated. Until then Yale had had no how-to courses at all: debating, like journalism, was learned by doing and by oral tradition passed down by those who had gone before. The notion of a "speech" course—to say nothing of the "speech" major that one now sees in some catalogues—would rightly have been laughed out of New Haven. What was inaugurated, as a result of Buckley's agitation, was a course called The History of the Great American Orations from Jonathan Edwards to Franklin Delano Roosevelt, two-thirds of which is history and the rest of which is students' modern adaptations of the orations they have studied.

But this was virtually a divertissement for Buckley the crusader.

Persuaded from childhood that the forests of the academy were congested with the dragons of atheism and communism, he had no difficulty descrying this overpopulation almost from the day he passed the first thicket. As a debater, as a student journalist, and as a citizen of Yale and New Haven he strove unceasingly to save his world, and from the beginning there was visible that moral contradiction so frequently to be noted in passionate ideologists: a dedication to a cause unquestionably moral in its foundation and its essence, yet so intense that it is virtually unaware of (and certainly indifferent to) the indecency of the means to which it will resort, and, when confronted with it, will deploy those further blatant intellectual dishonesties and short-cuts—today he and other intellectual conservatives like to use the adjective "prudential"—that it is the first to denounce in its adversaries. Bill Buckley has always been guiltless of that "sin of scrupulosity" that he charged to me when I confessed my aversion to some of my allies and their means.

Two persons who were significant in his development at this period were Kendall and Bozell. Both came under his influence, yet reciprocally extended theirs over him. It is true that Buckley won Bozell away from the mild Protestantism and, as Buckley called it in 1971, "utopianism" with which he had arrived at Yale; Buckley's own assistance to Kendall during the elder's slow journey along his peculiar road to Damascus has already been mentioned. But all these men were constantly shoring up one another as they exchanged very nearly identical ideas. They were indeed, in the sense of the late Albert Jay Nock, three Isaiahs preaching under divine letters patent to The Remnant—Buckley admits today, to some degree, to such a concept of himself—though what Nock, who in his late years was often Will Buckley's guest at Great Elm ("when I was a callow teen-ager," John Buckley said: "the conversations with my father were clearly over my head"), would have thought of some of their intellectual and philosophical dodges is an interesting subject for speculation. And they were indeed, too, a very tiny minority in their days at Yale: numerically Buckley did not exaggerate. The majority, however, was not composed of those godless collectivists whose fiery breath (he said) was burning truth and goodness alive; most of the students, like most of that more or less élite (in a very restricted sense) that they represented, were decent enough fellows who could not have cared (or known) less about what was going on in the world, and whose instinctive self-interest would be, in any crisis, the worst enemy that would rear up to thwart their natural decent impulses. The relatively large minority that was concerned believed in a kind of humanitarian liberalism that was perhaps more sentimental than intellectual, as unrealistic in its way as Buckley in his, and hence dangerous not (as he contended even then) because it was the natural gull of the Left but because it was susceptible to any mountebank from any quarter who knew how to further fuzz its congenitally clouded vision.

Kendall had few followers among faculty or students; Buckley had somewhat more; Bozell was the one who showed the greatest interest and made the greatest success in achieving positions. Buckley got as far as the executive committee of the Conservative Party in the Yale Political Union; Bozell, having left United World Federalists because, quite logically, he found that membership incompatible with his rapidly growing anti-Communist activism, sought and won election in his junior year as head of the Political Union, while Buckley was concentrating his activity, in a kind of prevision of the career he would make, in debate, journalism, and what used to be called on the Left of my youth *agitprop*, in all of which he could function most effectively if he were not hobbled by ties to any organisation or rigid responsibilities to any established constituency. He ranged beyond the university and into the general political sphere, into which he endeavored, when he became chairman of the editorial board of the *Yale Daily News*, to lead the university in one sense while at the same time striving to make it a bulwark against the heretic and the infidel from without. In his junior year he was broadcasting from New Haven under the auspices of the Connecticut Forum of the Air, which made him a member of its board of directors.

Here he was in close contact with one of his major targets: the Yale Law School, in the person of Professor Thomas I. Emerson, one of its more radical teachers, who was also a member of the Forum's directorate. Buckley would be asked to broadcast when a conservative point of view was wanted, Emerson says, and, when Ralph della Selva, the head of the program, "wanted a liberal or a partial radical, he picked me. As far as personal relations were concerned, Buckley and I got along very well. I always found him to be, somewhat surprisingly, moderate in his personal relations, and affable and quite charming and even attractive in some ways."

Through the years there has been no diminution in this quality, and I can attest to the utter absence of calculation in Buckley hospitality and cordiality to the known enemy. Here at least one is dealing with a very assured man, whatever dilutions this security may or may not undergo in public.

"When we met to decide on programs and who might be on them and so forth," Emerson recalled, "he was very cooperative: there was no serious difference of opinion as to what the program should be and who should represent different sides. I would say there was really not even any feeling of antagonism. However, when we got on the air, he was a rather formidable debater, and he was much better than I was. He used to talk circles around me, by and large. He of course always took a very conservative point of view [Buckley in fact made speeches on behalf of the Presidential candidacy of Thomas E. Dewey, then Governor of New York, whom Roosevelt had defeated in 1944 and whom Truman was to defeat in 1948, the year under discussion], and I was taking the Henry Wallace-Progressive Party-liberal point of view. . . .

"I used to try to figure out why Buckley was such a good debater and tended to overwhelm the opposition, at least as far as I was concerned. I remember analysing it at the time. One factor was that, in taking the conservative point of view, he was reiterating a very familiar position, a position that all of us at that time had been brought up on: rugged individualism and the less government the better, everybody taking care of himself, and so on. Simply by reason of the fact that he was expressing something that had been drilled into all of us prior to the New Deal, he sort of started off with a point of view that other people could understand and accept without too much elaboration on his part. The second thing was, it seemed to me, that he always appealed to a short-range self-interest in people—it was a very individualistic nineteenth-century post-Civil War kind of attitude in which he appealed to the immediate interests of people, whereas most of the problems that were arising as society got more complicated, and as the government and the New Deal got into more things, tended to be more sophisticated and in part more long-range, and required a broader, more objective point of view to appreciate them. So it was difficult for anyone arguing with him to get into the sophisticated areas of the liberal side.

"Finally, he was very keen in finding the weaknesses of the liberal side, very perceptive about where they were going wrong.

. . . He was very expert in putting a person on the defensive by pointing to the failures and the difficulties of the liberal program. In addition to all that, he was a hit-and-run debater. He would make his points very rapidly, very decisively; and before anyone could really reply he'd take off on another point, so that one could never get around to answering him. He was quite aggressive: he used to hog the microphone a good deal."

William Coley said much the same thing: "One of Buckley's great strengths as a public debater is that he touches the irascibility of his opponents beautifully and most of the time they fly off the handle. He stretches his allotted time and ignores his opponents'. He's a point-scoring kind of man, which is what makes him an extremely good debater by Oxford Union standards. He really thinks of life as scoring off the other guy. Most voters, if they sense nothing else about him, are put off by the feeling of his scoring off people: they're entertained, but they mistrust him."

Both judgments could have been made with equal accuracy twenty-five years ago or yesterday, in spite of the differences between the two men who made them. "One reaches a point," Coley has observed, "at which it is no longer possible to separate the man from his ideas"; but Emerson, in spite of having been publicly smeared by Buckley in the 1950's as at least an instrument of the Communists, still makes the distinction. It is perhaps precisely because of this distinction that Emerson, unlike so many on the Left who are afflicted with the wishful astigmatism so often characteristic of that orientation, recognises the Buckleys and their circle as dangerous. "I think essentially he has a fascist mentality and an ability to put himself across to people that are very dangerous," Emerson said of Bill Buckley.

Fred Rodell, who in times past was known to his Yale Law School students as Fred the Red because of his political positions— though he was never so far to the Left as Emerson, with whom, in fact, Rodell has vigorously disagreed on the question of cooperation with Communists—is inclined to believe that Buckley is rather less dangerous than he was ten years ago. Rodell was also his target both during and after Buckley's time at Yale (Buckley regarded Rodell and Emerson as enemies of the country, with their colleague Fowler Harper—who was occasionally Willmoore Kendall's lawyer—and Dr. Linus Pauling), and his review of *God and Man at Yale* was merciless. Yet their personal relations remained cordial when they encountered each other—chiefly at political meetings and on debating platforms, as well as occasional television broadcasts. To Rodell, Buckley's dangerousness is sharply limited: "I think he has a personal inborn decency which would stop him from going too far. . . . He has the same streak of gentleness as his mother." It is for this that Rodell, however arrogant and silly he may occasionally consider Buckley, has "always felt friendly toward him as a human being." After a debate in South Carolina to which Mrs. Buckley had come from Kamschatka to see her son triumph and in which Rodell, to his own surprise, had crushed him, Fred the Red felt constrained to apologise for having done so in his mother's presence.

Both Emerson and Rodell reject the notion of Buckley as a demagogue. Like others who have debated him, in college or since, and observers of his performance whether in print or on television, they are convinced of his sincerity, of the thorough genuineness of his fealty to the positions he takes, whatever the sharp practice—if not worse—by which he advances or defends them. It is, of course, precisely this honesty that makes the able man far more dangerous than the demagogue. A McCarthy (either kind) or a Kennedy—or a Nixon—is a threat only to common decency, since one can be certain that he will always change position to save face, to say nothing of skin; a Buckley, like a Lenin or a Trotsky (or a Torquemada, whom Bill Buckley in ideological passionate pursuit of the Devil irresistibly brings to mind), having been brought by reason and faith to embrace a view, will never change convictions for mere advantage. Such men are the greatest possible menaces; not only do they resist: they attract at least as much through their firmness as through the substance of their allegiances. Unfortunately, they frequently do not scruple—since they do not always commit the sin of scrupulosity—to use whatever chameleon offers to turn his complexion for them.

Bozell paced Buckley through Yale, and James Buckley was already in the Yale Law School when Bill entered the college; two years later Reid became a Yale freshman. Neither Rodell nor Emerson recalls James Buckley as a law student (he must have been as unobtrusive in the Law School as he had been as an undergraduate); both remember Bozell, who went on to take his law degree there, though without great specificity—they do not share the view held by some conservatives, particularly among the thirtyish lawyers on the staff of Young Americans for Freedom in Washington, that Bozell was brilliant as a legal mind, most especially in the field of constitutional law (he is the author of a book purporting to demolish what is called "the Warren Court"). Reid, who was to follow Bill as a debater and a member of the board of the *Daily News* (Reid became vice-chairman, but never chairman, as Bill was to be) and a vigorous campus protagonist of the Right, never made the same impress, though some members of the faculty remember him as brilliant and possessed of a certain flair for writing, which must have been more pronounced in his youth than it is today. Bill Buckley's nearest competitor (if that is the word) in the clan was his future brother-in-law. It was Bozell who went into the arena while Buckley remained for the most part on the minor Olympus of his newspaper, his broadcasts, and the debating team. Known then as Leo B. Bozell Jr., he campaigned for (and won) the leadership of the Yale branch of United World Federalists (an organisation, it is bemusing to recall, that at that time included such a one—subsequently to be hotly defended by Buckley—as the late Senator Thomas Dodd of Connecticut). Bozell devoted much time to a crusade against the growing Progressive Citizens of America and their leader at Yale, a New Haven graduate student named Pasquale Vecchione, who publicly denounced Bozell as a liar— Bozell having made the standard charge that all the Progressives were Communists or, worse still, dupes of Communists—and "a junior J. Parnell Thomas." (Thomas was the holier-than-everybody former chairman of the House Un-American Activities Committee who had made a titillating career out of ruining perfectly decent people at random until he was found to have put his hand into a till: a far more heinous offense; so he became—briefly—a guest of the taxpayers. But it was not this kind of thing that Vecchione was ascribing to Bozell.)

Bozell's ties with the Buckleys were tightening. In Weiss's course in the history of philosophy "Brent was a much abler person than Bill—more intelligent, better focused, more mature—and then he became converted to Catholicism about the time he got involved with Bill's sister. From that time he became a more and more reactionary Catholic, with less and less to say to anybody who didn't accept his faith." Bill Buckley was his closest friend as well as his partner on the debating team. In 1949, the year before his graduation from Yale, he married Patricia Buckley (in the same year his childhood Omaha friend, Ann Harding, married John Buckley, who has never remarried since her early death). For some years Bozell was to be virtually a Buckley until he and his wife, whose temper was a family byword, were swept out of politics by their total religious involvement. At her marriage an honors graduate of Vassar, where she had majored in music and shown no special flamboyance, Mrs. Bozell had suddenly gained a certain notoriety early in 1949 by publicly denouncing President Sarah Gibson Blanding of Vassar as an unwitting aider and abetter of the Communist conspiracy.

Miss Blanding was one of the thousands of persons eminent in the arts, the professions, education, and related domains who were sponsors of the Cultural and Scientific Conference for World Peace that was to be held on 25 May 1949 at the Waldorf-Astoria and that had been denounced in advance by the State Department and many other sources as "a sounding-board for Communist propaganda"—partly because it had Soviet backing, partly too because one of the luminaries was to be the Russian composer, Dmitri Shostakovitch, who had only recently accepted party chastisement for the unsound politics of his music (McCarthyism by whatever name having no national or ideological limitations). Mrs. Bozell, who had been a member of the editorial board of the lately established student conservative publication, *The Chronicle*, offered herself as an apostle to the chief Gentile of Poughkeepsie and made two journeys up the Hudson to carry the light to her elder, who, Mrs. Bozell wrote several years later in *The Freeman*, "was anxious to further Communist propaganda, or she was too naïve, too misinformed, or perhaps too unintelligent to fulfill her responsibilities as the head of a college." The crusader would appear not to have been suffused with Christian charity. Her epistle to the godless was a twenty-eight-page brochure of her own composition.

A year earlier, in her senior year at Vassar, she had made it clear that, like her brother Bill, she was not to be taken in by any nonsense about academic freedom and the search for truth—a search for which there was no need, since the truth was already available on demand. One aspect of this not altogether revealed truth was the "widely dawning fact that [the Progressive movement for Wallace] was nothing more nor less than an instrument of Soviet foreign policy." Now Mrs. Bozell found it necessary to explain to Miss Blanding that such a cultural and scientific exchange (she surrounded the substantive with quotation marks) as the proposed Waldorf celebration was "traditional Communist double-talk for Communist propaganda." Both these notions were already part of the family folklore, and the generic Buckley position on cultural

exchanges and academic freedom a quarter-century later has altered
only in that it has begun to petrify—though it has not prevented
Bill Buckley from making more than one pleasant journey to the
exurbs and even the citadel of that atheistic Communism he so
enjoys attacking; nor has it stopped him from invoking, in innumerable campus lecture halls, the very right the existence of which he
challenges. (To this, of course, he or Burnham or Russell Kirk
would reply that there is no inconsistency because it is not a question of academic freedom in the search for truth, but rather of the
academic duty to disseminate truth already found.)

While Mrs. Bozell was wrestling with the ghost of Lenin for
Miss Blanding's soul in Poughkeepsie, her brother was vigorously
attacking from the flank through his editorials in the *Yale Daily
News*, of which he had just become chairman by unanimous vote.
The controversy was almost immediately picked up by the press,
and the usual pundits made the usual observations consistent with
their political fixations, with the usual minimal attention to the
facts and the merits. The older alumnae of Vassar rallied to their
young colleague, and not long after the battle had begun there was
triumph for the House of Buckley: Miss Blanding withdrew her
sponsorship from the conference "reluctantly . . . since I am aware
that by so doing I will give comfort or even aid to that small but
increasing group of Americans who appear to be willing to abandon
our tradition of democracy, freedom of ideas, their expression and
their interchange." Her reason for so doing, she said, was doubt
whether the participants in the conference would "represent a
sufficiently broad point of view." But it seems rather painfully
evident that she had been compelled to recognise what José Ortega
y Gasset had found out twenty years earlier: "In the United States,
to be different is to be indecent."

"Miss Blanding Sees the Light," Buckley titled the *Yale Daily
News* editorial in which he congratulated the lady with a complacency beyond measurement and paid tribute to the missionary
zeal of the "young Vassar alumna"—whom he did not name—
who had carried the evangel to Poughkeepsie. The Buckleys were
on their way.

VII

Buckley was a good student at Yale in spite of the remarkable diffusion of himself that he had already begun to practice. His was what was called a divisional major, in history, economics, and political science; he studied widely also in philosophy, history, and literature, and taught freshman Spanish, which was almost a second native tongue for him; he read extensively; he spent a fair amount of time flying, having acquired a pilot's license; and he worked indefatigably for the *Yale Daily News*, which, even more than his debating and his broadcasting, was the real expression of his life at the university. When, according to the custom, he took over its control for a year beginning with his second semester as a junior—the chairman relinquishes to his successor in the second semester of his senior year—he so shaped it that those issues can be at once recognised as his more than twenty years later, both in substance and in style.

Before he became chairman it was, from a purely journalistic point of view, a good college paper, much superior to the general run then or now. During his tenure it was markedly better than it had been before, and more often than not it could be called almost professional; after his departure it remained influenced by the improvements he had made in it. But it was only for the one year that the *Yale Daily News* made one think often of William McKinley, and sometimes of William Randolph Hearst Sr.

It was no courses in journalism, graduate or undergraduate, that endowed the paper with an able staff. Such things did not exist at Yale. Each year's editors and staff imparted to the apprentices what they themselves had learned by doing (and, one supposes, by observing too, since there were then several good New York newspapers available daily in New Haven). There was one paid, permanent member of the staff, like the permanent undersecretary who keeps a ministry going efficiently regardless of changes in cabinet. He was—and is—Francis Donahue, who first went to work for the *Daily News* in 1923, when he was thirteen. His apprenticeship taught him makeup and layout, and he went on to function as advertising manager and chief salesman, serving both national and local accounts. What the students learned about these arcane arts they acquired from him, though he did not attempt explicitly to teach them. It was customary, at the end of the academic year, for the chairman, the business manager, and the managing editor to divide the paper's profits, if there were any, but according to Donahue, "they'd be lucky if they got forty cents an hour, all those hours they put in."

Donahue knew James, Bill, and Reid Buckley at the *Daily News*, but his sharpest memories are of Bill's year as chairman, and his unqualified admiration and affection for Bill are instructive. There is much of the attitude of the loyal family retainer in the best sense—no note of servility, but also none of criticism or even question. It is a kind of hero-worship that has persisted unabated, and it may be summarised by his own reply to the researcher for an *Esquire* article who asked to interview him about Bill. "I said to him," Donahue told me, " 'If all the important men in the world were put into one room, including the Pope, and God appeared to me and said: "Go and pick a brother out of that room," I'd go and pick Bill.' " Donahue was an important guest at *National Review's* fifteenth anniversary party in New York in 1971, and Buckley's devotion to him is strong. The Young Mahster of Great Elm was the Young Laird to Donahue, and he behaved as the ideal liege wants his ideal lord to behave, in private and in public. Above all, he assumed, most attractively, the burden of identity. And it is very likely this that is one of the most telling factors in the Buckleys' ability to arouse and hold the affectionate and at times aggressive allegiance of the hard-hats of every social and economic level, the men and women—though more especially the men— who hunger for a demigod to follow. One cannot help thinking of the feudal vestiges that informed the South and that persist so often still in both master and servant.

Though Yale University was not in regular session and the Oldest College Daily, as it frequently calls itself, was not being published in July of 1969, when Donahue reached his sixtieth

birthday, a special issue was produced and the handsomest tribute
—as well as the longest and the best written—to "A Unique Man
of 'Special Importance,' " as the bank of the headline called him,
was paid by Buckley, who went to New Haven for the celebration.
Donahue is probably one of the few men outside the narrow
worlds of family and conservative thought who could influence
Buckley, who wrote of the time when he was chairman and
worked daily with Donahue: "When he was pleased with me as
chairman he would sign a letter 'Your friend Francis.' . . . There
were other occasions [when] a tart note from Francis explaining
the morphology of publishing economics [would be] signed 'Your
employee Francis.' "

There has never been any real difference between Donahue's
politics and the Buckleys' in spite of party labels. (One has always
been troubled by the hyper-conservatism of those who have most
to gain from a more humane society, like those poor and ghetto
students in open-admission public colleges whose arch-reactionism
so bewilders their radical instructors.) When Bill Buckley's son,
Christopher, entered Yale as a freshman after a year of merchant-
marine experience that followed his graduation from prep school,
Donahue was of course already predisposed in his favor, but he
speaks of Christopher with a certain surprise: though he likes him
and admires his ability to form friendships across—or, more accurately, regardless of—lines of any kind, Donahue was by no means
sure that this young Buckley would automatically embrace the
conservatism of his family and its retainers; in any event Donahue
was looking forward to repeating with Christopher, on the staff of
the paper, his experience with Bill.*

Of this Donahue is full. Arranging unrestricted access to and
reproduction of whatever I might wish from the files, he explained
the machinery for choosing each year's chairman. The board of
editors—chiefly juniors—which itself is elected by the staff at
large, nominates and elects its chairman, vice-chairman, managing
editor, and business manager from its own ranks. Bill Buckley,
Donahue said, was the unanimous choice even of those who detested
his politics because "they had so much respect for him, and he
stood so much above all the rest of them." Reid Buckley, who was
vice-chairman two years later, was "nothing like Bill," Donahue
said. "He got along with everybody. But he would never attack
anything like Bill does. If Bill heard of something, he'd go out and

* Donahue need not have worried. See page 348. C.L.M.

chase it down. But Reid went straight up the middle." Of James he has little to say because Donahue had already gone off to war when James was on the board of editors. To Donahue, too, Bill has more warmth than his brothers.

Donahue could never be persuaded to go flying with Bill, who would sometimes take a three-hour flight "and then go upstairs and write his edits." Some of Donahue's recollections of Bill Buckley's chairmanship seem not to accord with the evidence of the paper itself, to say nothing of the chairman's comportment since in print and in public. That "Bill would fight for a cause at the drop of a hat if he thought it was right" is apparent enough. But it was rather surprising to be told that "Bill always used to give the other guy his day in court." Donahue elaborated: "He'd come over to look at the dummy I was making and he'd say: 'I don't want those ads on the editorial page tomorrow: we've got a lot of anti-Buckley communications.' And I would have to take the ads off and make a new dummy so we could run the anti-Buckley communications, of which there were *many*. But he always gave the other guy a chance to have his say." In a sense this was not untrue: Donahue's emphasis on the number of anti-Buckley communications was warranted; and a surprising number of them was printed. But very often the last word would be Buckley's; and certainly the selection and display of news and feature material could frequently be called biased. On the other hand, two days a week his political antagonist and vice-chairman, William J. C. Carlin, wrote the editorials according to his own lights. Donahue recalls too that, though Buckley and Weiss, the philosopher, "never got along too well, they did have deep respect for each other. If somebody belittled Weiss in some way, Bill took that guy apart."

Though Buckley (who, according to Donahue, missed Phi Beta Kappa by a hair) took one course with Weiss (in which he received a grade of B), their contacts arose predominantly out of Buckley's other activities, particularly his editorship. "He was the most extraordinary editor of a college newspaper that Yale had ever seen or I had ever heard of," Weiss said. "The faculty and the students waited every day to have the issue appear. It was electric, dynamic, horrendous; to read it was to be shocked. He was violent, reactionary more than conservative—and incredibly bold. In addition, Bill was the leading debater at Yale, and a very effective debater he was. He organised anti-Communist rallies; when he attended lectures by Communists, he would get up and say they should be thrown in jail.

"I liked him," Weiss continued, "because he was able to take as well as give. He was ready to listen to you, to attend to what your difficulties were, although he didn't accept them and perhaps didn't understand them, and I think it made no difference to him finally—nevertheless there was a sincere consideration for the fact that you were saying something different. . . . He was a charming human being—and still is. Remarkably courteous, and civilised, he was a polite, considerate, and thoughtful host." Weiss, like Coffin, recalled the dinner party at the Coffins' at which Mrs. Weiss had said to Buckley: "Bill, what are you always afraid of? Why do you pull down the curtains?" But to this, as to her observation about the gas chamber, no reply is recorded.

His journalistic career at Yale began, as I mentioned earlier, with the letter to the editor of which he was a co-signer in the first semester of his freshman year. By the time he wrote his second letter, on the subject of the scholarships for blacks, he had begun to "heel" the paper: it is only in the second semester of the freshman year that Yale permits students to start extra-curricular activities of this kind. The *Daily News* put its aspirants through the usual apprenticeship, in which everyone had to do everything at least until his principal abilities emerged, and in March of 1947 Buckley and Thomas Guinzburg were elected to the board for the next academic year. Since by-lines were very sparingly used in those days, it is very difficult to be certain which of the stories that appeared thereafter were Buckley's; one's suspicion that the April, 1947, interview with Burnham was his is dispelled by the fact that Burnham remembers clearly that they did not meet until three years later. In May, however, and again the next spring Patricia Buckley appeared as a writer of letters to the editor (with due indication of her Vassar allegiance) in which, with some cavalier disregard for the niceties of the language ("The male sex has never made any attempts to hide his wish . . . but . . . their ego is sharply deflated"), she took a kind of embryonic feminist stance —not a liberationist position, since she championed women's right to seek men who could keep them well—that must surely have long since been forgot when she attempted in 1971 to slap Ti-Grace Atkinson for an alleged insult to the Mother of God.

Bill Buckley's work for the paper was still anonymous, though

in March of 1948 it announced his election as the following year's
chairman. But his name did appear in May of 1948, when Professor
Kendall—whom Weiss recalls as "an earnest, intense man, rather
low in the academic hierarchy, who had no real future at Yale"—
was compelled to make what Weiss called a "really abject" apology
in the *Yale Daily News* for broadcast attacks on the followers of
Henry Wallace, and Buckley, who had taken part in the program,
issued an accompanying statement. Kendall made his act of con-
trition because "on April 18, 1948, over the facilities of Radio
Station WAVZ, on a Connecticut Forum of the Air program, I
stated in effect that people who work for Henry Wallace have in
effect transferred their loyalty to the Soviet Union. . . . On reflection, I realise that I then did not have, and that I do not now
have, any basis in fact" for such a statement, "and I therefore
retract" it, both in general and with reference to one Nathaniel
S. Colley, whom Kendall had assured that he included in the
charge. Buckley's statement asserted that "no one who listened to
the program could have justifiably construed Professor Kendall's
charges of transferred loyalty as inclusive of every follower of
the Wallace camp. He stated rather that the Wallace *movement*
was inspired and dominated by the Communist Party"—the italics
were Buckley's—and after the broadcast he made the charge to
and about Colley off the air, though in the presence of others. The
retraction, Buckley argued, was offered only because of the
expense of litigation and the probability of further publicity for
the forces of darkness. "It is tragic," he perorated, "to witness an
attempt to humiliate a universally respected scholar by the use of
legalistic chicanery on the part of individuals who know just when
to get righteous." He could hardly have known, of course, that
eighteen years later he would sue—and exact a retraction from—
a Connecticut neighbor of whom he sought five hundred thousand
dollars for having asserted on a television program that Buckley
"sells hate." And he concluded his statement by asserting that
Colley, "through his support of Henry Wallace, is—be it unwittingly—furthering the ends of the Soviet Union." What is
more, a terse but vigorous leading editorial in a parallel column,
censuring Kendall because he "should have been more precise in
his remarks to Mr. Colley," endorsed the comment by a number
of lawyers that "if the apparatus of the law can be used to extract
a retraction of this kind, we can only regard this as a grave threat
to civil and academic liberty." The incident is relevant to a num-

ber of analogous occurrences that were to follow, in some of which it was Buckleys who repeatedly threatened to resort to "the apparatus of the law."

Bill Buckley could not yet use the *Yale Daily News* directly for the furtherance of his views and the defeat of his adversaries'; but he was quoted in its news columns when he made news, as he legitimately enough did in the fall of 1948 by campaigning for Dewey and ridiculing the notion that the "Red Dean" of Canterbury, Hewlett Johnson, had the right to be heard; and for more extended coverage he resorted now and again to the letter columns, in which sometimes he would be answered by other Republican students who found him "anachronous." No one questioned the propriety of devoting the better part of a correspondence column in the paper, however, to one of its editors, more especially the man who in two months would take over as chairman of its editorial board. But, when he denounced Dean Johnson's ideas as "brazen disregard for established fact," another conservative student publicly rebuked him and asked whether indeed he did not mean "brazen disregard for Mr. Buckley's unalterable convictions."

Coincidentally with the outgoing board's imposition of a two-hundred-fifty-word limit on letters to the editor, Reid Buckley made his first newspaper appearance, with a letter denouncing a new League for Reaction that actually was not really very different from his brother's viewpoint and proposed practices. But Reid urged that, by the way of showing wicked political groups that their paths would be rocky, "in this case the *News* drop usual reportorial procedure for subjective reporting." Reid appeared once more as a letter writer to protest the "unfair" Christmas vacation burdens of reading and writing imposed by the faculty. He was already suffering, apparently, from what so many of his and his family's friends and acquaintances have identified as the problems created by his need to emulate and yet be distinct from Bill. But this is a matter to which one must return in a different context.

Bill Buckley's board formally assumed charge of the *Yale Daily News* with the issue of Monday, 7 February 1949. Certain results were immediately apparent, the chief of which was a totally unprecedented emphasis on religion. This was manifested both in editorials and in disproportionate news coverage of anything of a religious cast. The point of view was not specifically Catholic, but it was unmistakably Christian, and it was insistent. The only subject to which comparable attention was permitted was whatever could be gathered in under the infinitely expandable umbrella of "fighting Communism." Attacks on freedom of expression and particularly on academic freedom became chronic; individuals were singled out for denunciations that were not always scrupulously accurate (no taint here of "the sin of scrupulosity"); McCarthyist rhetoric had its model in the *Yale Daily News* while the man who was to give it its name was still out rousing the Wisconsin rabble.

I have mentioned the smug congratulations bestowed by The Young Mahster on the president of Vassar College after her *confiteor*. Yet, with his superb flair for recognizing his opponents' weaknesses, Buckley in his editorials took the impeccable position that the eminences who insisted on Shostakovitch's right to take part in the peace meetings could hardly reconcile this principled stand with their equal insistence that Walter Gieseking and Wilhelm Furtwängler, the pianist and the conductor who had not behaved precisely heroically during what our German allies now call the *Vergangenheit*, be forbidden even to cross the border, let alone perform in the land of the free and the home of the brave. Shostakovitch had just publicly acknowledged that his music was riddled with bourgeois betrayal, and Buckley must have enjoyed writing: "Those men who feel that Gieseking and Furtwängler do not merit American hospitality because they cooperated with a tyrannical government have a fine opportunity to assert their consistency." This virtue, however, was not altogether available to Buckley, who in the same editorial had listed Thomas Mann among "well known fellow travellers and avowed Communists"; when the novelist's nephew, Charles Luke Eliot, wrote to protest, Buckley replied in print—as if referring to sacred scripture—that he had based his statement on "Mann's sponsorship, participation in or contribution to twenty-nine Communist fronts, functions and publications, and membership in five fronts classed as subversive by the Attorney General." *O sancta simplicitas.*

A similar exercise in apprentice character-assassination—though it was obvious that journeyman status was well within his reach—has remained a classic in the incunabula of the Buckleys. Even Carlin, the vice-chairman of the *Yale Daily News* board, was constrained to protest publicly, and such a breach of front was most rare at Yale. Professor Raymond Kennedy (he vanished during a field trip in the Southwest Pacific a few years later) taught Sociology 10, a course for freshmen and sophomores that was always overflowing. Conceding that Kennedy taught it well, Buckley

devoted an editorial of almost eight hundred words in March of
1949—four weeks after he had assumed the dignities of his office—
to an attempt to prove that Kennedy was wrongfully employing
his course for the propagation of atheism, blasphemy, and sacrilege
in tender minds that could muster no defenses against this emissary
of Beëlzebub. Out of two semesters' lectures Buckley strung together a half-dozen ostensible quotations in support of his statement
that "Mr. Kennedy never makes the positive assertion that God
does not exist. Instead his beliefs form an inarticulated hypothesis
for his thesis. [Even then the bourgeois existed to be *épaté* by
Buckley.] Ridicule and slant have always been more effective."

How Buckley prepared his case is interesting. The sole evidentiary materials were of this level: "This place Limbo—all I know
is apparently the flames there aren't as hot as in hell. That's where
all the Greek philosophers are, along with unbaptized babies."
"Chaplains accompanying modern armies are comparable to witch
doctors accompanying tribes." "Religion is a matter of ghosts,
spirits and emotion." The three other quotations used by Buckley
were not quite so inflammatory as these; none would ground the
charge of "undermining religion through bawdy and slapstick
humor." (One is always baffled by these believers in an almighty
God who are so fearful lest he be incompetent to fortify his faithful against the seducer: could he be that Baal whose prophets
Elijah so unfeelingly mocked?) The editorial was titled "For a Fair
Approach."

Students and faculty members replied at once, indignantly.
Carlin wrote a long letter defending Kennedy's right to propound
his theories and, not incidentally, providing context and background for his chief's extractions from the lectures. In sum, he
took the position of more than a few genuine conservatives: that
the function of education is not to tell one what to think but to
impel one and assist one to think. "If any student is willing to
accept uncritically every opinion and interpretation with which
he is confronted," Carlin said, "he doesn't deserve to be at Yale.
For the most part, moreover, Kennedy's presentation . . . is . . .
always more objective than yesterday's editorial." Edmund H.
Volkart of the Department of Sociology wrote to castigate Buckley
for having asked Volkart general questions and then made it appear
that in replying he was attacking a colleague and friend; the letter
reminded Buckley of the title he had given his editorial. The
chairman of the department inquired whether the editorial repre-

sented the editorial board's policy or the author's own view; in the latter case, he suggested, it ought to have been signed. Buckley replied, "Yesterday's editorial and all *News* editorials represent ultimately the point of view of one man. The responsibility is the Chairman's."

Finally Kennedy was given two columns for a very detailed reply, in which he explained to the vulgar precisely what sociology and anthropology are about, what his own philosophy of teaching was, what the facts of his course material were; Buckley: "References to genitalia are as effective in the classroom as they are at a bachelor dinner"; Kennedy: "It happens that symbols of fertility in many primitive religions (especially in Southeast Asia, my field of specialization) take a sexual form." Kennedy concluded: "I hate to criticize a young man (the editorial writer) in this way, but the Chairman is growing up now, and he should learn that in the world of adult men attacks upon the integrity and honesty of another man will not be excused on the ground of youthful brashness." But, if he had learned, there might have been no *National Review*; certainly there would have been no *God and Man at Yale*; and the Buckleys might have spent the rest of their lives totally unnoticed except perhaps for their oddity in not having descended to the general level of public discourse.

There were other ramifications that, viewed from what was then the future, offer the whole schema of what was to come. A Buckley editorial denounced the proposed bonus for veterans (that same bonus that Bill Buckley later condemned his brother for refusing, once it had been voted) on principle; but it went on to denounce also its ally on the subject, the American Veterans Committee, for taking a stand on the Taft-Hartley Act. "What in the world," Buckley asked, "has the Taft-Hartley Law to do with 'veterans' as a group?" He reminded the AVC of its own slogan, "Citizens First, Veterans Second," and bade the boys "take this slogan more literally and more conscientiously." As if indeed they were not doing precisely that. And apparently it had not occurred to him that his ideological antagonists might have turned his own sophistry against him when the Yale student newspaper sat in judgment on some other labor legislation.

Or when the *Yale Daily News* issued an editorial "Call for an Indigenous Communist Party." One is rather perplexed by this document, from which a certain disinguousness seems to coquette in spite of its ostensible good sense. It was inspired by the contemporary promise made publicly by a number of radicals that, in the event of war against Russia, she would command their allegiance. This position, the editorial argued, was forced on many of them by the fact that the only existing Communist Party in the United States was Russian-owned and -operated, and theirs was the cruel dilemma of abjuring either country or creed: therefore it was meet that "they should have the opportunity to give vent to their opinions in a legitimate, indigenous American communist party. This would make everything a lot easier."

Communism almost displaced God for a time and the question of free speech vexed Buckley into a temporary heresy from which he quickly and lastingly recovered. A number of letters had criticised or ridiculed his crusade against Miss Blanding, and others had corrected his public statements that there was not a single non-Stalinist or anti-Stalinist radical party in the United States: better-informed students provided him with the names of several. The Political Union held a forum on the rôle of government in society, closely following Professor Emerson's attack on the Federal Bureau of Investigation for its unconstitutional violations of the First and Fourth Amendments. The paper's coverage of Emerson was minimal, but it devoted five or six times as much space to the stereotyped rhetorical defense offered by the chief of the FBI, the perennial and now late J. Edgar Hoover, though it was not rich in fact. The coverage of the forum, then, was so one-sided as to leave the unsophisticated reader with the impression that there could be no honest and/or intelligent support for anything but the merest dumb-show of government. And yet, when Yale banned a public appearance by Shostakovitch—an action to which the paper dedicated a disproportionate share of its front page—an editorial questioned the decision on practical, if not philosophical, grounds and indeed back-tracked to a degree from the interdict on the Red Dean that Buckley had supported. "There is a sobering experience to be got," the paper counseled, "from witnessing at first hand the intellectual prostitution, the staggering dissimulation of the Communist Party line."

To those who do not care about moral concerns, this is cogent reasoning and is to be recommended to "liberals" I have known who would stifle the Buckleys of the world in their editorial rooms. But it would be difficult to locate another such relapse in the decades since. For within weeks Buckley was editorially defending Yale for its self-contradictory decisions that José Felix Lequerica, formerly Foreign Minister of Spain under Generalissimo Franco, might speak on the campus and that Communists might not. The specious reasoning of the editorial's hypotheticals and conditionals —what might have happened in Spain, in the view of its author, if God had not stood with Franco (where else could he have stood, after all?)—hardly fortified the position, nor was it helped by the publication of a letter pointing out that Lequerica had made it a condition precedent of his appearance that no Spanish Loyalist be allowed to attend and that the university had acceded to the stipulation. (A day later it was announced that that future resident of and apologist for Spain, F. Reid Buckley, had been elected an associate editor for the forthcoming year.)

The mentality of the denunciation of scholarships for blacks emerged again in the spring of 1949 when the paper was aligned by its chairman against a bill in the Connecticut Legislature that would have penalised religious or racial discrimination in schools aided by the state: Buckley called this an unwarranted interference that went against "tradition." A second editorial attacked the bill from another point of view: it had been supported by demagogy, distortion, and emotionalism, "the most disturbing elements of democracy." Pot and kettle had established their perdurable dialogue.

Perhaps the high low point (if it may be called that) of Buckley's editorship occurred in these early months: certainly he was rarely to repeat its ridiculousness. One May evening, in an outburst of juvenility, occupants of a freshman dormitory began throwing things out their windows into the streets; an especially popular item was toilet paper, rolled and other. No one would pretend that this was defensible or, for that matter, important—no one, that is, except the chairman of the *Yale Daily News*, who had no difficulty understanding the real significance of the event as well as its cause: the "supercilious iconoclasm" of a large number of the freshmen's teachers, men who were "flabby in their convictions, mealymouthed and variable in their allegiance when they assert their beliefs in God, integrity and good." Man, obviously, was at Yale, and at his frailest; but where was God? Two of the supercilious iconoclasts, at least, replied, and in a second, self-exculpating editorial (he had not yet acquired the tactic of dismissing an error as a joke) Buckley explained that his charges did not apply exclusively to Yale though they were characteristic of it. Pointing out (irreproachably) that educators should worry less about method and (very reproachably) that they should concern themselves with moral purposes, he stated the thesis that has not changed since: "The obsessive conviction on the part of so many social scientists that liberality and intellectual curiosity demand indecision in appraising the fundamental truths that underlie Western Civilization gives rise to an atmosphere which is contagious and to which many freshmen succumb—atmosphere that teaches that cheating is all right if a proctor doesn't catch you, and that immorality is excusable if proper precautions are taken, that social order is purely a product of adjustment in a constantly changing world, that the ideas of absolute good and evil are unintellectual and reactionary." Demagogy? distortion? emotionalism?

Buckley must have spent the summer of 1949 perfecting his positions, for the second half of his tenure as chairman of the *Daily News* more than justified the attitudes described by Professor Weiss. It is worth noting that he has clung as firmly to his valid positions through the years as to the others; one was exemplified in an excellent editorial in September of 1949 that sharply condemned the university authorities for yielding to pressure from the Veterans Administration (which administered the funds available under the GI Bill) and reducing substantially those humanities courses that were not eliminated to please the hacks who could not distinguish between a university and a trade school. There was even a good word for the American Civil Liberties Union, "which bans communists from membership" and thus is "the only decorous civil rights committee of which we have knowledge." Buckley has never been very well informed about the ACLU (though he was quite right about its decorum): it did not then nor has it at any other time, past or present, set up any criteria for membership. Perhaps he was thinking of the resolution adopted by its board of directors, during the intense emotionalism of the 1940 war situation, that barred office or employment in the Union to adherents of any totalitarian doctrine. In any event, he was attacking the abortive effort to form a civil-liberties committee at Yale, which was really thwarted by the division within its ranks on the admission of Communists to membership and (presumably) protection. Emerson favored the eminently correct position against any exclusions; it was Fred, nicknamed the Red, Rodell who wanted to keep the Communists out.

As if he had never admonished the American Veterans Committee to mind its manners outside the artificially narrow realm in which he acknowledged its competence, Buckley campaigned vigorously throughout the fall of 1949 for the Right in every issue, local, national, or international. The terms "traitor" and "fellow traveler" appeared more often in the *Yale Daily News* than "lackey" and "running dog" in the entire Marxist press. The steel strikers were denounced, and the editorials invoked the spirits to favor United States Steel. The faculty of Yale was denounced as a hive of "Reds," a fantasy challenged by Professor Fowler Harper of the Law School (whose widow was later to win a libel action against Buckley), and after much debate the Political Union upheld him. When the *Harvard Crimson* reported that Yale was palsied by the fear of constant FBI loyalty checks, the *Daily News* sponsored a panel debate on the FBI's rôle in the colleges and the moderator was the paper's chairman, Buckley. Louis Nichols, who in the hierarchy of the Bureau shared in the aura of America's Yezhov—J. Edgar Hoover—appeared for his chief; other debaters included Cleanth Brooks of the Yale Department of English, Rodell, Harper, and Kendall. The paper's news coverage was quite fair; its editorial position, of course, was totally in favor of the FBI and the nascent loyalty/security program, to say nothing of the probative value of a suspect's "associations and associates."

Buckley's pursuit of the diabolical Communists and his defense of the various Saints George who sallied out against the dragons went far beyond Yale or even New Haven. Larry Adler, a musician, and Paul Draper, a dancer, sued one Hester McCullough of Greenwich, Connecticut, who had publicly called them Communists. In the autumn of 1949 the public temper was such that this label, if applied without foundation, was as actionable as that of Nazi. Buckley was outraged that they should have a ground for litigation, and the more outraged that they retained as their counsel the very respectable New Haven firm of Wiggin & Dana, which also represented Yale and was to be the employer of his brother James for several years. Editorially Bill Buckley demanded that Wiggin & Dana "wash their hands of the business" and turn it over "to some firm willing to play around with the laws to protect squeamish pro-Communists." For weeks Mrs. McCullough could be sure of front-page attention in the *Yale Daily News*, though she had no connection with the university.

Family influence on Bill Buckley's thinking was plain, in spite of one public printed disagreement with Reid over Lafayette College's refusal of a hundred-forty-thousand-dollar bequest to create scholarships for "American-born students, Jews and Catholics except." Bill, in a splendid demonstration of Olympian disinterestedness (after all, though he was a Catholic, he had enough money, and he was at Yale), to say nothing of a certain deviousness, thought this was pretty stupid: after all, the testator had the right to his bigotries, and acceptance would simply enable Lafayette to channel other moneys to the lesser breeds. Yale, Bill wrote, ought to ask the executor for the money and "hope that he has discretion to channel it to an institution that knows how to keep money and principle from clashing." But Reid wrote that "such a position is so impartial, however, as to show a curious lack of intelligent discrimination . . . to refuse the money is admirable."

Where the brothers did not disagree was in politics. It was clear how Bill could write an editorial urging the designation of Senator Robert A. Taft as the Political Union's man of the year because he was a "bulwark against the socialization of this country," or another praising the isolationism that had prevailed well into the Second World War, or a third insisting to his fellow-students that it was the Christian's duty to "assert his belief that he has apprehended the truth." It is difficult to conceive of any notion, in Christian, Jew, Moslem, or Marxist, that has been more ruinous to the human race. Reid Buckley, whose by-line was more than once the only one in the paper in his brother's final weeks of command, and who in March of 1950 was to be elected vice-chairman for the following year, also utilised the letters columns to denounce the whole concept of academic freedom, endorse loyalty and security investigations of college faculties, and demand the removal of teachers who espoused the wrong ideas.

Not everything that Bill Buckley advocated as his tenure ended was suspect. A series of seven editorials on "Faculty Policy at Yale" could well be reprinted monthly at every college in the country: it was a reasoned analysis of the problems of salaries, "publish or perish" (which is, if anything, a worse scourge now than ever), the quality of teaching, etc., and it concluded with impeccable recommendations: greater quality control of teaching, including due weight to the opinions of students, and at least as much emphasis on teaching as on publishing, which, Buckley pointed out (in another unfortunately timeless, placeless truism), was too often valued above teaching and accepted as an excuse for sloppy teaching. Another editorial suggested that between graduation from school and entrance into college young men (nothing was said of women) would benefit by a year of ordinary employment, particularly those young men who had always been cushioned in wealth.

And then he returned, by way of coda, to his already old tunes. Two editorials titled "What To Do?" called for the preservation of free enterprise by the elimination of Leftists from faculties: "the majority of scholars flock to the leftist banner." It was stated as an axiom, and it was not examined. Buckley urged that rich donors stipulate in their gifts to universities that the money be used to employ Rightist teachers whom the donors ought to name. He did not reply to critics who recognised this as a call for implicit prior restraint and a rejection of Jefferson's belief (in which, admittedly, it is not always easy to persevere, given the daily behavior of that unchallengeably inferior race, the human) that truth "will prevail if left to herself."

That Yale housed enough just men to stay the hand of God was evidenced two days before Buckley was to hand over the *Daily News* to his successor, Garrison McClintock Noel Ellis. A letter with seven signatures acclaimed Bill Buckley as Yale's Undergraduate of the Year and Taft as its Graduate of the Year because of the zeal and effectiveness with which both had championed the conservative cause. And in the issue of 20 January 1950 Buckley bade public farewell with a certain grace and without mention of the singular achievement that was reported on the front page with the modesty that he has always periodically shown. President Charles Seymour of Yale was to resign in July of 1950, and Buckley had resolved that the *Daily News*'s annual banquet should honor him. Thereupon Buckley wrote to the presidents of five other universities, inviting them to attend, but his initiative was nowhere reported; the story stated only that, as outgoing chairman of the board of editors, he would speak. The presidents who accepted his invitation (none refused; some he was to attack savagely not long afterward) were James R. Kilian Jr. of the Massachusetts Institute of Technology, Harold E. Stassen of the University of Pennsylvania, Dwight D. Eisenhower of Columbia, Harold W. Dodds of Princeton, and James Bryant Conant of Harvard. Buckley's basic theme in his address was "the necessity of fostering active Christianity in the higher institutions of learning."

He was on somewhat sounder ground in his valedictory editorial, in which he recalled his sin in assailing "the stereotype liberalism which, paradoxically enough, has prescribed rigid limits to tolerable opinion in mid-twentieth-century America." *Plus ça change.* . . . And he confessed to having earned much of the criticism he had received as a result of "the fatal attraction of facetiousness, the compelling urge to jolt, to ridicule, to pound square on the nose." It is difficult to resist such a paragraph as this:

"We are the first to admit that ours is not the art of persuasion. We deeply bemoan our inability to allure without antagonizing, to seduce without violating. Especially because we believe in what we preached and would have liked very much for our vision to have been contagious."

VIII

IN THE SUMMER of 1950, having applied to and been accepted by
the Yale Law School and the Yale Graduate School, Bill Buckley
married Patricia Taylor of Vancouver, who had been a Vassar
roommate of his sister Patricia and of whom his sister is supposed
to have told the family: "Pat looks like a queen, she acts like a
queen, and is just the wife for Billy." Whatever is to be said of
her in this book is of necessity second-hand, for the Buckleys,
whatever the deficiencies of their attitudes toward the feminist
movement, have two admirably un-American habits: they refuse
to make capital of their women and they keep their private lives
private.

(As this book was in work, the radio was reiterating an expensively vulgar magazine's "message" for its article on "the celebrated Kennedys and its famous sons," of whom it observed:
"They made family a metaphor for nationhood." It is difficult to
imagine the Buckleys, if one of them attains sufficient public eminence, similarly divvying the loot and the limelight even unto the
in-laws and the in-laws of the in-laws.)

Bill Buckley did not enter either the Law School or the Graduate School "because the Korean war came up, and I thought that
it might be a considerable struggle, so I decided to be a little bit
more mobile." He continued to teach Spanish at Yale, and he began work on *God and Man at Yale* in a small house that he and
his wife had taken in Hamden, just outside New Haven. John
was by now working for the family companies; James, still un-
married, was living in New Haven and working for Wiggin &
Dana; Reid was a junior at Yale (this was the year when, at
twenty-one, he married the very young Betsey Howell of Hart-

ford, a Protestant whom he had met at a Western ranch). Of the sisters, Aloïse was raising a family and writing an occasional magazine piece; Jane had just married William F. Smith, a Protestant graduate of Villanova and the Yale Law School (he never practiced); Priscilla was working for the CIA; Patricia had married Bozell, who was now in the Yale Law School; and Maureen and Carol were still in school.

Rollin G. Osterweis recalls visiting Patricia and Bill Buckley in Hamden during this period, especially a white-tie Christmas Eve throughout which Buckley played a magnificent recording of *The Creation* on a splendid machine—and the Osterweises waited for it to be over; they were not musical, but they liked their hosts. On other occasions Buckley, who of course kept up his intimacy with Kendall, showed some of the manuscript of *God and Man* to Osterweis, who begged him: "Bill, don't publish that book. Sit on it for ten years and then publish it." But, he recalls, Buckley replied: "Rollie, I can't. . . . I wait ten years and I won't publish it." This was precisely what Osterweis wanted, because he feared that the publication of the book would give needless offense to a number of people, damage Yale, and cost Buckley friendships that he valued. But Buckley was as adamant as Osterweis himself had been at a similar age when an older friend had tried to dissuade him from going ahead with a questionable book. The friendship between Osterweis and Bill Buckley has never declined.

Though James Buckley was also in New Haven then, Osterweis did not know him well. But his recollections of Reid are warm, especially of the night when Osterweis, Reid, and another debater were at West Point for a tournament and Osterweis became ill. Though a championship was involved, Reid and the other student, Jerry Butler, would not hear of Osterweis's being taken home alone in a taxi to New Haven: they drove him back in his car. Osterweis remembers Patricia Bozell at this time as beautiful and headstrong, a young woman of decided views. Richard Sewall, who teaches creative writing at Yale, recalls Reid as a good student (Osterweis, like Weiss, believes Bill's is a better mind), who recently suggested huge state loan funds to help needy college students on long-term financing (lending, for example, thirty thousand dollars to a Yale student, or ten thousand to one attending a school costing a third as much), arguing that, "if they had this financial commitment, they would be less likely to tear down their schools." Sewall recalls too that Reid was the better student in creative writing, which was called Daily Themes; Bill's fiction, Sewall says, always read like an editorial.

In spite of his own family's wealth and the fortune of his bride's family—the Taylors were multi-millionnaire shipbuilders—the Bill Buckleys did not, apparently, live with great luxury. The Korean war did not require Bill's services, and, when he had finished his book, he and his wife went to Mexico for a time with some notion of going into business and living there. But, in spite of his father's hopes, he was not interested in business. He became associated with the latest incarnation of *The American Mercury*, which had suffered a succession of degradations after its dazzling prime under H. L. Mencken and George Jean Nathan; by the early 1950's it was a badly written and worse edited voice of the extreme Right, including such groups as the National Economic Council, of which the late and notorious Merwin K. Hart was a leader and which had gathered in almost all the pillars of the old America First organisation—it had succumbed to the war. Will Buckley Sr. was a friend of Hart, and so was Buckley's South African business associate, Douglas Reed. *The Mercury* was rather motley in its population, including Ralph de Toledano, who had once been a kind of liberal; Eugene Lyons, a renegade from the Left; Karl Hess, who was about Bill Buckley's age and vehemently reactionary, and a few similar types. Bill Buckley represented a real acquisition for this rather seedy publication, already suffering from an earned reputation for barely disguised Fascism and anti-Semitism, because the publication of *God and Man at Yale* had made him an overnight national notable.

Subtitled *The Superstitions of "Academic Freedom,"* the manuscript had arrived late in 1950 at the offices of the Henry Regnery Co. in Chicago after innumerable rejections by New York editors. Regnery, a Germanophile conservative of a very old school, had founded his firm for the publication of books congenial to his view, and most of them, though he was a Protestant, turned out to be the work of Catholic authors. Kevin Corrigan, who was then a Regnery executive and is now director of news for a Spanish-language television station in New York, said that *God and Man* arrived accompanied by its reputation of rejections, as well as some question whether both title and subtitle were not "just a gag of some kind. Now we know it was a Buckleyesque thrust calculated to raise hackles." Regnery himself, Corrigan declared, was instrumental in the acceptance and publication of the book, though it proved costly.

"Henry's own extraordinarily complex personality played a tremendous part in the Buckley story," Corrigan said, "because Henry represented that older tradition in book publishing which was personal publishing. Henry believed that a view that was not a popular one had a right to be heard. And this book was somewhat more surprising coming from a very young man. Henry was able to raise something on the order of ten thousand dollars for promotion, which was terribly important. This unknown boy who had these provocative ideas was supported by a publisher in a very real way. Henry got behind the book and we all did a lot of work on it." Corrigan's brother at Yale, a classmate of James Buckley, had been a guest at Great Elm; his father, a doctor who became Ambassador to Venezuela, had been host to Bill Buckley and some of his sisters in Caracas. Corrigan himself, charged with the promotion, read everything about the Buckleys that he could find.

"It was interesting to observe a very real resistance to what Bill Buckley had to say," Corrigan continued. "At that time television hadn't really come into its own, and there were two important radio shows in Chicago: the University of Chicago Round Table and the Northwestern Reviewing Stand. The Chicago Round Table would not touch Bill Buckley. They would not let this young man appear on the Round Table." But then bigotry has never been the posted preserve of the Right. Corrigan, who was later to engage in published polemic with Buckley—though principally over their differing interpretations of Catholic doctrine rather than over politics—explained too how Regnery's adherence to his principles imposed financial loss on him; at the same time a clue was provided to a much later break in the conservative movement.

Regnery at that time was publishing in paperback the Great Books that were being used by discussion groups in the course devised by Professor Mortimer J. Adler and the Committee on Social Thought of the University of Chicago, one member of which was the eminent Austrian philosopher and economist, Frederick A. Hayek. The subtitle of Buckley's book "deeply wounded the sensibilities of the academic community," Corrigan said, "and my own personal view is that the loss of the Great Books Foundation,

an offshoot of the whole Great Books movement and a very
important back-list item, was the direct result of publishing the
Buckley book." Buckley, who went to Chicago from Mexico for
the radio appearance, was taken to lunch with Hayek, whom
everyone expected to be basically in accord with Buckley and
who deeply differed with him on academic freedom, which for
Hayek, regardless of his personal conservatism, was or ought to
be inviolate. Later Hayek and Buckley appeared on the same
platforms and in the same publications, and Hayek even wrote
for *National Review,* until the two men broke over a vulgarity
perpetrated by the magazine and a gratuitous insult inflicted by its
editor.

God and Man at Yale is especially important because it was, to
mix one's Biblical figures though hardly inappropriately, the star
in the east that was to lead the wise men of the Right to the Rose
of Sharon, and too because it offered to a broader public than
Yale an insight into not only the fanatically sincere beliefs of its
author but also the reprehensible means by which he was only
too ready to further his high moral cause. The first of the elders
of Zion to know the star was John Chamberlain, once a critic for
The New York Times and *The Wall Street Journal,* in 1949 one
of the editors of that lower-middle-brow instant-culture film-strip,
Life. Since it needed a certain amount of text to separate the flossy
photographs, and it pretended, like everything under the aegis of
Henry Luce, to a certain intellectuality, it also had an editorial
page, and Chamberlain had been dispatched to Yale, of which he
and Luce were graduates (Luce had also made a handsome contribution to the *Yale Daily News*), in quest of data on which to
base an editorial on education. During his mission he encountered
and was captivated by Bill Buckley, and he composed a fulsome
and not wholly honest introduction that helped materially to
draw attention to the book when Regnery brought it out in
September, 1951, in a hard-cover edition that sold for three dollars
and fifty cents.

The timing could not have been better. The Archangel Douglas
was brandishing his flaming sword against the fiend in Asia (the
struggle never became considerable enough to wrest Bill Buckley
from the pursuits of peace); the Communists, to judge by contemporary tocsins, outnumbered the rest of the world by the
thousandfold, and the new David out of the Middle West was only
beginning to dig the mud for his sling. Like most of his domestic

allies, moreover, he had no learning and less style, and he was too preoccupied with his own fortunes. What was needed was elegance and disinterestedness, and what used to be called glamour until (in Saul Bellow's phrase) the publicity intellectuals who became courtiers (courtesans?) in the sixties firmly implanted *charisma* in the American jargon. Chamberlain was only the first to hail Buckley; publication of *God and Man* brought the pledge of allegiance from Eastman, Burnham, Kirk, Henry Hazlitt (an eminent conservative economist), and the rest of the sages of the Right, to say nothing of the subalterns and other ranks, once these had got over their native distrust of anyone who could make a decent sentence—a diffidence, unfortunately, that seems today to be even stronger among those who profess to be the vanguard of the true, the beautiful and the good. The subject of panegyrics in *The American Mercury, Time, Life,* and the militantly know-nothing *New York Daily News,* and of a few lengthy attacks elsewhere, as well as of innumerable and generally favorable newspaper reviews, the book made its author an instant attraction on the lecture circuit, to which he has never ceased carrying his good tidings.

One of the major analyses of it was made in *The Atlantic Monthly* by McGeorge Bundy, then teaching government at Harvard and not yet vulnerable by reason of participation in the mid-century treason of the intellectuals. Another, by Fred Rodell, appeared in *The Progressive,* subsequent to Bundy's. These two very different scholars arrived at virtually identical conclusions concerning both the thesis and the argumentation of the book. It argued that Yale was pullulating with "atheism" or "secularism" and "collectivism." Bundy wrote: "As a believer in God, a Republican, and a Yale graduate, I find that the book is dishonest in its use of facts, false in its theory, and a discredit to its author and the writer of its introduction." Rodell, quoting Max Eastman's adjectives for it in *The American Mercury*—"brilliant, sincere, well-informed, keenly reasoned, and exciting to read"—asserted: "I'm afraid I found it —in almost exact antonyms—muddled, dishonest, inaccurate, sloppily argued, and dull."

Essentially the book is merely a much expanded restatement of the thesis of Buckley's *Daily News* editorials, "What To Do?" Rodell sums it up quite accurately: "What Buckley wants and asks is that Yale's alumni quit giving money to Yale until they have thus forced Yale to fire all faculty members who do not believe in and affirmatively teach (wherever these are even remotely relevant

to their courses) the divinity of Jesus Christ and the economic
gospel according to Adam Smith. It is just as simple and just as
sinister as that." And Rodell, at least, saw at once how great the
danger was and where it lay. It is imperative to quote:

". . . I should consider Buckley's balderdash scarcely worth a
booknote, were it not for the widespread attention it has received.
But it is precisely that attention which I find far more shocking
and sinister than the fact that one bigoted boy has written an
ignorant attack on Yale and on the whole concept of the free
university. For almost all those who have called attention to
Buckley have either praised him, though usually with reservations,
or at least have tempered their criticisms with praise—and so,
whether wittingly or unwittingly, have added fuel to his Philistine
crusade."

What neither Buckley's highly placed admirers nor his professionally anti-intellectual champions even mentioned—any more
than he did himself—were his own religious allegiance and social
and economic provenance and the quality of the evidence he professed to be adducing under the presumption of good faith. In some
instances it might be argued that persons unfamiliar with Yale
would be in no position to assess the evidentiary material presented;
but certainly there could be no excuse for ignorance of the fact
that he was a Roman Catholic from a rich, reactionary family long
identified with the extreme Right—circumstances that might well
have influenced his views and impaired his objectivity in the domains that he had chosen to examine. The technique of falsification employed in his editorial attacks on Professor Kennedy was
broadened in his book to cover the Yale departments that he had
found wanting: religion, economics, political science, and so on.
Those of a lecturer's or a textbook's words that ostensibly bolstered
his charges were cited at length; other observations from the same
source that made Buckley's accusations ridiculous were merely
ignored.

The one meritorious point raised in the book, however, ought
to be brought out. Every year a Yale senior is invited to address
the February Alumni Day, and the 1950 speaker, his book tells
us, was to be Buckley. He was invited to offer his speech for what
amounted to preliminary screening, and, because it was in effect
a synopsis of the book, he was (in my view, altogether wrongly)
forbidden to deliver it without certain modifications, which he
properly refused to make. It is reprinted as the sixth of the book's

seven appendices (the last lists all colleges and universities using the textbooks that Buckley would have put on his own *Index Expurgatorius*) and it amounts to no more than a warning, in the direst tones, that there were people on the Yale faculty who believed neither in the divinity of Jesus Christ nor in that of free enterprise so-called, and that the alumni had better see to it. Buckley contended that only those who paid the major part of a university's costs—the alumni, he said—had the right to determine how it should be run, what it should teach, and who should be the teachers. The primitiveness of the thinking was not really disguised by the relative refinement of its expression. In his book Buckley expressed the deepest distress because the biographies of candidates for election to the Yale Corporation—as its board of trustees is called—are silent on the men's political, philosophical, and economic beliefs (though he was quite right in saying that they could usually be presumed from the data given) and because similar silence is maintained with respect to the beliefs of prospective and actual members of the university administration and faculty. It would thus be possible for exponents of horrendous notions to accede to positions of power, and this is part of what he called "the hoax of 'academic freedom.' "

Principally young Buckley argued that it was the university's duty to inculcate the truth in its wards, and he rejected the notion that the scholar must forever be seeking truth. Truth was what the people in power said it was, he argued in essence, and the teacher had no business inciting inquiry: this was the snare of liberalism, its cowardly refusal to take stands. For values had been discovered and confirmed far back in humanity's past, and that modern man should question them was presumptuous: we have Christianity (though at times he would extend his *nihil obstat* to some other faiths to the extent to which they granted diplomatic recognition to his kind of God) and we have the free market, and who could ask for anything more? He did not mean, he explained, that the student should not be exposed to the fools and heretics: But, "while reading and studying Marx or Hitler, Laski or the Webbs, Huxley or Dewey, I should expect the teacher, whose competence, intelligence, and profundity I take for granted, to 'deflate' the arguments advanced. . . . Ultimately, of course, the student must decide for himself. If he chooses to repudiate the values of his instructor, he is free—and ought to be free—to do so." But it is the responsibility of both institution and teacher "to

steer the student toward the truth as they see it. But can they do
less than that?"

Only recently Garry Wills, a former ally and associate of
Buckley, has challenged his right to call himself a conservative
rather than a reactionary. In *God and Man* Buckley wrote: "I
hasten to dissociate myself from the school of thought, largely
staffed by conservatives, that believes teachers ought to be 'at all
times neutral.'" He added: "I believe such a policy to be a lazy
denial of educational responsibility." And so he was able to patron-
ise in his book "the wife of a prominent professor at Yale [who]
once told me that 'Yale ought to have a course on Communism,
and this course,' she added earnestly, 'should be taught by a man
who is neither pro-Communist nor anti-Communist.'" He was
able too to deplore in his book the fact that the chairman of the
Department of Religion "does not seek to persuade his students to
believe in Christ" and the further fact that the Yale Christian
Association's publication did not require its employees to swear
allegiance to the Cross and persisted in a "steadfast refusal to
proclaim Christianity as the true religion."

As for the teacher denied employment because of his beliefs,
"he will be out of a job; hence, in effect, will he not have been
persecuted for his beliefs? Yes. Similarly, if no one votes for an
incumbent, he too will be out of a job. He, too, in the realistic
analysis, will have been persecuted for his beliefs. In a democracy
it is proper that, in this sense, he should be." And why? Because
of the free market—that same free market that, according to some
of Buckley's current friends, precludes or ought to preclude state
intervention to curb venereal disease because one who contracts
syphilis has a tort action against the donor. In higher education
"every citizen in a free economy, no matter the wares that he plies
[*sic*], must defer to the sovereignty of the consumer. It is of the
essence of freedom that citizens not be made to pay for what the
majority does not want." It would be futile to quote this against
Lucifer in later contexts because subsequently he became very
much less concerned with freedom for the majority unless it were
his majority; and anyway, as his father had pointed out years
earlier, "eighty per cent of the people" were unequipped for
freedom.

Its nature, furthermore, was extremely restricted, as his illustration in this connection showed: he took the hypothetical case of
one John Smith, a Socialist economics teacher at Yale. "Let us bar

him from teaching because he is inculcating values that the governing board at Yale considers to be against the public welfare. *No freedom I know of has yet been violated* [emphasis added]. We still cling to the belief in this country that, acting in good conscience, we can hire whom we like."

Obviously Emerson was right when he observed that the facts of life had moved far beyond Buckley's apprehension of them. It is clear still, in talk with Buckley, as it was then in what he wrote, that he has never really faltered in his touching resemblance to Pippa. Not only has he the baldest idea of morality; Weiss was eminently correct when he said of Bill Buckley, in the acme of understatement: "I think that what he's insufficiently aware of is what it means to be out of luck. . . . I think he's a certain kind of innocent: he thinks people operate ideologically." And, for all the devout Catholicism, he is incapable of hearing the bell.

The book cost Buckley many of his Yale friends, though some of them ultimately recovered from it. When he first visited the campus after its publication, only Kendall, Osterweis, and Weiss, of the faculty, were genuinely cordial to him. Osterweis and Weiss certainly disagreed thoroughly with the book; but they firmly believed that he was entitled to a full hearing. It has long been the fashion (particularly among "liberals") to laugh at him and it; but the paperback edition is in its twelfth printing, and it is credulously swallowed whole by Young Americans for Freedom and an ever growing number of their elders. The persuasiveness of its language and the sinuousness of its syllogisms offer no clues to the falsity of its premises or the violence that has been done to its supporting "facts." And above all it tells a nation that has always distrusted the intellect (and this is the only betrayal that might be charged to Buckley, but it is a formidable one) precisely what it has always wanted to hear.

Since the frightening labels such as "collectivism" were left unexamined, no reader could divine, even after he had finished the book, that some of what was being taught at Yale at that time—and denounced by Buckley—was straight out of Herbert Hoover while none of the "collectivist" teaching went as far as some of the New Deal and subsequent legislation; the social security that so exercised Buckley was (even if for the wrong motives) recognised as indispensable even by Bismarck before Will Buckley was born, and in a far less democratic system. One has the right, too, to wonder whether Bill Buckley did not feel personally threatened by an idea he encountered in Theodore Morgan's *Income and Employment*, a text published by that well-known radical house, Prentice-Hall (the italics were added by Buckley; the passage deals with the desirability of high inheritance taxes): "*It is not allowable in a democracy* to set up the goal of establishing a family dynasty."

He was more careful with names than he had been in the *Yale Daily News:* he mentioned very few. One was Emerson's, whom he pilloried for being president of the National Lawyers' Guild, an association of progressive and radical lawyers that had broken off from the extremely conservative but semi-official American Bar Association, though many kept up both memberships simultaneously. The presidency of the Guild and Emerson's outspoken progressive views and advocacy of complete freedom of expression were the sum of the evidence that could be mustered against him, so Buckley was compelled to equate him with the famous Harvard astronomer, Harlow Shapley, whose crime was the chairmanship of the Waldorf-Astoria peace conference that had made the Right so warlike. Rodell was right: the most damning indictment of Yale to be found in the book was the proof that in four years the university had been impotent to modify the "dogma in which [Buckley] was obviously indoctrinated before he ever got near the place" and his "blatant disregard for intellectual tolerance, intellectual curiosity and intellectual humility." It is only in very recent years—perhaps since the extremely graceless television alley-fight with Gore Vidal, who is in so many respects his mirror image —that this criticism has become somewhat less applicable. (In the autumn of 1971 Rodell asserted that he would far rather have seen Buckley, who is not a lawyer, appointed to the Supreme Court than some others, if only because of the quality of his mind and his concern for language: Rodell is as elegant a stylist and as passionate a lover of the word, and these grow fewer daily.)

Bundy's November, 1951, review in *The Atlantic Monthly* (which in December printed a reply by Buckley that Rodell called "proof positive of Buckley's disingenuous intellectual dishonesty" and that Bundy demolished) cited reports that Will Buckley, who was immensely proud of his son's book, had sent a copy to every living Yale alumnus, though there is no verification. Mrs. Buckley, according to her namesake daughter, made a point of visiting every bookshop she could manage and asking for it—a promotion scheme that must date at least to the beginning of commercial bookselling and that must have been utilised by every novice author's proud connections. One may question Rodell's 1952 contention that "Buckley by himself, without his boosters, could be and would be ignored," but there is no doubt that John Chamberlain's introduction to the book and his vigorous defense of it in his own magazine, *The Freeman*, as well as Max Eastman's review in *The American Mercury*, gave it a tremendous momentum. It is quite conceivable that Rodell, like most intellectuals then, genuinely considered the American conservatives and reactionaries a permanent minority, though there was little in the nation's history and less in the current news to ground such a wishful belief: it was the flood tide of loyalty and security obsession, of the kind of Red-baiting that got that shoddy opportunist Richard M. Nixon well on his way, of the McCarran and McCarran-Walter Acts, with their provisions for detention camps for the dissident and malice toward all aliens, of that epitome of *canaglieria*, Joseph McCarthy. Without such enthusiasts as Chamberlain and Eastman the book might have had harder, slower going: but it was superbly apposite to its time. Yale might well issue its official rebuttal through an eminent Episcopal bishop who was also a member of the Yale Corporation and a resident of Lakeville—Henry Sloane Coffin, uncle to William Sloane Coffin Jr.—and this might satisfy at least some of the alumni, to whom he was designated the Corporation's apostle; but what he had to say, regardless of its merit, was unlikely to reach very far beyond the relatively small world of Yale graduates. While more of them were probably for Taft than for any other American politician, the mistake made by their adversaries was to suppose that, immediate belly issues apart, either the "respectable middle classes" or the majority of the rest of the country, however receptive to a certain meliorism, would really reject conservatism.

IX

ONE NEED NOT BE an admirer of the Buckleys to recognise and regret what has been done to Bill Buckley by that Moloch that taints as well as devours—television. Like everyone who has thought to exploit it, he has had largely to become its creature. While it may well have brought him to the knowledge of millions who might otherwise have lived whole lives in ignorance of him, it has presented him on its terms, and they have not always been his; nor have they often made him or his thinking appear better. There is indeed a considerable anomaly in the eagerness of so fastidious a man and so emphatic an élitist to make the most of this epitome of vulgarisation at the price it unfailingly exacts. Certainly nothing in the years immediately after the publication of his first book would have led anyone to expect such a descent among the groundlings.

The fact that he had made a Scarlet Whore of Moscow out of a university that, in Rodell's words, was at that time "as stuffy and reactionary and conservative politically as it could be," aside from the Law School and its New Deal liberalism, should have been somewhat of a clue, however, to something of what might come; so too should have been the pleasure with which he accepted accolades from people whom he might much more reasonably have been expected to forbid to speak to him on the street (as, for instance, my own father interdicted all professional politicians and their menials). But initially Buckley continued to move on a reasonably decent level. Max Eastman had become his enthusiastic admirer; Kendall presented him to James Burnham; he was introduced to Russell Kirk, whose book, *The Conservative Mind*, had just appeared, at the Michigan home of Professor John Abbot Clark, who had just reviewed *God and Man*—favorably, of course —in *The Chicago Tribune*, then as now an arch-reactionary journal. Buckley had come under the influence of Frank Chodorov, a former radical who had moved over to a kind of Right-Wing anarchism, not all of which Buckley could ever embrace; but he admired and loved Chodorov, a much older man (when in his last years Chodorov had to be under constant care in a nursing home and had no money, it was Buckley who anonymously met all his expenses until Chodorov's death).

Bill was still the only Buckley to attract attention in the great world. Reid, while playing Pygmalion to his very young wife, was finishing Yale under the shadow of his much more dramatic brother and the handicap of a rather exaggerated notion of his own significance. He considered himself a writer of remarkable promise, unjustly overlooked by contemporaries and elders alike. Yale had a "scholar of the house" program, in which each of its colleges selected certain of its most gifted members and, in Weiss's description, "freed them of all their courses, had them under the guidance of some faculty member, and met them once a week to discuss their work." Reid Buckley applied for the program, and, when he was rejected, told the committee: "You are doing a terrible thing: I am a genius." Some Yale teachers who knew both brothers felt sorry for Reid because of the presence that Bill had left behind him even after his departure and that seemed virtually to exclude any other Buckley. Not long after his graduation from Yale, Reid and his wife moved to Spain.

His motives, according to those who knew him then, were several. He was quite serious about being a writer, and he has always worked unbelievably hard at it—he spent nine years on his first novel, *Eye of the Hurricane*, and one feels that its reading lasts about as long; his journalism (chiefly for his brother's *National Review* and his brother-in-law's *Triumph*) is just that. He felt, rightly, that writing ought to be a full-time occupation, and he had no wish to hold a job or be a business man; on the other hand, the income from his share of the family fortune would not allow him to live in the United States on the rather grand scale he liked, whereas Spain was cheap, Catholic, conservative, and quiet. At times he is said to have dabbled there in export/import trade and in real estate, but, in later years, when his mode of living strained his resources, he resorted to periodic American lecture tours, chiefly at colleges: his general subject being, of course, the propagation of the conservative faith.

In these early years of the 1950's few other Buckleys were conspicuous. Priscilla, whose service as a reports officer on the European desk of the Central Intelligence Agency produced a bride for her brother James in the person of her colleague Ann Cooley, had gone to Paris for United Press. James himself, finding the practice of law to be less and less gratifying and not too likely to fill that rural life that he loved, yielded to pressure from his father, who was at the time short-handed, and left Wiggin & Dana to join the family firms; when he was not traveling for them, he spent half his week in Sharon and the other half in a small apartment that he rented in Manhattan. "I found I just plain was not enjoying the practice of law as much as one ought to like doing what one's doing as one's principal occupation," he said. At Wiggin & Dana, however, "I was very lucky in that a lot of my classmates that went to these huge firms in Wall Street would be thrown into one department and spend all their time worrying about this type of work. I had a balanced exposure to the law in a shop of highly competent men—it was a good practice—so that I think I had a far better exposure to what the practice of law would be like and a lot of my contemporaries didn't."

Patricia Buckley Bozell, however, could not confine herself to her private life as the wife of a law student at Yale: her concern with the enemies of the republic was too overpowering. When *The Freeman*, Chamberlain's Right-Wing monthly, published a running controversy about radical teaching at Vassar late in 1952, from which neither the accusers nor the accused stood forth with any brilliance or, indeed, convincingness, she joined it and in January, 1953, the magazine printed her three-page attack on the college, members of the faculty, and its president, based largely on the controversy over the 1949 peace conference that had so exercised the Right and on evidence skillfully selected from two or three students' experiences and various writings by Mary McCarthy, the novelist and critic, with a view to "proving" that Vassar, like the rest of the American higher-education industry, was a conscious collaborator in the furtherance of atheism and Communism. This was a major part of the Buckley canon, as promulgated for years by Will Buckley and unquestioningly accepted by all his children—no one ever rebelled at this or other indoctrination, Priscilla Buckley said in 1972, because "it was never forced on us; ideas were offered to us, and when we disagreed . . . if someone had said Franklin D. Roosevelt was a great man, he would have been gently laughed at."

Whether lamentable or otherwise, it seems to be the unassailable fact that almost no one is capable of teaching "objectively"—a conclusion one reaches from having taught as well as having been taught. It is only the most pallid of persons who have no convictions, no principles; and it is only the least human who can keep these out of their teaching. One will cheerfully concede that one has never studied under a teacher who did not transmit or try, even if unconsciously, to transmit his values, as one has always been aware that in one way or another one cannot prevent oneself from doing the same thing. I do not know that this is necessarily a terrible thing, even if the convictions thus advanced be or seem palpably wrong-headed: what is unforgivable is that, whatever the teacher's beliefs, he penalise the dissident for his dissidence. I find it quite impossible to believe that at any time in the history of this country its educational system at any level has been other than predominantly and even militantly on the side of Dr. Pangloss; it is precisely forty years since an ancient (for America) and honorable university very frankly denied me a degree because of literary heterodoxies that have since become quaintly old-fashioned, and I have known too many teachers both Left and Right who, honestly or otherwise, assume the right to evaluate the student on the basis of his beliefs. In this country, to cite Ortega again, to be different is to be indecent, whether on the Left or on the Right. None of the Buckleys pretended to a belief in "objectivity" of teaching— all of them ridiculed academic freedom by any definition: what they advocated very openly was in fact the teaching of revealed truth as revealed to them. There is thus the same hypocrisy in Mrs. Bozell's rather strident denunciations of indoctrination at Vassar that is evident throughout *God and Man at Yale*; and one is left with the same uncomfortable moral certainty that by no means all the evidence has been presented. That, of course, has something to do with the Sharon conviction that "all Buckleys always have to win."

There is an anecdote that is in point. One evening at this time Bill Buckley was drinking with friends at the Lime Rock Lodge, a very pleasant establishment in the little village of the same name a few miles south of Sharon. Bill bet ten dollars that another man in the group could not consume the entire contents of a jigger of whiskey by the sole means of spooning it up on the flat end of a toothpick without getting drunk; no time limit was imposed. It was, for some of those present, one of the most tedious evenings they had ever spent; but the other man spooned bravely on until, when only a few more toothpick-loads of whiskey were left in the jigger, he was still very obviously sober. Buckley jostled his elbow so that he upset the jigger, spilling what was left; then Buckley demanded that the other man pay up because "you didn't do what you were going to do, you didn't finish it." There was very nearly a fight. The story was told to illustrate the point that "Bill isn't doing things to make a buck or get ahead—it's almost gratuitous, just for the sake of hurting somebody or making somebody look foolish." It seems very much the same kind of cruelty that Yale colleagues noted with distaste in Kendall, of whom it was said that he was "abstract and quite brilliant and quite cruel." But, though Buckley might well agree with Kendall that it was the sacred duty of the Athenians to put Socrates to death because he challenged the existing order, he is not wholly abstract; and his cruelty, like so many people's, co-exists quite easily with a great gentleness and a genuine susceptibility. He is not afraid to weep and he would be the last to think it unmanly in anyone.

Having now made a position in the vanguard of the intellectual Right, Buckley prepared to dirty his shoes somewhat more than some of his supporters might have been willing to do. With his brother-in-law Bozell, who by now was out of law school (and who was to become a speech-writer for Joseph McCarthy), Buckley began work on a book about McCarthy and his antagonists even while the controversies aroused by *God and Man* continued. Quite predictably, these spread to the Catholic as well as the general press, and Catholics divided on the issue of Buckley according to their political orientations. *The Tablet* of Brooklyn, like its California counterpart, *Tidings*, saluted what they hoped was the latter-day Torquemada; the Jesuits' *America* and the more modern *Commonweal* took very different positions.

In a smaller publication, *Catholic World*, one Father Christopher E. Fullman, O.S.B., under the title of "God and Man and Mr. Buckley," pointed out that "God does not need Mr. Buckley to defend Him" and indeed that Buckley's notions of the way the world ought to be seemed widely divergent from what religion had given us to understand were God's. Several popes, notably

Leo XIII and Pius XI, Father Fullman added, had all but anathe-
matised that very Manchester Liberalism that Buckley was so
vigorously upholding: the classic nineteenth-century free-market
philosophy, which pretended that in the ideal free state the play
of supply and demand would take care of everything, including
the body, the mind, and the soul. Buckley's economics, Father
Fullman argued, was conscienceless, and hence counter to religion
and morality, because it was wholly materialistic. And indeed it
was no less so than the most rigid Marxism, unlike which, however,
it was indifferent to the general good, except as a kind of by-
product of individual good. Buckley replied in the same publication, contending that the popes cited by Father Fullman had
denounced Socialism and that anyway their encyclicals on such
non-ghostly matters were not always easy of interpretation. His
own line of argument, after citing his awareness of the most undeniable crimes of Manchesterism, his benevolent consent to anti-
trust laws and codes of fair business practices, and his unshakable
resistance to such wickednesses as "egalitarian tax laws, . . . capitulation to the demands of special interest groups [by which he meant
labor, the poor, minorities], . . . the increased power and centralisation of the government," was of the order of the statement of his
refusal "to believe that Pius XII should be so naïve as to believe
that the right to private property can long endure in a society that
has abandoned natural laws and any meaningful concept of private
ownership" and of his question: "[C]an the pre-eminence of the
family and the primacy of Christianity long withstand a public
educational system that is forbidden from teaching religion, or a
government that refuses on the one hand to aid the private schools,
while bent, on the other hand, on razing incomes so as to make
the maintenance of private schools a luxury impossible to indulge?"
In this mass of postulates, suppositions, and utter fantasies all put
forward with the same dogmatism as so many expressions of unalterable fact, logic was bound to be strangled; so was truth.

It was at this period, too, that Buckley became acquainted with
an interesting type named Marvin Liebman, now resident in London, who was to be an intimate participant, if not an instigator, in
a large number of curious Right-Wing endeavors. From 1938 to
1945 Liebman was a devout member of, successively, the Young
Communist League and the Communist Party, resigning in protest
at what he regarded as the unjust expulsion of Earl Browder, who
had long been the party's leader. He went to work for the Inter-

national Rescue Committee, but it was not until 1951 that he was
swept up in that tidal wave of conversions that poured over the
land with the blessings of McCarran, McCarthy, Nixon, and their
like. The light that Liebman saw through the waters was, naturally,
green—his retirement to London and the pleasures of theatrical
production was made possible by his not unimpressive earnings as
an organiser, promoter, and fund-raiser for his new friends. Suddenly recognising what a peril to the world was the Soviet Union,
in 1952 he set up Aid to Refugee Chinese Intellectuals; a year later
he launched the Committee of One Million Against the Admission
of Communist China to the United Nations, which was the god-
child of Alfred Kohlberg, an importer who had made a fortune
out of non-Communist China and who became known as the "one-
man China lobby." Buckley was soon in contact with Kohlberg and
Liebman, who flirted now and again in later years with the John
Birch Society and evidenced the totality of his ecumenical spirit by
toiling vigorously for both the American Jewish League Against
Communism, Inc., and the Christian Anti-Communist Crusade.
Most of the organisations that enjoyed his services were also listed
at Marvin Liebman Associates' office address and telephone number
in New York. All were thoroughly imbued with the spirit of
McCarthy, who, mercifully for his country, died in 1957.

McCarthy's apologists declare that he was an honest man who,
like themselves, believed that the republic was imminently menaced by the world conspiracy of Communism and who undertook
to drive the Communists and their agents out of government and
the military. His principal technique was the innuendo, the smear
of association—perfectly stolid middle-class people could be ruined,
under his aegis, for "consorting" with their Communist parents or
sisters or grandparents—the inference drawn from imagination.
By the law of averages he was bound occasionally to be right, since
he accused so many; if he did not denounce them as Communists
or Communist dupes, he harried them as homosexuals. He was the
Senate's equivalent of the House Un-American Activities Committee; and both were to be championed in Buckley books. To
Buckley's credit (or discredit, given his undoubted intelligence),
he never questioned the good faith of either; and certainly he
whole-heartedly backed the goals of both.

McCarthy and His Enemies, which was published in 1954 by
Regnery (in 1970 the copyright was transferred to Arlington
House, Buckley's connection with which will be discussed pres-

ently), had a remarkable prologue by another of those converted radicals, William S. (formerly Willi) Schlamm. An Austrian radical Marxist, he had found it expedient to leave the Continent for the United States in the late 1930's. According to James Burnham, he was never a Communist, but rather associated with the "Two-and-a-Half International of Vienna," which aspired to build a bridge between the Socialist Second International and the Communist Third International; Schlamm's own politics then were described as being quite like those of the Socialist Revolutionaries of Russia who took part in the 1917 Revolution but who were not Communists. When the tidal wave caught him up, it deposited him on the doorstep of the Luce publications; he picked himself up, went inside, and found it so comfortable that he stayed—as Luce's right hand—until his permanent return to Europe a few years ago. It is said that before the war he was the editor-in-chief of various extremely radical Berlin journals—Ralph de Toledano says one of them was *Die Rote Fahne*, the Communist Party's organ, but this seems doubtful since Schlamm never held a Party card. From the connections he enjoyed in America—and his continued contributions to the John Birch Society's *American Opinion* and, much less frequently, Buckley's *National Review*, of which he, like Burnham and Willmoore Kendall, was a founding senior editor—one can assume that he has not resumed his old European alliances.

Schlamm proposed as fact McCarthy's disclosure of "the immense Communist infiltration of democratic government and free society," though there has never been a shred of evidence to support such a preposterous statement. McCarthy's victims, direct and indirect, were only a few thousand—though the number, like the statistics of the concentration camps, is irrelevant to the moral question—largely because he was stopped by the public outcry provoked by his own porcine stupidities and by that common-law and statutory presumption of innocence that, Buckley and Bozell wrote, "will long remain the major barrier in the way of an effective security program," because (and the italics are theirs) "*justice*, we are saying, *is not the major objective here.*" In *The Catholic World* in 1952, quoting from illustrious eighteenth-century authorities, Buckley had written that "I confess that I consider the *genus* State as 'begotten of aggression and by aggression,' and as 'the common enemy of all well-disposed, industrious and decent men,'—hardly equipped, on the basis of its historical performance, to superintend the common good"; it sounds like something out of Kendall's early days as a kind of Rousseau libertarian. Less than two years later Buckley and Bozell were arguing that security was paramount to justice and that all that mattered was the needs of the state. Citing, as they did in their book (though without always acknowledging the heinousness of them), all the gutter tactics of McCarthy, the breaches of common decency and good faith on which he relied for much of his "evidence," even the dozens of misdoings for which they themselves criticised him, they were able to say that "McCarthyism . . . is a movement around which men of good will and stern morality can close ranks." In January of 1954 the Gallup Poll showed that fifty per cent of the population looked on McCarthy with favor and only twenty-nine per cent disapproved. "It was a melancholy time," Richard M. Rovere wrote in *Senator Joe McCarthy,* "and the Chief Justice of the United States was probably right when he said that, if the Bill of Rights were put to a vote, it would lose."

That simple statement has always been true—more than one survey on that very issue, undertaken for the American Civil Liberties Union, has ended in the same disquieting result. What Americans—some Americans, at any rate—take pride in as their nation's dedication to freedom and justice is an illusion, and the Buckleys, who do not share the illusion, know that theirs is the position of the majority. Bill Buckley today does not believe in the ACLU's interpretation of the First Amendment: he would silence the advocates of certain doctrines, though, as he said recently, "I take the Oliver Wendell Holmes position as a prudential matter: as an absolute matter, I agree with Harry V. Jaffa* that there is no right to speak that way." One should always bear in mind that most people would agree, and that that Ortega whom Buckley and I admire for such thoroughly contradictory reasons was absolutely correct in what can properly be called his warning about liberalism in the intellectual and philosophic sense: it "is the supreme form of generosity; it is the right which the majority accords to minorities and hence it is the noblest cry that has ever resounded in this planet. It announces the determination to share existence with the enemy; more than that, with an enemy which is weak. . . . It is a discipline too difficult and complex to take firm root on earth."

---

* A conservative professor of political science who wrote for Senator Barry Goldwater the sentence that, some think, helped to defeat his Presidential attempt in 1964: "Extremism in the defense of liberty is no vice, moderation in the pursuit of justice is no virtue."—C.L.M.

And Buckleys will always see to it that it never threatens to take root.

"Buckley was never as close to Joe [McCarthy] as I was," de Toledano (who at least once attacked McCarthy) said, "but of course Joe loved him and loved to have him around: he gave a sort of intellectual patent to the McCarthy movement. To the best of my knowledge, Bill was never involved in any of the behind-the-scenes maneuvers." Buckley deplored de Toledano's attack on McCarthy, the basis for which was McCarthy's assaults against the Eisenhower Administration, which de Toledano found "tactically very stupid, like the John Birchers saying Eisenhower was a Communist: Eisenhower was never smart enough to be a Communist."

Buckley admired McCarthy then and admires him still today. One of his few differences with a man whom he admired extravagantly, the late Whittaker Chambers, arose over McCarthy, of whom Chambers observed, in letters to Buckley and Regnery after McCarthy had been angered by reading the galleys of *McCarthy and His Enemies*, that he did not know what he was doing, that his intelligence was not equal to his energy, that he was "a heavy-handed slugger who telegraphs his fouls in advance," who "has to learn from consequences or counselors that he has fouled," and who "thinks this is a superior technique that the rest of us are too far behind to appreciate." But Buckley was not: it is too often his own in his television duels with people whom he has invited to his *Firing Line* program: he will enunciate what purports to be a damaging quotation, then ask whether the antagonist upholds or disavows it, and, if the reply is a factual denial of ever having said or written the matter attributed, Buckley will then persist in demanding that the non-author confirm or repudiate it.

The friendship with Chambers, which was to endure until Chambers died in 1961, was launched by correspondence at the beginning of 1954 after Chambers reluctantly refused Regnery's and then Buckley's request to write a jacket blurb for the McCarthy book. It was not that Chambers disapproved of McCarthy's objectives as he saw them: he found the man a less than desirable champion; but that is a complicated question not really germane to this book and certainly not to be potted into a worthless sentence or paragraph. The correspondence led to a request by Buckley to be allowed to visit Chambers and to bring along Kendall, who had defended Chambers vigorously at Yale during the Hiss trial. For the next seven years Buckley and Chambers were staunch friends.

And, of all the people Buckley came to know in this period, Chambers was probably the most remarkable. Buckley had read something by de Toledano and written him a complimentary letter, whereupon de Toledano, then at *Newsweek*, had asked to be allowed to review *God and Man*, which he had praised highly. De Toledano was a friend of Chambers, whom he much respected, and, rather contradictorily, of Victor Lasky: they had written *Seeds of Treason*, another anti-Communist book. Lasky is a kind of journalist, who nowadays appears sometimes in *Human Events* and other far-Right publications and who made rather a good bit of money by cutting-pasting-inventing books about John and Robert Kennedy. At public dinners he drops cigar butts into coffee cups.

De Toledano was also a friend of one Richard Nixon, then Vice President of the United States, to whom he introduced Buckley at Buckley's request. "There sat these two guys," de Toledano told me, "both very articulate men, practically just making stupid talk about the weather, both of them—Nixon being completely impressed by Bill, meeting this great intellectual, and Bill being completely impressed with Nixon, the Vice President of the United States. And for about ten minutes there was this inane back-and-forth, both of them tremendously ill at ease, until I said something to start the conversation going, and then it was fine. I've often wondered about Bill's real feelings about Nixon as a person. In both men you have what I call sexual aloofness."

(Here one must mark a distinction. De Toledano is quite right, and the observation is not a frivolous one. But unquestionably, in both Bill and Jim Buckley, this aloofness does not preclude an unmistakable sexual presence, perceptible to men and women alike, without which they could not exercise the personal attraction that both possess. It is the same sexual presence that was to be noted in and exploited by John and Robert Kennedy or John V. Lindsay; but one has not heard of its being sensed in Nixon.)

Another of the men whom Buckley met at this time and with whom he still maintains some connection was Roy M. Cohn, a young man from New York who became counsel to McCarthy's Senate subcommittee and whom some people blame for McCarthy's destruction. Cohn, who remained active in various anti-Communist organisations supported by Buckleys and who has spent a good deal of time and money fighting criminal prosecutions, thus far successfully, was involved much later in the founding and development of the Conservative Party of New York State, largely a Buckley creation, and was among the guests at *National Review*'s fifteenth-anniversary celebration in 1971. Such an association is an extraordinary contrast to Buckley's deep friendship with Chambers.

At this time Chambers was in a quite unhappy position, hailed by some of the worst savages on the Right for the wrong reasons, thoroughly distrusted by other leading rednecks for equally wrong reasons, and generally despised, largely without examination, by everyone from just left of center all the way over. An extraordinarily complex and deeply emotional man of superior intellect, cultivation, and sensibility, he had for years before the war worked for *Time* and belonged to the Communist Party, rising quite high in both. In a certain sense he was an American analogue to André Malraux: the totally engaged intellectual, long a radical activist (frequently he carried a gun for reasons more practical than romantic-revolutionary), who, having found himself constrained to go over to the Right, could not wholly abandon—or betray—his past or universally embrace the sharers of his new bed. Chambers's work in the party's intelligence section had much to do with the change in convictions that compelled him not only to leave the party but to regard it as a very real menace to his country and to the whole of Western civilisation, and the philosophical and experiential foundation of his views was of course far more solid than that of Buckley's thinking, and so therefore was his sense of moral obligation to disclose what he knew to various investigative bodies. It was his testimony that led in 1950 to the perjury conviction of one of his dearest personal as well as political friends, Alger Hiss, a former State Department official. The case aroused international controversy that has not yet subsided altogether; but one has lived long enough to have learned not to sit in judgment on the protagonists of this profound tragedy of friendship.

Chambers was, fortunately, a constant writer of letters (even though he destroyed many of them unmailed; but enough have survived to fascinate any student of the human psyche or of that era), and those to Buckley have been made into a book with a foreword by de Toledano that gives some idea of Chambers's background; much more emerges from the letters themselves. (Buckley's replies are not included; they are now the property of Mrs. Chambers, and besides, Buckley says, he made no copies of the rare letters he wrote to Chambers; chiefly he replied by telephone.) It is obvious from them and from the explanatory material inserted wherever necessary by Buckley how much he loved and respected his friend, and how warmly his friendship was requited, yet how honestly his friend assessed and addressed him.

By the middle of 1954 Buckley had conceived the idea of an intellectual conservative magazine, the tentative name of which was *The National Weekly*, and among those whom he attempted to recruit for its board of editors was Chambers, whose letters elucidate his reservations. In large part he felt that his recent notoriety could only militate against anything with which he was known to be associated; in at least equally large part he had a genuine lust for privacy and anonymity—he was content to work his little farm in Maryland, to enjoy his books and music with his wife, and to write when he felt that he must. He wanted, too, considerable further assurance as to the direction and tone that the periodical would take, and he was by no means certain of his ability to work with all the persons whom Buckley was soliciting for the board: Kirk, Burnham, Schlamm, Chamberlain, Kendall, Eastman, de Toledano, Suzanne La Follette of the Wisconsin Progressive family that had sent two men to the Senate, and Frank S. Meyer, another recent defector from the orthodox Communist Party, in which in the 1930's he had begun to distinguish himself as a theoretician and detector of heresies (the latter rôle he kept up on the other side, according to some of his friends there, until his death in 1972). Chambers's great problem seems to have been that of so many, once they have attained full intellectual growth: the inability to deceive oneself sufficiently to pledge blind allegiance anywhere and enter into unconditional open-ended *Blutbrüderschaft* sight unseen. But the same scrupulousness—or, as Buckley would call it, scrupulosity—that preserved him from the snare of "all the enemies of my enemies are my friends" prevented him also from even the appearance, to the hostile world, of a division with anyone else on his side of the field.

While he was being consulted by Buckley and the others involved in the midwifing of what was ultimately to be called *National Review*, Chambers's basic attitude toward Buckley had crystalised permanently. On New Year's Day, 1955, he wrote to Buckley: "After your visit here last spring, when my wife was asking the usual questions, I said of you: 'He is something special. He was born, not made, and not many like that are born in any time.' That is not, of course, the way I am accustomed to judge people. It has happened to me only twice before. . . . What you will do with your special grace I do not know. I shall watch with great interest. And not watch only. My counsel, which you invoke, is yours for the taking."

It was not seldom invoked—not always followed, not always rejected, but never dismissed. During the gestation of *National Review*, Chambers was frequently consulted in the flesh, by letter, by telephone. He thoroughly approved the idea of a new magazine, but not one that would attempt to lead a narrow crusade, like Chamberlain's *Freeman*; and he saw a potential audience of a half-million readers for this fluid voice of an evolving conservative philosophy on a reasonably high level. Schlamm, whom he had long known, discussed the project at length with him; Chambers felt able to work with him, Buckley, Burnham, Chamberlain, in spite of some or even many differences of view within a shared ideology. He was by now prepared to break his silence about the Eisenhower Administration, though for long he had forborne because "I would not give anything to the common enemy."

The question of Eisenhower, Nixon, and McCarthy was a vexed one for Buckley and his group. Some wanted to support them all, if only because they saw no other hope for their side; some divided in various ways; a few would have repudiated. Chambers wrote to Schlamm (the letter is included in Buckley's book): "I chiefly say: 'Give them a little more rope.'" One had always the feeling that Chambers experienced a certain distaste, indeed an attainder of dignity and decency, in any association with any of them, however tenuous, in spite of his endorsement of their ends. Yet he was very close (improbably) to Nixon, with whom, sometimes very clandestinely, he consulted; and one looks askance at this, as one marvels at Buckley's surprise, many years later, that Nixon should "betray" his conservative supporters on China and economic controls: one cannot believe that any middling intelligent person could be surprised at any shoddiness in a man whose whole career was one of last-minute opportunism, coupled occasionally with desperation, and whose intellectual apogee was the Rose Bowl football games.

In the summer of *National Review*'s conception Chambers stated the problem as he conceived it; there is no record of Schlamm's or Buckley's reaction except their utterances and actions in the years that followed. "History tells me," Chambers said, "that the rock-core of the Conservative Position, or any fragment of it, can be held realistically only if conservatism will accommodate itself to the needs and hopes of the masses—needs and hopes which, like the masses themselves, are the product of machines. For of course our fight . . . is only incidentally with socialists or other heroes of that kidney. *Wesentlichen* [essentially], it is with machines. A conservatism that cannot face the facts of the machine and mass production, and its consequences in government and politics, is foredoomed to futility and petulance." The machine, he pointed out, had come to stay, and with it "those gigantic yields and that increased man-hour productivity whose abundance spells bankruptcy and crisis—or controls." Chambers might have become as ardent a worshiper of God as any religious could desire, but such *aperçus* of conservatism as his could have had no place then in the lying-in home.

Buckley, however, labored continually, both before and after the birth, to get Chambers on to the governing board. Liberally financed by his father, Buckley, with Schlamm's help, was out in search of further funds at the same time; here Liebman is said to have been of considerable usefulness. But money was not the major problem: there was always more where the first batches had come from. Brains are rather harder to come by. Kirk, approached early to accept an editorship, had "declined, on the grounds that I write for many magazines and don't wish to be committed to just one, and that it is imprudent to be listed on the masthead as an editor when actually one is so remote in space [Kirk lived in deepest Michigan; *National Review* was to be published in New York] that he cannot assume any real editorial responsibilities or attend meetings of the editorial board." Kendall was Buckley's only academician (his place has now been taken by Jeffrey Hart of the Department of English at Dartmouth, a disciple of Burke in politics if not in manners—he is the sort of person who answers his correspondents at the bottom of their letters); and Kirk has speculated whether Kendall had not adhered to the Right at least in part because he "loved to quarrel with people and essentially to take the losing side: since the conservatives tended to be the losing side, he determined to join them."

Chambers made his choices more solidly. While he too was a former radical—indeed a former Communist, whereas Burnham (though Buckley would have been almost alone on the Right in understanding the differences) had been a Trotskyist and Schlamm at most a Socialist Revolutionary—he was one of the least suspect to the Right because he had not only recanted but acted; and his was a genuinely creative mind. But he was less in search of a new authority than the others, and his experience in the party, with the reflections to which it had led him, had made him wary of new commitments without the most exhaustive analysis and, what was far less likely, the most profound conviction. To the end of his life he was incapable of not examining every question thoroughly; and it is not of this fabric that zealots are made. So he wrote for the magazine occasionally, often reviewing books; but it was not until several years later that he could finally be persuaded to join the board of editors; not much more than a year after that, he resigned from it, partly because of his health and partly because of his principles.

He had always been forthright. "Your belief that NR [*National Review*] is full of readable copy troubles me," he wrote to Buckley in October, 1957. Something more than a year later he told Buckley that *National Review*'s article on *The New Class*, Milovan Djilas's controversial book, was "a nasty little job, sophomoric and vicious." Chambers himself was a notable elevation on the magazine's topography, virtually always avoiding personalities and evidencing love and respect for thought and language greater than those of any other of its authors, including its founder and editor-in-chief. In the controversies over the Eisenhower Administration and over foreign policy that occasionally arose among the editors (for the most part, before his acceptance of a post among them), Chambers's position was judicious and comprehensive: he had passed beyond partisanship and could look quite Olympianly on Schlamm's bloodthirsty demands for war *à outrance* on the godless Soviets, as he could on Burnham's far more subtle proposal for an American challenge to Russia to join in a mutual and total withdrawal from the whole of occupied Europe. After a visit from Brent Bozell and Frank Meyer, who by then had become one of the editors of *National Review* and who described what was going on inside the offices, some of it corroborated in a letter from Buckley, Chambers wrote: "The level of discussion, the personal assaults . . . is shocking. It is not even the tone of mayhem in the Politburo. It is the tone of unenlightened kilkenny in a district cell."

It was then and still is the tone of half of almost any issue of Buckley's magazine.

X

ONE OF THE EARLIEST CONSEQUENCES of the publication of *God and Man at Yale* had been to thrust Bill Buckley forward as an attraction for the lecture and debate circuit. (Another was to launch the family's voyages on the untidy seas of libel litigation and the threats of suit: the first potential plaintiff was Bill, and his adversaries were the editors of the *Harvard Crimson*—a story to be dealt with presently, though briefly.) The appearance of *McCarthy and His Enemies*, at just about the time when McCarthy had begun to get a small part of what he had earned—television was broadcasting the hearings of his ridiculous charges of Communist infiltration of the United States Army and letting a huge public observe just how contemptibly immoral he, his associates, and his methods were; and censure by the Senate was not far off—heightened the demand for Buckley, and not only in the cultural backwoods: he was the only literate defender ready and willing to carry the fight for McCarthy to the enemy, and the enemy had enough intellectual curiosity, very often, to want to hear what might be said for its black beast, as well as to gain some notion of the manner of man not too unlike itself who had elected to throw himself, as he had put it, athwart the twentieth century and cry *Halt!*

A digression is not out of order here. Nothing is easier—or more misleading—than to discredit one's opponent (seemingly) by relegating him to some past era or holding him in abeyance for an age yet to arrive. But there is no inherent sanctity in any period, and no special merit in the passionate embrace of one's own: that is like automatic patriotism. How indeed is it possible for anyone of any sensibility, however much he may enjoy the innumerable mixed and the few relatively untainted benisons of "our time" or "today's world," as the middle-brow jargon calls it interchangeably, to do so without at least an occasional sardonic jab of conscience—conscience social, political, esthetic, moral (if I may be forgiven the archaism)? Besides, Buckley's roadblock—like those thrown up occasionally from the Left—is by no means unselective: one keeps a *laissez-passer* always close to hand for what serves one's purpose, one's convenience, one's pleasures. One has yet to encounter a single scorner—including oneself—of television and its complacent herds who declines all opportunity to exploit it. The irony in the case of Buckley's *défi* to his time is that he has increasingly become the creature of some of those aspects of it that he affects most to contest.

Buckley on the platform did not disappoint those who had gone to hear him, whether to mock or to pray; and certainly none hit any sawdust trail in his presence: the mockers mocked harder and the adorers adored harder too, whether he lectured alone or appeared in debate with various stalking horses of the other side. Undoubtedly these barnstorming experiences and observations fueled his aspirations to publish a conservative journal of opinion, as the publicity and the development of his abilities helped to create a market for his articles in periodicals beyond those of purely Catholic interest. Very quickly he began to shed the pompousness that had so often hallmarked him at Yale; this was no doubt the effect of a mounting sense of sureness in *terris incognitis*.

Often he would take on local champions wherever he was booked; in built-up areas his debates would usually engage him against some accepted representative of what was already beginning, in the mid-1950's, to be called "the Liberal (or liberal) Establishment"—a phrase sometimes credited to Buckley; but that does not matter: it was substantially accurate in that those people called themselves liberals in another instance of the progressive degradation of language and ideas. The liberal of whom Ortega and other Europeans were thinking when they used the term was generally a classical economist and, far more important, always a genuine practitioner of toleration, not condescension, whatever his politics. No sich animule has existed in this country in any numbers since its inception. Certainly what have been called liberals in the United States since the First World War have been a gross caricature of the term, with very few honorable exceptions. Ample evidence on this point may be had from the membership secretary of the American Civil Liberties Union, who can cite the statistics of withdrawals whenever the Union has defended the rights of the Right. Whoever aspires to be a liberal ought to ponder the observation of Paul Weiss: "As a philosopher, I can't be bothered too much about how people differ from me: everybody differs from me."

There have been few such people among Buckley's adversaries. At various times there was virtually a traveling repertory company touring the provinces: Buckley and Dwight Macdonald, critic of the arts and society on the side of the self-acknowledged angels; Buckley and (as Chambers so aptly called him) little Arthur Schlesinger, son and namesake of the historian and later one of Camelot's inadvertent jesters and very advertent pitchmen; Buckley and James A. Wechsler, editor and commentator of the *New York Post*; Buckley and Murray Kempton, also a writer then for the *Post* as well as for periodicals and probably the only one among Buckley's antagonists who was at least his peer in intellect, cultivation, and prose; Buckley and John Kenneth Galbraith, Harvard economist, *camelot du roi*, occasional wit, Buckley's annual ski companion in Switzerland later, and possibly second to Kempton in *virtù*. What they debated about in the beginning was the liberal/Communist plague as Buckley saw it, and necessarily too McCarthy. As the decades trudged on, the first theme was kept shining, but of necessity the second tended to lose its attraction when the Senator's corpse did not emerge on the third day. The major subject, however, is infinitely flexible and has always allowed of perfect modulation to whatever was the gnawing problem of the moment: the intransigence of blacks who would insist on claiming human rights, the wickedness of central government, the unending efforts to drive almighty God (who, granted the epithet's validity, should not have needed mere human help) out of the schools and the society, the propagation of the faith by napalm and personnel bomb among the unbred heathen of questionable complexion, the duty to hurl across the plains of Hungary and Poland in a jehad against the brutal Slavs, their later presumptuousness in reaching first into "outer space," and the whole wearisome catalogue down to the rights of Jews in the Soviet Union, a subject of rather more apparent concern to the Right than the condition of poor whites, blacks, and browns—or for that matter Jews—in the United States.

Wechsler, who was one of Buckley's most frequent antagonists at the invitation of schools, colleges, women's clubs, political groups, etc., is also perhaps the most balanced in his recollections

and in his appraisal, possibly because there was never a friendship
between them or, obviously, a subsequent rift. Buckley and Macdonald were friends for a while, but neither could resist the temptation to plunge his rapier into the other or take the thrust in
particularly good part, though Buckley would seem to have been
a millimeter less the prima donna; a mutual friend's attempt to
reconcile them at a lunch was a fiasco. Macdonald said in 1957 that
Buckley could not write, had no sense of humor, and lacked intellectual curiosity—rather a grab-bag of petulancies. Schlesinger has
occasionally attacked Buckley, in terms that would lead one to
believe that it must have been he of whom Macdonald was thinking. Galbraith's and Buckley's criticisms of and attacks on each
other are intellectual rather than personal, and much resemble the
courtroom and newspaper exchanges between opposing lawyers
who thoroughly enjoy each other's company. Kempton, who has
been as close a friend of Buckley as anyone would be likely to be
who originated and remained so far outside Buckley's own circle,
has a considerable ambivalence about him and about the family.
He has had a great deal of social contact with many of the Buckleys, and there can be no question of the reciprocal respect that
exists between Kempton and Bill Buckley. Though Kempton has
often written very sympathetically of Buckley as a person, he has
remarked also that "Bill Buckley doesn't really have many feelings.
He can say: 'I think you're a dangerous Communist agent but I
love you,' and there can't be much feeling in that kind of thing."
This is reminiscent of William Coley's explanation of the decline
of his close friendship with James Buckley: "There comes a point
at which you can't separate the man from his ideas." One is not
quite certain that this is or need be always true: too many instances
to the contrary come to mind. Kempton, one is inclined to believe,
oversimplifies; it is not difficult to think of people whom one has
loved dearly in spite of the visceral certainty that, in a given set
of circumstances that is not beyond the range of probability, one
would be exchanging gunfire with them.

I remarked to Kempton that, when one reads Buckley on music
or sailing—and on virtually nothing else: here he writes with
grace of soul as well as of style, and with love—it is almost impossible not to feel *Christ, one could like this man,* just as one leaves
James Buckley's company with regret that such a nice guy is
a captain in the host of *Massenmensch.* Kempton replied that Bill
Buckley's feelings for such things, as for individual persons, are far

deeper than his political beliefs—and one cannot be sure that this is damning. A contrast was drawn between the urbanity of most of the Buckleys and the fanatical medieval Catholicism of their brother-in-law Brent Bozell; Kempton observed: "None of the Buckleys really believes very much in anything except Buckleys."

And in this the resemblance to the Kennedys—if Kempton is correct—is frightening. Every man who has made his way to power has believed primarily in himself—perhaps exclusively; how else could anyone have the sheer gall to *arrive*? I do not mean to suggest that I view Bill Buckley—or, indeed, any Buckley—as an aspirant to office, but that hardly implies that none of them aspires to power, to a power far more real and ominous than that of public office, which is so often the merest façade.

Wechsler, however, seems never to have shared Kempton's skepticisms. Buckley and Wechsler have debated up and down the eastern seaboard, and the only ugliness that ever attended any of their encounters did not arise between them. In the spring of 1954 *The Lakeville Journal*, the enterprising weekly serving the Buckleys' part of Connecticut, became involved with George V. Denny Jr., a local resident who for years had conducted a reasonably good radio program entitled *Town Meeting of the Air*, in a proposal for a series of local public meetings and debates on public questions. The programs were known as *Lakeville Journal Opinions Unlimited*, and a debate on McCarthy between Buckley and Wechsler was scheduled for the last Friday in April; the paper appeared on Thursdays. By way of stimulating interest in the forthcoming debate, the paper published reviews of the participants' latest books in its issue of the preceding week.

Wechsler's *Age of Suspicion*, a political autobiography, was discussed by Clyde Brion Davis, a novelist and former newspaper man who lived in Salisbury and who was virgin of any politics whatever. His review of Wechsler's story—youthful enlistment in the Young Communist League at Columbia University, abandonment of the party in 1937, and a life of consistent fighting against all forms of totalitarianism ever since—did not overlook the attacks to which Wechsler had been subjected for seventeen years, and most bitterly and dirtily by McCarthy, on the ground that his renunciation was a fake; and Davis called the book a "remarkable document" that should be read by "every American who wants no part of dictatorships whether of the Communist Left or the Fascist Right." Buckley's and Bozell's *McCarthy and His Enemies,* however, was shredded by Hal Borland, another professional writer and newspaper man resident in Salisbury and noted primarily for his books and essays about nature. Borland cited the authors' avoidance of such embarrassments as the actual number of persons injured by McCarthy's casual slanders, to say nothing of their condonation of virtually everything done by McCarthy and the sleazy Roy Cohn. Borland quoted, too, such Buckley-Bozell aphorisms as this: "Man's only absolute freedom is his freedom to earn salvation. . . . The Russian serf, even within the area in which he is allowed by the State to act, can triumph over evil every bit as effectively as can the American freedman." Borland added for himself, with shocking grammar: "Reading those lines and thinking of McCarthy's definition of heresy and McCarthy's framework of salvation, cold shivers run down one's back. The implications are appalling." For the greater part he condemned McCarthy and McCarthyism; of the book he says at the start that it "throw[s] a surprisingly clear light on" its subject and, toward the end, that "there is a chilling air of absolutism all through this defense of McCarthyism."

The day before the scheduled debate Buckley sent a telegram to *The Lakeville Journal* saying that he would not appear, for reasons to be explained in a following letter. In this document, which *The Journal* subsequently published, he denounced Borland's review as "a sustained and vicious misrepresentation of my book"; and he denounced the paper for having allowed this wrong to be done by a man who "has worked for *The New York Times,* to which he continues to contribute." Then came what Buckley likes to call the gravamen: "A sentence in the review of my book reads: 'Throughout the book, the authors reason, with McCarthy, that since Communists hate McCarthy, all who disagree with any phase of McCarthyism are Commies of some degree.' This statement is a lie. . . . I have been libeled by my hosts." The letter made it plain that Wechsler was not involved and that Buckley would in fact be debating him soon afterward in Brooklyn. Denny telegraphed to Buckley, urging him to reconsider, but Buckley stood firm and repeated: "I have been libeled." The matter went no farther, but it left some people in that part of Connecticut very leery of criticising a Buckley again.

What fascinates Wechsler today in Bill Buckley is the extent to which he has changed "from the guy I debated in the fifties"— their relations ended in 1961, when Wechsler was invited to participate in a *National Review* forum at Hunter College (which could not have been held without the intervention of the American Civil Liberties Union on Buckley's behalf) and found that it was loaded in the sense that he was deprived of equal question-and-answer time. But he is still deeply touched by the letter of condolence that Buckley wrote some time later when Wechsler's young son died tragically; and he recalls Buckley's consideration in driving many miles out of his way late at night, after a debate on Long Island and Wechsler's immediate departure for another city, in order to convey Mrs. Wechsler back to her home in Manhattan.

The change that Wechsler sees in Buckley he attributes to the encroachments of "critical introspection." Somewhat the same observation has been made by Weiss and Coffin, who speak of his "mellowing" and "maturing." Buckley's debating tactics have not much altered since the 1950's—the same sharp practices persist, some of them further sharpened—but his thinking, in Wechsler's view, has grown up from the manifestations in *God and Man at Yale* and his articles after graduation for *Facts Forum*, the organ of H. L. Hunt, the grotesquely Right-Wing Texas oil billionaire, and *The American Mercury*, which listed him successively as associate and contributing editor and with which he broke when its owner, Russell Maguire, made anti-Semitism part of its policy. (Some years later, in fact, Buckley warned *National Review*'s staff and contributors that it would boycott anyone who wrote for *The American Mercury*.) "I think today he is more conservative than radical Right, as he was in the fifties," Wechsler said in the autumn of 1971. "He has done a rather skillful job of dissociating himself from the lunatic fringe of his movement." Perhaps, Wechsler supposes, his brother's entry into politics has somewhat deprived him of "the luxury of being a maverick."

Reflecting on Buckley as his interlocutor on so many platforms and Buckley as the public man whose column Wechsler himself was influential, years later, in persuading the *Post* to buy, he contrasted the genuine charm that Buckley is not sometimes above exploiting, and the spontaneous grace with which he so often renders services great and small even to enemies, to that other side of the man that to some minds simply cannot co-exist with his virtues. "The vulnerability of Buckley," Wechsler said, "is in his extraordinary inhumanity in dealings with [one supposes Wechsler meant *utterances on*] agricultural workers, blacks, etc. This is so hard for me to equate with the warmth of his relation to Chambers, of his one gesture to me. He's good with humanity only in terms of individuals; in terms of mass—Kent State, for example, whatever one's political views, was a human tragedy—he is capable of the utmost horrible callousness." And then Wechsler did sound somewhat like Kempton: "I wonder sometimes whether the game isn't the thing—is he really so moved by the crisis of Western civilisation?"

The question is inevitable. I did not go up and down the East Coast debating Bill Buckley; we had met once only, before this book was conceived, with the utmost mutual hostility and a rather craftsmanlike exchange of personal insults, on a television program in Chicago several years ago. Since then I have read, I suppose, all his published writings ("No wonder you look so aged!" he said when I mentioned the apprenticeship), and more than enough of what has been written about him on all sides; and we have held a couple of civilised conversations in his offices at *National Review*. The composite impression of all this is that the answer to both terms of Wechsler's question must be *yes*. Of course Buckley enjoys the game: he is civilised, after all, and part of being civilised consists in refusing to lose the joy of play. But I believe he is quite as "moved by the crisis of Western civilisation" as anyone else who professes to be, and certainly more genuinely by far than such slobs of the intellect as Timothy Leary or Richard Nixon; unfortunately I think he has a skewed view of the nature of the crisis, perhaps a certain responsibility in its intensification as far as the United States is concerned, and consequently an almost altogether wrong set of proposals for its resolution. There is no reason —no valid reason, at least, if one is not inordinately eaten up inside —to suppose that concern is necessarily incompatible with style, or even with elegance. I do not pretend that Bill Buckley is always elegant; but even when he is behaving most badly he has style.

And Buckley's concern, of course, is by definition rather restricted, since his conception of Western civilisation has impassable frontiers. His style—in the broadest sense—had begun to become evident when he named his first boat, and it was given a certain rehearsal in his earliest venture into the world of libel, real and other. About a month after the publication of *God and Man*, the *Harvard Crimson* published a review by one Gordon Hall ("a sort of professional keeper of the anti-Right-Wing tablets," Buckley called him recently), who wrote: "William Buckley is even more of a Fascist than he is cracked up to be." Buckley not only threatened suit (in those days many people, including those who ought to have known better, regarded "Fascist" and "Nazi" as synonyms) and demanded a retraction by Hall and the *Crimson*, but insisted on the publication of a statement to the effect "that anybody who was familiar with my work—my work at that point was simply one book plus what people had happened to read at Yale—that such a conclusion was completely at odds with my writings." Buckley compelled the signature of this apology by Hall and by each of the editots of the *Crimson* individually.

One of the bases of style, at least sometimes, is *khutzpah*.

XI

SITTING ON A PLATFORM at East Carolina College one night in 1962, awaiting his turn to reply to Bill Buckley in a debate, Fred Rodell, who at times virtually thinks in limericks, scribbled among the notes he was taking:

> As I leafed through the *National Review*,
> Having nothing much better to do,
> I assumed that the date
> Was 1898
> Instead of 1962.

Obviously, the eminent authority on the Constitution and the Supreme Court—probably unique in possessing a photograph of the entire "Warren Court" with an individual dedication to him from each of the justices—was not being a strict constructionist. *National Review* was founded, essentially, on a thesis first stated by Buckley in *God and Man at Yale*: "I myself believe that the duel between Christianity and atheism is the most important in the world. I further believe that the struggle between individualism and collectivism is the same struggle reproduced on another level." The first statement in the credo makes one think of a time far earlier than 1898: it verges on the fanatic position that was ultimately to separate Brent Bozell and his wife from all the rest of the Buckleys: the absolute rule of the City of God and the subjugation of the City of Man. Whether by *Christianity* Buckley really meant *Catholicism*, as his own faith's dogma requires him to equate the terms, becomes irrelevant, morally and philosophically.

Volume I, Number 1, of *National Review*, A Weekly Journal of Opinion (it subsequently became a fortnightly), carried the

date of 19 November 1955 and listed its editor and publisher as
William F. Buckley, Jr. (the comma was later dropped). Its editors
were listed, in this order, as James Burnham, Willmoore Kendall,
Suzanne La Follette, Jonathan Mitchell, and William S. Schlamm;
"Associates and Contributors" catalogued L. Brent Bozell, John
Chamberlain, Frank Chodorov, John Abbot Clark, Forrest Davis,
Max Eastman, Medford Evans, Karl Hess, Russell Kirk, Eugene
Lyons, Frank S. Meyer, Gerhart Niemeyer, E. Merrill Root, Morrie
Ryskind, Freda Utley, Richard Weaver. There were Foreign Con-
tributors too: in London, F. A. Voigt; in Paris, Eudocio Ravines;
in Taipei, John C. Caldwell; in Vienna, Erik v. Kuehnelt-Leddihn;
in Zürich, Wilhelm Roepke. For the most part these were Right-
Wing professors; repentant Stalinists, Trotskyists, and free-lance
radicals; and journalists of middle and low degree. Mitchell has
seemingly vanished; Chodorov, with whom a few years earlier
Buckley had worked to found the Intercollegiate Society of Individualists, was a gentle theoretical Right-Wing anarchist who
has since died; Davis was a journalist; so was Evans, who now is
managing editor of the (White) Citizens' Councils' publications
and a major writer for the John Birch Society; Hess defected to
the New Left in a protracted trauma that began in 1968; Niemeyer
teaches at Notre Dame; Ryskind is an aging gag writer from the
days of the big Broadway musicals; Freda Utley, long a vehement
advocate of the Arab cause, was a lapsed Communist; Root and
Weaver were college teachers in the Middle West. Voight has
dropped from sight, with Ravines and Caldwell; v. Kuehnelt-
Leddihn, a vehement monarchist and militarist, has remained with
National Review throughout and is also correspondent for the
Bozells' relatively new fundamentalist Catholic magazine, *Triumph*;
Roepke is a passionate free-market economist whose most famous disciple was probably Ludwig Erhard, the man who briefly
succeeded Konrad Adenauer as Chancellor of West Germany.
Only Burnham, of the original editors, remains in that position,
in which he was joined by Meyer; Evans' son, M. Stanton Evans,
appears in the list of contributing editors; Kirk is a regular contributor of a column called "From the Academy"; and Niemeyer
continues to write for the magazine. Chamberlain, La Follette,
Ryskind, and Schlamm are named in the inventory of contributors, but they are most infrequently represented by their work.

The first issue carried a full-page "Publisher's Statement" accompanied by Buckley's "own views, as expressed in a memoran-

dum drafted a year ago, and directed to our investors." These were not numerous. The major part of the initial capital was put up by various Buckleys; some sympathetic souls rallied by Liebman, Hess, de Toledano, and others had also invested cautiously: according to the "Publisher's Statement," there were altogether "more than one hundred and twenty investors," among them "over fifty men and women of small means," who "invested less than one thousand dollars apiece in it." One must infer that *small* is a relative adjective. Among the investors was Robert Welch, later the founder of the John Birch Society, who put up two packets of a thousand dollars each at different times. Some of those who invested and/or lent money to the corporation assigned their shares and liens to others, such as Harding College, the incubator of Bible-thumping Know-Nothings in the Ozarks, which was headed by an old-time missionary, George Stuart Benson.

In the early years, the statements of ownership, management, and circulation required by law to be filed annually listed the same persons and institutions, with almost no exceptions, among shareholders owning or holding one per cent or more of the stock and known bond, mortgage, and other security holders with more than one per cent of these outstanding liabilities. No member of the Buckley family except William Jr. appeared on either list, and he was included only among the stockholders; but there were various names well known on the Right Wing in addition to Harding College: Alfred Kohlberg, the "one-man China Lobby" who was so close to McCarthy, was one; another was the reactionary Foundation for Social Research in California. Besides these and other known conservatives, two major New York hospitals were listed both as bond and as share owners; so was something called the 119 East Thirty-sixth Street Corp.; so too was a stockbroker partnership.

From the start, however, all the voting stock was owned by Buckley. The company was then called National Weekly, Inc.; in 1959 its assets were sold to a new firm, National Review, Inc., of which Buckley is the sole stockholder. This corporation also employs Buckley to appear on television and, in the words of William A. Rusher, since 1957 the publisher of *National Review*, it "contracts to make Mr. Buckley's services available to the producers of *Firing Line*." Until 1958 members of the Buckley family —to quote Rusher again—"were among the principal financial supporters of *National Review*. Since then, the burden has been

shared by all of those who contribute to our annual fund appeals."
These are letters sent to all the magazine's subscribers and to
persons on mailing lists of conservative organisations (*National
Review* subscribers also find themselves the recipients of fund
appeals on behalf of Catholic militant organisations over the signature of William F. Buckley Jr.). Its paid circulation in 1971
fluctuated between one hundred ten and one hundred twenty
thousand, a derisory figure for any publication in terms of profit-
ability today in spite of every effort to keep down costs: *National
Review*'s senior executives do not expect salaries comparable to
those that they might command in profit-making enterprises. Both
circulation and advertising, however, have steadily increased—one
suspects the advertisers of sentiment rather than calculation, but
the circulation is indubitably six or seven times what it was fifteen
years ago, and the magazine is not cheap, nor is anyone compelled
to buy it.

There has always been, too, a considerable interplay between
National Review and such outright fanatic Right-Wing publications as *Human Events* and *American Opinion*: all three share a
number of writers, make publicity for one another, and probably
share mailing lists, though *National Review* rarely admits to its
pages some of the ruder and less literate rousers of the respectable
rabble who appear in the others. Relatively early, however, as we
have seen, Buckley refused to publish or employ anyone who
wrote for *The American Mercury*, whose policies, though not so
extreme as those later to be embraced by his brother-in-law Bozell,
were too much for him.

"The largest cultural menace in America is the conformity of
the intellectual cliques which, in education as well as the arts,
are out to impose upon the nation their modish fads and falla-
cies, and have nearly succeeded in doing so. In this cultural issue,
we are, without reservations, on the side of excellence (rather
than 'newness') and of honest intellectual combat (rather than
conformity)." Such unimpeachable sentiments, which might have
come from anywhere, appeared in *National Review* under Buckley's signature. Unfortunately, so admirable a standard has yet to
be reached or even, in a favorite word of Willmoore Kendall and
his admirers, adumbrated in *National Review*, from Vol. I No. 1
on. Indeed, it is this very falling short of excellence that is part of
the Buckleys' strength: that quality is not much appreciated in
this country. "Every time I hear the word *excellence*," Edward

Vater, Dean of Students at Middlesex Community College in Connecticut, told D. D. Paige, the Pound scholar who headed the college's Department of English in 1970, "I wonder what the guy really wants."

The "Publisher's Statement" in that inaugural issue, in fact, set rather a higher tone than has since been maintained: "[*National Review*] stands athwart history, yelling Stop, at a time when no one is inclined to do so, or to have much patience with those who so urge it. *National Review* is out of place, in the sense that the United Nations and the League of Women Voters and *The New York Times* and Henry Steele Commager are *in place*. It is out of place because, in its maturity, literate America rejected conservatism in favor of radical social experimentation. Instead of covetously consolidating its premises, the United States seems tormented by its tradition of fixed postulates having to do with the meaning of existence, with the relationship of the state to the individual, of the individual to his neighbor, so clearly enunciated in the enabling documents of our Republic." This is pretty much the summit of the statement, which began then to breathe somewhat harder: "There never was an age of conformity quite like this one, or a camaraderie quite like the Liberals'. Drop a little itching powder in Jimmy Wechsler's bath and before he has scratched himself for the third time, Arthur Schlesinger will have denounced you in a dozen books and speeches, Archibald MacLeish will have written ten heroic cantos about our age of terror, *Harper's* will have published them, and everyone in sight will have been nominated for a Freedom Award." This might have done for a college newspaper; but excellence?

What is of rather more interest is another passage in the same essay: "Radical conservatives in this country have an interesting time of it, for when they are not being suppressed or humiliated by the Liberals, they are being ignored or humiliated by a great many of those of the well-fed Right, whose ignorance and amorality have never been exaggerated for the same reason that one cannot exaggerate infinity." Thus girded in the armor of one against the world (though not in any fashion to make one think of Stephen Dedalus, save for the contrast), Buckley proclaimed his thoughtful optimism "in a world dominated by the jubilant single-mindedness of the practicing Communist, with his inside track to History." As Wechsler was to observe later: "One turns . . . to Buckley and his adherents for an examination of conservatism because, alas, it is almost they alone who hold aloft the flag and proudly bear the label. Like nervous liberals in politics who prefer to be known as 'middle-of-the-roaders,' few of those in public life who share Buckley's world view desire to be known as conservatives." But that second statement describes a situation that the Buckleys have labored not unsuccessfully to change in the years since it was written.

The magazine's first issue made its obeisance to excellence with an article by Senator William F. Knowland of California, a Republican who was close in his views to McCarthy and Nixon, on how to maintain *Pax americana*; another by Aloïse Heath (the eldest of the Buckley children) on her attempt to incite her fellow-alumnae of Smith to overthrow what she was pleased to call the Communists in its faculty by refusing to give money to the college, with the result that Smith's fund campaign received more donations than ever before; and a "humorous" piece of Morrie Ryskind. What *National Review* listed as its departments included a professional reactionary, Sam Jones, on what was happening in Washington; Kendall on "The Liberal Line"; Bozell on "National Trends" ("stuffing the subversion problem into a closet"); an anonymous contribution on foreign affairs; a survey of the Left by an initialed author; a discussion of problems of constitutional law by C. Dickerman Williams, Buckley's lawyer and a former member of the board of directors of the American Civil Liberties Union; Mitchell on labor; Burnham on "The Third World War" (a standing head later to be partly superseded by "The Protracted Conflict"); Hess on the press; "From the Academy," by Kirk (who still covers this domain for the magazine), and Ryskind again, on "Arts and Manners." The book-review section, which was headed by Meyer (who discussed "Croce on Liberty"), included pieces by John Chamberlain and Freda Utley, as well as one by Philip Burnham, James's brother, who was managing editor of *Commonweal*. Schlamm was not represented, nor was Suzanne La Follette, who in fact functioned as managing editor until the publication began to become something of a family fief with the advent of Priscilla Buckley, whose administrative competence and considerable tact more than compensate for her negligible literary attainments.

Rusher, who has been the publisher for fifteen years, was at first a mere subscriber. A 1948 graduate of Harvard Law School, where he had founded a Young Republican Club, he was associate counsel to the Senate Internal Security Subcommittee under the notorious Robert Morris. Rusher was still in contact with the new generation of Young Republicans in the Harvard Law School, who, having set up a rachitic journal called *The Harvard Times-Republican* (it died very young), had invited him to write for it; clippings were sent by a mutual friend to Buckley, who excerpted Rusher at length in a *National Review* column then called "The Ivory Tower." They met at a lunch in January of 1956, and soon became friends. Rusher has a mind as good as Buckley's, as sound a culture, and the undoubted advantage that enures from first-rate training in the law. Their views coincided completely, and so did their methods.

When Morris decided to leave the Senate subcommittee, Rusher had no desire to remain and began to look for a job. He asked Buckley whether the family oil enterprises might not need a lawyer, and "he surprised me by offering me, instead, the job and title of publisher of *National Review*." In this position, which he assumed in July, 1957, Rusher has made many conservative friends and not a few conservative enemies: not because of any quarrel with tactics indistinguishable from Buckley's, or over philosophical matters, but solely because of personality clashes. No one contends that he has the charm and warmth of almost all the Buckleys; indeed, those who dislike him attack him for what they regard as an inhuman, pompous coldness; and this is the dominant personal impression he conveys in his weekly television appearances in a Corporation for Public Broadcasting program called *The Advocates*. Roger Baldwin, on the other hand (who founded the American Civil Liberties Union and is still, in his late eighties, a vigorously independent radical), speaks of Rusher as a man whose company is to be welcomed socially and intellectually.

Within a year more Buckleys were beginning to be involved with the publication. Priscilla, who was still in the Paris office of United Press, wrote an occasional article not devoid of the archness and italics that seem to be characteristic of all Buckleys when they employ the written word; Maureen, who, after her graduation from Smith, had rejected her father's urgings that she go to law school and chosen instead to work with words, became an editorial assistant and continued with the magazine after her marriage to Gerald O'Reilly (now vice-president of a perfume company) until the demands of her increasing family made it impossible; Aloïse wrote more articles, most of them almost ex-

cruciatingly arch when they were not totally savage and superbly
scornful of inconvenient fact, as well as occasional book reviews;
reviews served also to bring Reid Buckley into the list of occasional contributors—later he descanted on the esthetics of the bull-
fight, following a rather well-known example, and offered other
essays of which one can say no better and no worse than that they
were typical middle-brow magazine articles.

Some of the early *National Review* associates, such as Revilo P.
Oliver, parted dramatically with the Buckley circle; others, such
as the late Gen. Charles A. Willoughby, whose only claim to attention was his wartime association with Douglas MacArthur,
simply faded away without anyone's ever really noticing. Hess,
who had worked with Buckley in fund-raising—approaching such
men as H. L. Hunt, for whose *Facts Forum* Buckley had written,
and Leander Perez, the Louisiana racist whose bigotries caused him
to be barred from the Catholic Church, of which he was a member (he believed that integration was hatched from a conspiracy
of Communists and Zionists)—and in an equally unsuccessful
effort to set up regional editions of the magazine, wrote for it only
twice, though his name remained on the masthead for several years,
a common *National Review* practice in such circumstances. "Arts
and Manners" was soon transferred from Ryskind to Schlamm;
later it became public property.

Hess, Oliver, and Eastman were by no means the only persons
whose expulsions from or repudiations of the *Sanctum sanctorum*
were, at the very least, definitive; the particulars will be examined
presently. A number of other early associates were lost in similar
fashion, including some whose names rarely or never appeared on
the masthead or in the table of contents. At one time Buckley and
his colleagues were quite close to Ayn Rand, the novelist who
founded a self-styled school of social and political thought that
she denominated Objectivism (others called it merely egocentricity
à outrance), and to a number of free-market economists whose
thinking extended into politics and what might loosely be called
sociology: Murray Rothbard, now a darling of the Right-Wing
libertarians; Milton Friedman of the so-called Chicago school;
Ludwig von Mises and Frederick A. Hayek of the Viennese school.
Garry Wills, a professor of classics at Johns Hopkins University,
was for a long time a leading figure in the group and an esteemed contributor to the magazine. So, much more briefly, was

the Rev. Dr. J. B. Matthews, the hired witness for the House
Un-American Activities Committee.

For some time it was a weekly publication, with a supplement,
available separately, called *National Review Bulletin*. Ultimately
both these were made bi-weeklies, so that each appeared during
the week when the other did not. The *Bulletin* is usually an eight-
page newsletter that omits the amenities of the magazine proper:
literary, film, and dramatic reviews, notes on the luxuries of New
York living, etc.; it concentrates on what passes for "hard news"
in these circles: the latest misfeasances of the multitudinous enemy,
with much invective-laden analysis, and little "items" about personalities. These rarely—but occasionally—descend now to the
kind of thing that was not infrequent ten years ago in a *National
Review* department called "For the Record": "A prominent
American journalist is a target of Soviet blackmail for homo-
sexuality. U.S. authorities know it. His syndicate doesn't—yet."
It is appropriate to add that both publications, like Buckley's
own writings, are inordinately attentive to the sexual activities
and even possibilities of those who have taken the commissar's
kopeck or in any other fashion transgressed against the conservative canon. Buckley's attacks, on television and in print, on Gore
Vidal's monotonously vaunted bisexuality are perhaps the best-
known example; but he finds it difficult to mention Jean Genêt
without the epithet "sodomist"; and, when Kenneth Tynan, the
British critic, wrote that "I want my wife to have another child,
and I want to see that child learn to walk," Buckley found it
necessary to remark that those in the West who were seeking to
destroy the Communist Peril were "engaged in trying to make
just that possible, the birth of another child to Kenneth Tynan,
always assuming he has left the virility to procreate one." It is
difficult indeed not to be vehemently neutral against both the
literary exhibitionists and the men who cannot let slide a single
opportunity to comment on their actual, probable, possible, and
speculative sexual characteristics.

Other targets of opportunity are taken too, of course, beyond
the singular relish for the sexual. Both the *Bulletin* and *National
Review* itself are under the responsible editorship of Buckley or,
when he is not physically available, Burnham; and it is often difficult to tell which has written a given unsigned editorial: both go
unerringly for the enemy's groin. One of the legendary occasions

of this kind of attack occurred after Dag Hammarskjöld, the Secretary General of the United Nations, was killed in the crash of a plane in the Congo. A long editorial in the 25 November 1961 issue of *National Review Bulletin* said that when his body was found an ace of spades was discovered between his shirt and his underwear. After brief speculation to the effect that the card might have been placed there by an assassin, if indeed Hammarskjöld's own mysticism* did not incline him to superstition, the editorial (which was written, though not signed, by Burnham) took up the notion that Hammarskjöld had been keeping the card in reserve for some opportunity to cheat during a game, since obviously any man who had dealt as he had done with the problems of the Congo and Katanga would have no moral problem at all about cheating at cards.

There was only one letter of protest, according to Buckley, and it was written by Hayek, who said that this "seems to me to overstep the boundaries of common decency. I am convinced that a magazine that allows itself such inexcusable allegations does more harm than good to the cause that it intends to serve." Hayek added that he wished to have no further connection with *National Review* and to receive no further issues. Buckley replied that he was "astonished that you read into it what you did. I understand it to be an attempt at logical fantasy, after the manner of Grand Guignol, by which one explores in mock solemnity, for the sake of effect, every alternative explanation for a perplexing phenomenon." Buckley added that there must be something else in Hayek's mind, since this was so trivial a matter, to have inspired such a letter "written by a gentleman-scholar to an enterprise written (for the most part) by gentlemen-scholars of congenial spirit and common political concerns." He added that there was in other journals "a quality we seek always to avoid at *National Review*—namely mercilessness."

Hayek replied that he could see nothing playful in the paragraph and that he and Buckley differed on "standards of what is admissible in attacks on public figures." He denied any animus against *National Review* but repeated his wish not to have anything further to do with it. Buckley thereupon rebuked Hayek because his refusal to "consider such obvious possibilities as that you failed to identify the proper meaning because the *jeu d'idee*

* "Dag Hammarskjöld's rather defecated mysticism"—*National Review*, 21 January 1972.

[the accent is missing in the letter] was not written in your native
tongue bespeaks a pride which, before it is fully spent, might do
more harm to the cause we serve than a dozen lapses of taste by
an editor of *National Review*. . . . [I]t is a matter of public concern that you are capable of making such unstable judgments."
In a postscript falsely accusing Hayek of having written that he
must " 'openly' proclaim your disassociation from *National Review*," Buckley notified Hayek—who was writing and lecturing
in English before Buckley was born—that "I am compelled to
circularize our correspondence among a few common friends."
But what Hayek had written was that, "when my impression is
that a journal that means to aid a cause similar to mine does grave
harm to the reputation of that cause, I ought openly to say so."

The actual processes of putting out an issue of *National Review*
are much the same now as they were in the beginning, with some
allowances for the lessons of practical experience and the growth
of its staff. A number of conservatives, about as many of its hostile
readers, and some who look at it from a purely professional point
of view feel that in the years since Buckley has been so widely
diffusing his activities, it has lost much of what was good in it
in its early years, both in style and in content. Buckley himself
said late in 1971 that he had had complaints to this effect from
his own editors. "All the articles are approved by me," he said.
"I have never since the outset pre-read the columns [that is, such
standing departments as Burnham's or Kirk's or, before his death,
Meyer's], and I've never pre-read the book section. The only difference between *National Review* now and, say, ten years ago
is that ten years ago I wrote much more of the editorials than I
now do."

In his only "personal" book, *Cruising Speed*, he describes the
operation of the magazine in such a way that one can only shame-
lessly borrow from it. Editorial meetings are held on Tuesdays
and opened by Rusher, who makes recommendations based at
least in part on reader appeal. Jeffrey Hart, a professor of English
and history at Dartmouth, a former speech-writer for Nixon and
Ronald Reagan, and the producer of a singularly nasty syndicated
political column, takes part, as does Burnham. Priscilla Buckley,
managing editor and hence coordinator, presents her own list of
recommended subjects. Meyer, who for years led an extremely
reclusive life in Woodstock, New York, never attended. Junior

editors and writers are present and report on their individual fields
—such as "the kids," as Buckley calls them not unpejoratively.
Buckley (in his absence, Burnham) then makes the assignments
and indicates the length of each, and everyone goes to lunch. In
the afternoon the writers turn in their copy to Priscilla, who
sends it upstairs to her brother; when he has edited it, he returns
it to her for retyping. She handles all the outside contributions,
such as reviews, foreign correspondence (which is irregular: the
masthead lists reporters in London, Munich, Africa, Athens, and
Guelph, Ontario) and a sub-department called "Delectations"—
restaurant reviews, shopping notes, etc.—usually covered by a very
literate and fastidious woman, Nika Hazelton. Priscilla Buckley
also buys the verse turned out indefatigably by W. H. von Dreele,
a rather personable, no longer young bachelor whose doggerel is
almost invariably quite different from his social self. Though he
may have as many as four pieces in any given issue, he supports
himself by working in the public-relations department of IBM.
One is told by the Buckleys that he has a numerous and enthusiastic following that includes God's vicar in Washington, James
Reston. This is a fair sample of the poetic excellence that he contributes:

GETTING IT ALL TOGETHER

So long, Silas Marner;
  Adios, Jane Eyre.
Latin grammar's boring;
  Shakespeare is a square.
Who needs mathematics?
  History's a drag.
Screw the corporations;
  (Business makes them gag).
Cuddle up with Dylan;
  Puff a little grass;
Knit a Panther dolly;
  Hiss the Army brass.
If you had a hand in
  Spawning one of these,
You don't have an offspring:
  You have a disease.

For each such effort, be it of four lines or of forty, the poet
receives twenty dollars; and two little books of them have been

published, with suitable cartoon illustrations. He is listed as a contributing editor, with James Jackson Kilpatrick, a conservative newspaper columnist represented, like Buckley, by the Washington Star Syndicate, and one Will Herberg, who teaches philosophy and culture at Drew University in Madison, New Jersey, writes occasionally for the very Right *Human Events*, was a member of the advisory assembly of the American Conservative Union, and is on the committee of the American Jewish Association, which Eugene Lyons formed in 1968 for the convenience of anti-Communist, pro-Israeli, conservative American Jews.

These, no doubt, are the kind whom the dean of *National Review*'s foreign correspondents, v. Kuehnelt-Leddihn (whose ancestors were still running bare-bottomed through the Böhmerwald when the Moors and the Jews had made Spain a pinnacle of Western civilisation), had in mind when in *National Review* in 1971 he congratulated them on what he was pleased to call their "westernisation" by reason of their exposure to Christians. Buckley professed surprise that this might be found offensive and assured me that his correspondent, who is "very meticulous about scholarship, presumably . . . [was] referring to the Russian Jews." The author of *Liberty or Democracy*, he is an anti-Nazi monarchist, according to Buckley—"a splendid man, brilliantly learned."

Rather surprisingly, Elspeth Huxley covers Africa for the magazine, which, equally surprisingly, occasionally receives contributions from Alec Waugh and his nephew, Auberon (one wonders whether either would suffer his work to appear in a British periodical of the same intellectual level). The breveted London correspondent is Anthony Lejeune, a lifelong conservative, educated at the Merchant Taylors' School and Balliol, where he read law. He was called to the Bar but elected journalism as a profession after post-war service in the Royal Navy. He and Buckley, who is three years older, have been friends since their youth, and Lejeune has always worked for Right-Wing publications such as the late Lady Rhondda's *Time and Tide*; he is also a mystery-story writer and editorial director of Tom Stacey, Ltd., a London book publisher. The firm's first book was by Enoch Powell, M.P., Britain's leading white supremacist, many of whose conservative political ideas Lejeune shares.

His friendships are all at the highest social level and virtually exclusively at the most conservative. He broadcasts regularly to South Africa on British affairs, on which he writes for newspapers in Indianapolis, Cincinnati, Boston, Richmond (Virginia), Omaha, and Orlando, as well as for *National Review*. A close friend of Randolph Churchill, he is described by those who know him as perceptive, intelligent, and erudite; and he is certainly more literate than a number of *National Review*'s contributors; like many of them, he professes to see a pronounced Left bias in television. Rather curiously, he thoroughly disapproves of his country's Conservative Prime Minister, Edward Heath, and his election methods. In contrast, he wholeheartedly admires Buckley, is firmly convinced of the importance of his future in American politics, and is ready at any time to do everything that he can to help Buckley. Lejeune's own political contacts at the highest rank in Britain are impeccable and intimate, and this fact can hardly damage Buckley.

At present there are four Buckleys on the staff of *National Review*, though in the summer of 1971 the number rose to six because of the temporary employment of F. Reid Buckley Jr. and his brother, (William) Hunt Buckley. Besides Bill and Priscilla, there are Jane Buckley Smith, who has not remarried since her divorce from William F. Smith, and Carol Buckley Learsy, who, one is astonished to learn, really took the course offered (at what prices!) by the computers of the Famous Writers' School in Westport, Connecticut, before it became known through the courts that electronics was being used there to "teach" creative writing. Mrs. Smith, who does her work in Sharon, where she lives with her children about a mile from Great Elm, handles the magazine's correspondence as it is assigned to her—for "maid money," she says. Mrs. Learsy, who goes to the office, occupies the bottom rank in the assistant-editor category, according to Priscilla: she opens and distributes correspondence, does a certain amount of copy-editing, and is responsible for a considerable share of manuscript reading. There is a very large flow of unsolicited material, Priscilla Buckley says—very little of it comes from literary agents or people of any stature, literary or other, and most of it is impossible.

Priscilla first joined the staff in 1957, at her brother's insistence, but only on her own terms: six weeks' vacation every year, divided to suit her pleasures (like her brothers, she is very fond of a variety of outdoor sports, including fishing and hunting); this stipulation is still in force. Early in her tenure she took four months off in order to work on a biography of her father, but he, who knew how to interpret his first stroke, preferred to concentrate his remaining energies on his business, and the project had to be dropped. She seems ideally suited to her job as managing editor—not only because of her obvious competence but because of her personality: she is quite as shy as reputation says she is, though a great natural charm helps her to master the shyness. She has never made and will never make a public speech. Paradoxically, she is far more relaxed with a stranger than either Bill or Jim, and there is no reason to suppose that she is exerting an iron control. Bill cannot sit in the same position for thirty seconds in the privacy of an office conversation—not because he is uneasy or apprehensive but simply because he is hyperkinetic: his legs are constantly shifting position, his body twists constantly in his chair, his head assumes an infinite number of angles—yet his tone and his manner are quite easy. Jim, who has something of his sister's shyness, sits much more quietly than Bill but his hands work constantly with one or another object from his desk. Priscilla simply leans back in her chair and talks, or listens.

Another factor in her aptness for her work is her fondness for having her own life and freedom of movement. There is no paradox in this: hers is a job that she need not take forever with her. She has no tendency toward political activism; her only work outside *National Review* consists in the directorships in some of the family companies that she had to assume after her brother's election to the Senate constrained him to relinquish them.

XII

Most of the Buckleys are combative in their several ways, not all of which are public. The eldest served their apprenticeships in the controversies that preceded and accompanied the early part of the Second World War; they were journeymen by the time their younger siblings entered the tradition. Aloïse, for instance, had not made much public stir between her early America First letters to *The Lakeville Journal*, before she married, and her appeal in the early 1950's to her twenty-eight thousand fellow-graduates of Smith not to give the college a penny until it had got rid of the Communists on its faculty—the result of which, as noted, was the biggest single annual total of contributions in Smith's history.

She wrote sporadically for her brother's review—he complained that she was grandly indifferent to deadlines—and occasionally, too, for such periodicals as *The Ladies' Home Journal.* Otherwise she busied herself with the concerns that would naturally beset a woman who had ten children and nine brothers and sisters, all very closely bound; she was active in church affairs but she attracted no special attention in her own town, West Hartford, regardless of her views, which were strong, and her expressions, which were unambiguous. Her writing, irregular though it was, was her only public manifestation, though for the most part to a highly restricted and totally like-minded audience (the Right, like the Left, talks largely to itself). She suffered from the general susceptibility to the temptation to be arch (though she could be quite amusing without), as in a *National Review* piece called "The French Have a Word for It": ". . . I did get interested in French semantics. I mean, when I see madness, I look for method; and when you ask for a serious and get a glass of beer, or ask for a put-in-pleats and get your hair set—well, in West Hartford we call that madness." She could also, like the others, be savage, though with less skill: "The nearer Dr. Spock gets to the oriental horizon, the closer he comes to the educational level of the U.S. poverty program." In the chapters that she wrote for the family's privately printed memorials to the father and to Maureen, the sister who died of a cerebral hemorrhage at the age of thirty-one, there is no savagery, but the archness contests with an excess of sentimentalism and italics to the denigration of what must have been very deep emotion. Aloïse was a woman who put her political hostilities into the rearing of her children, who, by her own published boast, could and did parrot the wildest fantasies of McCarthys and worse. "My father's grandchildren," she wrote to *Time* in 1958, "are an intellectual elite by heritage."

But those who love the Buckleys loved Aloïse Heath especially. They thought of her as "the really brilliant one in the family, so far as writing is concerned. She had a remarkable wit," Irene Corbally Kuhn said, "and a really warm and bubbling spirit. She must have been a remarkable mother, too, because she brought her children up to be able, after their terrible grief, to feel that life without a mother was not life, so they turned to her closest friend and persuaded their father to court her, and he remarried, and the children are devoted to her."

Other friends of the Buckleys tend to make an implicit division among them: the volatile, highly visible ones—Aloïse, Patricia, Bill, Reid, Maureen—and the more settled—John, Jane, James, Priscilla, Carol. Jane supposedly shares the views of all the others and indeed in some respects is even more vehement, but she never or almost never is heard from, though she has, rarely, written a highly acerb and contemptuous letter to *The Lakeville Journal* about those who dare to differ. She is of course anti-Communist as that is understood in the Buckley circle, and for a long time she made it a point, when opponents of the Vietnam war held their Saturday vigil on the Sharon Green, to drive back and forth endlessly with her lights on and her car loaded with children. She can at times be as off the mark—whether deliberately or otherwise—as Bill: dismissing the participants in the vigil as "silly," she proposed that, "if they want to show their opposition to the war in a meaningful way," they "work in the Sharon hospital every Saturday instead." Unlike Priscilla, whose tact is so great that she will drop a painful subject out of consideration for others, Jane is reputed to press on ruthlessly and to evidence utter contempt for any and all whose vision she finds clouded.

John is much more of a controversialist, in spite of his quieter inclinations, but he restricts himself to local arenas. In these, however, he is easily as savage and as superior to the norms of civility as any of his siblings. At the same time, he is the epitome of cordiality and courtesy in his personal encounters even with those whom he most fiercely assails in public; and it is such people who testify uniformly to the fact that this is true of almost all the Buckleys. Among the enemies, too, it is always Priscilla who is singled out as the exception to whom the general inventory of anti-Buckley criticisms is inapplicable. But everyone has remarked on the fact that no Buckley has ever done anything to assist local activities such as the Sharon Playhouse, though the elder Mrs. Buckley did once contribute twenty-five dollars for a summer-school scholarship. That even this gift was made is attributed by Judson Philips, the mystery writer, to James Buckley's wife. (As long as John's wife was alive, the two were known as John-Ann and Jim-Ann for purposes of identification; one wonders why not Ann-John and Ann-Jim, if the pairing was indeed essential.)

John Buckley's major antagonists in the local area over the years have been Philips (with whom Priscilla plays golf), Mrs. DeLancey Ferguson, who lives in the neighboring Falls Village, and Robert H. Yoakum, a syndicated columnist on politics and public affairs who, like John, is a resident of Lakeville. To Yoakum, as to Emerson, among many others, all the Buckleys are dangerous regardless of their prominence or lack of it, simply because of their capacity to embody and promulgate the kind of thinking that is characteristic of the American majority (even if sometimes not immediately visible to casual observers) and to cloak it with respectability, style (which most of its followers certainly lack), and felicity of phrase. Like Emerson, who in 1948 so inflamed Bill Buckley at Yale by his advocacy of Henry Wallace, his championship of basic freedoms, and the study on *Loyalty in Government Employees* that he prepared for the American Civil Liberties Union, Yoakum regards the Buckleys' propaganda for their version of freedom as essentially a call for Fascism; and, again like Emerson, he challenges the chicaneries to which they are ready to descend in debate whether formal or informal, as well as the club of the threat to sue for libel.

John Buckley is the kind of man whose private letters often

went out in 1967 and 1968 with stickers bearing the picture of
Barry Goldwater and the legend "Goldwater in 1964" in which
the "4" was penciled over with an "8." As he told the man from
The Times, "I revel in being a capitalist . . . my only regret is that
I am not a more successful capitalist." He is also a courtly and
cordial host to a more hostile interviewer; and yet, like his brother
Bill—and all the rest of us whose tongues are often sharper than
our wits—he sometimes cannot resist the seduction of the forked
phrase. Comparable to Bill's insolent suggestion to Frederick A.
Hayek that the professor was deficient in English, John's letter to
a learned lady old enough to be his mother began: "I have long
since come to the realization that having rational discourse with
you is an impossibility—but it *is* fun to try," and concluded
(à propos her behavior, not his own): "*Quelle audace!* (What
audacity!)." And this was followed by "Genteel and sincere best
wishes"! What is more, he undoubtedly meant just that.

The lady in question—Mrs. DeLancey Ferguson—has never been
confronted with the threat of a libel action even after her letter to
The New York Times in November of 1970 in which she identified
herself as one "who has never believed that a Buckley in any office
would be anything but a distressing event to anyone with a viewpoint to the left of the late Senator Taft." What has particularly
roused John Buckley over the years has been Mrs. Ferguson's
insistence that Communists are not solely responsible for human
suffering and her tendency to believe that Communist régimes may
change with time, whereas nuclear war seems to her an unreasonable price to pay for their possible elimination. Above all John
Buckley cannot—and I believe he really cannot—recognise the fact
that Communism can be extremely alluring to peoples that have
been kept in misery for centuries by exploitation for profit. Consequently Mrs. Ferguson and Mr. Buckley have sporadically exchanged public and private correspondence of genteel asperity for
many years.

But, when one C. H. Stevens criticised the Buckleys rather intem-
perately in a letter to *The Lakeville Journal*, John (like Bill years
earlier, after the unfavorable reviews of *God and Man at Yale*
and *McCarthy and His Enemies*) publicly cried *libel*; further, he
threatened suit (as Jane Buckley Smith was to do subsequently
against Yoakum after James Buckley's election to the Senate; but
that controversy requires a place unto itself). Robert Osborn and
Yoakum have been John's major antagonists—Osborn since 1940,

when John wrote his first public letter and insinuated that Osborn might be less than a hero—and Philips, who has a column in *The Lakeville Journal*, has been in a slightly lower rank. There is a certain monotony to the *casus belli*, which in the end seems almost always to resolve itself in Communism, as seen by Buckleys, and sharp practice if not worse, as charged by the others and disconcertingly documented by Yoakum. He is the not infrequent beneficiary of private correspondence as well, sometimes with such enclosures as the decision by a United States District Court in Georgia that black school children are inherently, biologically, and genetically inferior to whites, as shown by various tests and testimony (one of the witnesses having been that curious "social scientist," Ernest van den Haag, who is a pillar of *National Review*).

At times the private letters, though always exemplarily framed on both sides, seem barely able to remain within the bounds of gentility. All the male correspondents (except Osborn) are on first-name terms and their children go to the same schools; the elders encounter one another at clubs; appearances are always preserved. Only the Stones of Hotchkiss, who are also far from the Buckleys in their social and political views, have been able to maintain a genuine friendship with them, but, as they have said and John has confirmed, that has been possible only through tacit accord on certain conversational taboos.

Though the elegant side table in the reception lobby of Catawba's tasteful mansion in Murray Hill is discreetly but plentifully stacked with the latest issues of *National Review* and its *Bulletin*, John plays no part in the magazine or any of its ramifications, or in his brothers' political careers. He did, he says, contribute money to James's Senate campaign, but offered no counsel and was asked for none except on the question of gun-control legislation. John, who says of hunting: "That's my life," was of course opposed to it; James, who as a matter of principle has never hunted or caught a living creature, was equally opposed on both philosophical and practical grounds—as indeed is every intelligent person of any political persuasion whom one has ever encountered (such legislation being on a par with the question formerly asked of prospective visitors and immigrants to God's Country: whether, if allowed in, they intended to assassinate the President). John had nothing to do —apart from moral support—with Bill's campaign for the Mayoralty of New York, and his only connection with the New York

State Conservative Party has been that of a contributor of money. He is convinced that such a third party could only fail on any scale larger than a given state with a given set of political circumstances; but, unlike Bill, he firmly believes in the necessity of an ultimate realignment of parties, on the British model, so that Conservatives and Radicals respectively can be clearly identified and largely relieved from the pressures or the temptations of unprincipled and emasculatory compromises. Like his brother, he rejects such Right radicals as George Wallace or Robert Welch: "not conservative at all," he says, quite accurately; but he refuses to allow them to be placed as *Right* radicals. The word "radical" would appear to have an exclusively Left connotation for him— that certainly is where he situates Wallace—and he prefers that men like Welch be called simply *extremists*. This is the term that John Buckley prefers, too, for his brother-in-law, Bozell, of whom, in spite of the philosophical rupture, he remains enormously fond.

There was an interruption in Patricia Bozell's activist career after her mission to the president of Vassar in 1949. For years she remained in the relative obscurity more or less enforced on a woman who has ten children, leaving political education to her husband. After his collaboration with Bill Buckley on *McCarthy and His Enemies* and some time as a writer of speeches for McCarthy, Bozell practiced law, but his mind was preoccupied with public perils and he was a regular contributor for a while to *National Review*; then his appearances became more sporadic. He wrote also occasionally for other, farther Right journals; and he earned a great reputation among the young lawyers on the staff of Young Americans for Freedom as an authority on constitutional law because of his book on *The Warren Revolution*, published in 1966 by Arlington House and chosen as an alternate selection by the Conservative Book Club. Its tenor, of course, was to the effect that Chief Justice Earl Warren was abusing the judicial process to the end of turning the country away from God, Edmund Burke, and Adam Smith and toward Marx, Lenin, and Lucifer. Though he had written some first-rate speeches for McCarthy (who often had difficulty reading these aloud), Bozell had concluded ten years earlier that this was an unworthy spokesman who was not even a conservative, as he told Richard M. Rovere of *The New Yorker* in 1956, but more and more of a Left-liberal-welfare-stater.

It was not long before Bozell, already remarked among his in-laws for his typical convert's zealotry, began to move from politics toward religion, and his wife moved with him. Roger Baldwin recalls lunches at *National Review*—in courteous acknowledgment of a New York Civil Liberties Union victory for the magazine over the Yahoos of the city's Board of Higher Education —at which in the very early 1960s Bozell expressed views that "were not of this world. He was opposed to Pope John. . . . He rather jestingly remarked that he [Bozell] was back in the thirteenth century with the other popes." But Baldwin felt that Bozell was fundamentally in earnest, though "he was very restrained, I should say, in expressing his opinions. He had no heat about it; he was very cool and calm." Baldwin's impression was that Bozell was a mystic and a medievalist. Not many years later the coolness and calm were to vanish, when Bozell declared that America must be destroyed for the salvation of the world's soul and when in 1970 he led his Sons of Thunder, in their red bérets, in a march against abortion during which he brought his five-foot wooden crucifix down on the skull of the policeman who attempted to herd the marchers into a restricted area. (For this Bozell was arrested on a minor charge and paid a small fine.)

All this started to come into the open when he and his wife founded *Triumph* in September, 1966, though much of what was to come seems, with hindsight, to have been predictable from articles that he wrote for *National Review* in earlier years. Bill Buckley has always called himself a libertarian, and, however effectively one may quarrel with this optimistic self-description, one must concede that he has always allowed for the right of at least a little difference of opinion and opposed the grosser forms of invasion of privacy, whether physical or intellectual/emotional. He would indeed probably endeavor to prove his libertarianism by the fact of having published in his magazine his brother-in-law's anathemas. Nonetheless, in his recent and most nearly self-examining book, *Cruising Speed*, Buckley, having started with the necessity to define abortion as something other than murder, wrote: "On this point I have become estranged from Brent Bozell, who founded a few years ago *Triumph* magazine, an organ of militant Catholicism which has elided now into an organ of militant anti-Americanism, reflecting the evolving intractability of its editor and his associates. The whole subject weighs heavily, and for once I find Catholics to the right of me, notwithstanding my own conviction that abortion is gravely, tragically wrong."

Buckley then quotes at length from an anonymous (though highly literate) correspondent who had attended the Christian Commonwealth Institute in Spain, organised by *Triumph*'s editors, in the summer of 1970 (the Bozells send their children to school in Spain, when they are old enough, because of a total loss of confidence in Catholic schools in the United States). But, in his correspondent's account of unanimity on "the desert that was America and how soon the blood of Christian Martyrs would be needed to nourish the cactus," or his accurate observation about *Triumph*—"every phrase is a funeral . . . *Triumph* is, I most forlornly believe, as hostile to the American ethos as any revolutionary organ on the hard Left"—there should have been nothing to surprise the editor who in 1961 published in *National Review* Bozell's call for a combination of infiltration and blackmail of the Republican Party by what he called a single-minded conservative cadre, or, a year later, the same author's observation that the philosophy of freedom—of the desirability of freedom—is of necessity an enemy of virtue and that the maximisation of freedom, in Hayek's phrase, means in effect that *"virtue must be made as difficult as possible"* (the italics are Bozell's).

Bozell plunged himself into such Catholic thinkers as Professor Frederick Wilhelmsen, who directs his CCI, and he battled his way to the innermost layers of Professor Eric Voegelin's philosophic and religious writings, especially on Gnosticism (a subject that for centuries had received an absolute minimum of attention outside the seminaries). Having found that this ancient heresy resembled modern Liberalism in that both believe that salvation for men and nations is to be had in this life and on this earth, he found also that Liberals can no longer escape the recognition that "the gnostic dream of an earthly paradise can be realized (as Khrushchev knows), not by changing society *but by changing man*, by transmutative surgery on the soul. *It follows that if Gnosticism is ever to triumph it will triumph in the Communist form*" (again the italics are Bozell's).

His wife has adopted all his thinking, with some modifications of her own. She is opposed to the welfare state, but opposed even more to allowing people on welfare the possibility of not having children (except, of course, through the discipline of chastity). "Catholicism," she says, "has collided with the secular political parties, so we refuse to be identified with them." She finds it quite possible, too, to say: "I think abortion is worse than Hitler's murder of the Jews. Unborn babies are more defenseless than the Jews were."

Her attempt to strike Ti-Grace Atkinson, the women's-liberation pioneer, at a meeting in 1971 at the Catholic University in Washington ought not to be exaggerated. Some people who have known the Buckleys all their lives have found it to be merely Patricia Bozell's normal mode of expression. She is obviously a woman of passionate convictions, all of which were outraged when it was suggested that the Mother of God (to use that metaphysically curious term dear to Catholics) had been simply and impurely exploited by male chauvinism. Some might think it presumptuous, however, that a mere mortal should pretend to punish an insult to an all-powerful divinity. There is no good reason to rehearse the banalities of either of the adversaries: in her own way, each made quite as notable a fool of herself (and not at all of the other) as did Bill Buckley and Gore Vidal in 1968. Mrs. Bozell, who is managing editor of *Triumph*, is as simplistic in her views as her husband: whatever the Church laid down through the Council of Trent in 1563 is right; scientific reductionism is the root of all evil, or anyway of a large proportion of it; "Christ constrains us to love Jews too much to treat them as anything other than men in need of Christ." *Und so weiter.*

The Bozells' Christian Commonwealth Institute and its summer sessions at El Escorial, Spain, under Wilhelmsen, a leading Mariolator, are a reasonable summary of their views and *Triumph*'s. In a full-page advertisement in the magazine, whose address it uses, the Institute talks about "Shaping the Post-Modern World" and, under "Politics," "The Mandate of the Christian Tribe." On the subject of "Christian Formation," one can only quote: "Since Christians mean to influence history, spiritual conditioning is not a private luxury but a tribal need." Fifty American students are accepted at a cost of one thousand fifty dollars for two months (in 1971), though undergraduates in colleges or universities got rebates of two hundred fifty dollars. "The new Christian tribe is forming here . . . preparing themselves to shape the modern world," the Institute announced.

The Institute is the formal pedagogical arm of the Society for the Christian Commonwealth, the aim of which is rather less general and inclusive than that of the Institute: the Society seeks "to recruit and train those men and women who will be able to

introduce authentic Catholic action to America's public life." The
SCC, which is not unsympathetic to the John Birch Society, knows
better, however, than the Birchers do: it knows that no mere
human Conspiracy is at work to destroy men's souls and that,
when at last "the typical Bircher" penetrates the private office of
the Chief Conspirator, he will find that "the One behind the desk
(or lurking in the back room) is a Spirit, for whom," Bozell wrote
in October, 1971, "there is only one rebuff: Begone. What he may
be brought to know even better is that Satan can be spoken to in
that way only by Christ, or by men adequately armed with
Christ."

To Randal Cornell Teague, executive director of Young Americans for Freedom, Bozell is a tragic figure because he "was
regarded . . . as probably one of the top five constitutional scholars
[a view unechoed in my experience], a man who wrote *The Warren Revolution* as the start of the most detailed treatise on the
history of the Supreme Court, and then rejected the whole thing.
You know, Brent genuinely prays to see the Second Coming, because he's going to run out in his front yard and look up at the
clouds and see the coming of Christ and say: 'Aha! We outdid them
—the liberals have had it.' He's adopted the theological position
that we only exist on earth for the fulfillment of Christ and must
reject all politics, all concerns of the government. He rejects the
Constitution of the United States as the most anti-Christian document ever written because it committed the heresy of total separation of church and state."

One is tempted to dismiss the Bozells, with a certain pity, as
far less dangerous, if only because less in the world, than the rest
of the Buckley circle. But, if this century has taught us anything
(and this is indeed doubtful, the more so as the contempt for
intellect and history spreads among the educationists and, consequently, their prey), it is the lesson of the ostensibly laughable
fanatic minority. On the other hand, the Bozells' fanaticism is much
too pure and too disembodied to lure even those who may be able
to comprehend it, if indeed it lends itself to understanding. To the
outer world it looks very simply like a return to the philosophy
of the Holy Inquisition, and its conception of the sin against the
Holy Ghost is simply stated by Patricia Bozell: "Many American
Catholics have come to transfer their first allegiances from Church
to state."

The offender who brought forth the denunciation, furthermore,

was that distinguished conservative convert to Catholicism, Clare
Boothe Luce, and the accomplice that shared the guilt was identified as *National Review*, because of its publication of Mrs. Luce's
article more or less favoring permissive abortion laws. The importance of this is that it is "the last act of the capitulation by
America-first Catholics to the ideology of pluralism." It is not, Mrs.
Bozell explains, that the church does not recognise variety in
society; but that "does not ordain variety in the moral order—the
moral law is one . . . the Church is uniquely authorized to define it.
But since its origin is nature and nature's God, the law's application
is universal. *All* [her italics] are governed by it." It is difficult not
to be amused by Mrs. Bozell's final wild punch at her brother Bill:
". . . the awesome responsibility for the change in moral attitudes
can be laid in significant part to the likes of Mrs. Luce and her
Catholic friends at *National Review* who play the democratic game,
the secular game, the pluralistic game in violation of their faith."

In 1972, its sixth year, *Triumph* was having a difficult time financially. Like *National Review*, it was resorting to pleas for financial
help from its readers, though much more frequently. Its semi-
monthly newsletter, *Catholic Currents*, has had no better success,
though its manner is somewhat less apocalyptic. The Bozells, indeed, represent a somber tone not otherwise to be remarked in the
Buckley circle or in conservative groups generally except those of
an equally fundamentalist or primitivist character. One would not
be surprised to find *Triumph* predicting the end of the world in
its next issue. There is, after all, a story—which cannot be verified
—that the first issue had been set up in type and the forms were
awaiting only a few minor rectifications before being locked up.
It was late, and the editors decided to let the final touches wait
until morning. During the night the forms were struck by lightning
and melted, whereupon Bill Buckley is reputed to have remarked:
"Well, if you can't read that. . . ."

Refusing to give me his version of his break with Bill Buckley,
who discussed it at length in *Cruising Speed*, Revilo P. Oliver
informed me that "certain members of the Buckley family and
persons closely associated with them have played parts of some
significance in the history of the last days of the American Republic," which, earlier in this letter, he also called "this doomed
country." He might have had in mind the late Maureen Buckley
O'Reilly, and perhaps even the youngest of her brothers, Reid, as
well as the more prominent siblings and Bozell.

Will Buckley wanted Maureen to be a lawyer, but she would have none of this. After her graduation from Smith she found a job as an editor with a film company of no great pretensions; but it was a step toward what she wanted, which was a career associated with the drama and with what has come to be called the communications media (or, in those trade schools now called colleges, communications arts). With a college friend she took an apartment in New York in 1954; but the film job proved a disappointment and in February of 1955 she began nine months of unpaid staff work for The Christophers, a Catholic dramatic group that staged plays in the theater, on radio, and on television. This was a job that she seems to have enjoyed, and she left it only when Bill was launching *National Review*, which she joined with even greater enthusiasm. Father James A. Keller, O.M., the director of The Christophers, was extremely sorry to lose her; he continued occasionally, when her time permitted, to enlist her as a consultant, and their friendship went on until her death in 1964.

Fully indoctrinated in her family's *religio rei publicae*, and further stimulated by generous readings in her father's good friend, Albert Jay Nock, a fascinating, highly civilised Right-Wing libertarian who had been a friend of Mencken and an intellectual agitator of the 1920's, Maureen was as dedicated to *National Review* and its causes as she had been to The Christophers, even after her marriage to Gerald O'Reilly in 1957, until she began having children. Initially she dealt with correspondence from readers, whether complimentary, curious or crotchety (now the domain of her sister Jane), letters-to-the-editor (if she did not like them, they did not appear), editorials, research—whatever had to be done by a small staff. In his contribution to the family's memoir, James McFadden, assistant publisher of *National Review*, speaks of her as the one member of the staff who never (or almost never) lost her temper or even grew angry, though she allowed no one to scant her when it was a matter of recognition—and the one member who dared to beard the editor and founder and even Schlamm, a man for whom there were no greys and who was incapable of viewing anything otherwise than ideologically, usually as the product of a conscious decision arrived at out of evil intent. Since he looked on Eisenhower as the reigning incarnation of Belial, Maureen papered his office, during his vacation, with pictures of that ineffectual Prince of Darkness.

She was also a competent and hard-working researcher and

reporter—responsible, too, for the actual writing of many pieces that appeared under more celebrated signatures—and it was largely as a result of her work that her brother and employer was able to make one of his more resounding attacks, replete with a full complement of those embellishments that make one turn away in anger and start moving reflexively into his enemy's camp. Then, unfortunately, one too often discovers that the said enemy is hardly the comrade one would choose, and again one is constrained to remember the fundamental lesson that the enemies of one's enemies are not necessarily on that account less maculate.

The leopard this time was the late Reverend Representative (or does one say Representative the Reverend?) Adam Clayton Powell Jr. of New York, who had made a considerable success of the clerical trade and the race business, a well-known friend of the poor who went about his spiritual, egalitarian, and proletarian chores in a Jaguar and an Austin-Healey alternately, and who lived generally in a style rather different from those of his parishioners and constituents (for a long time, until his final illness, he found it prudent to reside outside the reach of United States writs). "The Ordeal of Adam Clayton Powell" was a thorough job of research and reporting in the field (which included Harlem) as well as the library; published in June, 1957, it was followed in December by "The Wheels of Justice Stop for Adam Clayton Powell Jr." and in May, 1958, by "Who Obstructed Justice in the Case of Adam Clayton Powell Jr.?" The Reverend and Honorable Mr. Powell was the object of insinuation and investigation having to do with mysterious comings and goings of funds, and a federal grand jury took an interest in him until a few days after he made a sudden switch of position in 1956 and bade his disciples to vote for the re-election of Eisenhower, whereupon the pursuers (as the common law so aptly used to say) dropped matters. As a concerned citizen, Buckley was or purported to be aghast; and indeed there was a good deal to be aghast and worse at.

But it is not to be left unnoticed that when, some ten years later, his white conservative friend, the late Senator Thomas Dodd of Connecticut, was under comparable suspicions and no deity emerged from—or threw sand into—a machine, Buckley was a prime champion against what was loudly termed smear and malice. Now the Reverend and Honorable Powell is and was hardly the model that a good radical would hold up before his young (one of the Buckleys' greatest complaints was Powell's close ties with the Communist

Party); and it is hard to imagine that a moral conservative would much like his children to grow up to be like the Honorable Dodd (who, however, consorted with generals and industrialists and their public-relations viziers and paymasters). The Buckleys assiduously marshaled against the Reverend and Honorable every scrap of fact and quotation available, especially what came from a pro-Communist paper called *The People's Voice*; but the same kinds of weapons, turned later by others against the lay Honorable, who had been approvingly quoted and lavishly lauded by the very far Right, were most righteously denounced. Buckley was horrified by the fact that former employes of Dodd had taken their evidence to the press and the authorities; he was struck verbose with admiration by the fact that Thomas A. Bolan, an Assistant United States Attorney in New York and a close friend of McCarthy's hired man, Roy Cohn, having resigned from his federal job, in which he had been charged with preparing and directing the Powell investigation, had gone at once to tell all he knew to Buckley and *National Review*. It is not irrelevant to add that Powell was a vehement advocate of the civil-rights crusade and Dodd was at least equally vehement against any tinkering with the divinely ordained color scheme.

To dispose of the matter: Buckley brought up Powell's tax case in every issue for a while. In May of 1958 he ran an editorial curiously entitled "The Jig Is Up for Adam Clayton Powell Jr.," shortly after he had obtained all the grand jurors' names and addresses and sent each one a copy of his December, 1957, article. All this was given due—or undue—publicity, and, predictably, the grand jurors asked to be recalled, with mutterings about retaining Bolan as independent counsel; and, again predictably, they indicted the Reverend and Honorable on tax charges. The case went to trial in the spring of 1960, and, after five weeks of prosecution testimony, it developed that there was no evidence of tax evasion; the charge was changed to improper deductions, and a hung jury —ten for acquittal, two for conviction—could not be made to agree. The government—not improperly criticised by *The New York Times*, on purely legal grounds—finally conceded that it could not prove its case, and dropped it.

Maureen's closest friend in the family, it is said, was Reid, who was three years older. Not many years after his removal to Spain, he began wandering periodically back to Sharon and Camden, sometimes with his wife and their four sons, and at about the time when Maureen went to work for *National Review* Reid began to write a novel, *Eye of the Hurricane*, which was finished in 1966 and published by Doubleday in 1967. It rather accurately reflects what can be learned of its author from his writing, his friends, and sparse correspondence: he refused to be interviewed during his stays in this country while I was working on this book. Much given to active sports, such as hunting and fishing, and enthusiastic about watching bullfights, he is a very intense man whose convictions seem almost as explosive as Patricia Buckley Bozell's. Like Frank Meyer, who obtained a New York teaching certificate in order to be able to educate his children at home, Reid Buckley believes that all children should be taken out of organised schools and taught at home; but he has not followed his own precept. Some eighty per cent of his lectures, he says, are given at colleges and universities: their purpose is "the proselytising of the conservative philosophy."

He writes screenplays as well as novels, and some of them, produced in Spain and elsewhere, were scheduled for release during 1972, having been directed by one Antonio Isasi, responsible for works called *Istambul* and *They Went to Rob Las Vegas*; another, according to Buckley, was done for Paramount but was found to be (he does not say why) "politically untouchable." His first novel carries the notice to the reader that it is the first of a tetralogy to be called *Great South Bay*, and it is worth some examination.

It preaches, of course, the social-political-theological doctrine of the family, though it is not explicitly Catholic and it does—in its most nearly contemporary parts—use some short bad words in some short bad dialogue: Reid Buckley is no literary or intellectual rival for his brother. The whole presentation of the 562-page gothic is pretentious packaging indeed for its ponderous symbolism, its clumsy oligarchic propaganda, and its rather pathetic flogging of that very dead horse, St. Franklin of the Blue Eagle. There are acknowledgments to one hundred persons living and dead, including two saints (Joseph and Anthony), sixteen kinfolk by blood and marriage, and a clutch of domestics both house and field, concluding with the hallmark of archness: ". . . each of whom, more or less chronologically and in various ways and degrees, is personally and directly culpable for this book; and each of whom, among the living, is naturally expected to purchase a minimum of ten copies apiece [*sic*]." This is followed by a bibliography (for a novel!)

with twenty-two entries in history, political science, fiction, seamanship, philosophy, geography, etc.

The story starts in 1895—the chronology goes back to 1644—and stops for breath in 1938. There are some surprising insights into themselves by some of the characters, and one sentence that has a writer's touch: "The gale did not recede; only Jonathan's emotional commitment to it." Most of the book, unfortunately, consists of passages like this overture to a breakfast episode: "Gaunt, gristle-bearded, stoop-shouldered, crazy-eyed Jeremiah Wooster was first on the scene," and the woman who was cooking "crepitated" her reply to his question when it would be ready. I will cite only one further sentence: "Himself the incubus, it was as though turgid loins were rubbing interiorly, lobe on erotic lobe, inspiring the friction of a ravening desire." In other parts it is quite clear that the author has read *Ulysses*: one could wish he had not. *The New York Times* summarised the novel without comment; *Library Journal* said it was "the kind of old-fashioned melodramatic novel (tangled family relationships, skeletons in the closet) that went out of fashion fifty years ago, but which dedicated amateur writers try vainly to revive. It is written without any considerable literary style." *Choice* quotes its subtitle: *A Novel About Faith and Hate, Love and Betrayal, Man and the Sea*; it concedes some convincing details of reportage but calls the author "much less convincing when he deals with Love, Lust and Co."

To Russell Kirk in *National Review*, however, *Eye* was "reminiscent of Santayana's *The Last Puritan*." Kirk did not like the short bad words—"hard on the stomach and the heart"; though he concedes the impossibility of genteel description of "love frustrated and lust triumphant in a powerful nature." Buckley, he found, took the reader "from the world of Norman Mailer to the world of Joseph Conrad." Kirk was quite carried away, and he concluded: "As social historian and as master of character, Fergus Reid Buckley will make his mark."

His second novel, which is not part of the tetralogy, was scheduled to be published in April, 1973, by Doubleday. Titled *Servants and Their Masters*, "it's a social criticism of a functionless society," its author wrote to me. "It's also my *Pickwick Papers*."

His youngest sibling, Carol, is probably the least spectacular and the least driven of all the Buckleys. Born five years after Maureen, she was brought up virtually alone and, she told Susan Sheehan of

McCall's, "missed out on the living abroad and on the group lessons and group pressures. My childhood was also rather lonely. To me, my older brothers and sisters were 'they' and 'them.' " She was the only Buckley to be sent to a Catholic college, which she left after two years; for the next nine years she lived in Virginia with her fox-hunting Protestant husband, a Yale graduate and occasional engineer, to whom she bore four children, and whom she divorced; she is now married to Ray Learsy, a Jewish business man in the export/import trade, and, according to the article in *McCall's*, thinks of herself as a lapsed Catholic. In many ways she is a lapsed conservative too, at least in that she has none of the passion for politics and boycotts that the others show. Nor, in all probability, would she share the view of Reid—second only to the Bozells, despite his divorce and remarriage in 1972, in the fundamentalism of his Catholic beliefs—that this is a "pagan society" that is "a whole climate savagely against our sort of family closeness . . . against the faith." Their mother, however, told L. Clayton DuBois of *The New York Times*, when he asked her her reaction to Carol's divorce and remarriage: "I believe God will judge Carol by her standards and conscience, not by mine. . . . He will be more understanding than I because he knows more than I do."

The Buckleys have often said, with visible sincerity, that their debt to their wives is great. There is every reason to believe them, if only because of the wives' very consistent preference for privacy. James's wife was by no means enthusiastic about his entrance into politics, and she kept herself quite apart from it, as Bill's wife has remained aloof from his activities as a publicist and a polemicist. Reid's wives have followed the same rule, as John's did. This is equally true of the men who have married into the family, with the exception of Bozell: Benjamin Heath, who married Aloïse; William Smith, Jane's former husband; O'Reilly, Maureen's widower; and Carol's former husband, Thomas J. Charlton, and her present one, Learsy. It is as if—again with the exception of Bozell—marriage to a Buckley by no means necessarily implies participation in that Buckley's public life. Hence Buckleys-by-marriage must remain outside the jurisdiction of this book.

XIII

National Review could not be enough for Bill Buckley; his debating career had to continue too. The range of his opponents had widened long since to include people like the late Norman Thomas, the aging but still incisive leader of the Socialist Party; his young future successor, Michael Harrington; Norman Mailer, the sometime novelist; Steve Allen, the comedian; various of the narcissists to be found any week in *The Village Voice*, and an occasional dark horse. The combination of the magazine and the debates kept his intellectual muscle tone high, however it might have tended to induce a certain repetitiousness of movement; occasionally too he was writing for magazines not his own; and all this was of considerable assistance in tending toward formulations of his political and social philosophy on a fairly broad scale. At the same time, of course, he was becoming more and more the creature of those mass forms that any man of taste must despise but that few can resist with any consistency; so that ultimately he was to be dependent on them not only for the maintenance, not to mention the growth, of his prestige but also for at least some of the shaping of both his ideas and their expression. I do not mean that he consciously talked down or accommodated himself to any lower common denominator; rather, it gave him added delight to bedazzle the burghers, and they in turn could never be certain whether they were more resentful or flattered. But audiences expect certain patterns of behavior from anyone who ventures into any aspect of what is called show-business; and the microphone, the camera, and the platform are heady drugs for which one always pays a little price that, in solitude, one might rather sneer at. Moreover, the lecture circuit and the broadcasting studio do not gladly suffer discourse on the level below which it will be simply barred from truly cultivated society; so that the baseness of the medium, like the innate character of any form, must inevitably to a degree infuse itself into the substance.

The most obvious illustration is the Buckley of his 1959 book, *UP From Liberalism*, as against the Buckley of *National Review* (then or now) and the show-business audience. Even then everything in the United States had already become a show for the entertainment of as large an audience as possible—whether the sending of troops into Little Rock, the frenetic haste to match the Russians' successful launch of a satellite, the newspaper and television coverage of an earthquake, the strangely named World Series of baseball, or the presentation of ideas—or, in recent years, such fascinating spectacles as fire-bombing, the slaughter of civilians, the mobbing of dissidents, or the interrogation of prisoners: it's all a great show and everybody likes a show, so there's enough variety to let you take your pick. It is not to Bill Buckley's credit that more often than not he goes gladly along with this; and it hardly comports with his not unfounded claim to a certain level of cultivation and even fastidiousness. It is about as honest as the use of street jargon to their followers by men as highly articulate as Bobby Seale or Eldridge Cleaver, or the affectation of drug-pusher communication by doctors of philosophy.

UP From Liberalism—the entire thesis of which is given away by its title—is at least a serious effort to present a serious set of ideas, even if one may find them almost without exception untenable, and even if more than a modicum of intellectual dishonesty doses their exposition. This consistent dichotomy between undiluted integrity of belief and purpose and amoral resort to flagrant distortion and falsification, as well as often despicable personal attack, is a justification of means by ends that is totally unacceptable in people who call themselves moralists and pretend to the standards of, say, a Nock, an Ortega, or any of the Catholic thinkers whom Buckley has so often invoked. Such opportunism in even the noblest cause taints whatever it ostensibly furthers, as in the case of Buckley's otherwise admirable and ultimately successful effort to obtain the release of a man convicted of murder and sentenced to death because of that very denial of due process that the Buckleys support: only by exploiting the decisions for which he had always castigated "the Warren Court" was Buckley able to save Edgar H. Smith Jr. of New Jersey.

Neither in his diatribes against liberalism nor in his tributes to
Ortega has Buckley ever even alluded to Ortega's characterisation
of liberalism. *UP From Liberalism* barely mentions his name. First
published in 1959 (it was reprinted in 1968 by Arlington House,
in which Buckley has a financial interest through Starr Broadcasting Group, Inc.), with an introduction by Barry Goldwater and
a foreword by John Dos Passos, another pilgrim who progressed
from the Left to the farther Right, it is dedicated to Bozell, Burnham, Chamberlain, Chambers, Kendall, and Meyer. It is divided
into two parts: The Failure of Contemporary American Liberalism,
which is quite long, and The Conservative Alternative, which is
relatively brief ("He is considerably handicapped by the fact of
having nothing to say," *The St. Louis Post-Dispatch*'s review
rather fatuously summed up, as unperceptively as The Associated
Press, which located Buckley in the "die-hard band of extreme
conservatives").

Now there cannot be much disagreement among honest men as
to the proposition that American liberalism—if indeed it ever
existed—is a failure better passed over in silence. If the word is
taken in its Manchester sense, then the failure is obvious especially
in the economic aspect: the inequities and incapacities and, above
all, the inhumanities of the free market need no further rehearsing.
But that is not what Buckleyan conservatives—or most others in
this country—mean when they use the term: they have in mind
a hybrid that is perhaps almost liberal in the social/cultural/politi-
cal sense—in that it allows for a fairly broad, though by no means
an unlimited, pluralism and a measure of individual freedom unrestricted (at least in principle) by class or wealth that has yet to
be matched or even challenged in any other philosophy—with a
highly contradictory intolerance of its enemies and an inevitable
infringement of economic freedom for the preservation of civil,
political, and individual liberties. When conservatives attack liberalism for its undeniably illiberal suppression of anti-liberals, they
are on impregnable ground: this is a most unworthy and untenable
dereliction, whether the enemies they are attempting to eliminate
are of the Right or the Left. Here the traditionalist conservatives
are far more admirable in that they make no such lofty professions
of freedom but allow no one to linger in error: "certain kinds" of
freedom, notably in terms of speech and assembly, simply cannot
be allowed.

But the real core of the attack is twinned: the growth of the state's power and, especially, the use of that power to combat certain kinds of injustices and ruthlessness. Calling themselves unmitigated believers in the philosophy of the free market not only in economics but in every aspect of human life—with the specific exclusion of the realm of ideas—they are concerned really only with the most primitive form of survival of the fittest. The freedom that they would preserve, for example, is the freedom, when one works for a barely living wage, to provide unhelped against illness, emergency, and old age; to retrain oneself, when half one's working life is over and the free market has made one's trade obsolete, for a new occupation; to combat the oppressions of large corporations by buying stock in them and taking part in stockholder democracy. Platitudinous though it be to say so, this is a philosophy of purely material values, regardless of the religious vestments in which the theistic among its adepts attempt to cover its sores.

An examination of *UP From Liberalism* offers a reliable schema of Buckleyan argumentation and philosophy at its most serious and best. The references that follow are to the Arlington House edition. It is not the intention of such an analysis to bring forth, even as a by-product, any exculpation of American liberalism, which, though its heart may be less impure, is guilty of virtually every charge that may be or has been made against it from Left or Right, and certainly of stooping quite as low as any of its accusers: to liberalism, as to Buckleyism, virtually no weapon is too repellent to be used.

This point was made by Murray Kempton in *Commentary* when the book was first published, though Kempton spoke more gently in his rebuke of both the Buckleys of the world and the so-called liberals for their employment of the double standard. There can be no exoneration for liberals who used the same kind of paid traitor-cum-liar whose employment by Joseph McCarthy they denounced without cease. But, Kempton observed, Buckley's "skill at debate seems to me, when indulged, a serious disability, diverting him from the reality of human existence . . . the exercise of a superficial skill results in contamination of private feeling by official rhetoric and a turning of public self into a caricature of private self." Kempton could not regard Buckley as no better than his followers; quite the contrary, he counted among Buckley's advantages not only his independence of economic pressures but his passion and his restive intelligence; Buckley, Kempton said correctly, "is the repository of values insufficiently attended in an America which has come to believe that all social and spiritual development can be covered without any reference outside Freud, Marx, Henry Ford, the Reverend Daniel Poling, and Edward L. Bernays—that, in a word, the twentieth century destroyed all previous values"; Kempton added that, though "Buckley would deny with passion that he accepts this notion of the universe," he behaves in this book as if he did.

One of Buckley's troubles has always been definitions. Certainly one would squirm if one were compelled to offer a valid definition of American liberalism in the mid-twentieth century, and in all probability one would grasp the evasion of description. But Buckley says (pages 36–37): "Because liberalism has no definitive manifesto, one cannot say, prepared to back up the statement with unimpeachable authority, that such-and-such a man or measure is 'liberal.' But one can say that Mrs. Roosevelt was a liberal, and do so confident that no one will contradict him [I will, and do]. And say the same of Arthur Schlesinger Jr. and Joseph L. Rank and James Wechsler and Richard Rovere and Alan Barth and Agnes Meyer and Edward R. Murrow and Chester Bowles, Hubert Humphrey, Averell Harriman, Adlai Stevenson, Paul Hoffman. The *New Republic* is liberal, so is the *Washington Post*, the *St. Louis Post-Dispatch*, the *Minneapolis Tribune*; much of *The New York Times, all* [his italics] of the *New York Post*, save that oasis in which it publishes my dispatches. These men and women and institutions share premises and attitudes, show common reactions, enthusiasms and aversions, and display an empirical solidarity in thought and action, on the strength of which society has come to know them as 'liberals.' They are men and women who tend to believe that the human being is perfectible and social progress predictable, and that the instrument for effecting the two is reason; that truths are transitory and empirically determined; that equality is desirable and attainable through the action of state power; that social and individual differences, if they are not rational, are objectionable, and should be scientifically eliminated; that all peoples and societies should strive to organize themselves upon a rationalist and scientific paradigm."

There is enough truth in all that to make it seem a good deal more plausible than it is. But there is a reminder of Sartre in the suggestion that X is a liberal because people say he is. None of the names on the list is above challenge; what is undebatably liberal about the *New York Post* is precisely the fact that it does publish Buckley and other columnists with whose philosophies it profoundly disagrees. The beliefs that Buckley ascribes to his liberals are in some cases admirable, in others not even theirs at all: what is wrong in a faith in human perfectibility and social progress, even if one is too misanthropic to share it, or in the resolution to use the state for the protection of equality of rights? and is no truth transitory or empirically determined?—this is almost Calvinist. What "liberal" agitates for the elimination of social and individual differences on the ground that they are objectionable because not rational? or for the mechanist, quantified society? Or does Buckley, perhaps, hold his truths to be self-evident?

No one has a full nelson on the half-truth, either. It is rather amusing, though, when, on page 51, Buckley reports Robert Maynard Hutchins' statement "to the effect that Orthodoxy had closed down American freedom to the point where it had become hazardous to contribute money to Harvard University," and his own footnote to this revelation actually quotes Hutchins: "Now, after McCarthy's attack on Harvard, they [the foundations] will hesitate to give money to the University." Well, to the unjaundiced eye these are not quite the same thing. Still, one feels rather sorry for the ineptitude of the self-betrayal. Now, on the same page Buckley approvingly quoted the Rev. Dr. J. B. Matthews, cleric turned paid informer, for having written that "the largest single group supporting the Communist apparatus today is composed of Protestant clergymen." Buckley added that the adequacy of Matthews' so-called documentation was not relevant, but he said Matthews "finally reckoned that, percentagewise, more ministers had been gulled into supporting Communist fronts than teachers or lawyers," and the liberals thereupon did him out of his new job with McCarthy. Out of charity one forbears to comment on the unBuckleyan butcheries of English.

One is less concerned, too, with Buckley's pious defense of the Wisconsin martyr's memory than with his own more refined brand of McCarthyism. He takes an unconscionable time discussing "The Liberal" and his various manifestations—"In Controversy," "As Indoctrinator," "In Action," "And the Obliging Order," "And the Silent Generation"—and citing assorted individual misbehaviors, not one of which is without its counterpart on the conservative side, with the aim of discrediting ideas that he has nowhere very clearly identified; instead, he succeeds in sniping at a great number of people, and quite often with some foundation, since American "liberals" are indeed not very liberal or, for the greater part, any more ethical than Buckley himself. As my father explained to me in 1919, when I childishly asked how policemen could succeed in their profession: "It takes one to spot one."

It is when Buckley comes to "His [the liberal's] Root Assumptions" that the book reveals itself to be largely a new and more polished edition of *God and Man at Yale*. The liberal, like the democrat, is characterised by his "instrumental view of life" and "the transfer of attention from subject-matter to method." In clear, the preoccupation is with method rather than content, with freedom rather than with its uses; and this is wrong, Buckley says. But having stated a highly arguable proposition that compels earnest consideration, he ridicules his own position by asserting: "Intellectuals have tended to look upon democracy as an extension of the scientific method, as the scientific method applied to social problems." Who are these intellectuals? Where is the evidence of their tendency? Then there is the rhetorical device of challenging the principle of democracy—which is certainly far from invulnerable—with this kind of question: "Can a nation with a strong socialist minority ever be stable, when the shadow of socialism renders private property perpetually insecure?" No definitions, no illustrations—merely articles of faith, reinforced by this guide to policy: "I certainly do not suggest that the existence of a Communist minority is good reason for doing away with democracy, though I would say it is sufficient reason for doing away with Communists."

In this dissection of the liberal's root assumptions, Buckley's own are more fully shown. He is not totally wrong in his argument that "the claims that are made in behalf of democracy, the showpiece of the liberal ideology, are illusory, because the attributes imputed to it are wholly extrinsic to democracy itself." But from this he proceeds to the proposition that democracy is to be permitted by the white West only to "politically mature people among whom there is a consensus on the meaning of life within their society." He has just finished chastising the United States for its behavior toward certain democratically chosen but abhorrent governments in other countries, and he is quite correct; but how is anyone any better qualified to determine who else shall or shall not enjoy these perils and privileges, and by what criteria? This leads to the "generic question whether the minority in a democratically organized community is ever entitled to take such measures as are necessary to prevail, politically and culturally, over the majority [pages 156–57]. . . . In the South, the white community is entitled to put forward a claim to prevail politically because, for the time being anyway, the leaders of American civilization are white—as one would certainly expect, given their preternatural advantages, of tradition, training and economic status." The saving exception does not really save, of course; things are indeed made plainer, if possible, by the bald statements of prevailing cultural superiorities and the right of preserving them, and by the complete silence on the causes and remedies. It is not enough to deny any biological ground for differentiation.

"The humbler claims for democracy are not only legitimate but realistic," Buckley says at page 160. "It is right that the views of the individual who stands to be affected by a law or ordinance should be canvassed. It remains only to be added that standards exist by which to appraise the man's views. And that if these views argue for barbarism or regimentation, it is proper to circumvent them, even if, in doing so, democracy is flouted; as it deliberately is under the Constitution of the United States."

Whose are the standards, what are the standards, by which to appraise "the man's" views? Why is circumvention proper (dogma is not enough, save perhaps among theologians)? One would be interested to have an explanation of the constitutional circumvention, too. As he moves toward the peroration of this first part of the book, Buckley becomes rhetorically more impressive (when not downright flashy) and factually more unreliable (not to say fanciful): "The call by liberalism to conformity with its economic dispensations does not grow out of the economic requirements of modern life; but rather out of liberalism's total appetite for power. The root assumptions of liberal economic theory are that there is no serious economic problem; that in any case economic considerations cannot be permitted to stand in the way of 'progress'; that, economically speaking, the people are merely gatherers of money which it is the right and duty of a central intelligence to distribute."

By way of coda, Buckley proposes to lay to rest the nonsensical fairy tales of Professor J. Salwyn Schapiro in *Liberalism: Its Meaning and History*. Schapiro having traced the liberals' embrace of *laisser-faire* in the nineteenth century and their repudiation of it as reactionary in the twentieth, when liberalism moved to protect the individual against not only arbitrary acts of government but arbitrary acts of private organisations too, Buckley whips up his rhetoric to a climax: "The only autonomy liberalism appears to encourage is moral and intellectual autonomy; solipsism. And that is the autonomy of deracination; the philosophy that has peopled the earth with atomized and presumptuous social careerists diseased with hubris; the pestilence that breeds those 'squalid oligarchs who detest the world of silence and of freedom' whom, Russell Kirk charges conservatives, it has fallen to us 'to keep at bay.' "

Hence it is hardly necessary for him to say: "I do not understand liberalism as a historical continuum." Liberalism, he concludes, is an infinite maximisation of choices, the nature of which is unimportant; whereas to the conservative that is of the first importance because man's "first choice was so catastrophic." And thus he offers "The Conservative Alternative," first reviewing "The Failure of the Conservative Demonstration." This failure, as far as Eisenhower's Modern Republicans were concerned, consisted of too much deviationism and accommodationism—theoretical insufficiency, Buckley calls it; as for the Right Republicans, their "rhetorical extravagances" (!) were their undoing, for they were forever crying *Wolf!* when not even a cockroach was about. Buckley offers some warnings.

"Communism is *not* idealistic and for the most part does not appeal to idealistic people; our position, adequately defined, is *not* materialist and is *not* 'hard to defend' [as Eisenhower said he had found it in conversation with Marshal Zhukov], and is *not* burdened by a primary appeal to the 'selfish in man' [as Eisenhower said Zhukov had described it]. . . . The distinctive challenge of our time . . . is to resist the philosophical infiltration of the west by Communism. That infiltration is the end toward which the great engines of history are busily working, the grand synthesis whose name, in one of its phases, is Coexistence, and whose meaning, for the west, is death. . . . Liberalism cannot teach Mr. Eisenhower to talk back effectively to Mr. Khrushchev; but conservatism can."

Hence conservatism must learn not to waste its fire on such facts of life as social security. Make no mistake: it is still, economically and philosophically, wicked: economically because it can never pay its way, philosophically because it appeals (fraudulently) to the desire to get something for nothing and because it deprives the taxpayer of the freedom to suffer old age with nothing instead of with almost nothing. This example, he pointed out, he was taking as a synecdoche (Buckley has, in print and on the air—rather less in private—a proved arsenal of recondite technical terms): his thesis is that "Conservatives have failed to alert the community to the interconnection between economic freedom and —freedom." Because:

"It is a part of the conservative intuition that economic freedom is the most precious temporal freedom, for the reason that it alone gives to each one of us, in our comings and goings in our complex society, sovereignty—and over that part of existence in which by far the most choices have in fact to be made, and in which it is possible to make choices, involving oneself, without damage to other people. And for the further reason that without economic freedom, political and other freedoms are likely to be taken from us." (That economic freedom might mean freedom from economic chaos and from the slavery of poverty did not, of course, occur to him.)

No explanation, of course: another article of faith. Rather, the demonstration that the conservative must make is simply this: "Give me the right to spend my dollars as I see fit . . . and, if I must make the choice, I will surrender to you my political franchise in trade, confident that by the transaction, assuming the terms of the contract are that no political decision affecting my sovereignty over my dollar can be made, I shall have augmented my dominance over my own affairs." What was that that Zhukov was so wrong about in his little chat with Eisenhower?

The loss of freedom by attrition is what should be the concern of conservatives, their aspiring leader asserts; and this attrition is primarily the work of the centralisation of power in an ever more pervasive state. "The answers of liberalism create worse problems than those they set out to solve. Conservatives cannot be blind, or give the appearance of being blind, to the dismaying spectacle of unemployment, or any other kind of suffering. But conservatives can insist that the statist solution to the problem is inadmissible." What is to be done, then? "It is to maintain and wherever possible enhance the freedom of the individual to acquire property and dispose of that property in ways that he decides on." Out, then, with "monopoly unionism, feather-bedding, and inflexibilities in the labor market"—though not a word of the analogues on the other side; "where residual unemployment persists," it must be coped with locally. "Let the natural desire of the individual for more goods, and better education, and more leisure, find satisfaction in individual encounters with the marketplace, in the growth of private schools, in the myriad economic and charitable activities which, because they took root in the individual imagination and impulse, take organic form. . . .

"I will not cede more power to the state. I will not willingly cede more power to anyone, not to the state, not to General Motors, not to the CIO. I will hoard my power like a miser, resisting every effort to drain it away from me. I will then use *my* power, as *I* see fit. I mean to live my life an obedient man, but obedient to God, subservient to the wisdom of my ancestors; never to the authority of political truths arrived at yesterday at the voting booth. That . . . is certainly program enough to keep conservatives busy, and liberals at bay. And the nation free."

I have dealt at such length with this relatively old book for a number of reasons. It is thus far the last philosophical effort of any substantial length by Buckley (his projected commentary on Ortega's *Revolt of the Masses* has unfortunately been abandoned since he wrote some twenty-five thousand words of it in 1964–65), it is a predominantly serious book, and it embodies essentially, on a reasonably high level of discourse, all his current thinking on the matters at issue—his ideas are substantially what they were when he entered Yale in 1946, with some minor peripheral modifications brought about by experience and further study. His subsequent books—apart from *Cruising Speed*, the record of a week of his life in late 1970, and *The Unmaking of a Mayor*, the analytical account of his 1965 campaign—are all compendia of articles for *National Review* and other magazines, occasional pieces, speeches, etc.; and the political substance comprehended in them is very well summarised in *UP From Liberalism*. In this respect—though not necessarily in its literary quality—it represents Buckley at his peak.

It is therefore almost a shock to turn from this book, devoid of authentic humanity though it often be, to the *pettegolezze* that have cheapened almost every issue of *National Review* and its *Bulletin* from the early years on. What some saddened conservatives call its "undergraduate note"—which, they are quite right in maintaining, was far less discernible in the *Yale Daily News* under Buckley's editorship—is viewed as "more affected than it is instinctive. It's adopted for certain purposes." These friendly critics fear that such material and such a tone alienate many people who might otherwise be more inclined to take the magazine seriously. One explanation is seen in the character of the original subscription list. "The original circulation list of *National Review*," I was told, "was built out of the supporters of Joseph McCarthy. Buckley was in close touch with him; there were lists of such people. There was therefore a desire to cultivate and continue this support and thus the tone is in part determined by the approval of the initial readers: there was not an early enough attempt to reach a wider audience. It was of course made later. But much of that tone still lingers; partly because of people who go out to make readers for the magazine and who say: 'Well, you're too intellectual, we can't understand it and we're not going to give you any more help if you're so intellectual and abstract.' "

Partly, too, the spirit of fun—however malicious and, often, unfunny—is responsible. In the earliest days there was a very strong division of opinion between Buckley—supported by Priscilla—and John Chamberlain and Suzanne La Follette, both of whom had come from the much more serious (and often stodgy) *Freeman,* which was not the same brilliant, wide-open journal that it had been under Albert Jay Nock, its founding editor. Chamberlain and Miss La Follette wanted *National Review* to concentrate on lengthy, meaty essays; but the Buckleys won. As a consequence, its claim to be a thoughtful voice of conservative opinion is somewhat vitiated—once more the mentality of show-business has dirtied *National Review* with the same determined mediocrity to be found in any mass-circulation magazine. Somehow, when the spirit of fun is made flesh in *National Review*, it is almost always overweight. And it is less at ease with the rapier than with the chamber pot. For example: "Conservatives are organizing a Paean for Earl Warren. They're going to gather at the Supreme Court and Pae on him."

XIV

National Review is published out of a seedy, skinny old former apartment building, in which it occupies a number of small floors, on the southern edge of Murray Hill, somewhat to the south and east of Catawba's exquisite quarters, and in some contrast to its editor's New York residence (in 1954 he bought a waterfront house in Stamford, largely because of his passion for sailing)— the Park Avenue duplex, in the Lenox Hill section, that he purchased from the estate of that austere Secretary General of the United Nations of whom *National Review Bulletin* had written so disgracefully. *National Review*'s building also houses Caribbean Enterprises, Inc., the company that attempts to make money out of chartering out Bill Buckley's two boats, the luxurious and beautiful *Cyrano*, a cruising yacht, and *Suzie Wong*, a racing boat. (Sometimes Buckley's charter firm hires out Buckley's big boat to Buckley's radio enterprise, Starr Broadcasting Group, Inc.)

By the time the magazine was five years old Buckley was not only setting forth his views in it and other publications over his own by-line but also being interviewed, and sometimes he said things that pleased him (if not everyone else) so much that he would use them again and again. He spoke very frankly at that time to Dan Wakefield of *Esquire*, and none of the views he set forth then has substantially changed:

"If I lived in South Carolina, I would vote for segregated schools in my community; in Stamford, where I live, I'd vote for integrated schools. I hope that if I lived in South Carolina, I would take a position aimed at doing what I could to increase the opportunity of Negroes to the point where I no longer felt segregation was necessary."

Africans will be ready for self-government "when they stop eating each other." (When, twelve years later, the representatives of Zambia in the United Nations danced a jig to celebrate the admission of the People's Republic of China, *National Review* commented editorially that all that was missing was "a pot to boil George Bush in." Bush was the American Ambassador to the U.N.)

"I would rather be governed by the first two thousand names in the telephone directory than by the Harvard University faculty."

"Under certain circumstances dictatorship is best. I'm interested in human freedom and the kind of government that maximizes it. I think I would have more freedom under Franco, for instance, than I would have had under the Spanish Republic." (A year or two later, John Buckley said that *National Review*'s editorials about Spain had been most helpful in obtaining concessions for the family companies in the Spanish Sahara.)

It is rather more difficult to condemn Bill Buckley in toto when he expresses fear of the quality of mass education—though "schooling" would be the more accurate word for what is attempted in this country, where education in the real sense is dreaded—or when he insists that "one of the great self-delusions of democracy" is the notion that everyone is qualified to vote. It is conceivable—though remote—that in some utopia everyone may indeed be qualified to vote (and immune to disease, somatic and psychic); but in a society in which the dominant tradition has seen to it that virtually no one—including most of its own believers—is qualified to vote, one is compelled to Winston Churchill's grim conclusion that democracy is merely the least bad form of society thus far evolved. I cannot forget the extremely brilliant student anarchist who, after a year or two in the great dirty world, remained as much an anarchist as ever and yet "cringe[d] whenever I hear 'All power to the people.' "

It was students less thoughtful than this one who were to flock —often in sheer lust for something, anything, that looked like security, like a belief—to Young Americans for Freedom, which was incubated partly in the shabby *National Review* building, partly in Marvin Liebman's public-relations office on lower Madison Avenue, partly on the acres of Sharon (Kempton has said that, as the student of Soviet Russia must be a Kremlinologist, the student of American conservatism must be a Sharonologist). What is more, in spite of the divisions that have more recently appeared in this Legion of Light—between traditionalist and libertarian, between religious believer and secularist, between young wowser and what used to be called free-lover—its consistently increasing ranks have turned unceasingly to Bill Buckley as the man whom they most admire (though, since the 1970 election, he has had to share some of his honors with his Senatorial brother). There are, it is true (particularly in the intellectually scrawnier areas, like New Mexico), some not-so-Young Americans for Freedom (they stop being young on their fortieth birthdays) who find Bill too pink—and, though they admit this less readily, too bright; possibly the two are in their case synonymous—as there are, in regions less resistant to refinement, even fewer who wonder lest The Founder be somewhat too much the man of authority.

That YAF enjoyed the backing of all the Buckleys from the start may be taken as axiomatic. Its Sharon Statement drew extensively on the late Will Buckley's program for his private school; his widow has always extended her blessing and the hospitality of her home to wandering members; all the Buckleys have contributed money to it; several have given it their active aid. In return for their patronage and for making themselves manifest in the flesh at annual YAF conclaves, Bill and (since his entrance into politics) Jim have enjoyed hero status: a poll of the Young Americans showed that Bill was by far the man that most of them would like to be, and at their 1971 convention they rallied in most impressive numbers to Jim Buckley as successor to Nixon or Agnew, impartially. To dismiss YAF as a joke is to show a remarkably short-sighted sense of humor. They are predominantly middle- and lower-middle-class, and determined to rise: the epitome of the sociologists' upward mobiles. And they number hundreds of thousands, steadily increasing: the cadres, to borrow the "revolutionary" jargon, of the ruling class that they fully intend not to replace but to prolong. The Buckleys are their natural heroes, who in their charm and cultivation and success are equally natural identification figures for the groundlings.

All this derives naturally from adherence to what has become known as The Sharon Statement. Based on Will Buckley's charter for his private school and elaborated by Bill Buckley, a number of *National Review*'s house philosophers and the very practical former YCL man, Liebman, this latter-day Sermon on the Mount curiously ignored what, in a letter, Whittaker Chambers had tried to impress on Bill Buckley as a fundamental of any true conservatism: civil liberties. "Why, for example," Chambers wrote a year before the birth of YAF, "should we leave it to the Liberals to give tongue against the frightening developments in wire-tapping?" Civil liberties, Chambers tried to show his acolyte, "by rights . . . belong[s] to the Right"; as Whitney North Seymour Sr., once president of the American Bar Association and vice-chairman of the board of directors of the American Civil Liberties Union, emphasised five years later: "It is impossible to over-estimate the stake of the true conservative in the constant strengthening of civil liberties, for the whole principle and practice of liberty under law are what it is always most essential to conserve. Once either the principle or the practice is corrupted, the conservative is in as great peril as the innovator."

The Sharon Statement's primary concern with freedom, however, was economic—"political freedom cannot long exist without economic freedom" and "the purposes of government are to protect these freedoms through the preservation of internal order, the provision of national defense, and the administration of justice; . . . when government ventures beyond these rightful functions, it accumulates power which tends to diminish order and liberty; . . . the market economy, allocating resources by the free play of supply and demand, is the single economic system compatible with the requirements of personal freedom and constitutional government, and it is at the same time the most productive [not, be it noted, the most equitable] supplier of human needs; . . . when government interferes with the work of the market economy, it tends to reduce the moral and physical strength of the nation; . . . when it takes from one man to bestow on another, it diminishes the incentive of the first, the integrity of the second, and the moral autonomy of both [the young moralists, like their elders, are apparently incapable of conceiving of any incentive other than gain]; . . . the forces of international Communism are, at present, the greatest single threat to these liberties; . . . the United States should stress victory over, rather than co-existence with, this menace." There was also the obligatory obeisance to states' rights, described with restraint as "the genius of the Constitution."

In 1965 and 1970—the fifth and tenth anniversaries of the Sharon Creed, "adopted in Conference at Sharon, Connecticut, September 9–11, 1960"—YAF staged what it called Returns to Sharon, where Mrs. Buckley Sr. held open house for those in attendance. These celebrated the formal inception of the organisation: the fruit of all those trysts in Manhattan. It at once acquired a National Advisory Board, which included, of course, Bill Buckley; some other members of that original group, such as Irene Corbally Kuhn, were still among the several hundred advisers listed as of 30 April 1971 on the back of the stationery. These comprise almost seventy members of Congress: James Buckley, naturally, and, among others, Representative John M. Ashbrook of Ohio, a close Buckley associate for years who in 1971 was put forward as the conservatives' nominal candidate for the purpose of forcing Nixon to repudiate what they consider to be his betrayals of the cause, and the Goldwaters—Senator Barry Sr. and Representative Barry Jr.—the notorious Senator Karl Mundt, the equally notorious Representative John Rousselot, the Birch leader who headed YAF's latest fund appeal, and the arch-reactionary Senator Strom Thurmond. The lay or non-Congressional members similarly represent a roll-call of reaction: for instance, Cmdr. Lloyd N. Bucher of the *Pueblo*, the spy ship seized by North Korea; Taylor Caldwell, the extreme Right novelist; John Chamberlain; Gen. Mark W. Clark, who commanded the Fifth Army in Italy during the Second World War; Devin Garrity, who heads the very conservative Catholic publishing house, Devin-Adair; former Senator William Knowland; William Loeb, the arch-reactionary New Hampshire newspaper publisher who has attained a certain national eminence; Clarence Manion, former dean of the Law School at Notre Dame and a charter member of the John Birch Society; Adm. Ben Moreell and a number of other unreasonably far Right military men; Governor Ronald Reagan of California; and a herd of *National Review* editors and contributors and former clients and associates of Marvin Liebman, including such individuals of real stature as Russell Kirk, whose presence in these milieux always surprises.

While YAF's subsidiary heroes have included the elder Goldwater and Reagan, in whose various campaigns the members have worked as fanatically as any other militants, the prime hero has always been Bill Buckley, who has now been joined in that exclusive Pantheon by his senatorial brother. Randal Cornell Teague, the young lawyer who is now executive director in the national headquarters, attributes the Buckley cult in part to the family's rôle in the creation of YAF and, more important in his view, "the fact that Bill Buckley contributed more to YAF than any other person." Teague pointed out also that a surprisingly large number of young campaign workers and voters aligned themselves with

James Buckley: "The movement itself was in need of a hero, and to a great extent both the Buckleys fill that vacuum." But Teague added that "there are people who are dissatisfied with Bill because they feel that he doesn't have the gusto that he used to in 1955 to 1965, let's say, or '64, when he was really the bugaboo in everybody's hat." (This view has been expressed frequently by other senior Young Americans for Freedom and by many older conservatives in various parts of the country, who cherish nostalgic memories of Bill Buckley's 1965 campaign for the Mayoralty of New York and who felt badly let down by his 1968 blow-up at Gore Vidal on television: something was lost then, I have frequently been told, and he has been much more sobersided ever since; on the other hand, the Rev. William Sloane Coffin and Professor Paul Weiss, among others, have viewed this sequel as a certain mellowing or maturation; and Buckley himself is inclined to dismiss both views with quick scorn.)

In any event, he has always been extremely close to YAF, which is precious to him, and he and Teague are in frequent contact both by telephone and in the flesh. Today YAF is, in the current jargon of both sides, a much more "viable" organisation than it was in its earlier years, and not to take it seriously is to be rather unperceptive. In the first five years it was overshadowed by the growing radical movement among the young, by which it is still in an organisational sense outnumbered; and its initial biases toward religiosity and strait-laced private conduct were hardly alluring. As the taint of hedonism began, however, to corrupt even these lofty circles—divine lightnings were notably inactive even when wickedness flaunted itself in the very streets—and, at the same time, a scarcely acknowledged hunger for subordination to authority began to spread among those who found an independent conscience an insupportable burden, the ranks began to grow. A certain realism also came in with the new recruits, as the mock political convention that was part of YAF's 1971 annual meeting in Houston showed: there were 1577 voting delegates present at this imitation nomination of a Presidential candidate, and exactly forty-six of them pledged allegiance to Nixon. But they did vote authorisation for a campaign fund of seven hundred fifty thousand dollars to put "a real conservative" on the 1972 ticket. On the first ballot, Reagan got 258 votes, James Buckley got 210 and Vice President Agnew got 208. Buckley's name was then withdrawn, and in the end Agnew (*faute de pis?*) won 976 and Reagan dropped to 204; Nixon lost four of his die-hards. Thereupon the group nominated Buckley by acclamation as its Vice Presidential candidate. When he disavowed any such ambition for 1972, he was unquestionably sincere: "I'm not ready," he is reliably reported to have told close friends, and this is quite credible even if one cannot altogether believe any elected official who tells one without qualification that he does not want higher office.

What was important about this action by youngish people who will be dominating their communities' economic and political activities for a long time was, first of all, their recognition of Nixon's failure as a conservative and their endorsement of the "suspension of support" that had recently been announced by Bill Buckley and the *National Review* ruling class but from which James Buckley had publicly dissociated himself; the second important lesson was the Senator's very strong attraction to a group that had otherwise begun to suffer the kind of sectarianism that has always beset the Left. "Bill," Teague said in summarising his conversations with Bill Buckley on the subject, "really expected a great deal from Nixon, whereas most other conservatives did not expect anything." This majority, obviously, included the overwhelming preponderance of YAF. It remains a mystery that a man with Buckley's intellectual equipment could ever have taken Nixon seriously as a person, and the only explanation must be Paul Weiss's belief that Buckley is a victim of the notion that everyone always acts from reasoned, ideological motivations, whereas an observer less shackled by dogmatic preconception would have recognised the man for the desperate careerist, ignorant of scruple throughout his life, that he has always been: not evil in any conscious sense, but evil only with the consummate evil of mediocrity, guilty only of the sin of total moral autism.

This seeming repudiation of Nixon by YAF, however, is to be taken seriously, like Buckley's advocacy of Representative John Ashbrook's rival primary candidacy (which will be discussed in greater detail presently), only so far: "It's a matter of strategy as to what one should do in '71 to try to exert pressure on '72 itself," Teague explained. "I think that's the real key. . . . If the Democrats nominate some really crazy person and there's a chance that Nixon might lose, I would really expect to see most YAF members out there trying to help Nixon. In 1968 we supported Reagan all the way down the line—in the twenty-five-man board of directors there were two for Nixon, twenty-three for Reagan, none for Wallace—and in Miami in '68 we just turned out gobs and gobs and gobs of people, YAF people, for Reagan, very few for Nixon; and yet, once Nixon had the nomination, YAF mounted a very good effort, I think, toward the Nixon camp." In this one hears very clearly the master's voice.

It speaks in the first instance to Teague, for practical purposes, though there are the conventional elected officers and directors scattered through colleges, graduate schools, and professional schools predominantly in the Midwest, the West, the Southwest, and the South—the only institutions of any consequence that are represented are the University of Pennsylvania (to my surprise) and the University of Southern California, which is twice blest. There is a paid staff of twenty-three, the top five of whom—the executive director, the director of regional organisations, the programming director, the chapter director, and the editor of YAF's monthly organ, *New Guard*—draw salaries comparable to those of junior executives in private industry: the highest is just under twenty thousand dollars a year. The offices, in an excellent apartment building on Massachusetts Avenue in Washington, are pleasant without being imposing. The chapter director, when I saw Teague, was *en mission* in Saigon, whence he telephoned during our talk. The Washington office appoints the various state chairmen, because "they are really administrative officers and function under the complete direction of this office"; but chapter chairmen are elected.

Not a great deal of money is collected or spent. The Washington headquarters costs $723,000 a year, and $700,000 more is spent on regional operations and raised through regional offices precisely where one might expect them to be: in Houston, Atlanta, New Jersey, and Seattle. All production of literature and mailing pieces is done in the Washington quarters. Dues, according to Teague, range from one to ten dollars a year and represent 1.81 per cent of YAF's income. "Ninety-three per cent of our income is from direct-mail solicitation," he said, "and the rest from chapter chartering fees, *New Guard* advertising and subscriptions, film sales and rentals, legacies, conventions, and miscellaneous. The average contribution runs $11.17. In the eleven years we have been in operation, the total number of people who have ever given YAF five hundred dollars or more is ninety-three people. And the largest contribution we've ever received is three thousand dollars." None of the ninety-three was a Buckley or a Buckley corporation,

Teague said; Liebman procured the initial financing from Charles Edison, a former Governor of New Jersey; Herbert Kohler Sr., who fought one of the longest and cruelest labor wars against a union in American history, and some of their friends.

Teague was occasionally self-contradictory on the Buckleys' closeness to YAF, though he claims credit for having brought about a considerable increase in communication and coordination among the conservatives—the American Conservative Union, *National Review*, YAF, the New York State Conservative Party, *Human Events*, and other minor entities, because it was "time we started having a little more coordination—the Left surely has it." By way of explanation of this rather startling constatation, he cited the closeness of thought and act (on certain monochrome matters) between Senator J. William Fulbright and *The New York Times*. Before he took over, Teague said, there was extremely little contact between YAF and the Buckleys—two years without a telephone call, even to discuss YAF's leadership-training projects, in which ostensibly Bill Buckley was deeply interested. Teague names M. Stanton Evans as the author of The Sharon Statement, though, he says, Buckley looked it over. "His position," Teague said, "is that YAF was going to have its own internal political problems, and he was going to stand back from them." In the next sentence he is expatiating on the intense closeness to YAF that Buckley feels, but he insists that the Buckleys almost never provide advice or cooperation. Teague and his second wife were at Great Elm when DuBois was interviewing Buckleys in 1970 for his long story in *The New York Times Magazine*, he told me, "and at dinner Mrs. Buckley Senior said: 'You know, that *New York Times* man asked me how many children I had,' and she said: 'I felt I should tell him that I had more than I had because I feel YAF is a child of mine: it was born in my house, I carried it in my womb as if it were one of my children.' "

In 1969, responding to the fragmentation that was beginning among the older conservatives, YAF suffered "a rupture along philosophical lines: the traditionalists, the libertarians, and a great deal of fusionists in between." The traditionalists won overwhelmingly; the disciples of Karl Hess and Murray Rothbard walked out. "They said they left on philosophical grounds," Teague asserted, "but, as Bill pointed out in Houston this year, you could say they left because they lost." The greatest proportion of defections occurred in Massachusetts, New Jersey, Pennsylvania, and

California, but "almost every one of those people that left YAF came back—still as libertarians and so forth, but they came back." The reason, Teague explained, was that "YAF is where the action is in the conservative movement."

Though it publishes a large number of the writers who appear in *National Review* and not a few of the hacks to be found in *Human Events* and similar journals, the YAF organ, *New Guard*, maintains—curiously—a consistently more adult tone. There is no sign of the adolescent peevishness that can erupt from a philosopher like James Burnham or a man of the great world like Bill Buckley. On the other hand, there are few signs of anything but the stodgiest earnestness in the service of a gospel the meretriciousness of which ought to be evident even to its preachers and pupils. Indeed, there are some indications of such perception from time to time, as in a review of Frank Perry's film, *Diary of a Mad Housewife*: the critic is amazingly attuned to the film's point of view and contemptuous of the upper-middle-class social/cultural syndrome at which the title character rebels; indeed, he sees (correctly) that "the drama of degeneracy of *Diary* is acted out all around us. . . . The answer calls for a rejection of the empty goal of status striving which is so much a part of American life and the substitution of a non-material value system." And, as is so often the case, there is every sign that the young would be thoroughly ashamed to indulge in anything like *National Review*'s traducement of Hammarskjöld after his death or Buckley's contemptible letter to Hayek.

Teague confirmed a rather interesting phenomenon to be observed in conversation with conservatives of various ages in many parts of the country. An increasing proportion has rejected the Buckleyan dogma that only a believer in God can be a real conservative, though there is still a strong *Triumph* faction in YAF. But there is an almost even split on the whole question of private heterosexual behavior and contraception—I met some remarkably loose livers, as the ancients used to say, among the YAF—though the ranks close pretty much against abortion: woman, by and large, remains a chattel, sexual and other. Even drug use, for a while, was to be observed among the libertarian factions, which could also hear the word "homosexual" without queasing internally. No position on drugs was ever taken because of the intense division. There was a period, too, when many YAF members were much taken with Ayn Rand's brutal philosophy of selfish enrichment and ruthlessness to the less competent.

The orthodox, however, still control the YAF administration, which, Teague said, "has quite a bit of contact with youth organisations around the world. At any one time we're probably sending literature out to about seventy to seventy-five leaders of youth groups, ranging all the way from economic-study groups in Europe all the way through anti-Communist student movements in the Orient and things like that. It gives you a sense of cohesion, a common sense of purpose." He was not more specific as to the identities of the leaders or their groups. This activity is natural enough, and no more or less sinister than the contacts between American and foreign Left organisations, junior or senior. There is no way of establishing at the moment whether liaison is maintained by YAF with actual Fascist organisations abroad; certainly Buckley denies, for his part, any contacts with the resurgent British, German, and Italian Fascists, while at the same time making no secret of his ties with extreme conservatives abroad.

One of the more misleading commonplaces is the notion that to be young means to revolt. The most dedicated workers for Bill Buckley's 1965 Mayoralty campaign and James Buckley's 1970 Senatorial campaign were young—very many of them too young to vote for their heroes. Most of the Buckleys' youthful acolytes, undoubtedly, come from homes or communities in which there is barely even the conjecture that something not quite so American as apple pie might exist within the borders; but a surprisingly large proportion is far more sophisticated than that. YAF represents the first major effort to form them into some more organised entity than their elders have ever been recruited for—to make an effective start toward breaking the silence of the majority, for majority it is, and majority it is likely to remain for the foreseeable future; there is indeed little reason to suppose that it will not become even larger. Even if one grants that most of the people, regardless of age, are merely apathetic most of the time, the very fact of their apathy, again regardless of age, of necessity moves them, in those rare moments of recognition, to what is known and "safe" and not threatening: the Right; and the more so when its spokesmen are as persuasive and coruscating as Bill or as persuasive and familiar-seeming as Jim. Some older Rightists, it is true, such as *National Review*'s laureate, W. H. von Dreele, can hardly contain their hostility to the influx of "the kids" into the movement and the magazine ("I don't like to read things by people nineteen years of age," von Dreele, the breveted bard, told me); but the wiser among the angelic host know very well how useful are these aspiring cherubim.

Inside and outside YAF, young people are attracted by the Buckleys, and not seldom, just as they were by the Kennedys and John Lindsay, purely glandularly. Some, of course, recover: I am thinking of a graduate student in political science who was brought up in the bosom of mid-Ohio conservatism and accepted it without question, from his twelve-year-old partisanship for Nixon in 1960. "After that failure Buckley was probably the strongest conservative figure left," he told me, "and I began reading him regularly a few years later, when I started at Ohio State. He was the only conservative with enough eloquence who wasn't a throwback to the old politicians: the only conservative who was a modernist. What interested me then was defending the values I had and finding a good defender. The values themselves were vague—a father-figure conservatism: more of a trust relationship, the old uncle or grandfather, rather than truly political. I was concerned not with issues but with parties and people—an emotional rather than an intellectual approach."

I asked what had changed his course: "Meetings and reading. I became a political science major and ran into two very grandiloquent instructors who were liberal versions of Buckley. Pretty soon I was learning that grandiloquence wasn't very important: I was forced to make decisions about issues, and for this you need fact. And I found very little fact supporting general conservative thought in any field." His own conversion, he thought, was the exception rather than the rule, because, among his contemporaries both at Ohio State and later in graduate school at the University of New Mexico, most shared his initial orientation and did not lose it regardless of the dangerous men who taught them. He and others, including some newspaper editors who should have known better, pointed out that few people in New Mexico then—in the summer of 1971, very soon after *Firing Line* had begun to appear on television there—had heard of the Buckleys and still fewer took them seriously, until and unless there was prolonged exposure, whereupon the younger people in particular began to be increasingly attracted.

"My own impression during the years of my admiration for

Buckley," my informant added, "came from reading him regularly in *National Review* and other magazines and his books, and it was personal rather than intellectual, though his presentation was the first I'd had that I considered to be an intelligent representation of political ideas and issues. He added a sophisticated note to conservative doctrine that was absent in Eisenhower—who had no doctrine. Nixon was a failure, and Goldwater had little or nothing to say. Buckley's appealing, but more in a literary than in a political sense. Actually, I'd compare my infatuation by Buckley with the general seduction of the American populace by the Kennedy family."

A much younger informant, a seventeen-year-old high-school student who has lived in many states and countries as the son of an Air Force officer and who aspires to West Point as the preparation for a career in law, told of having been interested in politics, and always having had a conservative view, except in his appearance, since the beginning of junior high school. He is fascinated by Bill Buckley's intelligence, "which seems to me to be great. And he always gives the people who watch his show a chance to understand more fully the issues he discusses. I'm attracted to him because I like to hear him speak, I like the words he comes up with, and he has the ability to point out flaws in his opponent much better than a lot of people. He seems to speak with facts and not from his heart, not with a lot of emotion mixed in. But I don't think it's right when he makes statements that aren't true. And he'll rattle off questions and start pressing the person when they're trying to talk. But you have to fight fire with fire. . . . Often on Mr. Buckley's show he's made to look like a bigot rather than a conservative, and he's not a bigot, he's just realistic, just the way I think and feel. I think Mr. Buckley could produce convincing arguments about anything that you could catch him saying." But this boy acknowledged that what remained with him was Buckley's rhetoric and brilliance; the substance of what he says "doesn't stick with me."

Some of it, however, did, as his conclusions evidenced: "Most of what he says on his show is very much in agreement with what I think; sometimes there's something I don't understand completely, or completely agree with. I think his feelings on the war, his feelings on nuclear weapons and even his social feelings are not unlike my own. So I can say that he is a good spokesman for me." I asked him about Buckley's habitual resort to the personal attack, the deliberate misquotation, the strategic interruption, the monopoly of the microphone, and the boy replied: "Well, I'd have to say I approve of this in my spokesman." But he was amused at the idea that Bill Buckley was "too pink," as some people in Sharon, Connecticut, as well as in Arizona and New Mexico, have alleged: "I would say that Mr. Buckley is as far to the Right as you would want him to be. I think that by the time you get so conservative that he seems too far to the Left, you're too conservative."

A twenty-nine-year-old geologist who had just got his degree told me that he had not known he was a conservative until he read Ayn Rand during his second year at Washington University in St. Louis; he was then eighteen. Like almost all the YAF people I interviewed in the Washington headquarters, in New York, and in various parts of the back country, he was the son of college graduates who had always barely managed to maintain a middle-class position and of whom he spoke the almost changeless litany: "Whatever they had, they worked hard to get. And they knew that education means a better job and more money." My informant himself was doing graduate work at Cornell when Bill Buckley was running for the Mayoralty of New York, several hundred miles away, and, though it was a difficult thing to do in his current economic position, he sent a twenty-five-dollar contribution to Buckley's campaign: he had recently joined YAF, subscribed to *National Review,* and begun to devour the free-market economists. It was interesting too to hear him ascribe his own adherence to YAF and Buckleyism, and the conversion of liberal students whom he had known on various campuses, to revulsion at "growing permissiveness, a general lowering of the quality of education in universities, and a decline of standards among students—low academic standards, low personal standards." The latter, he explained, meant chiefly appearance and allergy to cleanliness. One of the most intelligent men I met in YAF, the geologist, whose field work had brought him into close contact with the salt of the earth in all parts of the country, tended to correlate political conservatism in the main with a religious fundamentalism that he himself mocked but that he found very rife in YAF, among both Protestants and Catholics; only in Texas did he encounter rich men's sons and daughters in the ranks.

"YAF members will support the Buckleys for whatever they're running for," he said. "They have a very high opinion of the

Buckleys. I think just the fact that Bill Buckley runs the only national-circulation conservative magazine in the country puts him in the position where, even if one disagrees with some or many of his ideas, one still admires and respects him." The areas of disagreement turned out to be rather narrow: religion—many YAF members have no love for Catholicism—and sexual morality; but there is some resentment, too, that Buckley is as wealthy and talked-about as he is; he is occasionally spoken of as "the liberal establishment's conservative."

Both the geologist and a Texan, five years older, who holds a doctorate in mathematics and works in a government weapons laboratory, found the Buckleys insufficiently libertarian in the matter of the draft and of sex; but both agreed that there must be strict curbs on speech and assembly. So did a thirty-four-year-old professor of biochemistry, a Floridian who, like his parents, had voted for George Wallace in 1968. His admiration for the Buckleys, however, was tempered by a Mormon upbringing and the attitude toward Catholics that that entails. Others said that their ideal ticket for 1972 would be one consisting of Bill Buckley and Reagan. A few—a very few—observed that, as one of them said, "while Buckley's done more for the conservative movement than anybody else, in spite of this he's done half of what he could have done. He lacks commitment."

Such criticism of any of the Buckleys, however, is extremely rare in YAF circles, especially since the libertarian uprising of 1969, which has really eliminated almost all the Buckleys' critics. These in any event tend to diminish in number and vehemence in direct proportion to their geographical proximity to the Boston-New York-Washington megalopolitan area. On the whole, YAF is very nearly as single-mindedly loyal to the founding brothers as it was at its inception.

The period that led to the birth of YAF was also that in which Buckley recruited William F. Rickenbacker, son of the First World War aviator and later airline president, to the editorial board of *National Review*. Three years younger than Buckley, Rickenbacker is a Harvard graduate, a competent serious pianist and an occasional music critic, a master of eight languages in addition to his own, an athlete, a flier, an excellent financial analyst, and a firm believer in God and the free market—or, perhaps one should say, in the free market and God. He is also a perpetually adolescent smart-aleck, as his various essays in *National Review* attest (most notably his tirade against any kind of public-health legislation: he is a great believer in getting rid of venereal disease by lodging tort actions against its donors), to say nothing of the "Song of the Wild Goose" that he wrote in contempt of the Russians' pioneer woman cosmonaut and that *National Review* did not quite dare to print, though Buckley gleefully reproduces it in his introduction to Rickenbacker's book, *The Fourth House*, and again in his own 1972 book, *Inveighing We Will Go*; but one stanza ought to suffice to portray the poet's soul:

> Yon zombie astrobabe doth say
> All systems go, virago—
> Then padlaunched from the cuntdown, yea,
> She'll hump Yuri Garago.

Rickenbacker believes that, if Buckley and Thurmond had supported Reagan (or even merely abstained from backing Nixon) in 1968, Neanderthal (though to Rickenbacker, who always had at least the sense to wish no part of Nixon, he would seem Galahad) would have entered the White House in 1969. He argues that the conservatives backed Nixon in the hope of at least getting a few Cabinet positions, and that "only the incurably innocent may complain" of Nixon's betrayal of conservatism—a refreshing and accurate appraisal. What seems initially to have attracted Buckley was Rickenbacker's "hold of the English language" and "a streak of madcap irony that I have found very nearly indispensable in those with whom one cohabits in the house of ideology." (The earlier sample may be invoked again here.) Rickenbacker, who professes admiration for Mencken, Weaver, and Nock, is not Buckley's match, however, either as stylist or as ideologist—nuances tend to escape him; he is happiest with the dirk in language and the cudgel in ideas. Though he has left *National Review* to publish *Rickenbacker Report* ("the investor's edge in the best or worst of times"), he has not loosened his ties with the Buckley circle, where he continues to be esteemed, though his libertarianism (especially in economics) is more nearly pure (and therefore heartless) than theirs; indeed, one would be tempted, did he not profess religion, to wonder whether he had been trapped young by Ayn Rand. What is one to think, after all, of a rich man who refuses, even if in jest (*vide* Freud on the subject), to be interviewed unless he is guaranteed thirty dollars an hour?

Another of the early associates—one who was to attempt to lead a schism in YAF, if only by proxy—was Murray Rothbard, who teaches economics at the Polytechnic Institute of Brooklyn. Since his defection from the ranks (though he has begun again to appear in *National Review*), Rothbard has at times been the object of various disobliging and (occasionally) not wholly accurate comments by Buckley, into whose circle he was originally brought by Meyer after Buckley had published an article in *Commonweal* in 1952 in which he espoused a far more libertarian position than he takes today, though, Rothbard points out, Buckley made his libertarianism contingent on the prior defeat of the "international Communist conspiracy" by means of a totalitarian bureaucracy, which would be disbanded after victory. At that time Rothbard, an economist who had done all his undergraduate and graduate work at Columbia, was an analyst for the William Volker Fund. This, he explained, was "an obscure but important Right-Wing foundation [that] financed a large portion of conservative libertarian scholarship. Its money came from a big Kansas City merchant."

Another of the Fund's personnel was Frank Meyer, "and he introduced me to Buckley. Meyer had been the head of the Workers' School in Chicago, which was the second top training ground of the Communist Party, and a member of the National Committee. Then he became senior theoretician at *National Review*, after he retired from the Communist movement to his mountain top in Woodstock. I think John Chamberlain discovered him and brought him into the movement." Rothbard emphasised that so many of the early *National Review* people were Jews and/or former Communists, and he recalled an attack on them by Kendall that was based on this fact: none of the editors, Kendall said after his departure from the board, was a real Midwestern American Protestant but all were Jews or Catholics. Schlamm, according to Rothbard, was too eager for a war of annihilation against Russia for even his colleagues' stomachs, and Rothbard reminded me that since his return to Germany Schlamm had gained a huge following there through his constant irredentist cries for revenge on the eastern barbarians.

Rothbard was close to Frank Chodorov, the Right anarchist who had so strong an influence on Buckley in his early years and who founded the Intercollegiate Society of Individualists in 1953 with Buckley as president—it became the Intercollegiate Studies Institute in 1968 "because the head of it then said that the business men, their contributors, didn't like the word *individuals*, they considered individuals as sort of Communist." By 1960, however, a rupture had begun between Buckley and Rothbard because of Rothbard's rigid and rather unrealistic *laisser-faire* economics but also and more significantly because of his endorsement of Khrushchev's visit to President Eisenhower (whom Buckley was denouncing for shaking hands with the alleged murderer of countless Ukrainian peasants; when Rothbard offered the parallel of Eisenhower's responsibility in the deaths of countless German civilians, reason gave way to emotional casuistry and obfuscatory rhetoric) and his vigorous advocacy of a foreign policy based on peace. Ultimately, Rothbard says, Buckley made an infantile personal attack on him at a public summer session of the ISI.

"Meyer was visiting us once during the water shortage years before," Rothbard said, "when we had a dripping faucet and he was quite concerned about the shortage. My wife said the repair was up to the landlord, and somehow he got the idea that I was deliberately turning on the water to somehow screw the landlord, which is impossible in New York anyway because the landlord only pays a fixed amount for water. At any rate, this story went around the Right Wing, and Buckley said in public that Rothbard's the kind of person who runs the water to ruin the landlord." Several years later, after Rothbard had published a hostile analysis of the traditional conservatives in *Ramparts*—it is curious how ready all these people are to write for journals that they do not respect and would not read except, perhaps, in the line of duty— "Buckley said to somebody who'd raised my name: 'Oh, yes, Rothbard has been wandering around for many years and now he's found his home in the freak house.'"

The *Ramparts* article foreshadowed Rothbard's encapsulation of libertarianism in a conversation late in 1971: "Libertarianism is essentially a belief in individual liberty, first and foremost. And this means, as far as we're concerned, *laisser-faire* economics, civil liberties, and peace—I'm more extreme than the ACLU. Conservatism clashes with civil-libertarianism right down the line." Rothbard claimed to have Meyer's backing on this point to a considerable extent, though he said, quite accurately, that Meyer, though often privately critical of Buckley, would not criticise him in public or to outsiders. Rothbard's libertarians extend their advocacy of individual freedom to the whole range of private consensual conduct, including abortion, the use of drugs, and unrestrained utterance, in contrast to Buckley, who said late in 1971 that, as he

had often written, he still believed that "advocates of certain doctrines" did not have an absolute right to propound them: "I don't
think anybody has the right to say: 'Let's burn all the niggers.' "
(The illustration that he chose is interesting.) Another element in
Rothbard's break with *National Review* circles, he said, was the
strong monarchist sentiment there. Buckley's friendship with Otto
von Habsburg, the pretender to the non-existent Austro-Hungarian
throne, is anything but a secret, of course: Buckley neither hides
it nor flaunts it, and has himself disclosed that they are both members of a very secret group that meets in Europe two or three
times a year, without any fanfare, to discuss world problems from
a Right-Wing point of view and to weigh possible courses of
action. But Rothbard recalls discussions among his friends at *National Review* in which the theme was simply which monarchy
ought to be restored—Meyer, he says, favored the recall of the
Habsburgs to Austria-Hungary and of the Stuarts to the United
Kingdom. Others wanted a Habsburg monarch for America.
Bozell and many of his academic supporters are Carlists, according to Rothbard, and in fact Franco expelled one of them from
Spain for his efforts to gain support for a Carlist monarch. And
in a *New York Times* article in January of 1971 Rothbard denounced "Burnham's recent call in *National Review* for a new
Bismarck for America and for a re-evaluation of Fascism" as "the
logical culmination of conservative statism and obscurantism."

Rothbard's discourse in *Ramparts* (15 June 1968) blamed Joseph
McCarthy primarily for "transforming the Right Wing from an
isolationist and quasi-libertarian movement to an anti-Communist
one" (he describes himself as an extreme Right-Winger from his
intellectual beginnings—he is a year Bill Buckley's junior). Quoting Buckley's 1952 *Commonweal* article—endorsing "the extensive
and productive tax laws that are needed to support a vigorous
anti-Communist policy," in the furtherance of which "we have to
accept Big Government for the duration—for neither an offensive
nor a defensive war can be waged . . . except through the instrument of a totalitarian bureaucracy within our shores," Rothbard
emphasised that this was written at the height of the Korean war,
which, it will be remembered, Buckley was expecting to erupt into
a major conflict. Rothbard emphasised that *National Review* became the vehicle for propagating this anti-Communist militancy
throughout the Right, and that the influential positions of so many
former Communists in its editorial board served further to add

both expertise and authority to its preachments. Among those whom he listed as expiating their earlier profane love in this new sacred union were Chamberlain, de Toledano, and Herberg, the latter-day New Jersey theologist; and he cited (without naming him) Chamberlain's letter agreeing that the draft was contrary to civil liberties but that it must be excused because of the nastiness of the Communist cell at *Time* in the 1930s.

Led by such men as these, reinforced by Bozell and "another repellent political theorist," Kendall, whom he denounced in especial for his thesis of the majority's right and duty to suppress those who disturb it, the new conservatives were accused by Rothbard of having repudiated their former intellectual leaders—Mencken, Nock, Thoreau, Jefferson, Paine, who "either dropped from sight or were roundly condemned as rationalists, atheists or anarchists" —and their old basic thesis that the enemy was always, in whatever form, the state; instead, he asserted, the new heroes were "such despotic reactionaries as Burke, Metternich, de Maistre," and, in our own history, Hamilton and Madison, all of whom favored the primacy of order (one is reminded of the age-old maxim of every ruling class, "better injustice than disorder") and a strong élitist central government. The animating vision of *National Review* conservatives, Rothbard said, was the annihilation of the Soviet Union by nuclear attack, and he quotes such statements. It is his basic thesis that the new conservatives are simply oligarchs and indeed have every reason to form a united front with the liberals of consensus such as Daniel Patrick Moynihan and Sidney Hook; that Big Business is at least as great an enemy as Big Government (when they can be distinguished from each other), that America is becoming a corporate state in the classic Fascist mold ("As Gabriel Kolko pointed out, all the various measures of federal regulation and welfare-statism that Left and Right alike have always believed to be mass movements against Big Business are now not only backed to the hilt by Big Business, but were originated by it for the very purpose of shifting from a free market to a cartelized economy that would benefit it"), that "even the Cold War—including the war in Vietnam—was begun and maintained and escalated by the liberals themselves." Now this would be almost impossible to challenge; and Rothbard is again eminently right when he continues: "On the domestic front, virtually the only conservative interests are to suppress Negroes ('shoot looters,' 'crush those riots'), to call for more power for the police so as not to 'shield the criminal' (i.e., not to protect his libertarian rights), to enforce prayer in the public schools, to put Reds and other subversives and 'seditionists' in jail and to carry on the crusade for war abroad. There is little in the thrust of this program with which liberals can now disagree; any disagreements are tactical or matters of degree only." Substantially, this is as true in 1972 as it was in 1968.

Rothbard's piece points out that a number of independent Right-Wing libertarians were arriving independently and simultaneously at similar conclusions—one of them was Karl Hess; another was Jerome Tuccille—and that many young conservatives were aligning themselves with the Left against the draft, rediscovering for the nth time how close the true conservative and the true radical frequently are (for it is his thesis that the Buckleys and *National Review* are not conservative but reactionary—though he will not accept the further fact that in this they truly represent the majority of their fellow citizens). Burnham, he added, had specifically warned against this in his *National Review* column, appending as anathema: "Murray Rothbard has shown how Right-Wing libertarianism can lead to almost as anti-U.S. a position as Left-Wing libertarianism does." Yet one cannot help believing that the truly *conservative* position is not Buckley's or Burnham's or their friends' but Rothbard's:

"The Right Wing has been captured and transformed by élitists and devotees of the European conservative ideals of order and militarism, by witch hunters and global crusaders, by statists who wish to coerce 'morality' and suppress 'sedition.' . . . we have allowed ourselves to sacrifice the American ideals of peace and freedom and anti-colonialism on the altar of a crusade to kill Communists throughout the world; we have surrendered our libertarian birthright into the hands of those who yearn to restore the Golden Age of the Holy Inquisition."

That his school consistently refuses to recognise the inevitable consequence of uncontrolled economic libertarianism—precisely that evolution into the corporate state that he condemns and that invariably destroys *all* libertarianism—cannot be gainsaid. But it in no way dilutes the validity of his analysis, or the accuracy of his description. Rothbard was to be one of the earlier of the authentically conservative challengers of the majority dominating the American Right.

XV

"I FIND that Bill Buckley has a capacity to laugh at himself," Michael Harrington, who has debated him off and on for twenty years, very accurately observed; but this capacity is much more likely to be visible today than it was when Harrington first debated Buckley, and even today it emerges much more in private than in public or even in print. Harrington, who was with *The Catholic Worker* when these encounters began, and who became co-chairman of the Socialist Party, is three years Buckley's junior, a graduate of Holy Cross who abandoned the study of law after a year of it at Yale. "Part of the problem that Bill has had," he said, "is that he became a pundit much too early, and this really kept him, I think, from having the opportunity to study and develop."

But Harrington is properly shocked by those liberals (for lack of a better term) and supercilious members of the actual Left who shrug off the Buckleys. "I take them very seriously," he said, "because, for one thing, of the obvious trend in New York State, and certainly among Irish Catholic workers, who've been moving to the Right for thirty, forty years—certainly since the second Roosevelt election [1936], which was the last time they all voted solidly New Deal. The Conservative Party is a very serious development that could be a portent of significant changes in American political life. And the Buckleys obviously are the first family of this not inconsiderable phenomenon." A further element in the Buckleys' importance, Harrington believes, is the fact that their spokesman, Bill, is by far the best spokesman for the whole Right as well: "You've got a second string, which is really not very good and not deep at all."

Harrington's acquaintance with Buckley developed through debates and periodic social gatherings of leading figures in Catholic lay circles—men and women from the Right, including a number of *National Review* people, others of a more centrist position, such as people from *Commonweal*, and the Catholic Left as represented by *The Catholic Worker*. Harrington has also appeared on *Firing Line*, Buckley's television program, and, like so many others, is more than a little preoccupied with the contrasts between the private and the public Buckley; primarily because he is quite aware that neither, however he may contradict the other, is anything but authentic. "Objectively," Harrington said, for example, "his positions are anti-poor, anti-black, etc. Of course they are: there can be no doubt of that. What I can't resolve is the degree to which he is subjectively critical."

At times, too, Harrington has found that casual remarks made in the social atmosphere of the half-hour or so before a debate or a taping will be quite unexpectedly thrown in his face from the platform. On another occasion, in a television discussion of poverty, Harrington's concrete arguments and factual demonstrations were repeatedly countered by Buckley's "trying to drag in the question of socialism, or God—to get back to the generalities, which I kept refusing because we were there to talk about poverty and not abstractions. Being on *Firing Line* is sort of schizophrenic. There's no question that off stage Bill's an extremely charming, likable, friendly guy, and my relationship with him has always been very cordial. At the same time, on stage he can be a nasty, tricky, tough guy." This is an almost universal reaction. Yet the same man who evokes it is the man who, when Father William Clancy of Pittsburgh, a former editor of *Commonweal*, telephoned to ask assistance in enabling his archbishop, in anticipation of imminent elevation to the Sacred College, to meet some New York Catholic intellectual leaders, spontaneously turned over his apartment, his servants, and his cellar to Clancy and insisted that the priest choose the guest list—on which, Harrington emphasised, everyone was to the Left of Buckley, who was the paragon of hosts.

In his earlier polemic days, however, this would have been most unlikely. There is no sign of the capacity to laugh at oneself in his controversies with prominent and less prominent Catholics over those trends in the church that most threatened him—the social and economic concerns voiced by Popes John XXIII and even Paul VI; but in his subsequent attacks on the vulgarisation of the liturgy it would be much more difficult to fault him. It would be even more difficult to disagree.

For there is nothing presumptuous, I think, in the fact that a non-communicant protests the debasement of the Latin Mass to the vernacular. The Roman Catholic Mass, like the King James Version, the Book of Common Prayer, the liturgy of the Greek and Russian Orthodox Churches, and some parts of the Sephardic service, is less the property of a closed religious group than a basic treasure of the common wealth of culture, and against their esthetic desecration it is not only meet but mandatory that all who recognise the outrage protest it. It is hardly necessary to be a Christian, or even the vaguest kind of deist, to feel one's blood run backward at psalms or Nativity stories transposed to the literary level of a small-town afternoon newspaper.

But it is astounding, on close examination, when the same sensibilities that revolt at the debasement of beauty rebel even more fiercely at any effort to interfere with the debasement of human life. Pope John's *Mater et Magistra* and Pope Paul's *Populorum Progressio* and *Humanae Vitae* evoked from the Buckley circle the kind of anguished, angry shrieks that had been used only against the godless Communists, and they have not yet wholly died down in spite of the passage of years and the reasoned, compassionate positions—compassionate as much toward the psychologically as toward the economically impoverished—of those who, regardless of religion, evidenced a more Christian comprehension. But in fact Buckley's quarrel with many in his church had begun before the issuance of any of those frightening encyclicals; to a degree, in fact, it arose out of more venerable documents, Leo XIII's *Rerum Novarum* of 1891 and Pius XI's celebration of its fortieth anniversary, *Quadragesimo Anno,* on the one hand, and Buckley's fanatical adherence to Manchester liberalism, on the other. As Kevin Corrigan cogently pointed out in "God and Man at *National Review*" in *The Catholic World* in February, 1961, Buckley and his fellow-"conservatives" are in reality liberals as the word is correctly used, and political and economic liberalism is a paradoxical philosophy for one who calls himself a Catholic to adopt. Leo XIII rejected both the notion of society as the result of a social contract and the doctrine of the greatest good for the greatest number through the unrestricted operation of the free market; rather, he held, society is a natural, organic community ordained by God, whose will is expressed in "natural law"—the moral authority that bids man pursue good and flee evil, and that "resides in three natural institutions: the Church, the state and the family. Each, in its own realm, exercises authority and applies sanctions to man, who is created morally and naturally free by God."

Corrigan's analysis proceeds to the unescapable conclusion that the old liberalism that rejected the church's view was of necessity the matrix of the new, both of which, he says, share the same "root error"—a kind of Rousseauan belief in man's natural goodness. But, Corrigan shows, the blind religion of the marketplace could not assure the common good because of the market's inevitable susceptibility to distortion, whether temporary or lasting, and equally inevitably its restriction was imperative; but, he says—still very rightly—all the reformers perpetuated the original liberal error of believing economics to be an autonomous domain entirely immune to moral authority. How else could a Buckley have challenged an opponent to prove any difference between the common good and the sum of individual goods? Leo XIII and Pius XI were merely reasserting the moral content of life, even economic life (and one can certainly agree that an economics without morality, like a politics without morality, must of necessity destroy itself, not because it lacks a putative deity but because its rejection of morality robs it of any means of preserving itself against the combination of greed, aggression, and cunning that constantly reappears). Buckley, then, Corrigan argued, wholly flouted the teachings of the church in his espousal of a political/economic creed already condemned by the church because of its mechanistic unconcern with both morals and humanity. (What Corrigan did not, perhaps, sufficiently examine was the *hubris* of Buckley's and his colleagues' efforts to claim the authority of that same natural law and the quality of a moral philosophy for their wholly materialistic dog-eat-dogma.)

The Catholic World gave Buckley space to reply to Corrigan, and it was used as well to cite and attempt to refute other Catholics who had been critical: most notably Professor Francis E. McMahon of Notre Dame, who had really epitomised the whole issue by saying in *America* (17 October 1959) that Buckley's problem was "a woefully inadequate grasp of theological and philosophical principles." Others implied that he had not read the two encyclicals, or perhaps had not read them soon enough, Buckley said; and he proceeded to flaunt a series of rhetorical

arpeggi over several columns of the magazine without even con-
futing one of the arguments that had been raised against him.
Instead he claimed that thousands of loyal Catholics (including
"cardinals and bishops, and *monsignori* and priests") were also
loyal readers of *National Review* and supporters of his views,
and therefore he could not be promulgating ideas contrary to the
church's teaching. The fallacy was too obvious to require notice.
But similar controversies were to persist in the Catholic press;
and in general it was the retarded segment, such as *The Tablet*
of Brooklyn, that alone would uphold Buckleyism.

Pope John's *Mater et Magistra* of 1961, however, detonated a
real explosion on Thirty-fifth Street. "*Mater Si, Magistra No,*"
Buckley said in the editorial in *National Review* that dismissed the
encyclical as "a venture in triviality." To those of little faith or
none such ambivalence about Holy Mother Church—retaining her
in that rôle while revoking her teaching certificate—might seem
the occasion for no more than a superior smile; but that is to
under-estimate the traditional Catholic attitude toward the all-
embracing church and the infallibility of its chief priest as God's
vicar; for, though it be generally stated now that the said infallibility is not infinite but rather is bounded by matters of faith and
morals, there is a certain inconsistency, and not least for a Buckley,
in contending that the domain of men's relations with one another
is outside the jurisdiction of morals. Yet that is precisely the radical position that Buckley and his circle adopted—of far greater
importance, granted, in Catholic circles than elsewhere; but important even *in partibus infidelium* as an indication of the meat
upon which this Caesar hath fed. In short, Buckley made it clear,
the Pope of Rome was a know-nothing in the political and economic sciences—except, of course, when he said the things that
Buckley would have had him say. But to invoke the sanctity of
the church and the supposed authority of God against absentee
landlords, greedy monopolists, and prepotent oligarchs, to pretend that against these there existed, and the church and its deity
or his vicar proposed to champion, rights for the helpless, the
more or less enslaved, the unprivileged was to distort the supreme
moral law of Adam Smith.

In matters of sexual morality the Buckleys would have us all—
heathen, Turk, and Jew, to borrow from Blake—bound by the
sexologists in the Vatican and its overseas branches. As good
Catholics, Buckleys argue that the church must always be para-

mount to the state, which indeed (for them) exists by its sanction, and that the enemy of civilisation is secularism. Natural—
which is to say divine—law has ordained the uniquely right rules
for the relations of mankind on all levels, the devout Catholic
holds—but suddenly an exception is found through a casuistic
conclusion that economics and some aspects of politics have nothing to do with human relations but are so suprahumanly and
infallibly governed by abstract forces having likewise nothing to
do with morality that the church can only ratify the workings
of *force majeure*.

It is the same kind of opportunism that Buckleys are so ready
to denounce in lesser breeds and that made it possible for Bill
Buckley to appeal twice for help to that American Civil Liberties
Union that at other times he has been (and remains) so ready to
traduce. The first occasion (the citation is *Buckley v. Meng, 230
N.Y.S. (2d) 924,* decided in 1962) arose in 1961, when *National
Review* sought to rent the auditorium of Hunter College in New
York for a program favoring the French Right and opposing the
liberation of Algeria. President John Meng of the college, backed
by the city's Board of Higher Education, refused the application
(though the college auditorium had always been available to Left
and "liberal" groups of the most arcane and, sometimes, questionable descriptions) on the ground that *National Review* wanted
the premises for a purpose that was political and contrary to the
college's and the board's policy of primarily academic use of the
facilities. The New York Civil Liberties Union properly entered
the case as *amicus curiae* on the ground that this was a constitu-
tionally defective position, inasmuch as official policy approved
the leasing of the auditorium for non-academic purposes "compatible with the attitudes of Hunter College as a public institution
of higher learning." This, the court held, was unconstitutionally
vague in its delineations or unconstitutional in the principle of
selection that it embodied. The authorities did not appeal and
National Review's scheduled program went forward.

One side effect was Wechsler's cessation of debates with Buckley, as noted; another was the opportunity afforded to Roger
Baldwin to meet the leading figures in *National Review* at that
time and form some impression of them, colored to a degree by
his tendency to see in almost everyone else the reflection of his
own remarkable decencies. His view of them as men whose ethics
in debate were impeccable, for example, would hardly be sup-

ported by transcripts of such things as Rusher's concealment of
material facts, when presenting favorable witnesses on *The Advocates* on educational television, that would vitiate much of the
credibility of their testimony—offering, for instance, a professor
to speak in favor of public money for religiously affiliated schools
and making it appear that the professor's college was a lay institution without any selfish interest in the matter.

Buckley's second appeal to the American Civil Liberties Union
was made ten years later and the question was a more complicated
one: the issue of freedom of speech from prior restraint—on
which the ACLU's position had always been clear and unexceptionable—was inextricably interwoven with that of the closed-
shop labor-union contract. For years the American Federation of
Television and Radio Actors had had contracts with all major
broadcasters, under which any regular performer (in whatever
capacity, whether as a soap-opera actor, a solicitor of suckers for
products and services, a reciter of news and weather forecasts,
a commentator, a professional propagandist) must be a member
of AFTRA in order to ply his trade. The legality of the closed-
shop contract was almost hallowed by this time; the courts, with
the ACLU's blessing, had made provision for those whose con-
sciences would not permit them to enroll in these legions, the
expedient being to rule that they need not join or take part in
activities but they must pay the dues imposed on members of
comparable status—a decision, in short, that is rather an evasion
than a resolution of a problem that very nearly defies resolution.
Buckley's action against the union, initiated early in 1971, raised
a new issue: he contended that the AFTRA closed-shop contract
constituted an unconstitutional prior restraint of his freedom of
utterance by making it contingent on his membership in a specific
group—and, moreover, a group that he found repugnant.

Buckley's request was troubling to the ACLU. Some of its directors had long thought that the policy on the closed shop required review from a pure civil-liberties standpoint; some believed
that the closed shop represented a paramount civil-liberties good;
some, of course, were influenced wittingly or not by their own
attitudes toward Buckley and his views and associates. In any
event, the decision was not to be made lightly, and, inasmuch as
Buckley's case was not likely to come to trial immediately, Aryeh
Neier, executive director of the ACLU, wrote to him that the
whole question—in particular and in general—would be taken

up when the Board of Directors met in early October. Meanwhile
various ACLU committees began consideration of the several aspects of the problem and preparing recommendations for the
board. Buckley found all this rather irritating: it was not his way
of arriving at decisions. In the same week of June in which *New
York* magazine ran an article about his broadcasting operations that
caused him to complain of the reporting, *Nation's Business* published an interview with him in which he said that Nat Hentoff,
a columnist for *The Village Voice*, and Tom Wicker of *The
New York Times*, both far to his Left, were giving him support
—Hentoff by joining him as a co-plaintiff, Wicker by contributing to the cost of the litigation and authorising Buckley to say
so publicly; then the interviewer asked whether he had heard
from the ACLU since its statement that it was going to review
its position. He replied:

"My guess is that the executive director of the ACLU is favorably disposed to this case, but that he is going to face a lot of
trouble from those old trade-union types who put in a lot of
money to keep ACLU alive."

Retraction and apology came quickly from both Buckley and
Nation's Business. Six months later he could admit the enormity
of the gaffe and the laxity behind it: "Somebody told me, somewhere along the line, that the ACLU's consistent failure to move
on anything to do with right-to-work issues simply had to do with
their acknowledgment of reality: the reality being that they get
most of their contributions from the liberal trade-union side." (He
himself had contributed a thousand dollars after *Buckley v. Meng.*)
Later, he admitted, he had learned that this was simply not the
case. He was probably on much firmer ground when he told
Nation's Business that there were people on the ACLU's board
who "aren't going to want to see themselves identified with anything as scabbish as this."

After a great deal of study and debate the board did indeed decide not to intervene at that time in *Buckley v. AFTRA*. There is
nothing in the *acta* or in anything Neier has said in conversation
to indicate that he favored or opposed Buckley's position. The
board took the view—in my opinion, wrongly, but this was a case
in which no view could be arrived at easily—that Buckley had
suffered and was suffering no infringement of his First Amendment rights because no prior restraint had been attempted in that
the union had never sought to censor him or to prevent him—

except by requiring membership or tribute—from appearing on
the air; and that, further, it was prohibited from so doing by the
Landrum-Griffin Act, and any actual violation could be dealt with
in proceedings before the National Labor Relations Board. So
Neier wrote to Buckley in October, 1971; two months later
Buckley replied, taking issue with the ACLU on the ground that
the requirement of AFTRA membership as a condition of speaking on the air did indeed infringe his rights. At the same time, *The
Wall Street Journal* and that sad commentary on the Jewish intellectual, *Commentary*, were attacking the ACLU, without any
real ground, for almost never acting on behalf of the civil liberties
of the Right—a cavalier attitude to the facts worthy of Buckley.
Neier replied to Buckley early in 1972, putting forth the ACLU's
position but making it, in the opinion of any disinterested champion of free expression, no jot or tittle sounder:

"Under Section 8(a)(3) and Section 8(b)(2) of the National
Labor Relations Act, and the decisions of the National Labor
Relations Board and the Courts in interpreting those provisions,
you cannot be compelled to become a member of the Union, to
obey any Union regulations, or to be subject to any Union disciplinary proceedings. The most that can be required of you, and
then only under a Union security provision agreed to by your
employer, is that you tender to the Union an amount of money
equal to regular dues and initiation fees. The tender of such an
amount, however, in no way obligates you to accept membership
in the Union, be bound by any Union rules, or become subject
to any Union disciplinary proceedings."

Neier added that this does not constitute an infringement of
freedom of speech in the view of the ACLU. Citing Supreme
Court decisions to the effect that a union is required to bargain
for all employees, the ACLU saw no injustice in making all share
the cost of this representation; it cited further the contributor's
right to recover from the union that portion of his dues that is used
for political purposes that he does not approve. "If at any time,"
the letter concluded, "AFTRA should attempt or threaten in any
way to discipline you for anything which you might say or print,
or cause any broadcasting station or publication to refuse to employ you for any ideas which you may express, the ACLU will
stand ready to defend your rights."

One is tempted to resort to that ancient sneer, *pilpul*. These are
paper rights, of which the average union member is not likely to

be informed by his "representatives," nor are they likely to approve his invoking them if he ever finds out about them. In Buckley's case, it is true, economic weapons would be derisory; but the principle that he has invoked is a major one and ought not to be sacrificed to sentimental loyalties to *Solidarity Forever* and the 1920's.

And yet the standard here is no lower—unfortunately, too, no higher—than Buckley's in his first two books, his anthology called *The Committee and Its Critics*, his misguided test of the limits of the free market's tolerance, or his ambiguous break, if it was that, with the John Birch Society.

Subtitled *A Calm Review of the House Committee on Un-American Activities* and credited to William F. Buckley Jr. and the Editors of *National Review*, the anthology was published by Putnam's in 1962 and subsequently put into paperback by Regnery. Four of the authors—each chapter has its own—were not *National Review* editors: C. Dickerson Williams, counsel to Buckley and the magazine; Irving Ferman (mistakenly described as former chief counsel to the ACLU), once a director of the ACLU's Washington office; George N. Crocker, a lawyer who wrote *Roosevelt's Road to Russia*; and Ross D. Mackenzie, then vice-chairman of the *Yale Daily News*. The book is a much more professional and refined attempt to do for HUAC what Buckley and Bozell had sought to accomplish years earlier for McCarthy. In most instances the title of a chapter and its author's name are reasonably indicative of content.

Burnham examined—and vindicated—"The Investigating Power of Congress"; Kendall, who knew something of the matter from his service on the Latin American desks of the State Department and the CIA, as well as his academic infiltration of the hosts of darkness, dealt with "Subversion in the Twentieth Century"; Rickenbacker offered "A Short History of the Committee and a Chronology, 1946–60"; Karl Hess wrote about "A Year's Work (1958)"; de Toledano reviewed "The Hiss Case," of which he sought to make Nixon and HUAC the heroic discoverers; M. Stanton Evans, with a fine disregard for the record, both printed and cinematic, reported "The San Francisco Riots"; Buckley, already its historiographer, dealt with "The Campaign Against HUAC"; Williams discussed "The Committee's Procedures," conceding some procedural faults but forced to fall back on the defense that things were done worse elsewhere—for instance, in

Canada; Ferman's "Comment by a Civil Libertarian" was a disingenuous greywash (he would have "subversives," not "un-Americans," investigated) that itself challenged his description of himself; Crocker tried, eschewing any and all documentation, to twist the already tortured record into a semblance of achievements under the rubric "HUAC and Legislation"; and Mackenzie provided "A Record of the Committee's Work" that is no more than a mildly descriptive catalogue of hearings, consultations, and reports.

The majority of the authors—Williams and Ferman excepted—made amazing efforts in order to smear HUAC critics, especially civil-liberties groups, and distort or ignore their counter-evidence, as they tried to pretend out of existence the California Bar Association's fierce censure of the committee and its methods. Buckley's own chapter purported to show that there were only two sources of opposition to the HUAC: organised—the Communist Party and its fronts; and unorganised—"excitable and rebellious students," "arch humanitarians" and "doctrinaire advocates of the 'open society.'" All these latter, of course, were the dupes of the organised and constituted the Confused Majority, reinforced by the Purist Minority, "those who endorse the exact philosophical position of John Stuart Mill," the absolutist of freedom. This minority had not been tainted by the vile Reds, but it was blinded by ignorance of all realities, including Communism, subversion, and the "traditional American way of treating unassimilable minorities," which the author of the phrase nowhere defined or even, in the favorite locution of his senior, Kendall, adumbrated. But in the next breath it turned out after all that not only the Confused Majority but also the Purist Minority had been duped by the CP's systematic and comprehensive slanders of the committee. The italic synopses that preceded the chapters added to the pretentiousness of this very useless book—or, to be more precise, this book whose usefulness is defined by what it reveals of those who put it together.

The bit of sharp practice reported at this period by *Time* makes one think of Rickenbacker rather than of Buckley, though it is he to whom it is apparently quite accurately discredited. The University of North Carolina had invited Buckley to address it, and he did; but some of his audience, gathered to hear him descant on Freedom and the Welfare State, thought his pearls had a differently familiar luster. He was actually reading an article (the

one in which he questioned Kenneth Tynan's potency, in fact)
that he had written for *Playboy* for thirty-five hundred dollars,
then read in Chicago for a thousand; he was asking only four
hundred fifty in the less prosperous South. The sponsoring group
would not pay, however, and insisted that he scale down further.

The more-or-less rupture with the John Birch Society raised
questions of the same moral character. It led also to a rupture with
that strange fanatic, Revilo P. Oliver, who had always said that
it was Buckley who had first lured him from the classic world into
politics, and who did not communicate with Buckley again for
almost ten years until, having received an inquiry concerning the
book in hand, he sent copies of that letter and his own pathetically
insolent reply to Buckley and Bozell. *National Review* found it
impossible to do otherwise than denounce Robert Welch, the
founder of the Birch Society, for his grotesque attacks on Eisenhower and other equally likely agents as conscious tools of international Communism, and for some of his most extreme fantasies
about minorities. But at the same time the magazine emphasised that
it was not denouncing all Welch's followers, or even the society
as a whole—rather like Moscow's and Peking's distinctions between the imperialist American government and the peace-loving
American people. Thus *National Review*, sometimes under Buckley's signature, sometimes under other authors' names, sometimes
institutionally, frequently reiterated its conviction that there was
much that was good in the Birch creed and many fine fellows in
the ranks; and few indeed of the fine fellows have ever deserted
the Buckleys or their works—one has only to look at *Human
Events* or *American Opinion*, the Birch organ, to see how many
National Review authors appear there too. Birch eminences may be
noted also in fraternisation with *National Review* leaders on boards
and councils of such organisations as the American Conservative
Union and YAF—even with those who, like Kirk, have expressly
condemned the Birch Society. And Birch books were distributed
free to all the guests at the 1972 Washington's Birthday dinner of
the Conservative Party of New York, at which James Buckley
spoke.

Bill Buckley became concerned at the failure, or refusal, of
Oliver, a brilliant perfectionist scholar, to make those distinctions
that Buckley regarded as vital. Oliver believed, for instance, that
the Pentagon had rehearsed John Kennedy's funeral before the
assassination because of secret advance knowledge; and he had

definitive views on Final Solutions for those whom he considered
Gentiles. Some of the ideological company that he kept did not
at all please Buckley, who made the point. "Before you got me
interested in politics," Oliver replied, according to Buckley's
printed and oral accounts, "I'd as soon have split the skull of anyone
who split an infinitive, but in *politics* what matters is that you pull
together." The chasm became such that *National Review* dropped
Oliver's name from the masthead, but the friendship continued
until Oliver terminated it.

In *Cruising Speed* Buckley tells of asking Oliver why he thought
National Review had attacked the Birchers. Oliver offered three
possible explanations, of which, he said, he inclined toward the
first two: (1) Buckley had been misled by his editors; (2) he was
jealous of Welch's influence among conservatives and was motivated by vanity and the desire for power; (3) he was an agent of
the Communist Party. Subsequently, before Oliver proved to be
too extreme in his reactionism and his anti-Semitism for even the
Birch Society, the University of Illinois, at which he was teaching
literature, began proceedings to deprive him of tenure because of
his political views, and Buckley wrote a column fiercely defending
his rights and citing his professional record; at the same time Buckley denounced Oliver's notions about the Kennedy assassination.
A few days later Buckley received a little package in the mail. He
recognised Oliver's handwriting on the label; inside he found a
very small replica of a Florentine knife with a card: "To stab
your next friend in the back with, if you have a friend."

The Conservative Party of New York, which was to become so
closely identified with the Buckley brothers of Connecticut, was
not initially a Buckley enterprise. Two young New York lawyers,
J. Daniel Mahoney and his wife's brother, Kieran O'Doherty, were
its actual originators, and its purpose was to counter the state's
Liberal Party and what they viewed as the steady movement of
the Republican Party toward the Left, in the persons of such radicals as Nelson Rockefeller, Jacob Javits, and Richard Nixon. They
admired Buckley and *National Review*, they were thoroughly at
home with *The News*, the militant know-nothing tabloid, and
they were probably somewhat frightened by the Birchers. Mahoney and O'Doherty therefore in 1961 called upon Buckley,
who had broken with the Society, and Marvin Liebman, whom

they already knew from a heroic, if failed, joint venture to keep Khrushchev out of the United States. Liebman's Madison Avenue public-relations office became the forcing-bed and, through Buckley's enthusiasm, Frank Meyer was brought in to be, as it were, the Dr. Spock to the infant movement's nannies.

Liebman, who moved to London in 1969, is extremely reticent about all his connections with the Buckleys (whose name is the only Sesame to his door) and their associates, except to say that he knows and admires all of them. He will concede that, with his help, the Buckleys are on the way to the top in the United States, and he professes to maintain close and constant touch with them. This contradicts their and their friends' accounts. Liebman said in February of 1972 that he was short of money but "I can get money for anything out of anyone." Certainly he was not living like anything but a transplanted Seventh Avenue spender—though Seventh Avenue does not easily put down roots in British soil, which tends to reject the alien organ. Like Lejeune, whose extreme Right-Wing attitudes extend into his personal associations and whom, therefore, it is unlikely that Liebman really knows (neither mentions the other), Liebman, who is forty-seven, has never married. His Georgian-Victorian villa in London W.2 is most impressively and expensively done, staffed, and furnished. He has produced eight plays since he moved to London; half have failed. When he needs money, he returns to New York for a bit—thus he was there in the winter of 1972 while his close contact, Bill Buckley, was conferring with Right-Wing British politicians on his way home from Vietnam and Israel. Liebman says his plays are principally American-financed.

The London telephone directory does not list Liebman's home, but it credits him with a public-relations office in The Strand— where he is unknown because, investigators report, he has no office there. He has told British interviewers for three years that he handled political public relations for Goldwater, Reagan, and Nixon, and there seems no reason to doubt the association, at any rate, whatever the accuracy of the details, which tend to vary. He is often likened to Jack Valenti, who enjoyed, if that is the word, a relation with L. B. Johnson rather similar to Liebman's with the Buckleys and the Birchers. Small in appearance like Lejeune, who is otherwise quite unlike him in every way, Liebman is widely disliked and distrusted in London, and those who talk to him, especially in his own surroundings, have the uncomfortable feeling that "everything about him belies what he says. He is as reticent and as hard to find as if he were hiding a body on the premises."

On the other hand, he has identified himself as one of Nixon's 1968 campaign managers, and in July of 1969 he described one of his tricks for an interviewer from *The Manchester Guardian*: "At low points in the campaign, when the candidate wants love, . . . we have him walking slow and lonely up to the rostrum to win sympathy. . . . 'The Battle Hymn of the Republic' is played softly in the background. . . . At a middle stage we have him happy happy happy with his wife and children all around him." He professes unsullied Right-Wing sympathies, but his frightened reluctance to talk to anyone he does not know leads some interviewers to be skeptical, as is his friend de Toledano. Most of his friends, Liebman said early in 1972, are liberals, "but they forgive my sympathies and my activities if I'm just doing these things for money." He sold his public-relations and fund-raising business, he said, to finance his theatrical beginnings in Britain. These must have been far less complicated than simultaneous tutelage of the Committee of One Million Against the Admission of Communist China to the United Nations, the American Committee for Aid to Katanga Freedom Fighters, YAF, the American Afro-Asian Educational Exchange, Inc., the Emergency Committee for Chinese Refugees, the separate Jewish and Christian anti-Communist guerrillas, and the Committee for the Monroe Doctrine (which came to life in Bill Buckley's apartment), even though Buckley was at his elbow in all of them. One can only marvel at the sacrifices of these men, who, under such burdens—and the list is far from complete: it is merely illustrative—nonetheless assumed the patriotic obligation of rearing the Conservative Party, even as they continued to maintain avuncular watch over Chodorov's Intercollegiate Society of Individualists.

Not all New York conservatives agreed with Buckley and Liebman, Mahoney and O'Doherty, that a fourth party in the state was the best means of achieving their ends: some thought that the proper method, both philosophically and practically, was to oust what they called the liberals who had taken the Republican Party away from its exploited conservative rank and file. The chief devils among these liberals were Rockefeller and Javits, whose liberalism might be said to have been somewhat to the Right of Bismarck's and Winston Churchill's. Even the sponsors of the new party believed it could work only in New York State, where state-wide candidates of both parties are chosen only in managed conventions. As Mahoney observed with unimpeachable accuracy in *Actions Speak Louder,* his fond narrative of the party's birth and childhood, this system "translated into one blunt fact: at the state level, the 'ins' stayed in." It is quite probable that Mahoney is equally right (though perhaps for reasons that did not occur to him) when he says that without this democratic procedure, the prefabricated character of which even the official Republican leaders had neither the skill nor the common decency to try to hide, neither Rockefeller nor Javits could so often have been renominated. Hence the Conservative Party, the emergence of which should have been welcomed by every honest conservative but also by every honest radical or even progressive. Perhaps indeed it was; but honesty in political circles is almost as rare as intelligence; otherwise the Republican and Democratic Parties would not be the partners in crime that they have been for at least the past half-century.

Meyer's manifesto—or care-and-feeding manual—was commendably brief, and enthusiastically adopted by all the baby's nannies. Recalling the country's greatness, its foundation in "the free energy of free men," and its abject retreat before the "armed might and conspiratorial techniques of Soviet Communism" and "encroaching bureaucracy," as well as rising taxation and inflation unconnected with arms, labor-union power, and (the outstandingly valid count in the indictment) the accelerating rot of what passes for education in this country, Meyer sounded the tocsin against this decline of America into a "socialist society, in which the individual person will count for nothing." One cannot forbear here to observe how consistently these zealots of the individual devote their energies to the conservation of a culture (in the anthropological sense) and a political/economic system that are as implacably hostile to the individual as any dictatorship in history and that are the more effective because they chiefly use the most sophisticated of all weapons to enforce their ends: the public opinion that they shape.

First of all, Meyer's Declaration of Principles proclaimed, the Conservative Party dedicated itself to victory over Communism as "the lodestar of all our international action," which required total independence of the United Nations, since American action must be "determined by our just national interests, which are the interests of the free world." Corollarily, "internal sabotage and subversion" and "the Communist drive to infiltrate and undermine our institu-

tions" (*pace The Cross and the Flag*: ed. and pub., Rev. Gerald
L. K. Smith) must be ruthlessly suppressed. The other major purpose was a "return to the principles of the Constitution," which
meant not merely "the limitation of government to its essential and
necessary activities" (in itself an unexceptionable aspiration, until,
of course, interpreted) but also the "return of all possible activities
to the several States; of all possible activities of the States to the
local communities; and of all possible governmental activities at
every level to the private energies of individuals and non-govern-
mental associations." What this came down to was drastic reduc-
tion in government payrolls and hence in taxation, the emancipation
of "the working man, industry and the community at large from
the imperial domination of trade-union bosses," the end of all farm
subsidies and controls and of all governmental subsidies and favors
to industry, all of which together would put an end to inflation;
and, finally, "returning the control of education to the parent and
the local communities, and returning the content of education to
the fundamental principles of our civilization and the fundamental
skills of an educated man." In the ensuing ten years a great deal of
particularisation was to be undertaken; but in its initial simplism
(one must perforce put aside here the question of good faith) this
manifesto sounded like classic Manchester liberalism, various versions of anarchism, Midwestern Christianism, and what is now
called by these same friends of the individual "consumerism," with
unmistakable implications of unrestricted redneckery. These were
to come to fruition later in outspoken opposition to any kind of
racial integration, the advocacy of state subventions of religious
schools (the party's membership from the start has been heavily
lower-middle-class Catholic) and the restoration of religion in
public schools, demands for complete police autonomy, the end of
social services of all kinds, and whatever military action might be
necessary to overthrow whatever foreign government might be
labeled Communist. By the law of averages the party was bound
to offer something worth-while, and it did, in the form of opposition to ceilings on the earnings of persons receiving social-security
pensions, which are among the major grisly jokes of the American
charade of economic democracy.

In its first ten years the Conservative Party has not made much
numerical headway. It could not elect a Mayor of New York City
(to no one's surprise); but it did elect a Senator from New York,
whatever fragile explanations the ostriches may whisper to one

another beneath the sand while their buttocks are up-ended for another Conservative kick. Moreover, it has been recognisably effective in other than electoral ways; indeed, to any thoughtful person the question is why it has not rallied more adherents. But that must be discussed presently; and it would be foolish to suppose that all that the Buckleys want of their party is the accumulation of enrolled voters. It avoided the New York elections in the year of its birth, and came out of the nursery in 1962. Nine years later its name might have been substituted for that of YAF in a Columbia University student's letter to *Triumph*, in which he wrote that "YAF is composed to a great extent of lower-middle-class Catholics who love God, the Latin Mass, Bill Buckley and Spiro Agnew in that order" and who "realize that political conservatism is a means to an end, and that End is, ultimately, God."

Older Conservatives would probably hesitate to endorse publicly his conclusion that "some brand of political conservatism is the best political language with which to . . . keep the secularists from jamming their Hellish programs down our throats . . . and above all to ensure the liberty and exaltation of our Holy Mother the Church in America and throughout the world." Vincent J. Rigdon, who wrote this, was probably exalted; but his elders in the party, who rarely talk so freely, merely vote and live his way. And certainly they would come within the rebuke administered to Buckley, at the very time of the Conservative Party's incubation under his tender care, by Ronald Hamowy of *New Individualist Review*, the organ of the conservative Intercollegiate Society of Individualists. In November, 1961, Hamowy accused Buckley of "a polite form of white supremacy," hostility to civil liberties, advocacy of immediate war against Russia, and the aspiration "not so much to limit the state as to control it." He reminded Buckley, who defended colonialism with references to "the semi-savages" of the African nations, that freedom was a right, not something to be earned or bestowed. Hamowy's accusations would still apply (except perhaps for the advocacy of immediate war) to both Buckley and the party that he has nurtured.

Buckley's controversies during this period had a direct bearing on the inception of his syndicated column. His polemics with the leading Catholic publications—*The Catholic World*, *Commonweal*, and the Jesuits' *America*, which he had called "impudent" for criticising his attack on *Mater et Magistra*—his increasing output of articles in general magazines, usually in defense of his conservative theses, his widening activity in lecture and debate (one of the opponents whom he liked best was Norman Mailer) were creating a public. Television talk-programs found him a favorite of audiences: he was charming, handsome, adroit, and, for all his genuine high culture, simultaneously wholly attuned to the fears and desires of the average half-schooled, thing-dominated Americans who make up what the late novelist William Lindsay Gresham called half-contemptuously, half-affectionately "the desperate middle-class riff-raff," frightened beyond speech by anyone and anything different. Thus, though he might often risk the momentary resentment of his mass audiences by his intellectual snobbisms and exhibitionism, which was chiefly linguistic, he would not lose their hero-worship, because their values were essentially his too, and they knew it; and at the same time he could command a more or less respectful and frequently indulgent, if not affectionate, hearing from those who in turn condescended intellectually to him, as well as those who respected him, personally and intellectually, in spite of political conflicts. No one who was seduced even for an instant by the specious charm of any Kennedy may justly fling even a pebble at those who have fallen under the far more real enchantment of almost all the Buckleys.

XVI

ONE KENNEDY DEMOCRAT who has unbelievably managed to keep
that loyalty untarnished and at the same time to have become probably the most effusive of Bill Buckley's admirers is Harry Elmlark,
the man who alone is responsible for Buckley's having added a
newspaper column to all his other frenetic activities. Elmlark would
vehemently challenge the statement by a close Buckley associate
of more than fifteen years, to the effect that in the ten years since
he has been a television personality Buckley has not had a thought.
Yet one cannot ignore the question: how can anyone who devotes
so much of himself to television, a newspaper column, and popular
journalism save himself from being at least in part the creature of
these brainless media? And the part of him that is their creature
must of necessity renounce original thought.

The history of the column and the unlikely friendship that
soared out of it is told with great affection by Buckley in *Cruising
Speed*, and this same warmth is replicated in Elmlark when he
talks of Buckley—and, to a lesser degree, when he talks of Buckleys other than Bill: lesser only because he knows them less well.
Elmlark is about seventeen years older than Buckley, but he tends
to bristle at any notion that theirs is a surrogate father-son relationship. He is fiercely protective of Buckley—who hardly needs
protection beyond what he can provide for himself—and they are
equals in the intensity of their loyalty. Elmlark is president and
editor of the Washington Star Syndicate, which distributes all
kinds of finished and semi-finished goods from comic strips to the
meditations of *monsignori*, and it was as a potential recruit to his
stable that Buckley first attracted him. Their friendship, which had
various obstacles to overcome—the chief of these being Buckley's

intense disinclination to become a columnist—has since gone far
beyond their professional association; and the Elmlarks live only
a few streets away from the Buckleys in Lenox Hill.

"About ten years ago," Elmlark said, "I had a young man
working for me who was a conservative. 'You know,' he said, 'you
ought to get Bill Buckley.' At that time I thought of Bill Buckley
as some sort of fanatic or nut. The young fellow said: 'Harry,
you don't understand this guy. The papers are ready for him.' I
got in touch with about thirty newspapers without consulting Bill
Buckley, and the reaction was largely affirmative. So I said to the
young man: 'O.K., you go ahead and get Buckley.' Well, he tried
to get through to Bill and he couldn't. I did, because by this time
the letters were coming in in response to my offer, and telegrams
too. This, I think, was late February of 1962. As Bill says in *Cruising Speed*, I didn't meet him until the following May: we made
an agreement over the telephone, and later signed it. When we
met, we immediately became friends.

"And then we worked very closely. Bill needs somebody to
work with him on a column. He writes too much. I think I've
rejected only one of his columns, and for that I had to reach him
aboard a ship. It was when Churchill died, and I, being a little
square, said to him: 'This is no time to write a derogatory column
about Churchill—why don't you wait a few weeks?' The only
other time I objected to anything and had my way about it—I can
sense what Bill will insist on and where he is flexible—was, I think,
when Eleanor Roosevelt died, and he referred to her as 'the old
lady,' which he thought was a perfectly acceptable expression in
the South. I asked him to change it to 'the venerable lady,' though
he honestly didn't think there was anything wrong with 'the old
lady.' But his wife agreed with me, and in the end he changed it."

Sometimes, Elmlark said, Buckley will write his column in the
syndicate office: it takes him about a half-hour if no research is
called for. Occasionally an idea dropped by Elmlark in speculative
conversation will produce a column that is a recognisable mutant.
"If I think a passage is fuzzy," Elmlark added, "and a lot of Bill's
passages can be a little convoluted, I may ask him to make it a
little more lucid, and he does. But he will not yield on basic principles, and I wouldn't ask him to." On the other hand, when a
column needs cutting and Buckley is pressed, he relies on Elmlark's judgment. Occasionally Frances Bronson, the executive
secretary of *National Review*, will make the cuts, but Elmlark is

free to alter them. (Elmlark has also criticised Buckley in a very different field: he has not hesitated to object to what he regards as trickiness in debate on *Firing Line*. And, in still another area, Elmlark, who is Jewish, has been privately admonished by Buckley for not observing the prescriptions to which he was born.)

Buckley's incessant traveling creates occasional problems. At times the column simply does not arrive at all. Sometimes it comes to Elmlark on tape; occasionally it is telephoned from Stamford, Switzerland, or Hong Kong. Almost the only external force that can interfere with its production is the total lack of transmission facilities, as occurred when Buckley spent several days at American and Soviet scientific bases in the Antarctic with his brother James in January of 1972.

It took Elmlark days of telephoning even to persuade Buckley, in the beginning, to discuss the prospect of a column. He thought, as he recounted in *Cruising Speed*, to discourage the seducer by demanding what seemed an outrageous guaranty: one hundred fifty dollars a week. To this Elmlark retorted that he would guarantee two hundred, to begin on 1 April, though Elmlark was by no means certain that he could afford it. This rounded the victim's heels, and *On the Right* appeared in thirty-eight papers, large and small. All were conservative and none was in New York, though subsequently the "liberal" *New York Post* bought it at Wechsler's urging and has run it for years without censorship of any kind, no matter how it may outrage the editors' sensibilities or, for that matter, some readers'. For the first three years the Star Syndicate handled every aspect of the business; but since 1965 the actual sales and marketing have been farmed out to King Features Syndicate, an old Hearst corporation; Star edits and services the column, and Elmlark is probably almost the only man who calls Buckley to suggest that he write something differently, or drop it altogether—and sometimes Buckley goes along. At the time of the division of labor, according to Neal Freeman, executive editor of King, the column had only forty subscribers; it now has several hundred, and commands an income at the very top of its field. Freeman, incidentally, is on the boards of directors of *National Review* and, by appointment of President Nixon, of the Corporation for Public Broadcasting—Buckley's medium.

Elmlark's relation with Bill Buckley has troubled many of his shorter-sighted friends. In *Cruising Speed* Buckley pointed out that Elmlark abominates Nixon, whom Buckley used to admire and still prefers *faute de mieux*, and McCarthy, whom Buckley still admires; and few of Buckley's reactionary friends are puzzled by his ability to dine happily at the Elmlarks', whereas Elmlark's friends and business acquaintances alike assume that he is a front man for Fascism, or else they marvel that he can sit at the same table with the arch-fiend. One's own view is that this state of affairs conduces to one's having rather more regard for both parties. To quote Elmlark: "It's almost amateurish to assume that you can't have a close friendship with a man whose politics you disagree with, as long as that man is not evil." One is reminded, too, of a Jewish sergeant of the guard at Nürnberg who found Hermann Goering quite as delightful a companion as he was an evil man; whereas J. McCarthy was as repugnant as he was evil, and only transitorily dangerous. Nor is evil always to be equated with menace: no Buckley is evil but as individuals or *en bloc* they are very dangerous, precisely, in part, because they are not evil, just as Fiorello La Guardia, who also was not evil (but also not bright, and certainly not civilised), was equally if differently dangerous.

Elmlark, who describes himself as "not political," has virtually a free hand in editing Buckley's column when it requires cuts—its optimum length is supposed to be seven hundred words—and prides himself, rightfully, on the detachment with which he exercises this authority. Nor does he hesitate, when he thinks all or part of a column is in questionable taste, to say so and to make recommendations, if necessary by transoceanic telephone (Buckley spends two months of almost every winter in Switzerland). On some occasions what he says is followed; but in any event it is carefully considered. But he does not offer opinions, guidance, or counsel on anything else that Bill Buckley does or says, in whatever forum. When he disagrees, Elmlark, like other close associates who have had important differences of opinion with Buckley, voices his views only to Buckley and never to anyone else. I do not, in his or anyone's case, ascribe this reticence to any sinister influence exerted on the dissident, to any kind of blackmail, psychological or other: it seems the very natural loyalty of close friendship.

Like Jeff Greenfield, the youngish liberal (for lack, again, of a better word: certainly Greenfield cannot be called a man of the Left) who for some time was a regular panelist on *Firing Line*, Elmlark insists that Bill Buckley is not a racist, and not merely because he is capable of liking individual blacks. As if in corroboration of Paul Weiss's observation on Buckley's ignorance of what it is to be down on one's luck, Greenfield (though not Elmlark) says that Buckley's apparent racism is merely social snobbism and that what Buckley despises is not the black or the Puerto Rican, for example, but the boor and the poor. Certainly, when Buckley had Representative Ronald Dellums, who headed the Black Caucus in the House of Representatives, on his television show, his attitude toward Dellums was virtually indistinguishable from Dr. Johnson's (Sam, not Lyndon) toward the lady preacher. And what he has written, one would argue, requires careful study.

Like other friends of Buckley, Elmlark insists that what Bill Buckley may hate, when he does hate, is not persons but ideas; other sources say that there is one exception to his inability to hate persons, and the exception is supposed to be Gore Vidal. On the other hand, according to Elmlark, Buckley "is a man with a unique almost-genius for warmth and friendship," and for loyalty. "Bill happens to be in Washington today," Elmlark said, "and if I called him and said something terrible had happened in my private life, he'd walk out of his USIA meeting and fly back to New York. And I've seen him do such things for others.

"He's also the busiest man I've ever known. He's scheduled months in advance—for example, I called up early in September to ask him, as a favor, to deliver a speech in Dallas on November 28, and he said that the only time he could do it was in the evening on a Saturday or at noon Sunday or Monday. He always has everything in his life so awfully close. Of course, he's got a lot of people doing things for him: always a car and chauffeur, he has a secretary who has another secretary, he has me and his column. I'm protecting him in all kinds of ways. And he's got to have that. It's not because he's spoiled, it's because he has so much to do."

Part of Elmlark's protectiveness, and of his loyalty to his friend, was reflected in the fact that before agreeing to be interviewed he, like other people round Buckley, asked him whether he objected. (Many who have known Bill or other Buckleys refused to be interviewed at all; others were careful to insist that a line be drawn between the private and the public Buckleys in answers to any questions.) On the other hand, Elmlark and Teague were instrumental in breaking down the Buckleys' own resistance to trading with the enemy. In Elmlark's case the motivations were two: not only the obvious but also his concern that as many as possible of the aspects of his friend's character be made clear, especially the contrasts between the public and the private *personae*:

the slashing, unscrupulous (the word was not Elmlark's) fighter
in print and on television and the private man who will never allow
a social situation to turn into a serious political argument, who is
the epitome of the amenities. Elmlark is charmed equally by James
Buckley, whose much more modest personality is immediately
attractive even on television, but it is Bill who is his great friend.
Bill, Elmlark says, knows very well (and assumed when he ran in
1965 for the Mayoralty of New York) that he could never be
elected to any office, if only because of his intensity and his refusal to talk or behave down—which is not at all inconsistent
with the fact that so many of his views require no dishonest modifications to accord almost wholly with the entire arsenal of Middle
American parochialism; but Elmlark is most dubious whether
James Buckley could ever have been elected to the Senate if he
had not been Bill's brother. "I've told Bill a dozen times if I've
told him once," Elmlark said, "that, if he'd been elected Mayor,
this city would be a shambles now." When I protested that it was
a shambles anyway, Elmlark agreed, but insisted: "Bill would have
made it worse." One reason, according to Elmlark, is Buckley's
refusal to compromise with anyone on anything.

His more offensive remarks on the living habits of the poor and
the black, Elmlark said, have been made "because Bill can't resist
a wisecrack." This was to be noted years earlier, when he was
chairman of the *Yale Daily News*; and one is hardly qualified to
cast the first or even the thirty-first stone; but this is a remediable
frailty in all its possessors. Moreover, it is the more damaging when
it appears in print, and Buckley's column is guilty almost as often
as his television program. A propos the creation of a committee
at Princeton University in October of 1971 to inquire into the
workings of the FBI, Buckley noted that Warren Beatty, the actor
who had the male lead in *Bonnie and Clyde*, a film about a folklore gangster couple, was a member of the group; then Buckley
added: "Did you know that Warren Beatty was interested in
public justice? That was the true meaning of the gleam in his eye
when, as Clyde, he took Bonnie to the bank." In the same column,
he descanted on another committee member, Ramsey Clark, most
recently Attorney General of the United States before he entered
private practice and accepted retainers from clients whose politics
offended Buckley: "Mr. Clark, who is a splendid fellow, wrote,
alas, the most perverse book about morals [*Crime in America*]
since de Sade, the jurisprudential equivalent of *The Greening of*

America." Or, in February of 1972, this from Peking, whither, as a journalist, Buckley had accompanied his quondam hero now clay from soles to groins, Richard Nixon, of whose behavior at a state banquet he wrote: "And then . . . [Buckley's suspense] and then, he toasted Chairman Mao, Chou En-lai, the whole lot of them. I would not have been surprised if he had lurched into a toast of Alger Hiss."

Buckley has, quite justly, castigated our unlovely custom of trial by press. But in his one eye there is a mote and in his other eye there is a beam. He is as entitled as anyone else to his opinion of the guilt or innocence of criminal or political defendants, but it is characteristic of him to deny the very possibility of political trials in the United States, as in the cases of Angela Davis and Daniel Ellsberg, and then to convict the defendants as common criminals in his column, even, at times, after the courts have set them free. On 29 July 1972, for example, a Buckley column explained very precisely, like a sentencing judge who also has the second sight, how and why Ellsberg, who made public the Pentagon Papers, clearly intended (according to Buckley) to help his country's enemies and damage his country. Ellsberg's crime, Buckley said, comes under the Espionage Act, whose authors' goal was clear: "What they meant to discourage was the kind of thing Benedict Arnold did." One can entertain quite solid doubts of Ellsberg's saintliness and, even, of his motivations without doing one's best, through one's wide public influence, to assure his conviction of a crime of which he is neither guilty nor even formally accused.

Buckley's column, which is called "On the Right," is not, however, always there. It has been used more than once for causes not wholly congenial to the rest of the Right. One, of course, the most sensational, was his nine-year battle for Edgar H. Smith Jr., who was convicted of first-degree murder in New Jersey and sentenced to death in the most suspect of circumstances. The elementary protections of due process (never esteemed by the Garden State) were not extended to Smith—quite as Buckley would not have had them extended to any defendant, if he had had his way: this was one of his major complaints against "the Earl Warren Court"—and in any event neither the licitly nor the illicitly adduced evidence was especially convincing. Buckley took up Smith's case after Smith wrote to him from the death house in Trenton; he used the television screen, his own and other magazines, and his column to fight for a new trial, at the very least, in which Smith would enjoy the rights enunciated by the Supreme Court of the United States; he helped to finance Smith's various legal moves; and in the end Smith was set free after having been forced into a base mercantile transaction unfortunately character-istic of the indifference of the American courts to justice and of their dedication to vicarious revenge.

"I dispute the proposition that justice is better served by accept-ing the so-called Warren reforms," Buckley explained. "This does not by any means suggest that I am not prepared to take advantage of the Warren reforms in order to help someone that I think is innocent. If Edgar Smith had been executed in 1958 I would harbor the belief that an innocent man had been executed. I do not, however, think that on that account I would have been justi-fied in making the correlative statement that the establishment of the law was, net, disadvantageous to justice." Thus, he explained or sought to explain to me, his behavior on behalf of Smith in no way conflicted with all his prior, present, and potential attacks on the courts' concern to protect defendants' rights to the detriment of what Buckley and the Right conceive to be law and order.

Another of the surprising uses to which Buckley put his column was the ends of Amnesty International; still more astonishingly, he was for a long time a member of its board of directors, in such company as that of Roger Baldwin, the founder of the ACLU, and Maurice Goldbloom, an old Socialist and a consistent public opponent of the current Greek régime so cherished of the Buck-leys and their group (Burnham most blandly—and unsubtly—whitewashed it in The New York Times for Christmas, 1971). Amnesty is dedicated to the release of purely political prisoners—a category that, beyond question, it is becoming more and more difficult to delimit—and in a number of cases Buckley wrote able pleas for persons whose causes it had embraced; so much so that, when he left the board of directors for a less responsible place on its council, because in his three years as a director he had been unable to attend a single board meeting, Mark Benenson, the ex-ecutive head of the organisation, wrote to Buckley to say that he had done more for it than many people who had attended all the meetings.

The story of this resignation is variously recounted. "I also told Benenson," Buckley said to me, "that, as long as I couldn't attend the board meetings, I didn't want to be that close corporately to an organisation which I thought had not satisfactorily resolved some questions that societies face on the nature of political dissent. As you know, Amnesty limits its defense to people who express a conscientious objection to policies, and they do not defend people who advocate direct action. But my own feeling is that it is, as a practical matter, extremely difficult to draw the line between people who advocate dissent with certain policies and others whose dissent in effect catalyses a violent action. And that's why I simply told them I would feel more comfortable not being a member of a corporate body whose decisions people were by inference entitled to assign to me as a member of the board."

To Baldwin, these are "distinctions that one with a generous mind ought not to make." Buckley, he added, "is a very quick fellow to take very fine positions." According to Goldbloom, who was trained in medieval philosophy as well as Socialism, Buckley's resignation was prompted by Amnesty International's support of people who had conscientious objections to the Vietnam war. Buckley, Goldbloom elaborated, "objected to supporting Antinomians.* At my suggestion, Mark Benenson wrote back to him that these people were not Antinomians but quite the reverse: believers in the doctrine of natural law, which takes precedence over civil law, and their position was actually the Catholic position on just wars; and Buckley agreed to come back to the national council."

For more personal causes, however, Buckley did not exploit his column. He kept it independent of his Mayoralty campaign of 1965 and of his brother's Senatorial campaigns of 1968 and 1970. Nor has he used it especially to further the Conservative Party of New York, though he has naturally and properly employed it for the propagation of the conservative faith. Appearing three times a week—initially it was planned to run once weekly—it maintains a level not only higher than one might reasonably expect in the light of such frequency but also well above that of any other comparable column now that Murray Kempton has withdrawn from that arena. Buckley and Kempton were the only real men of letters among the practitioners, just as they were virtually the only ones

* The Antinomians held that faith alone was required for salvation. Their origins may be noted in the New Testament (Romans vi: 15ff.), though they flourished about the time of the Reformation. They repudiated even the idea of obedience as legalistic, and claimed authority both from Martin Luther and from St. Augustine.—C.L.M.

who had any justification for taking the world as their province. Buckley now has more than four hundred papers with many millions of readers or potential readers, and not all these papers are conservative nowadays.

Few of them edit him except for space; he rightly insists on freedom of expression. In one instance he withdrew his column from a subscribing paper. This is what Elmlark calls "the ultra-liberal, not Left-Wing, paper in Madison, Wisconsin": the *Capital Times*. Miles McMillan, the editor, Elmlark continued, "is a hard liberal, as I am. He used Bill's column in a way which I considered journalistically sort of reprehensible. His attacks on Bill in his own column in his paper were almost continuous. Now, I think it's perfectly all right to attack another writer, but, if you feel that strongly about him, you shouldn't have him in your paper: you should drop him. He used Bill because Bill is widely read and because he could see the copy and write a column of his own on it. Well, finally he said that Bill couldn't make a living if it weren't for anti-Communism. I suppose Bill is a professional anti-Communist, but he's a highly talented guy." The result was Buckley's refusal to sell the column to McMillan, who was obviously a poor judge of other people's capacities to support themselves.

Some fourteen papers, on the other hand, canceled their subscriptions to "On the Right" in the summer of 1971 after *National Review*'s so-called "Pentagon Papers hoax." In each case it was made clear that the action was taken not because of anything in the columns but purely because of the hoax, if hoax it was (and, whether it was that or worse, or better, it was hardly worth so much notice). In spite of these defections—and none of the papers was of great consequence—the column continues to have a huge distribution and to bring in a revenue among the very highest in the field of serious commentary: neither Elmlark nor Freedman will specify, and indeed the exact figure is probably not a matter of legitimate public curiosity. Like his television and lecture remuneration, Buckley's share of the syndicate income is paid in to National Review, Inc., which gives him a salary of thirty-eight thousand dollars a year.

The column has also helped, over the years, to fill out the books that Buckley publishes steadily (*The Unmaking of a Mayor* is devoted solely to the title subject): *Rumbles Left and Right*, in 1963; *The Jeweler's Eye*, in 1968; *The Governor Listeth*, in 1970; and *Inveighing We Will Go*, in 1972. These consist chiefly of brief

essays on virtually any subject that may interest him, though most
of the pieces get back inevitably and indeed monotonously to God
and the free market in one form or another, with asides of graduated
acerbity and roughly uniform unfairness on whatever incurs the
author's disapproval—the young, women's liberation ("chicklib"
is the *National Review* term), social security, welfare, radicals of
all Left categories. Thus he is able to add the respectability of hard
covers—and later the further diffusion of soft ones—to the exposition of political fundamentalism and some cultural sophistica-
tions that have already been laid before the readers of the newspapers that carry his column. Hence he has an excellent instrument
for the reinforcement of Middle American prejudices and the leav-
ening of them with decent rhetoric, which, however, not seldom
takes wing into mere exhibitionism quite comparable to more material forms that are to be found among the recently moneyed. In
this Bill Buckley seems to be quite apart from his siblings (except
his epigone—to use another of his favorite words—Reid): they
handle language quite competently but without bedizenment.

There are parts of the country, notably the Southwest, where
the column has no great distribution and where educational television stations have only laggardly begun to carry Buckley's program. Newspaper editors in this outback seem for the most part
to be indistinguishable from their customers—certainly they speak
hardly more articulately, and in many cases less—and their reaction to Buckleys in general is parochial to an extreme. Very often
their real reason for not taking the column, the orientation of
which would certainly please both them and their subscribers, is
their uneasiness in even the teletyped presence of a man who can
read and write, and this is manifest in conversation with them.
"He's that entertainer fella," they will say; "the one that had that
fight with that swishy fella on the teevee." That is how they really
talk. Their suspicion of both Bill and James Buckley as "city
fellas" is its own caricature; but it is, incredibly, genuine: the East
is Satan's fief, as far as they are concerned, and they prefer the
kind of columnist who might be likened to a lay Billy James
Hargis or Oral Roberts. Bill Buckley himself has the proper sovereign contempt for such attitudes; "entertainer," to him, "is simply
a term in the glossary of disparagement, and I'm used to the whole
glossary."

Its users would hardly be likely to buy Buckley's—or anyone's
—books; but all his have sold well and then gone into successful

paperback editions. Tom Wallace, who was his editor at G. P. Putnam's Sons—"though one doesn't edit Bill Buckley"—recalls that little had to be done (or would be suffered by the author to be done) to Buckley's copy. "People who publish Buckley," Wallace said, "are doing advertising, promotion, and publicity and providing distribution, rather than providing editorial services." Wallace had obtained Buckley as a Putnam's author simply by telephoning him when Buckley's earlier publisher, McDowell Obolensky, was going out of business; like Buckley, though five years later, Wallace was a graduate of Yale and its *Daily News*, and he had met Buckley at *Daily News* banquets. Buckley's books, Wallace said, average twenty thousand copies in hard cover before they go into paperback, and most of these books are reprints of articles and speeches. This in itself is ample evidence of his potential influence, without any prestidigitation about the number of probable readers per copy: it is the fact, lamentable or otherwise, that only a minuscule percentage of the population, usually reasonably literate, determines elections and policies (if only by deciding who the candidates shall be), and that a substantial part of that group reads Buckley. So, obviously, does a good part of the middle class that buys paperback non-fiction and that is concerned with public matters partly philosophically, partly (probably largely) in terms of what it costs in taxes to pay for what government does, and of the creatures of dark that constantly menace comfort and "security."

Buckley is in a sense the editor's ideal writer, according to Wallace: he turns out clean copy that requires minimal editorial attention, he is much more nearly punctual than the huge majority of authors, to whom a deadline is something purely metaphysical, and he is never necessitous enough to come pestering—or send his agent—for an additional advance. His agent, in the occurrence, is Wallace's wife, Lois, who is with the William Morris Agency and who finds Buckley an ideal client, not only for all the reasons hereinabove set forth but for one final cause that would make any writer the darling of his agent and his publisher alike: he is sure to be a money-maker.

Tom Wallace takes Buckley seriously most of the time, and believes simultaneously that for most conservatives—of whom Wallace does not consider himself one; nor is he a radical—he is "too clever by half." Wallace adds that "Bill probably doesn't reflect a broad range of conservatism," and in this he reflects the prevailing view among "liberals" that is precisely one of the chief elements that make the Buckleys dangerous. Wallace is bemused— and in this he is quite representative of the great majority of his fellows—by "the twinkle in his eye." Of course he is quite right in his contention that "half of Bill's rôle is the gadfly rôle; I'm not sure he always takes himself seriously." To Wallace, Buckley and *National Review* are not dangerous because they are "responsible"; he sees the danger from the Right in such sheets as *Human Events* because they are "marginal."

This is a curious if perennial astigmatism that should have been corrected by modern history, if by nothing else. It is difficult to think of any country in which public affairs have been taken over by marginal or irresponsible factions. The marginals, indeed, are forever being left out, at the least, if not hunted down—witness the Trotskyists, or the Anarchists in Spain before Franco's victory; the irresponsibles are ignored in themselves and are dangerous only as they accept recruitment into other forces' ranks, as the rag, tag, and bobtail of the Right in this country largely falls in every four years behind whatever Republican has been nominated for the Presidency. There was nothing marginal about any of the factions that have seized power anywhere in this century, and nothing irresponsible: Fascists, Falangists, Nazis, Stalinists, nationalists of whatever variety have all been highly responsible, knowing precisely what they intended, how they proposed to accomplish it, and why their peculiar philosophies made them the mutually exclusive saviors of their respective countries and, in some cases, of the world. All of them, in fact, might be said to suffer from that tinge of Jansenism that Ralph de Toledano (more perceptively than any of Buckley's adversaries or critics on the Left) pointed out in the Buckleys' conservatism.

In one of the essays in *Rumbles Left and Right*, a reply to the educational philosophy of Robert M. Hutchins, former president of the University of Chicago, Buckley summarised that conservatism in what might much more fairly be called a manifesto on behalf of obscurantism: "We know that we have made no discoveries, and we think that no discoveries are to be made, in morality, nor many in the great principles of government, nor in the idea of liberty, which were understood long before we were born, altogether as well as they will be after the grave has heaped its mould upon our presumption, and the silent tomb shall have imposed its law on our pert loquacity." It is magniloquent prose; it is also damnable philosophy.

It is the philosophy, or part of the philosophy, that directly contributed to the Buckleys' support of Goldwater's Presidential candidacy in 1964 and Bill Buckley's effort to have a hand in the campaign. There are other illustrations of the philosophy in this book, in his introduction to which Russell Kirk, whose admirable study of T. S. Eliot would never conduce to the expectation of finding him saying such things as this, declares that Buckley "objects to mediocrity for the sake of normality; he detests the monster because he cherishes the true man." Sometimes, it is true, one is almost tempted to believe both parts of the statement: *vide* the dissection of a television person called Jack Paar, though in the end it is beneath Buckley's dignity, for adults do not play with dung. Or, again, try (it is impossible) to disagree with what he has to say in "Why Don't We Complain?"—that the almost universal apathy in the face of infinite discomfort, *Schlamperei*, and sheer brute inhumanity springs from the twin alienations wrought by ever more complex technology and the pullulation of remote power structures.

But is it conservative (one thinks back to Whitney North Seymour's statement) to propose, as Buckley does in "Catholic Liberals, Catholic Conservatives, and the Requirements of Unity," that "the distinction is not between 'just' and 'unjust' acts in relation to fighting Communism, but between relevant and irrelevant means of fighting Communism"? It is the more appalling in that, only a breath or two before, he had reiterated the truism that the end can never justify the means. For the apostle of truth, one must recall this, in the same essay: "A correlation has never been established between the extent of injustice and the appeal of Communism." Or this: "If there were no frictions [in the West for Communism to exploit], Communism would provide them." He would have his reader believe that the Freedom Riders did more than the segregationists to fuel Communist propaganda and that the Portuguese "have virtually wiped out discrimination on account of color" in their African colonies.

Nixon, Buckley said ten years ago, was "a moderate, a left-moderate." De Toledano has pointed out in conversation that Buckley could never really accept Nixon after his initial awe at meeting the occupant of the Vice President's office, and that Buckley's attitude toward the man has long been essentially one of condescension (though one must in fairness ask how it is possible not to condescend to that individual). This must be borne in mind when one considers, as we shall presently do, the whole Buckley group's "suspension of support" for Nixon in public statements in the summer of 1971. Goldwater was Buckley's man, well before 1964, not least because he agreed with Buckley (even if the facts of life do not) that "in America, as in all free-market economies, the only (lawful) way for one man to acquire wealth is by contributing to the wealth of other men. That is why in America it has never been the case that the rich got richer while the poor got poorer." Five years later, in a relapse from Jansenism, he was to observe in "Let the Rich Alone," an article in *The Jeweler's Eye*: "Some people *will* be rich. Some people *will* be poor"—the italics being his. One is reminded of a lady translated by marriage from exiguous survival to Fairfield County who, blacking out her parents' lives, opined that "the poor are poor because they want to be poor."

"Will Formosa Liberate the United States?" Buckley asked in one of the pieces in *Rumbles Left and Right*. This is a speech that he delivered to the National Defense Research Institute in Taiwan just about ten years before he sat at dinner in Peking with the man he no longer supported, Nixon, and the Chairman and Premier, Mao and Chou, whom in this oration he said it was America's duty to overthrow; pending which he pledged his allegiance to "nuclear stalemate, or the balance of terror" as an article of faith. This should hardly surprise in the mouth of a man who two years earlier, on the fifth anniversary of *National Review*, had derided "the great rationalist superstition, defended today by the reactionaries who cluster about the American Civil Liberties Union, that the free exchange of opposite ideas midwives truth." That this was not quite the contention of those "reactionaries," but rather a nondeclaration that he strove to put into their mouths, was unknown to his hearers and indifferent to him. In all such utterances he reminds one of Pontius in Roger Caillois' *Ponce Pilate*, when, having at last crushed out his conviction of Jesus' innocence in submission to the guiding principle of all rulers, "Better injustice than disorder," he accepts the suggestion of his military aide, Menenius, that he wash his hands of the matter publicly before the people in the traditional symbolic rite. Impressing on Menenius that the towel must be spotless and the pitcher and bowl of flawless silver,

he adds: "*Qu'au moins le geste soit élégant et le symbole irré-
prochable, si l'action est malhonnête* (At least, if the act itself be
dirty, let the instrument be elegant and the symbolism beyond
reproach)."

There was much less of such esthetic preoccupation in Buckley's
attempt to assist in Goldwater's Presidential campaign. In *National
Review* for 19 November 1963, many months before the Republican Convention that was virtually certain to choose Goldwater,
Buckley undertook to cleanse Goldwater of the smear of John
Birch Society affiliation by denying that this existed—and it did
not; but at the same time he made it clear that he himself (and,
by implication, Goldwater) agreed with "the general goals of the
Society's members," which he defined as the defeat of Communism and Socialism and the exaltation of Manchester liberalism.
And he denounced "genocidal assaults upon the membership of
the Society, and on candidates who refuse to condemn all members
of the Society," as "unreasonable and undiscriminating."

Buckley and his brother-in-law Brent Bozell, who had helped
Goldwater to write *The Conscience of a Conservative* (as Stephen
Shadegg, long Goldwater's political manager, phrased it in his
own book, *What Happened to Goldwater*), had requested and
obtained a meeting with Dr. Charles Kelley, a Goldwater adviser, in Washington in September, 1963, according to Shadegg,
for two purposes. They wanted, first, to propose the creation of
a committee of eminent academics to support Goldwater; in addition, they wanted to bring Goldwater together with a man who
wished very strongly to make a handsome monetary contribution
to his campaign. The dinner meeting turned out, to the surprise
of Buckley and Bozell, to include Denison Kitchel, a lawyer transplanted from Bronxville and the New Deal to Arizona, big business, and the direction of Goldwater's Senatorial campaigns, and
William Baroody Sr., who had begun his working life as a statistician for the New Hampshire Unemployment Division in 1937,
moved into the federal bureaucracy, and then progressed to the
Chamber of Commerce of the United States and the executive
vice-presidency of the hard-Right American Enterprise Institute.
Kitchel was a near-idolator of Goldwater and believed that his
hero was invincible, and Baroody was determined to keep *dilettanti* out.

Their presence prevented Buckley and Bozell from even men-
tioning the potential donor, Shadegg wrote, because "muckraking

columnists seem to make a scandal out of even relatively insignificant sums of money, and this offer of cash was not something to be discussed in front of Kitchel and Baroody; so Buckley confined his remarks to an elaboration of the committee idea." A few days later *The New York Times* said that Goldwater and his advisers had "repelled" Buckley and Bozell, "who wanted to join the campaign organization, they said, on the policy-planning level." *The Times* added that Goldwater's strategists did not want "more support from the far right."

Buckley and Bozell, according to Shadegg, were "offended and alarmed. It seemed obvious someone had talked." The brothers-in-law had no intention of joining the drive, Shadegg said, but sought only to give occasional help. Shadegg clearly implies that *The Times* had got its story through Baroody, who employed Karl Hess at the American Enterprise Institute and added him to Goldwater's staff as a speech-writer. In the end, Shadegg wrote mournfully, Kitchel, Baroody, and Hess took "possession" of Goldwater, and Buckley, Bozell, and Rusher, all of whom had made major contributions to building up his candidacy and gaining him the nomination through their public and private efforts, were thrown out. It is not difficult to infer that Shadegg believes that this was not unconnected with Goldwater's ultimate election defeat.

It is not inappropriate here to deal to some extent with Hess, a former Catholic who in his youth was rabidly Right until Murray Rothbard converted him to libertarianism and who now is at the far Left, working at the Institute for Policy Studies in Washington alongside such less volatile and more intellectually mature people as Marcus Raskin, who was one of the five men indicted in Boston in 1968 for conspiracy to violate the Selective Service Act and who is a Leftist by conviction at least as much as by sentiment. Having worked for de Toledano, Maguire of *The American Mercury*, and Baroody, Hess was for a time associated with Buckley in the inception of *National Review*. The break, essentially, came in 1969 with Hess's total immersion in libertarianism; now he is convinced that at the Institute for Policy Studies he has entered Paradise and will never again know any of the disillusions or irritations that he found on the Right. Because he believes, even more firmly than Bozell is convinced that he will see the Second Coming, that the world is about to embrace a kind of utopian anarchy à la Kropotkin, Hess sees no reason to take the Buckleys or their fellows seriously except in an abstract intellectual sense. "I didn't meet anybody on the Right that I can remember who I felt was really trying to change things," he said. "What they were trying to do was establish positions, commanding intellectual heights from which they could hurl their intellectual thunderbolts. There was no real sense that they wanted to change anything, and the clue was that they never changed the way they themselves lived."

While Hess in his proselyte's glow oversimplifies—one knows no other anarchist who expects the millennium quite so soon or so painlessly—he nonetheless is not unrepresentative of the fundamental fallacy among those "men of good will" who can conceive of danger only as change. Thus he misunderstands the very host in which he labored so long. The threat posed by the Right, except in most superficial fashion, is most certainly not change but, precisely, the resolve to prevent change—a resolve as blind as the adoration of change. One need not have a Fascist mind to question, with Buckley—and, for that matter, with Hess or with Herbert Marcuse—the inherent desirability of what is called progress, or, more trenchantly, to seek what progress really is. Indeed, change, as Ortega has shown, is one of the necessary elements in a true Fascist style: a kind of permanent revolution of the Right, and as much to be viewed with misgiving as a permanent revolution from any other quarter. It is not necessarily progress, any more than it is necessarily retrogression: it is movement, and we have come to bow down to movement for its own sake, almost regardless of its origin, its direction, or its destination.

XVII

"THE SELECT MAN," Ortega wrote in *The Revolt of the Masses* in 1929, "is not the petulant person who thinks himself superior to the rest, but the man who demands more of himself than the rest, even though he may not fulfill in his person those higher exigencies." Four years later Ramon Fernandez observed in an article in *Le Mercure de France*: "Fascism and Bolshevism, which govern the masses by adopting the vision and sentiment of the lowest, show that the contemporary élite assumes the faults of the mass it intends to govern." And in *The New York Review of Books* in February, 1972, Philip Rahv pointed out that "the aristocrat is a type in whom subtle manners and beautiful displays of consideration can easily go hand in hand with the crudest moral practices and presumptions." All of which goes far to explain why at times some of the Buckleys, and in especial Bill, make one reflect on some of the characters of Marcel Proust, though it is difficult to conceive of most of the residents of Proust's Faubourg St.-Germain exerting themselves to flatter the unsubtle susceptibilities of back-yard bigots in even a mocking campaign for office. But it was no character out of a fictional *catalogue raisonné* of aristocracy who observed, during his campaign for the Mayoralty of New York in 1965, that a principal problem for the ages was "the perennial question of the artists and intellectuals and their depressing political unintelligence." Bill Buckley, like all the Buckleys, is relentless in his vivisections of *Massenmensch* and mass values, and probably he is sincere: but his most enthusiastic New York backers are to be found in the lower middle class and the studiedly vulgar tabloid *Daily News*, among the newly propertied semi-skilled workers and the police force.

In 1964, when it was two years old, the Conservative Party had put candidates into the competition for city and state offices, with the blessings and assistance of various Buckleys and the backing of *National Review*; and, though none of them won, Professor Henry Paolucci of Iona College—a political virgin who played chamber music, had translated Pirandello, and is an enthusiast for capital punishment—had persuaded 119,971 residents of New York City to vote for him for the United States Senate. What he stood for and they, presumably, wanted was quite representatively expressed in Bill Buckley's speech to the diners gathered to celebrate their party's second birthday in that year. "We intend for the individual to survive the Twentieth Century," Buckley clarioned, and then his rhetoric modulated (one must always recognise craftsmanship): "We are still reluctant to accept the state as a sacramental agent for transubstantiating private interest into public good." Back to the old lure: the sum of all private goods equals the public good.

Richard Rovere has credited Buckley with the creation of the concept of "the Liberal Establishment"; Buckley modestly distributes the laurels, to his own exclusion, among Kendall, Meyer, Burnham, and William Henry Chamberlin, who, he said, introduced the notion into *National Review*. That Establishment, Buckley told the celebrants in his encapsulation of the gospel carried to the plebs by Paolucci and lesser Conservatives, had not yet been able to prevail in its alien-dominated endeavors—"our own intellectuals speak a derivative speech; speak in European accents," though he conceded the possibility of exception for Oliver Wendell Holmes and John Dewey, neither of whom he really much liked—to nationalise and secularise the nation, and it was conceivable, in the light of this failure and presumable enfeeblement, that the Conservative Party could be the vanguard by which "we [might] be saved from that dreadful century, whose name stands for universal ignominy, in the name of equality; and in the name of freedom, a drab servitude to anonymous institutional idealisms." There is no reason to suppose anything but the utmost sincerity in this revulsion against the twentieth century. The Conservative Party must bring the nation back to Adam Smith and his prophet, God.

Barry the Forerunner, however, cried in vain in the wilderness, and his head was served up on a charger for the pleasure of sinners; Paolucci went back to his nobler concerns and kept politics, as it were, for the sabbath. Nonetheless a trend had been described, and it was a real one: Paolucci had taken away enough votes from Kenneth Keating, the incumbent Republican Senator allied with Rockefeller, to help that hastily and never wholly naturalised New Yorker, Robert Kennedy, to wring election to the Senate out of the martyr's name. In the city, Kennedy's Liberal votes were barely thirty-five thousand more than Paolucci's Conservative total. And the city Republicans were a cross-breed anyway, as any observer knew: thus far their party had represented the only game in town for conservatives in spite of its infiltration by such "liberals" as then Representative John Vliet Lindsay, who easily won re-election against Kieran O'Doherty, one of the founders of the Conservative Party. It has always been largely a mystery why and how the two major parties have continued to exist separately as they have done in New York City, where neither of them can begin to be representative in any consistent fashion since each is so much the chameleon, indistinguishable from the other. For years conservative New Yorkers had either (sensibly) not voted at all or bitterly voted for a label that, for what they wanted, had long since lost all meaning. In 1962 some fifty thousand of them had voted in desperation for Conservative candidates for Congress and local office; in two years their number had doubled. Like those radicals who rightly curl their lips at the Democratic and Liberal Parties and, if they vote at all, vote for such parties as the Socialist Workers, these Conservatives were equally rightly sick of being diddled. But conservatives and radicals together could not have changed anything then, since, as is almost always the case, the overwhelming majority of the suckers would have lynched the first man to tell them what they were.

The Conservative Party wanted nonetheless to make a beginning, even if defeat was foregone. Its leaders had started in 1964 to weigh the possibilities of a Mayoral campaign in 1965 and to assay the potential sacrificial lambs who might be offered up. But until Lindsay, after the usual coquetting, had finally said *yes* to the Republicans, all this activity had been to a large degree academic. Neither Conservatives nor conservatives could accept Lindsay, who had thus far been a kind of colorless cut-rate Kennedy, any more than they could tolerate the amiably incompetent incumbent, Robert F. Wagner. Conservative leaders saw this as their opportunity to affect the Mayoral battle, at least, and perhaps to thwart Lindsay, for whom it seemed to be a first step along what he and his supporters hoped would be his road to the Presidency—though, after what one has seen in that august post since the Second World War, it is probably not too august for a man who could bring himself to enunciate the idea of *Fun City* as a pretext for voting for him.

Lindsay had announced his candidacy on 13 May 1965. Later that month Buckley (who in *The Unmaking of a Mayor* insists he had never been high in the councils of the Conservative leaders; Mahoney, in *Actions Speak Louder*, gives the unmistakably contrary impression) wrote a column, which appeared both in newspapers and in *National Review*, that offered "half in fun" a ten-point packaged program for anyone who cared to be a mayor anywhere. Subsequently he abandoned some of these ideas and modified others, after he had announced his own candidacy (on which he finally decided on 3 June). The originals included neighborhood vigilantes to prevent crime, repeal of the anti-narcotics laws and adoption of the British system, tax exemptions for black and Puerto Rican capitalists, rigorous enforcement of harsh penalties (as they seemed then) for violators of parking rules, a municipal right-to-work law with criminal sanctions, the full legalisation of gambling, the end of the taxi-ownership monopoly, compulsory work for all welfare recipients except invalids and mothers of children under fifteen, the assignment of children to local schools and compulsory vocational training, at the hands of administrators with extraordinary disciplinary powers, for dropouts under fourteen, and the exemption of children from the minimum-wage law (which, he really believed and believes, ought not to exist at all). At the *National Review* staff conference on the cover for the issue, Priscilla Buckley suggested a diagonal legend across the upper-left-hand corner: "Buckley for Mayor." This was supposed to be a joke, Priscilla argued, and everyone would know it was a mere metaphor.

Within a short time unidentified informants advised Buckley that, though he was a resident and registered Republican voter in Stamford, he was eligible to seek the Mayoralty of New York. He endeavored instead to persuade *National Review*'s publisher, William A. Rusher, to be the candidate: Rusher was more than acceptable to Conservative Party leaders. But the idea was wholly unacceptable to him; and so Buckley began to toy with its enticements for himself. In his book about the campaign he insists that he was in no way motivated by any animus, personal or political, against Lindsay, for whom one can recall no kind word ever on his part; and various journalists have over the years commented adversely on the amount and kind of attention given by Buckley to Lindsay since. The matter is hardly a major one. It is interesting, however, that James Buckley and Lindsay's twin brother, David, were close friends at Yale; James Buckley is the godfather of one of David Lindsay's children. Bill Buckley asked James to be his campaign manager, as John Lindsay craved the same service of his own brother, and James consented only after an amicable exchange of letters with his friend.

Lindsay had to be stopped, in the Buckleys' view, because of his threat to conservative Republicans, and, as Bill Buckley explained, it would have been a dismal exercise to attempt to eliminate him in a Republican primary campaign. That would have left only two candidates, Lindsay, whom Buckley would then have felt bound to support, and the trusty cog in the Democratic machine, Abraham Beame of Brooklyn: the "liberals" would have followed the Liberal Party in its support of Lindsay, who was rapidly manufacturing a glamour candidacy to the extent to which this was possible. Buckley, as Lindsay's advisers correctly guessed, had no illusions that he could be elected: he hoped to be able to divide the Republicans sufficiently to allow the innocuous Beame (innocuous in Buckley's eyes, at any rate, in comparison to Lindsay) to win, and Buckley aspired too to create the occasion to build something of a mass base for conservatism whether under its own or under the Republican ensign.

Two months before his announcement of his candidacy, however, Buckley had suffered—if indeed he had not brought about —a critical moment the effects of which can never be statistically measured; but it was revealing of the man and of his adversaries. He had been invited to address the annual Communion breakfast of the Police Department's Holy Name Society on 4 April 1965 in the presence of the traditional luminaries: the Mayor, the Police Commissioner, the Cardinal-Archbishop, assorted elective paladins of all origins. Now it would be dishonest to pretend that in his address Buckley once departed from his own tenets or sought to flatter his audience: the cops loved him because, when it comes to *lawnorder* and poor people and non-whites, the two last of whom are virtually interchangeable in his mind, he thinks exactly like a cop.

The six thousand Finest there present laughed whenever Buck-

ley poked at the press and anyone else who had ever spoken up
for defendants' and prisoners' rights; and every attack was made
in his customary cultivated rhetoric, without condescension to
the probable level of his audience—just as he was never to descend
to the language of the political club or the street, or to such pimp-
ing as the kissing of babies or the eating of "ethnic" foods for the
photographers. But what he said was in some of its implications
frightening: in essence, he was assuring the police that they were
above the law and he was studiedly minimising the racist actions of
their colleagues in Alabama under the aegis of Governor Wallace,
in spite of his sanctimonious ritual lament for their possible "excesses" in response to "the excesses . . . of those who provoked
them beyond the endurance that we tend to think of as human."
The provocators in question were the followers of the late Rev.
Dr. Martin Luther King Jr., who refused, in their orderly manifestation in Selma, to disperse when ordered to do so in violation
of the First Amendment. The record, in print and on film, is
available to those who would verify the marchers' "excesses."
Buckley also minimised the murder of a white woman from Detroit for her part in helping the blacks: it was to have been expected, given the locale, so why the nation-wide attention to it?
It was grotesque that he quoted T. S. Eliot—not only because of
the ambience but also because of the unbridgeable differences between the men: it is difficult to conceive of Eliot ever distorting
fact to advance a cause, especially one in which he believed as
a moral man. Buckley's peroration was in essence a denunciation
a priori of everyone who might ever be arrested by a cop, or who
might even reproach one.

No doubt what he said pleased his audience and the Conservative Party; and it was quite bad enough, from another point of
view, without any of the distortion and fabrication with which
it was presented or misrepresented to the public at large. Buckley
was accused of having said what he had not said, as the police
were accused of having reacted as they had not reacted; and this
by "respectable" newspapers. John Leo, an associate editor of
Commonweal, examined the entire array of press coverage and comment—the worst offenders were the *Herald Tribune* and the *Post*,
though *The Times* was there too—and found, for instance, that
of twenty-six quotations in the *Herald Tribune* nineteen were mis-
quotations, and, of the seven that were not, "at least two were
used unfairly. The ones he [the reporter] got absolutely straight,

and used fairly (here presented in their entirety), were 'ten days later,' 'acting under orders,' 'they might not proceed,' 'you must stand mutely' and 'the Governor of Alabama.'" Mr. Leo concluded: "I think Mr. Buckley's speech, on the whole, was quite objectionable, both in thought and rhetoric. But there is no doubt that he has been treated rather shabbily, first by being subjected to a Pavlovian liberal response on the part of New York papers and pressure groups, few of which seem to have troubled themselves to discover what he actually said, and secondly by the disinclination of the *Tribune* to apologize for a wretched story." In fact, had the names been changed, one would have thought Leo was discussing *National Review*'s coverage of a speech by Noam Chomsky. But thirty years in New York journalism would lead one to expect nothing else.

Buckley, however, had a weapon not readily available to most of his own victims—the money to hire a good lawyer. Libel actions against the *Herald Tribune* and the *Post* compelled reparation, not in money, which would have been irrelevant, but in apologies and retractions. "It was reassuring," Buckley wrote, "to ascertain that right, plus a good lawyer, can sometimes stimulate the dormant conscience"; and one hopes that some of his opponents may benefit by the same reassurance. Professor Fowler Harper, who died during the litigation, did successfully sue Buckley, Rusher, and *National Review* for having called him a Communist fellow-traveler who aided and abetted the nation's enemies: his widow received a public apology and cash damages. On the other hand, Dr. Linus Pauling, who also sued on the same ground, was denied a recovery on the postulate that as a public figure he was within the rule that permitted fair comment on public personalities in their public capacities even if it was inaccurate, provided there was no malice: unlike Harper, who could hardly have been called an activist, Pauling had been a militant partisan of disarmament, world peace, and various national and international radical causes since the Second World War.

Whether Buckley might, under that rule, have failed in a slander action filed at the same time as his libel suits against the two newspapers is a matter of conjecture. The slander defendant was Artie Shaw, band leader, writer, and film producer, who had and has a house in Lakeville and was an acquaintance of John and James Buckley. On one occasion in 1964, Shaw, a frequent visitor to television programs, had debated Buckley on the air with con-

siderable fervor. On the night of 5 May 1965, not long after the
Holy Name Society's breakfast, Shaw was being interviewed by
one William B. Williams on an American Broadcasting Co. program. The talk dealt at first with a new book by Shaw, but then
Williams recalled the program with Buckley and asked Shaw's
opinion of him. Initially Shaw tried to turn the question aside on
the sound ground that Buckley was not present to speak for himself. But Shaw is highly reactive to cant phrases (or some cant
phrases), and, when Williams asked whether Shaw did not agree
that Buckley was "a master of the forensic"—and it is not really
a very fine turn of language, nor a very novel one—Shaw began
to heat up. Williams then said that he thought Buckley had something to say even though it ran counter to Williams' own beliefs,
"and I think he does present it in almost a chilling fashion."

To which Shaw replied, according to the ABC transcript:
"Well, Bill, let's start with one thing. If a man sells hate, he's got
a very useful commodity. An awful lot of people looking for it."
Williams said: "Do you think he sells hate?" and Shaw answered:
"Oh, indeed he does. That's the basis of his entire commodity."
At this point Williams announced into the vacuum of the night
that Buckley, if he was listening, was welcome to "drop in" and
present his own case. Presumably Buckley had better things to
do, because his only reply was made two weeks later with the
filing of his litigation. Then he requested a public apology, which
he did not get. He then filed an amended complaint—the action
was initiated in Fairfield County, Connecticut—charging, among
other things:

> 3. Said words ["sells hate"] are false, malicious, and li-
> belous per se.
> 4. By said false and malicious words, defendant intended
> to charge, and hearers of said broadcast understood plain-
> tiff [sic: a stenographer's error?] to mean, that the plaintiff
> encourages the members of the white race to hate the
> members of the Negro race, to use violence towards them
> and to frustrate and defeat their proper aspirations. By said
> false and malicious words defendant further intended to
> injure plaintiff's good name, fame, credit and reputation.
> 5. Defendant used said words with reckless disregard
> of their truth. . . .
> 7. The said false and malicious words have injured plain-
> tiff's good name, fame and reputation and held him up to

public scorn, hatred, disgrace, scandal, contempt and dishonor. Said false and malicious words have caused plaintiff great mental anxiety and suffering.

8. The said false and malicious words have substantially injured plaintiff in his several business capacities as an editor, columnist, author and speaker, and sole stockholder of *National Review*, Inc.

Wherefore plaintiff prayed actual damages in the amount of five hundred thousand dollars, punitive damages, and counsel fees, costs, and expenses.

Quite aside from the manifest rhetorical deficiencies of the complaint—which (Rodell is right) would have been far better written by plaintiff's own hand—and the ritual mumbo-jumbo of such documents, Buckley had chosen to narrow the whole issue to hatred of one specific group, Negroes, though Shaw had never mentioned them. Buckley had never protested when *Time* quoted his defense of segregation on moral grounds, or *The Times* reported his dismissal of the citizens of the Congo as "semi-savages," or *Esquire* quoted him on African cannibalism as if it were current and quotidian, to take only three of numerous examples. One is curious at this seeming weakness in the complaint; but perhaps it did not matter too much, since Buckley was in a reasonable position to know that at that time, because of a combination of problems, some of which had attracted the attention of the press, Shaw was in no financial condition to fight a long lawsuit: indeed, neighbors helped him to pay his attorney's retainer. The lawyer thought that Buckley's Mayoralty campaign might induce him to withdraw his action; but this was unwarranted optimism. By October, however, Buckley was willing to settle for a full written retraction and payment of a thousand dollars toward his legal fees. Shaw balked at the money, and the case was still pending when the election came and Buckley was defeated—though neither this suit against Shaw nor Harper's and Pauling's one-and-a-half-million-dollar actions against Buckley, which were pending in the New York courts, was ever a factor, or even mentioned. On the day after the election, Buckley moved—unsuccessfully—for a change of venue in the latter actions; the final judgments were not announced until the following March.

It was six months later still—September, 1966—when a deposition was taken from Shaw in the Bridgeport office of Buckley's lawyers, assisted by C. Dickerman Williams. Neither his examination of Shaw nor the questioning by Shaw's own attorney, Edwin K. Dimes of Westport, brought out anything to strengthen Shaw's defense, which at no time raised the question of fair comment or public personage. No evidence was adduced that could support any strict construction of Shaw's statement about Buckley, though the charge of malice on Shaw's part was pretty well vitiated by the circumstances of the spontaneous and generally irresponsible give-and-take out of which broadcasters make money or think they make money. Shaw finally apologised and the suit was withdrawn. Buckley himself is inclined now to believe that in a similar situation today he would lose such a suit as soon as the defense moved to dismiss under the fair-comment rule.

Certainly the inching progress of this litigation did not preempt much of Buckley's attention during the campaign. Nor was the episode of the Holy Name breakfast the sort of thing that prompted Kempton to write, during the summer of 1965: "There are occasions when Buckley tempts you to remember Macaulay's grudging compliment to Burke, which was that he generally chose his side like a fanatic and defended it like a philosopher." On 4 August Buckley had explained his candidacy in what he called a self-interview delivered at the National Press Club in Washington. Anyone who is outraged by being appealed to invariably by every lickspittle luster after public office on the ground of race, religion, occupation, hair color, or sexual preference could only applaud Buckley for this:

"As far as New York politicians are concerned, a New Yorker is an Irishman, an Italian, or a Negro; he is a union member or a white-collar worker; a welfare recipient or a city employee; a Catholic or a Protestant or a Jew; a taxi driver or a taxi owner; a merchant or a policeman. The problem is to weigh the voting strength of all the categories and formulate a program that least dissatisfies the least crowded and least powerful categories: and the victory is supposed to go to the most successful bloc Benthamite in the race."

Asked (by himself) what he would do if he became Mayor, he replied: "I would treat people as individuals." This, of course, was and remains revolutionary; but how he would have done this threw the whole statement into doubt, because he proposed, as a passionate disciple of the free-market philosophy in universal applicability, to do away with precisely those safeguards that, if enforced, might make individuality possible again in this country.

It was very attractive to be told that Utopia would consist of security of life, limb, and property, assurance of employment without tribute to a union, guaranties of doing business without minimum wages, education without arbitrary color harmonies determined by the magic of numbers—especially if no allusion was made to the price necessarily to be paid for these boons: random arrest, vigilante violence, the continual risk of unemployment, starvation pay, the perpetuation of educational disparities, all of which together would mean the exacerbation of just that strife of blocs, racial groups, and classes that the free market was supposed in a vacuum to preclude.

His own candidacy, he said, was an attempt to restore the two-party system in New York because Lindsay's Republican platform was indistinguishable from Beame's Democratic program, whereas Buckley's Conservative agenda was "wholly congruent with the Republican national platform of 1964." Therefore, he continued, the outcome of the city election was of great importance throughout the country because of the general belief in the two-party system: "The two-party system would be damaged by the election to a very prominent position of an ambitious gentleman whose policies are left-Democratic but whose affiliation is Republican." Moreover, Republicans everywhere ought to be concerned by the candidacy of "a Republican running in New York, who refused to support the Republican Presidential candidate [and] now gladly supports New York socialists and is supported by them." This was the basis on which he was to solicit contributions to his own campaign from non-residents of New York and on which many people were to volunteer donations: most of the out-of-town givers seem to have been residents of the South and the Southwest.

It was alleged at the time of the campaign that Lindsay wrote all the things that appeared over his name, including the book reviews that he occasionally published, and Buckley was right in assuming, from the result, that this was probably true then (*tempora mutantur*: once he became Mayor he had a helot who confected these critiques for him to sign). Buckley's sneer was not frivolous: the style does tell something of the man, and one would be hard pressed to recall anyone who found any individuality or zest in the Lindsay who used to suffer himself to be impaneled for WBAI or television when he was still in Congress. On his unholpen merit he could not put together a more than

pedestrian paragraph. Change *paragraph* to *program* and the statement is no less accurate. Like the whole line of "liberal" candidates
over the past thirty years—Roosevelt removed himself from the
ranks after 1936—he offers a dull exposition of a tired, borrowed
agenda that no intelligent person expects him to try to realise.

Both Buckleys stand out in sharp contrast. They share the disconcerting quality of saying exactly what they mean: they really
do intend to do, if they are elected, the things with the threat of
which they frighten some of us and delight others. Both of them
say what they have to say with some respect for the decencies
of language; James Buckley's genuine modesty shows itself in his
discreet style, as Bill's arrogance and intolerance and often devilish
charm form the skeleton of his coruscating rhetoric. The Grand
Guignol offers a constant and nearly irresistible temptation to Bill
Buckley, and to a degree even his Mayoralty campaign had something of the Guignol side by side with the unquestionable seriousness of his resolve to stop Lindsay and to exploit the campaign
as a sounding-board for the pre-pubescent Conservative Party. But
he would never, even for the sake of Guignol, have been capable
of such a pronouncement as that of Tom Anderson of the Council
of the John Birch Society: "Where there is no poverty, there is
no freedom."

It may or may not have been coincidence that Buckley's and
National Review's break with that Society was virtually completed
in the summer and autumn of 1965, as his Mayoral campaign was
accelerating. The Birch organ, *American Opinion*, on whose masthead, as on *National Review*'s, Schlamm's name still flourished and
for which that implacable crier of holy war against the Communists continued to write, revealed in its 1965 Scoreboard that the
United States was sixty to eighty per cent under Communist control: such was the conclusion of an exhaustive analysis by Revilo
P. Oliver. It was becoming impossible for Buckley and Goldwater
to continue to draw their insuperable distinction between Welch
and all the perfectly good people who were still members of the
Society, or to proclaim their community of purpose with the Society as distinguished from Welch, who had told the world as
much years earlier in his *Blue Book*: "The men who join the John
Birch Society during the next few months or few years are going
to do so primarily because they believe in me and what I am doing
and are willing to accept my leadership anyway."

A special six-part section in *National Review* for 19 October

1965, preceded by a number of columns by Buckley in August, conceding the lack of any major ideological gap between Welch and those who believed in the Society's "paranoid and unpatriotic drivel," identified the Birch Society as a threat to American conservatism. Both Buckley and Frank Meyer developed this theme; Meyer demolished the worst of the conspiratorial fantasies; James Burnham pointed out that in its opposition to the Vietnam war the Society had aligned itself with the Left, though he strove still to hope that most of the members were only "misguided"; nonetheless he warned that any serious anti-Communist "will have to stay clear of the JBS." Oliver's idea that Burnham and Meyer had duped Buckley, or that Buckley was jealous of Welch's leadership, must be dismissed out of hand—the first on its face and the second virtually so: Welch was obviously in desperate need of a leadership rôle and Buckley was equally obviously far more complex and sophisticated and thus far more a man of ideas than of personal ambition.

But he was, in 1965, rather ahead of the times: the platitudinously though accurately named silent majority was silent but not yet wholly aware that it was the majority; it was still enjoying the titillatory thrills of fear and refusing to admit that it was manufacturing its own frights. In as little as five years, when James Buckley won election to the Senate, this majority would have begun to feel more confidence, though even then it did not grasp the fact of its preponderance in spite of having in 1968 elected its composite image to the Presidency. But its heart warmed when Bill Buckley, in his campaign, gave the sanction of his superiority and his language to its and his intentions for the lower orders. Sometimes his frankness and his schoolboy temptations to *épater le bourgeois* did not redound to his advantage, however. His honest admission that he did not expect election was misread to mean that his candidacy was not serious, whereas it was most earnest—on behalf not of himself but of his cause. Asked what he would do if, by a miracle, he did win, he retorted: "Demand a recount." It was a rather endearing answer, really, and the kind one would have liked to make in a similar circumstance: it was devoid of illusion. Mahoney is quite right in deploring, in his book, the fact that the press—and, by extension, radio and television— almost never paid serious attention to Buckley's policies and arguments but treated his candidacy as a continuous free entertainment and himself as its star. These elements existed, unquestionably, and

he was quite adroit in exploiting them; but in actuality he far over-
estimated the intelligence of New York journalists, and probably
their sense of responsibility as well (there are exceptions to this
anathema, but not many). They were ripe for such a concept as
Lindsay's Fun City, and they belonged in it.

Even *The Times*'s editorial writers discounted Buckley as "glib,
assertive and usually impossible." So he is, sometimes, and he
knows it (having stated a hypothetical protasis about himself to
me, he concluded by way of apodosis: "I'd be insufferable—more
insufferable"). He had to write a letter to the editor in order to
obtain consideration of his serious ideas about the city and its
needs. Paradoxically, it was only that shoe-rag, *The News*, that
took him really seriously and discussed, in the small words best
suited to its owners, editors, and readers, what he was after—
which was what *The News* was after too. Certainly it could only
sing hosanna to his principal running mates: a Queens housewife,
Mrs. Rosemary Gunning, for the presidency of the City Council,
and Hugh Markey, a Staten Island business man, for the comp-
trollership. Mrs. Gunning was notorious for having roused the
kulaki of Queens against the integration of the schools—Mahoney
says in his book that "she personifies everything that is sound and
decent in the mind and heart of New York City." *The Times*
thereupon, and rightly, congratulated the Conservative Party for
having, in spite of its own internal doubts of the wisdom of advertising its dominance by Irish Catholics, refused to truckle to
the opportunistic "ethnic" criteria by which the big parties had
always determined their choices of candidates.

One does not recall any paper, however, that mentioned the
fact that Liebman was in charge of raising the money to keep the
campaign going. It was shocking, however, in spite of the business
links of the prior and present generations, to find so eminent a
lawyer and social symbol as Frederic R. Coudert Jr. in the chairmanship of the Buckley for Mayor Committee. Freeman, who
was on the staff of *National Review* and syndicating Buckley's
column, was the right hand. Unlike the Republicans and the
Democrats, who set up lavish headquarters in expensive hotels, the
Conservatives rented an apartment in an aging Forty-fifth Street
building west of Fifth Avenue. The usual television circuses were
organised by the broadcasters, and for sheer entertainment value
and consistent literacy, of course, the shows were always Buckley's, I am told by all qualified observers: I had no television set,

and in any event one would prefer to base one's political choices on something other than shows; but it would appear that one's prejudices did cheat one out of some fairly literate diversion—and spare one from an inordinate, if not unconscionable, amount of tedium and billingsgate in equal measure.

For the campaign quickly degenerated, in spite of the unquestionable cultivation and breeding of two of the candidates, into the typical American orgy of vulgarity, dishonesty, manipulation, blackmail, and worse. It is painful to have to concede that the only candidate who occasionally attempted to bring the contest back to an almost decent level was Buckley, and he was far from consistent in this: he was also at least as bad as the others most of the time. In essence the battle was between him and Lindsay, since Beame was of no significance and his election could have made no difference to the city, the state, or anything else except the Democratic Party, which needed New York. But Lindsay was clawing his way up and Buckley was clubbing him down and at the same time striving to secure the first beachhead for the Conservative Party. That was at once visible and that was why the struggle in New York was the focus of nation-wide attention right to the end. Lindsay had at first attempted to ignore Buckley, but then had become frightened of him, especially as newspaper polls during the campaign indicated gains in his popularity. No doubt entire books could and will be written on the dubiousness of these devices and the perniciousness of the ways in which they are virtually invariably exploited.

In retrospect the wonder is that Buckley got so few votes, and the explanation probably lies primarily in his refusal to pander to "ethnics" and indulge in cheap play-acting. Quite as many bigots and *machos* voted for Lindsay and Beame as for Buckley—most of them, probably, because they did not trust the condescending amateur in politics (as they regarded him) who did not remotely "speak their language," but also very many because he had not promised them anything. In the big Fifth Avenue demonstration against the Vietnam war in late October, 1965, just before the election, most of the identifiable hooligans who stormed off the sidewalks—especially in the Eighties—to punch and kick the marchers while the police looked very ostentatiously the other way wore Buckley buttons and hats; but there was a great deal of nasty behavior against the "peaceniks" by good l.-m.-c. Americans tagged out for Lindsay and Beame. One is always adjured not to hold leaders accountable for the behavior of their hordes; but one must sometimes wonder how broad this exemption is.

A political campaign, of course, degrades anyone who takes part in it, at least in this country. It required a statesman of the caliber of Jacob Javits to declare on 15 October: "I fear for the freedom of New York City." This was the same day on which Lindsay accused Buckley, both directly and indirectly, of attempting to incite riot in the streets: he said that Buckley advocated "a radical philosophy full of hatred and division and violence," and that New York was a "powderkeg, and Buckley's doing his best to light the fuse." This kind of nonsense was in itself almost enough to make anyone vote for Buckley: if it did not, that was only because there were far sounder and more real reasons not to do so: but these were not unlike the reasons that for years have impelled a great many people not to vote at all, and certainly not for anyone who would allow himself to be drafted into either of the drossy hordes. One of the few accurate observations to be made by Lindsay was the much more sober and realistic comment of 9 October, to the effect that Buckley was "attracting a white-supremacy following." Of this there could be little doubt. Nor was it unfair, as we shall see, for Buckley's opponents to accuse him of wishing to set up deportation and even concentration camps outside the city for those whose offense to good morals was poverty. At the end of October *The Times* said editorially that his campaign was consciously oriented toward "brutish instincts," which it inventoried: "fear, ignorance, racial superiority, religious antagonism, contempt for the weak and afflicted and hatred for those different from oneself."

Unfortunately Buckley had no monopoly on some of these, at least. Timothy Costello, one of Lindsay's fellow-candidates and now president of a public college (who must have been singularly forgetful), would have had Buckley defeated because of his "propagation of the social doctrine of the Catholic Church"! It is conceivable, of course, that Costello meant "sexual doctrine," but then he should have said so; in any event, it was difficult to comprehend his conclusion that "a vote for Buckley is an anti-Catholic vote," and it is, of course, impossible to exculpate it or him. Buckley constantly opposed—for the record—the traditional politician's cynicism in appealing to racial and religious blocs; at the same time he took more than one opportunity to remind the electorate that his entire ticket was Catholic and Lindsay was

Protestant. (For once the Jews ran a poor third in this kind of citation.) Contemporary press accounts of the campaign are hardly reliable, since such things as *The News* selected and slanted their stories to favor Buckley and the respectable papers selected and slanted theirs to denigrate him. In the end the best source is Buckley's own book on the subject, *The Unmaking of a Mayor*. It provides some evidence whether there was any substance to Beame's contention that, although relatively few people were willing to take Buckley seriously, his "mask of humor" and his "twisted wit" concealed "sinister and evil philosophies."

Some of the things he said were quite unexceptionable, from any point of view: for example, this to a black audience: "The Jew with his crooked nose, the Italian with his accent, the Irishman with his drunkenness or whatever—they had a difficult time. But it was nothing like the great disadvantage you have suffered and which we white people need to face as a charge upon our conscience that we need to expiate. . . ." It was or should have been apparent even to someone with the mind of a policeman or a drill sergeant that the first three references merely symbolised stereotypes of prejudice; what is most interesting is that the "liberal" press, quite like *National Review* in analogous circumstances, quoted selectively so that the Irish stereotype was omitted and Buckley was made to appear anti-Jewish and anti-Italian. The balance of the excerpt was anodyne. But his own variant of his opponents' techniques, and some indication of his real views, came in the same setting when a member of the audience asked him about the report that he had accused the Harlem blacks of throwing garbage out their windows in order to wallow in it:

"I asked James Baldwin why some people do that, and he said: 'Why, that's a form of social protest.' This is an answer that is inexplicable to me. Why should people throw garbage out their windows?—in order themselves to wallow in it?"

The device is hardly a new one. On the other hand, it is conceivable that the newspaper editor who told him, after the election, that a single phrase had cost Buckley a hundred thousand votes was right in attributing to mere "stupidity" his appeal for votes not for himself "but for a vision of a new order." Buckley did not believe the editor's analysis; I myself cannot accept the parochialism of his having called it, in Buckley's words, "a red flag flourished . . . in the face of the Jewish community." It is difficult to imagine that only Jews remember the terminology of both Italian and German Fascism, or that those who remember it do so only in the context of anti-Semitism. "Vision of a new order" was indeed Anne Morrow Lindbergh's salute to Fascism in her 1940 book, *The Wave of the Future, A Confession of Faith*, which Buckley may or may not have read; but "new order" was the term used by Mussolini, Hitler, and Sir Oswald Mosley to describe their respective versions of Fascism (and the inspiration of Roosevelt's "New Deal"), and the fact was common knowledge in literate circles—of which Buckley was certainly a member. There was certainly, to use the legal idiom, a reasonable, if rebuttable, presumption that he knew this.

Let us examine the Conservative Party's position papers; the source on which we draw is *The Unmaking of a Mayor*. Buckley introduces them by rehearsing some of the comments that were made when they were issued: *The Wall Street Journal* found "concrete remedies," and *The New York Review of Books*, in the person of the late Paul Goodman, regarded them as "occasionally . . . inventive." (One of Buckley's less vital suggestions—special traffic lanes for bicycles—was indeed put into practice in different form six years later by Lindsay, though without acknowledgment of its paternity.) Buckley apologises for the fact that they are ideological too, because, as one of the more persistent popularisers of that very difficult scholar, Professor Eric Voegelin, he believes that ideology is the antithesis of philosophy, and he takes issue with Webster on the matter. The Conservative Party held certain presumptions, Buckley said, "in favor of realism (economic truth), private property (equity), the private sector (as opposed to the public), the individual (as opposed to the bloc)"; and, "to use James Burnham's example, conservatives know that you *can't* do away with Skid Row." Conservatives also believe "that politics should not, in the lofty phrase of Voegelin, attempt to 'immanentize the eschaton.' And conservatives believe, along with Dr. Johnson, that 'the end of political liberty is personal liberty.'" Against this background the Conservative Party issued ten position papers, dealing, respectively, with water (always a New York problem), welfare, education, fiscal affairs, crime, taxation, housing, pollution, narcotics, and transit. That wherever possible they were uncompromisingly on the side of the free-market approach as opposed to the social may be taken for granted. Their final form was imposed by Buckley, and it is virtually devoid of the kind of *enfant terrible* playfulness (told in a debate that he had twenty unused seconds in which to expound further, he declined: "I think I'll just contemplate the great eloquence of my previous remarks") that added an occasional trace of humane letters to the pedestrian muck through which he had committed himself to move.

Free enterprise would cope with the water shortage by the use of water meters (only a quarter of the city's users paid a graduated rather than a flat fee for water). Welfare recipients would have to be city residents for one year—provided they survived, by means lawful or unlawful—before they could receive payments; on the other hand, they would be allowed to keep enough of their outside earnings to spur them "to seek gainful employment"; all qualified recipents would have to work for what they got, or join vocational-training programs; fraud would be ruthlessly eliminated from the children's-aid program; and an experiment in the removal of chronic cases beyond the city limits, and in the rehabilitation of some of them, would be undertaken. It is extremely important to note that no word was said about the procedures to be employed, about due process of law, about the rights of the persons involved.

Buckley proposed that the concept of the neighborhood school be retained and reinforced, on the ground that the purpose of the school is to instruct, not to integrate: the school population would reflect the neighborhood population. There is nothing very immoral in this, and in the years since 1965 the position's merits have become very clear to people on all sides of the question of race. The proposal that Puerto Rican children be taught English is a first principle, and nothing could be more falsely "liberal" than the specious argument that one must not impose the culture of the ruling class on minorities and thus wipe out their own. (When Buckley talks about "the special needs of students of differing race," that is quite another matter, and he condemns himself.) In Italy, for instance, where there are as many dialects as there are towns, everyone speaks (from childhood) what amounts to two languages: the local dialect, for local purposes, and standard Italian, for communication with the man from across the river. This proposal, like Buckley's insistence on emphasis on intellectual progress "even at the expense of pseudo-democratic equality" and mass promotions, represents a vital weapon in the fight to overthrow the intellectual ghetto in which the minorities have so long been kept (in part, moreover, by their own actions): to reduce the standards of the schools to the needs of the least able, as I have heard "liberal" and even radical educationists propose in all seriousness, is to aggravate the intellectual pauperisation of those already subject to exploitation and to make it even more difficult for them to achieve liberation. As for Buckley's endorsement of decentralisation of schools, he was anticipating the Left. But his was the typical Right-Wing position on public education: as little of it as possible should be free—education, like mass transportation, medical care, and every other necessity of life, must pay its way even if this meant excluding a vast portion of the qualified population from access to it.

Such an attitude led logically to his view of municipal finances. It might be summed up, not unjustly, as "cut out most of the services and cut back the taxes paid by the owners of enterprises." Buckley proposed, instead, the introduction of a value-added tax, long known in Europe: a tax levied at each stage in the production of a commodity and based on the further value given to it by that process, the sum to be paid by the ultimate purchaser. It would have eliminated a swarm of existing levies (on gross receipts, on sales and use, on utilities, on occupancy, on cigarettes, on amusements, on hotel rooms) and the paperwork thereon attendant, and "it would maintain a broad tax base (which recognises the obligation of any business enterprise to contribute to the cost of the city services it enjoys)."

This approach is so eminently sensible that it would leave the innocent wholly unprepared and utterly open for what was probably the most vicious aspect of the program: crime control. Buckley began with the suggestion, which was reasonable enough, that the police force be increased; but then he proposed that it be removed from any civilian surveillance of its excesses. "Criminal-coddling" must end: parole and probation must be tightened, sentences must be longer, juveniles guilty of serious crimes must be punished more severely, their and their parents' identities must be made public, and bounties should be paid to informers. The only thing to be said in favor of this whole amalgam of savagery is its honesty in speaking only of punishment: at least it said what it meant and did not hide behind pretty talk of rehabilitation. There were in addition two acceptable proposals: state indemnification of victims of crimes of violence and financial compensation for witnesses in criminal trials. That is how it is stated; one must hope that it is comprehensive and means witnesses for the defense as well as for the prosecution, otherwise it becomes as reprehensible as the cash incentive to informers. One has to agree that the adversary system of criminal justice is a cruel farce—for many reasons, and not merely because it may sometimes (though not often) work to the advantage of the guilty, or inadequately, after the event, protect "the rights of the public" against the defendant (again fundamentally a question of vengeance): justice is not, or ought not to be, a mere game, like chess or tennis; but one cannot forbear quoting Murray Kempton's comment on this position paper: "This century has been a continual trial and failure of liberal notions. The prime article of its faith has been that, if you pay a man well enough, he will do things that pride or sense of public obligation should have made him do in the first place. There is every excuse for Bill Buckley to believe in this century: he hasn't been there." But what excuse is there for Bill Buckley the moralist to measure morality by the price that must be paid for it in dollars? Bill Buckley, Kempton concluded, "would redeem the bad citizen by making him a good bounty hunter."

Buckley made no friends by telling the truth, however, about the city's housing failure and by emphasising the fact that it was the poor who were its greatest victims. This said, however, he proceeded to demand action that could only make matters even worse (as subsequent legislative and executive cringing before the landlord lobby was to demonstrate): the end of rent controls because (he quaintly argued) they discriminate against the poor, the young, the old; and the surrender of all housing construction to the selfless hands of private enterprise "liberated" from "bureaucratic harassment." Part of the latter task entailed curbs on monopoly labor unions—a point beyond cavil—and "elementary steps to discourage the thoughtless flow of immigrants into the city." One wonders whether he meant to reactivate Ellis Island, and what criteria would determine the eligibility (or thoughtfulness) of the acceptable immigrants. On the other hand, Buckley's idea for the growth of many "self-contained working and recreational communities" in the city can be only praised.

Pollution afforded a concrete illustration of the conservative bias toward purely local control. Buckley would have kept the state and federal governments completely out of the city's problem, and this he would have dealt with by a combination of tax-relief inducements for compliance with recognised anti-pollution procedures and penalties for non-compliance. This represented probably the ultimate concession that anyone with his free-market philosophy could make to "our enemy, the state": municipal garbage disposal, a ban on bituminous coal, mandatory pollution-reduction devices on motor vehicles.

Otherwise it was only in connection with crime and the related problem of narcotics that Buckley would sweepingly add to the powers of the government as against the citizen. He was intelligent enough to recognise addiction as illness and not crime; but his prophylactic and therapeutic measures were harsh indeed. Suspected addicts would be subjected to tests; those who wished to be cured would be separated from those who did not, and each category would be "sequestered." The bad addicts would nevertheless be exposed to various psychological efforts such as those practiced by Synanon, the voluntary drug-cure group that claims considerable success; Buckley also advocated experiments with methadone. His proposals for sequestration, the constitutionality of which is at least questionable, were later to be taken up by many who had opposed them and him.

One may be certain that few conservatives agreed with his position paper on the city's traffic problem, for he emphasised the importance of mass transit and a variety of experiments designed to minimise the number of vehicles entering the city: special tolls for non-residents, flexible regulations for loading and unloading commercial vehicles, and the end of special privileges for foreign diplomats. This last item would certainly please the xenophobes in the bedroom boroughs. But his insistence on higher transit fares and economic self-sufficiency for the system antagonised a great many of the more far-sighted conservatives who had long since learned that public transport is as much a public necessity as public sewers and cannot be expected to support itself; that indeed without its optimum functioning any city must fall to pieces economically. Yet even while he was demanding self-supporting transit he advocated free rides for the poor.

And too, while he was issuing position papers and making campaign speeches, he was also delivering other addresses and writing columns and articles that had a direct bearing on the number of votes that he gathered for his Conservatives and the conservative point of view. He was saying such things as these:

"The moment is overdue for someone who speaks authentically for the Negroes to tell Mr. [James] Baldwin that his morose nihilism is a greater threat by far to prospects for the Negroes in America than anything that George Wallace ever said or did."

"Do we really intend to have a team from *Good Housekeeping* attached to every military unit of the United States, to pass on whether the Marines are fighting the war according to the highest standards of American moral hygiene?"

"If, yielding to pressure that is generally understood to be primarily Negro pressure, crime should increase, then so will resentment and ill-will increase."

"What goes on in the minds, always supposing that is the word for it, of the youth who fret and fuss and moan over a minimum wage of only a dollar and a quarter an hour, and strut their epicene resentment over a gallant national effort to keep an entire section of the globe from sinking into the subhuman wretchedness of Asiatic Communism?"

Hilaire Belloc had excited Buckley's admiration by winning election to Parliament in spite (or because) of his craftsmanlike insults to the electorate. But neither this nor the endorsements of such eminent Republicans as Clare Boothe Luce could achieve a Buckley victory. On the other hand, he and the Conservative Party did accomplish two of their real objectives: to establish the party in New York politics as a voice for the Right, and to poll more votes than the Liberal Party, Buckley's votes totaled 341,226, or 13.4 per cent of the total vote cast; the Liberals mustered only 281,796 of the 1,149,106 votes that elected Lindsay by barely a hundred thousand over Beame. The Conservative Party was now firmly established, even though it had failed in its third and perhaps dearest aim: to defeat Lindsay. Every dispassionate analyst of the results agreed that he would have defeated Beame, quite irrespective of Buckley, whose inroads—if indeed he made any—were at Lindsay's rather than Beame's expense.

"If I had been elected," Buckley reflected a half-dozen years later, "it would have been as a result of the kind of social revolution that would have given me a mandate which would have been difficult to gainsay." There is no exaggeration or self-aggrandisement in that evaluation: the vote that elected his brother to the Senate five years later, like the vote that would have elected him Mayor, was a vote above all for a certain set of ideas, a certain point of view, far more than a vote for an individual. The mandate of which he spoke would have been a mandate not so much to Bill Buckley qua Bill Buckley as to Bill Buckley qua the embodiment of Conservative/conservative principles.

Even without that mandate, however, the 1965 campaign for the Mayoralty established him and his party as influential factors in New York City, at least. Lindsay, having been elected in part on his promise to enforce some kind of curb on the arrogance of that lawless city within the city, the Police Department, appointed an anemic so-called Civilian Review Board—four of its members were civilians, but three were departmental deputy commissioners, and its powers were only advisory: it could merely hear testimony and recommend that the commissioner take disciplinary action. Nevertheless Buckley and his party fought it bitterly, and they cooperated assiduously with the interestingly named Patrolmen's Benevolent Association and other police groups to petition for the board's emasculation, if not its elimination. They were bitter when the board's proponents listed them among its adversaries side by side with the John Birch Society, the National Renaissance Party, and George Lincoln Rockwell, Commander of the American Nazi Party. This, they screamed, was guilt by association; whereas they had performed a public service by revealing that Lindsay's appointee as the board's chairman, Algernon D. Black, could hardly be expected to be objective because he was a leader of the Society for Ethical Culture, a member of the advisory board of the Congress of Racial Equality, a vice-president and director of the National Association for the Advancement of Colored People, and a director of the ACLU. Worse still was what Mahoney in his book called Black's "proclivity for organizations designated as Communist-front or subversive by the Attorney General, including the National Council of Soviet American Friendship, the National Federation for Constitutional Liberties, the American Committee for Protection of the Foreign Born (from which he had resigned in 1953), and the Committee for a Democratic Far Eastern Policy."

In 1966 the board's fate was put to a referendum. By a margin of almost two to one, Conservatives and conservatives destroyed it.

XVIII

Almost everyone who watches *Firing Line,* Bill Buckley's television program, is impressed by his proficiency and assurance; most viewers, like many persons who have appeared on the program, are indeed somewhat awed by the fact that almost always Buckley comes off much better than his guests. It is no denigration of his capacities, as it is no exculpation of some of his tactics, to point out that of necessity he enjoys a tremendous inherent advantage: it is his program. Like any other interviewer in any other circumstances, he determines the questions to be asked, the boundaries to be respected (or transgressed); he has prepared himself with these things in view, and he is free to be now the friendly helper, now the relentless harrier. Moreover, it is the man who runs the program who can set the pace. The guest, inevitably, cannot wholly or perhaps even largely anticipate what is likely to be done to him. He must be watching all directions, including the rear, at the same time; essentially he has to improvise his replies, and there is an almost irresistible pressure (even if it is only subjective) to reply immediately lest one appear at a loss or allow the antagonist the opportunity to unsettle one further. There have been very few *Firing Line* guests indeed who have been able to take the direction of the program, even for a moment, away from Buckley: the combination of the advantage inherent in his position with his unquestionable talents and (to be charitable) his flexibility of principle in certain circumstances is virtually invincible.

The notion of a regular television program, he says, was not initially his: it was proposed by a television producer named Robert Kline, and in principle Buckley had nothing against it. No doubt he must at once have recognised how useful it could be

financially to *National Review*, which was and is constantly operating at a substantial deficit, if it were a success. Kline sought
his financing for the program, naturally enough, among people
sympathetic to Buckley's points of view, and in the spring of 1965
several programs were filmed with money provided by Patrick
Frawley, who headed the Eversharp-Schick complex. Frawley
had previously contributed large sums to a number of Right-
Wing causes, some of them, such as Schwarz's Christian Anti-
Communist Crusade, already being helped by Buckley and Marvin
Liebman. A few of the filmed programs were given test runs
during the spring and summer of 1965, but then Buckley decided
that the venture should be tabled until the conclusion of his
Mayoral campaign. Frawley withdrew his financial support at
about the same time.

Once the political season was over, Kline went hunting again
for an outlet. He approached a number of independent stations,
and submitted bids to Buckley from WOR-TV, affiliated with
the Mutual Broadcasting System; from Metromedia, and from
another station with which David Susskind was associated: Susskind, who was hardly Buckley's hero, would have been willing,
apparently, to produce Buckley's program. One may be grateful that this hybridisation was never consummated. Of all the
offers, WOR's "seemed to make the most sense," Buckley said,
and in 1966 the program went on the air on a regular basis. It
was shown once weekly, in a desirable time period, with commercial sponsorship, and it was offered to other affiliates of the
Mutual network, many of which accepted it. This arrangement
continued for five years, though it had irksome aspects: for one,
the frequent interruptions for commercials; for another, the loss
of timeliness because of the mechanics of Mutual's syndication:
sometimes the lag between the filming of a program and its distribution would be as much as twelve to fourteen weeks.

Hence it was natural enough for Buckley and his producer,
Warren Steibel, to be interested in any reasonable proposal for
a gain in contemporaneity; when that was coupled with an increase in the number of outlets, it was, of course, all the more inviting. This was the potential offered by the growing educational
television network. The Corporation for Public Broadcasting
wanted the Buckley program, if only to counter its own reputation for being out of balance on the "liberal" side in its programming; it had one hundred seventy stations in its stable, and it could

assure Buckley and Steibel of a maximum of four weeks' lag between production and distribution of any given program: some could be done live (though very few were), and some could be (and were) broadcast within a few hours of taping. In the spring of 1971, then, working through a non-profit organisation called the Southern Educational Communications Association, with headquarters in Columbia, South Carolina, *Firing Line* moved to educational television. Most of the stations attempt to broadcast the program simultaneously; occasionally there are technical reasons why this is not possible.

From the beginning the choice of guests and the format of the program have been predominantly up to Buckley and Steibel. From the beginning, too, its revenue (a five-figure weekly sum from public television) has been paid to *National Review*, which keeps whatever is left after having met all the expenses of the program. These can be staggering, since it is frequently filmed in various parts of the United States, the British Isles, Europe, Asia, Africa, and oceanic islands. The *persona* of Buckley that the program presents is both like and unlike the private man: like in ideas, in precision and savor of language, in range of interests, in courtesy that is second nature even—or especially— when anger is most difficult to restrain; unlike in a certain irreducible minimum of formality, in tension perhaps associated with rigorous control of all the relaxed, spontaneous movement that characterises private conversation, in meticulous attention to appearance—no clue to the slightly disheveled, not recently shaved man in shirt-sleeves whose warmth makes it difficult to believe in what one has seen on the screen and whose immediate hospitality almost belies the caution that sometimes appears in his smile. Nor is it easy to assimilate the rapier incarnate of the screen with the author of the deeply moving little essays in which he has made farewells to people whom he has loved.

At times, unquestionably, he is quite deliberately outrageous in his program as he is in print or in person, and he will burden the air as well as the page with such evidences of his cultivation as *litotes* and *oxymoron, synecdoche* and *periphrasis, epistemology* and *eschaton.* On the other hand, it cannot be said that he seeks out adversaries unworthy of him—indeed, when he finds himself undermatched, he seems (usually) rather embarrassed and even uncharacteristically gentle. Nor does he schedule more friends than foes—if anything, the contrary. Generally, he arrives at the

studio where the program is being taped only a short time before
the business begins; during the make-up procedure he will talk
briefly with his guest (in the case of an old friend, he may arrive
earlier for the sake of more conversation—the brevity is in the
interest of on-the-air spontaneity), and after the program he
spends a quarter-hour or so with any interviewers who may have
turned up and then he leaves for the next item in his taut schedule.

The early programs were three-sided in that there was a moderator interposed between him and his adversary. Very often the
function was fulfilled by his lawyer, C. Dickerman Williams.
Panels of questioners were not a regular ingredient; when the
question period became more or less a fixture, he had a kind of
regular corps of three persons, drawn from various backgrounds
and points of view. One of these for some time—until Buckley
began to draw the question panel from the local studio audience
—was Jeff Greenfield, who had worked since his graduation from
Yale Law School a year earlier, in 1967, for the late Robert
Kennedy. Kennedy was one of the few persons who consistently
resisted every invitation to appear on Buckley's program: Kennedy had a keen flair for self-preservation, as Buckley inelegantly
noted when, asked his view of Kennedy's reason for refusing, he
replied: "Why does baloney reject the grinder?"

Greenfield was brought into *Firing Line* through his participation in a series of discussions among young people in Buckley's
home during the summer of 1968: *Eye,* an abortive Hearst publication aimed at the young, had arranged the talks. Buckley was
impressed with him, and dissatisfied with the existing question-
and-answer process; he asked Greenfield to join the program and
Greenfield remained with it until it moved to public television.
At the same time, Greenfield, who was not practicing law, was
writing speeches for Lindsay. Out of three years on *Firing Line,*
as well as his reading of Buckley's writings and other exposures,
Greenfield is convinced that, regardless of his language, Buckley
is very much the statist, especially in the field of speech and other
civil liberties. This is borne out by some of the things Buckley
said on the air long before Greenfield's advent. "I don't feel any
obligation to protect the liberties of the Nazi or the Communist,
or, for that matter, anybody who seeks class legislation or geno-
cide," he said to Leo Cherne of the Research Institute of America
in June, 1966, adding, on the subject of Commander Rockwell of
the American Nazi Party: "As a theoretical matter, I insist that

he has no right that I understand, issuing out of the Constitution of the United States, to stay out of jail." At about the same period Buckley told William Sloane Coffin that the clergy had no business speaking out on social, economic, or political questions (a point of view that one must confess to finding extremely sympathetic, for opposite reasons) even though the state ought not to be secular; but when Coffin asked whether proposals to compel prayers in schools did not ignore the rights of atheists, Buckley replied: "Well, I'm not particularly concerned about the atheists." To Greenfield, Buckley is as statist in his attitude toward civil liberties 'as the most ardent New Dealer about economic policies and the power of the government." Every anti-Communist act is "subsumed by Buckley under the general notion of the fight against Antichrist," Greenfield added.

Both as a panelist and, earlier, as an uninvolved spectator, Greenfield had noted that Buckley's handling of guests varied directly with the consonance between their views and his. With such people as Cherne, Mrs. Luce (who, in addition, is a woman and much his senior), or the late Senator Thomas Dodd, he was gentle and charming and helpful; with Noam Chomsky of the Massachusetts Institute of Technology, one of the founders of Resist and a leader in the campaign against the war in Vietnam, Buckley was harsh and hostile, as he was with Leander Perez, the Louisiana arch-racist, or William Kunstler, the radical lawyer, who did as badly for himself as for his less important clients. Few other persons, Greenfield said, aroused a personal antagonism in Buckley—but among those few were leaders of the Catholic Left. With Kunstler, as with Dr. Spock, Buckley has been savage, using even more than ordinarily all the unfair debating tricks that, as Greenfield pointed out, audiences and even parliaments have come to tolerate: the deliberate misquotation, the distortion, the excision from context, even the various modulations on have-you-stopped-beating-your-wife-answer-yes-or-no. Greenfield likened these tactics to the little advertisements for *National Review* that appear in other magazines: "Here's one that says—and this is a typical way that Buckley will use a word that I am kind of bothered by: 'At the very moment when parochial schools are being bombed by the courts as too religious. . . .' Well, that verb is quite deliberate: it raises the sense of the Weathermen, instead of saying 'attacked' or 'chastised' or 'limited' by the courts." Buckley's attitudes and behavior toward blacks, on or off the air, according to Greenfield, betray a prejudice not of race but of class: "He has a prejudice against poverty." It would be difficult indeed to pretend that he did not have that prejudice: how else could he have asked, in a column written in May, 1969, after a session with black militants in Watts: "Why don't the oppressed buy shares in Standard Oil?"

Views like this, expressed on his television program with all the additional emphasis of voice and manner and smile (or glare) and good looks, reach vast audiences that probably never or rarely see any printed word and might well have difficulty with it. But what they hear will convert many of them and reinforce many others. Even the use of language beyond a hearer's reach will not always—though it may often—antagonise him: very frequently he is grateful for the flattery of it even if he only dimly grasps its purport. No doubt thousands of television watchers were easily persuaded by Buckley that *Playboy* and its publisher, Hugh Hefner, sought to destroy religion. But Buckley did not mention the fact that he very gladly accepted Hefner's checks for articles that Buckley wrote for *Playboy*, whose hypocrisy, however, he was busily denouncing. This was rather akin to his introduction of Chomsky on a program devoted to American Power and the New Mandarins; Buckley attributed to him this statement: "By accepting the legitimacy of debate on certain issues, such as this one, one has already lost one's humanity." But, Chomsky pointed out, what he had said was not that at all: "I said that there are certain issues—Auschwitz, for example—such that, by consenting to discuss them, one degrades oneself and to some degree loses one's humanity. . . . Nevertheless I can easily imagine circumstances in which I would have been glad to debate Auschwitz"—by which he meant circumstances such that there might be a chance of mitigating or eliminating it. When Chomsky said, later in the program, that sometimes he lost his temper but would not do so that night, Buckley replied: "If you would, I'd smash you in the goddamn face." On another program, Anthony Marrecco, who had been one of the British prosecutors at Nürnberg, spoke of Dr. Goebbels as a radical Right-Winger, and Buckley snapped: "That's Communist propaganda"—he explained then that "the Right desires order, stability, and freedom" and therefore could not make an alliance with people who "indulge in crimes against humanity." Unfortunately this bland erasure of history would have gone unremarked by virtually the entire television audience and perhaps most of the population, the sense of history not being remarkable in this country, which can hold its own with Left or Right anywhere in the matter of crimes against humanity.

Buckley's behavior on his program is not always beyond the control of his adversaries. With a fumbler or a pathological narcissist one cannot always be sporting—the temptations are too many, more particularly when one is full of high moral scorn (the grounds for which may or may not exist), and it is almost impossible not to crowd, say, a Kunstler to the wall and knee him in the groin *ad majorem Dei gloriam*. Occasionally, however, Buckley will be pulled up short, very much to his own surprise. In the summer of 1971 Representative Ronald Dellums of California, whose color had brought him a certain condescension as the conversation progressed, again and again compelled his host to stick to the business in hand and to abandon the allurements of various irrelevancies. For instance, Dellums' comments on the crisis in low- and middle-income housing in American cities were interrupted by Buckley's supercilious reminder that there was a housing shortage in Moscow, whereupon Dellums reminded him that Moscow was beyond the jurisdiction of the Congress of the United States. Later that summer Buckley interviewed Mary McCarthy, the expatriate and ex-Catholic novelist whose opposition to the Vietnam war has so long and so deeply infuriated him; he very blandly spoke of Soviet Russia as "the society whose romantic aspirations you continue to identify with," and Miss McCarthy pointed out that she had never made such identification. Nonetheless Buckley continued to misrepresent her stands on various matters until she very clearly put her television finger on one of his basic techniques: "Don't ascribe positions to me and then attack them." This did not prevent him from insisting—with blatant disregard for everything that she has published—that she championed the Russian repression of domestic literary dissidents and of Czech, Polish, and Hungarian rebels against totalitarianism. It must have been embarrassing, too, to be publicly given lessons in contemporary history when he cavalierly attempted to make it appear that Eastern Europeans of his generation and hers could not remember anything but Communism and hence could not know how much better the old order had been—though in actuality by no means all the former gentry and aristocracy did think that.

"You know, Buckley," the Reverend Jesse Jackson, the black civil-rights leader, said to him a month or two later, "one who is *not* hurting cannot very well tell one who *is* how to holler." Buckley's retort? "The man who cured syphilis didn't suffer from it." The obvious explanation is only part of the explanation for the flippant *non sequitur*: there is also the show-business psychology that has so thoroughly tainted almost everything in America. The late Harold E. Fellows, when he was president of the National Association of Broadcasters in the latter half of the 1950's, wrestled unceasingly against it—the phrase was his critical reproach to the industry's insistence on turning everything, from a concentration camp to a Presidential budget message, into an entertainment. Once Buckley became a man of the media, it was almost inevitable that he would be infected by at least some of their viruses. Even if he resisted the verbal horrors of newspaper and magazine, he was not immune to the triviality of the broadcast. His detractors insist that he is inherently quite as shallow as television itself, but, if that is true at all, it is so only in the limited sense that he apparently spends little or no time and effort in the re-examination of thinking and positions and that he delights in titillating even when his deepest principles—and it would be the mark of the utmost unperceptiveness to pretend that he did not have them—are very thoroughly involved. Consequently, at times it would appear that he was as profoundly committed as a *Playboy* cartoonist, and yet this is not true.

Even some of his most eager detractors are constrained to concede the point. A woman journalist who has known and disagreed with him for years insists that "Bill Buckley is a little necessary" because he is serious, and her husband, who has known him longer and disagreed with him more bitterly, added: "I'd like to see far more of Bill Buckley's kind of eccentricity manifested on the Left, and tolerated from there. He's Little Lord Fauntleroy getting more and more exposure to rednecked idiots." The woman pointed out that Buckley was not a rednecked idiot and "it's the goddamned liberals who watch him and get excited about him. Everybody we know in New York watches that program—people can't wait for it." Her husband countered with what is probably the best insight into the growing popularity of *Firing Line*: "The masses watch him as they watched Christians being thrown to the lions, and that's what his TV show is." What he neglected to add was that the Christians in the living room derived a certain pleasure from seeing their fellow-believers in the arena.

A *Time* cover story in November, 1967, quoted William Sloane Coffin to the effect that "Buckley is as brilliant an adversary as he is bankrupt an advocate"—but that bankruptcy is deceptive: like all successful advocates, Buckley does not convince: he persuades, and far less by reason than by flamboyance. Indeed, the same article quoted his self-appraisal: "I feel I qualify spiritually and philosophically as a conservative, but temperamentally I am not of the breed." If he is less solid than, say H. L. Mencken or Alfred Jay Nock, whom he admires, he is on the other hand much more willing to play to the plebs, to sacrifice accuracy and logic for wit and witticism. When Staughton Lynd of Yale was describing his visit with the late Ho Chi Minh in Hanoi to discuss the end of the war, Buckley cut in: "Surely Hanoi isn't dependent upon Yale's vacation schedule for deciding how to press its foreign policy?" To Billy Graham—a most improbable interlocutor—he observed: "Charity without the Crucifixion is Liberalism." Debating the "Separation of Church and State" with Mrs. Madalyn Murray O'Hair, the crusader for atheism, Buckley used the iron pipe rather than the rapier: "I can't imagine adult people worrying about the establishmentarianism of religion in America. I'd sooner believe Eisenhower was a Communist."

One would like to think that he was joking again when, discussing what he was pleased to say was the ready availability of a clean clinical illegal abortion for three hundred dollars in New York before the law was humanised, he told Betty Friedan that the price "is not a sum that is beyond the reach of most women who live in New York"! But then one reflects that in conversation he asserted as dogma that a head of a family who earned sixty dollars a week in 1936, when social-security taxation began, could have amply provided for his family and his own old age by buying blue-chip securities out of earnings instead of paying for social security, and one recalls how accurately Professor Weiss pointed up Buckley's innocence of the economic facts of life—especially if in 1936 one was a head of a family and earning sixty dollars a week while the little Buckleys were all in their various private schools in various countries or with their various governesses.

There is one television declaration by Buckley that defies categorisation slightly more effectively than it resists analysis; one is tempted to ascribe its peculiar convolutions to the environmental influence of his fellow-columnist in the *New York Post*, Max Lerner, the world's greatest authority, who was his guest. To him Buckley said on *Firing Line*, presumably spontaneously: "I myself would care less whether something was said with integrity than I would care about whether or not the certain postulates continued to be present on the basis of which these particular observers would more likely than not get us into more of the same kind of trouble than they got us into in the past." Well, that ought to immanentise the eschaton. The subject was Communist China, and one was entitled to deduce by judicious context exploration that Buckley felt that the certified students of Chinese affairs had made a fool of the United States and that what mattered was not so much whether people told the truth as whether what they said was what he believed they ought to say.

What is most disillusioning—multilaterally—is to study the transcripts of these programs since their inception. Regardless of the intellectual and characterological endowments and the varying achievements of the participants, the overpowering preponderance of what is said is trivial beyond belief; what is even more staggering is the prevailing ineptitude of people whom one is accustomed to regard automatically as varyingly competent and articulate: Lerner, Lynd, Dwight Macdonald, Hefner, Spock, Nixon, Ralph Schoenman (whom Earl Russell had to dismiss after the Stockholm panels on war crimes in Vietnam), and other assorted politicians, authors, professors, lawyers, comedians, athletes: representatives of every species in the television zoo. A very few of Buckley's guests manage to retain some or most of their stature—such people as Dellums, Norman Thomas, Mrs. Luce, Kempton, Weiss, Neier, Rebecca West, Groucho Marx (one would so much like to have seen that!). Those who do not are not his victims: it is the medium itself that does them in, as it to a degree does everyone in.

The paradox is that it is precisely this irreducible degradation of everyone concerned that contributes materially to making Buckley dangerous. The medium, by trivialising him, his associates, and what they are doing, makes him thereby the more attractive to, the more self-reflecting of, the unthinking mass that makes up most of virtually any television audience. Very little of what is said by Buckley or by his interlocutors is particularly difficult to grasp or, at worst, to intuit; in especially intricate instances there is the play of eyebrows, the wink, the flashing smile and what he himself calls the "disconcerting sea of teeth," the urbanity relieved only by the stern Jovian frown or the outraged Torquemadan execution for the princeling of darkness who has just committed or even merely defended the sin against the Holy Ghost (whatever, at the moment, that happens to be). It is all a good show, and one need not listen too closely—indeed, it is much better if one does not, or one might backslide into reading, or conversation. But, taken with a card game and a glass of beer, *Firing Line* is likely to be amusing, vicariously gratificatory of a number of needs, and, above all, reassuring because in fact, whatever its proprietor's intentions, whatever, even, his beliefs and his own personal qualities, it is reinforcing what Ortega called "the characteristic of our time; not that the vulgar believes itself super-excellent and not vulgar, but that the vulgar proclaims and imposes the rights of vulgarity, or vulgarity as a right." And this is inevitable, since television is the philosopher's stone of vulgarisation, fabricated as if expressly for what that perceptive critic and novelist, Emile Capouya, calls the "well-intentioned egotist, [the] bright, stupid man not readily distinguishable from our happy era's dominant type."

To that type Buckley is always the winner because of its admiration for and befuddlement by his fundamental approach and technique. "Basically," to quote a man who has been able more than once to deal with him successfully, "his method of debating is to throw in a comment totally irrelevant to the subject being debated, trying to take the opponent off on a tangent, and then to follow that comment with a question to the adversary on still another subject. So the adversary has two choices: either he has to leave a sally unanswered, or he has to follow Buckley like a will-o'-the-wisp on whatever tangent Buckley has taken. Unfortunately, a good many of the people who debate him are inclined to follow the random sallies and skim over the surface of many issues with him. He's extremely glib, and able to deal with a large number of subjects, making witty and biting comments on a great many different issues. He is not capable of delving in any depth into any single issue. So, as a debating tactic, it is a good idea to ignore his random sallies and stick to the particular subject of the debate and lead him as far into it as possible, because he quickly gets out of his depth. He does not have the facility to debate effectively under those circumstances, and he'll fall back on name-calling, like the time he tried to dismiss Chief Justice Warren by saying he was a 'fanatic.' Or he'll resort to what I saw him do in front of a crowd of two thousand University of Wisconsin students, debating Norman Thomas in 1960. Buckley mentioned a book that had just been published and turned round to Thomas and rather snidely said: 'I don't know whether you've had a chance to read this book yet, Mr. Thomas.' In a stage whisper that went through the whole auditorium, Thomas snorted: 'Read it, he-e-ell! It's dedicated to me.'" But few of Buckley's opponents have either the occasion or the poise to administer the comeuppance, and so his flashy hit-and-run methods are highly effective with that great middle class that he truly represents, although one may well wonder whether he would be any more hospitable to it in his dining room than, say, some of the more prosperous and public militant black intellectuals would be to the imprisoned "brothers" if they were in the street again. It is rather reminiscent of the anguish that went up among the American Zionists when the real ones adopted a resolution—hastily repealed lest it dry up the dollar flow—to the effect that anyone who had held office in a Zionist organisation must within two years put his body and his citizenship where his mouth had been.

In such a moral climate a Buckley can only flourish, once he has allowed himself to become representative of it. He was quite capable, in his 1968 battle with Leander Perez on *Firing Line*, of quoting with approval Garry Wills's assessment of George Wallace's views as "a fusion of racism, nationalism and collectivism, which spells a kind of Fascism" and must therefore be opposed by conservatives; but neither he nor his appreciative audiences, apparently, would or could recognise how wholly separable from Fascism racism is (Italy, Spain, Greece, Austria before 1934, Latin American countries generally), and, racism quite apart, how close Buckley's own views are to Fascism, not only in his aggressive nationalism coupled with messianic anti-Communism and his preference for traditionalism over libertarianism (though he calls himself a libertarian), but also in his own kind of collectivism: the action of the state to enforce restrictions on private and religious practices as well as on expression and to compel (paradoxically) the operation of a free market in everything though the heavens fall and crush the individual (whom he professes so vigorously to champion).

The same curious morality has almost always been evident in his

choices of protégés, beginning with J. McCarthy; the only exception would seem to be Edgar H. Smith, Jr., whom he materially
helped to defeat electrocution and regain his freedom. One wonders still how any Buckley could have defended the singularly unsavory Roy Cohn. That, it might be argued, is largely a matter
of esthetics, given their community of political faith (though this
is to credit Cohn with convictions, and one is reluctant before
such naïveté); what is far harder to comprehend, especially in a
man who could throw off Ayn Rand for her materialism and
ruthlessness, as Buckley and Chambers did in 1957, is Buckley's
dogged attachment to the late Senator Dodd regardless of any
and all facts. One cannot help wondering whether Buckley would
have stayed with this hero had Chambers lived: Buckley has never
minimised Chambers' influence on him, and Chambers was a far
deeper thinker, a far better judge of character, and a man of far
more rigorous principle.

Granted that Dodd was a Catholic and a very traditional conservative, whose economics and politics were almost identical with
the Buckleys' and whose primary interests (outside the intellec-
tual/esthetic domain, in which Dodd was an unregistered alien)
were the same. Granted that Dodd was against crime, homosexu-
ality, some kinds of heterosexuality, birth control, abortion (on
both these the Buckleys were gradually to make some compromises of expediency, at least on behalf of the heretic, the infidel, and the darker-skinned poor), "pornography and obscenity,"
freedom of expression, and so on. His ethics were approximately
those of a professional fence or a writer who will hire out to
propagandise for the highest bidder. Ultimately, through persons
and processes quite as dubious as the Senator and his own ways,
some of his misdoings became a matter of knowledge so public
that his peers in the Senate, whose qualifications for casting the
first, or indeed any, stone may well be more charitably left un-
mentioned, bestowed on him in 1967 the distinction of being the
first Senator in the history of the United States to be censured
by the chamber for his financial misconduct. The vote was ninety-
two to five. Of course Dodd stayed in his heaven and all remained
well with the world.

The story came out in the sleazy way in which most such things
become known in this country. Once a member of the prosecution staff at Nürnberg, then a holder of state elective offices in
Connecticut (where, as in the forty-nine other states, it is assumed

that politics is a legitimate means of making a fortune), a Senator since 1959, and an eminence in the van of the crusades against Communism foreign and domestic, subversion, "security risks," crime, narcotics, and critics of the possible pernicious influences of television; chairman of the Internal Security subcommittee and a member of the Judiciary Committee, which passes on the fitness of appointees to the Department of Justice and the federal bench, and of the Foreign Relations Committee at the height of the division over Vietnam, the good Senator was also seeing to it that his close (and rich) friends were properly done by in their dealings with government, performing a little referral work for deserving members of the bar, accepting modest cash gifts from no doubt disinterested individuals and corporations, and so on. He was also a close friend of former Brig. Gen. (in the Illinois National Guard) Julius Klein, a national commander of the Jewish War Veterans who had set up in public relations and was representing the West German government and some of the biggest and oldest industries in that country; from time to time he facilitated things whenever the Senator wished to visit that New Jerusalem and come back to tell the taxpayers and investors of the United States what a splendid new democracy they were buying there (at quality prices). Dodd was also, now and again, the recipient of testimonial dinners, for which the guests paid substantially more than they would have done in the best of restaurants: they were given to understand that the cash was meant for political campaigning (except when, according to Dodd's defenders, nothing at all was said): but all the proceeds went into Dodd's private accounts. So did the profits of occasional double billing: charging the government for trips already paid for by what might be called his business friends. There were substantial receipts from such Right-Wing organisations as the *Reader's Digest*, the Institute for American Strategy, the American Medical Political Action Committee (the chevalier seeking to kill the dragon of "socialised medicine"), and the Freedom Forum of Tyler, Texas. One James Boyd, Dodd's former administrative assistant, got religion, along with three of his colleagues, and turned over to Drew Pearson, the syndicated columnist, a sheaf of fascinating documents that, rather unfortunately, did not belong to him, and Pearson made them public. Dodd thereupon "discovered" that Boyd and his friends had been engaging in Dodd-damned sexual activities and that it was for these that the Senator had discharged them. One may well hold one's nose at the whole mess.

Buckley, like Pearson, did not. He wrote a number of columns and *National Review* articles in defense of Dodd and helped to organise the Justice for Dodd Committee, the purpose of which was to rouse the nation against any investigation or censure; its membership was almost exclusively from the Right, and, led by Buckley, it was vociferous in a concern for Dodd's civil liberties such as it had not yet learned when he, as chairman of the Internal Security subcommittee, had shown almost as much interest in the civil liberties of his victims as had his exemplars, Joseph McCarthy and J. Parnell Thomas. Nor did the heralds of Justice for Dodd ever remark on the curbs placed on the chief counsel of the Senate Ethics Committee, or on its prohibition of any interrogation of Dodd or his wife. Buckley's articles about the case, and his subsequent attacks on Boyd's book about Dodd, were recklessly indifferent to the facts—for instance, by insisting that the testimonial dinners had never been touted as vehicles for raising campaign funds; or by pooh-poohing the double billing of Dodd's voyages— and consistently focused on the alleged sexual mis- and malfeasances of Pearson's informers. Robert H. Yoakum, the Lakeville author whose own column has consistently attacked the Buckleys —they have been his targets in the *New Republic* and elsewhere, too—reviewed favorably Boyd's book on the whole case, the revelations in which were undoubtedly important, though one is still rather put off by all the attendant circumstances. This provoked Bill Buckley to supercilious retort and minor distortion of Yoakum's criticisms of him (Yoakum had written that Buckley was "almost alone" in exploiting Dodd's charges about his former employes' behavior, but Buckley wrote that Yoakum "says that I alone bought the story"). Yoakum, in rebuttal, pointed out that Buckley's " 'research' did not even lead him to interview the people most deeply involved—people he has casually savaged."* As for Buckley's distortions of the facts, Yoakum had previously documented these in articles in the *Columbia Journalism Review* for spring, 1967 (page 14), and summer of the same year (pages 52– 53). More of the Buckleys were to move (in print) against Yoakum after James Buckley's election to the Senate in 1970.

* Buckley's letter to the *New Republic* appeared in the issue of 6 April 1968; Yoakum's reply was in the following week's issue.—C.L.M.

Bill Buckley's defeat under Dodd's banner did not discountenance him unduly. In October of 1967 he announced—fifteen years after *God and Man at Yale*—that he would enter his candidacy as an insurgent for a post in the Yale Corporation, opposing the slate of candidates selected by a committee, in order to protest against the university's unabated "liberal bias." He said there was an "almost total absence of conservatives on the faculty" and "the students simply don't have access to the conservative point of view." What exercised him at least as much was the decision by Yale to broaden and diversify its admissions. Here one must quote *The New York Times* of 21 October 1967: "Mr. Buckley, whose father was graduated from the University of Texas, decried Yale's move away from its role as 'the kind of place where your family goes for generations,' and said: 'The son of an alumnus, who goes to a private preparatory school, now has less of a chance of getting in than some boy from P.S. 109 somewhere.' " In order to be placed on the ballot for the post about to be vacated by William McChesney Martin, chairman of the Federal Reserve Board and former president of the New York Stock Exchange, Buckley had to collect the signatures of two hundred fifty Yale graduates on his nominating petition, and in this he succeeded. Only one prior member of the corporation had gained election in this way— William Horowitz of New Haven, the first Jew to be elected. Buckley hoped to be the first Catholic. Had he been elected, he would have had as a colleague Mayor Lindsay of New York, whose career in politics he had been and still was determined to abort. But the vote, which was announced in June of 1968, went in favor of Cyrus R. Vance, a rich man whom President Johnson had made deputy chief of the American team in the Paris talks that had recently been initiated ostensibly with a view to ending the war in Vietnam. Of the sixty-five thousand alumni eligible to vote, almost thirty thousand, a record number, did so. Yale does not reveal such statistics, but "it was understood," as the newspapers like to say, that Vance's margin was considerable. This was regarded as a blow to conservatism. Behind Buckley there was a third candidate, John M. Musser of St. Paul.

There was no way of determining where among the alumni the Buckley voters lived. It would probably not be inaccurate to suppose that they would be more numerous as one moved farther south and west from New York. As early as February, 1968, the *St. Louis Globe Democrat* told of reverend clergy in northern

California wearing buttons that said: "President Buckley." Bill Buckley—it was he who was meant at that time—had already discouraged Conservative Party leaders in New York who wanted him to run for the Senate against Javits in 1968: he would cite only "personal reasons" for his refusal to run, and it is conceivable that he had reached the conclusion later reported by various of his friends (and shared by many observers) that, regardless of his merits, his was not the kind of personality that seduces a mass of voters. In the event, it was in this year that his brother James was to make his first venture into politics on his own behalf: a campaign for the Senate that, as we shall see, was a very fruitful failure, to which, at the time, no one paid sufficient attention. In the outback, however, James was still unknown, while Bill's prestige was mounting. In California he could always be counted on to fill an auditorium of any size whenever he appeared. The same is true of almost every major hall between the coasts: he was aptly characterised by the *Globe Democrat*'s reporter, Art Seidenbaum, as "the educated man in the pop medium."

There are two other fields in which Buckley has been effectively at work with far less public attention. One is on the edge of government, or, more precisely, in the direction of American propaganda abroad, and this is the more recent activity, since it dates only from 1969. The other, which extends back fifteen years, is commercial broadcasting. Buckley's activity as a member of the United States Advisory Commission on Information, which in effect tells the President what the United States Information Agency ought to be doing and how it might best do it, will be taken up presently.

National Review bought KOWH, a radio station in Omaha, in 1957, with the hope that its profits would help to support the magazine. KOWH claims to have been the first rock-music station in the country, but an early competitor in noise made steady inroads on its revenue until 1964, when Peter Starr, Buckley's former newsboy in Stamford and later cabin boy aboard his yacht, came out of college and went to work as a salesman for the station. By early 1965 Starr had so rejuvenated KOWH and so incisively analysed its operations that he easily prevailed on Buckley to make him its manager—at twenty-three the youngest in the country. Soon thereafter KOWH was sold by *National Review* to Buckley and Starr, who then bought a second station in Sioux Falls, South Dakota. They soon expanded further, and, when Starr Broadcast-

ing Group, Inc., became a publicly held corporation in 1969, it
had added three black-oriented stations in Houston, Memphis,
and New Orleans, a country-and-western outlet in Little Rock,
and a station in Kansas City. Subsequently it moved into Dallas,
the Virginia-Tennessee area, New Jersey, Hawaii, Detroit, and
New York (WNCN-FM), acquiring a couple of television stations en route. According to a report in *New York* (14 June
1971), the whole cluster cost about fourteen and a half million
dollars and lost money until 1970, when a respectable net was
earned.

None of this would be of any great importance in itself, except
that there is a certain ambivalence behind the success of Starr
Broadcasting, and at least an apparent conflict with the views of
the chairman of its board, who is also its second largest share-
holder (about twelve per cent—Starr has fourteen). Rock and
"The Kids" have long been prime targets for Buckley, and he
has inveighed against both on moral, political, spiritual, intellectual, and esthetic grounds. In fact, he has often been quite right,
even when his legendary precision of language has betrayed him
(or, as some contend, he has betrayed it, as when, in an otherwise
delightful review of the new two-volume edition of the *Oxford
English Dictionary*, he used *début* as a verb—for which, to do him
justice, he made exemplary penance when the sin was brought
to his attention) into saying on *Firing Line* that the reason why
"The Kids" "hide in rock music is because they are philosophically jejuned and this is a way to make them sound sort of philosophical and heady and profound, whereas, in fact, they're just
sort of a shallow recapitulation of pre-Adamite notions about personal hedonism." But, though he is right as far as he has gone, his
colleague Frank Meyer had seen more of the truth when he said
that rock is "a constituent of the symbolism of revolt"—for that
is precisely how far too many of its dupes regard it, as they im-
pute the same political significance to their other drugs.

The issue is not major, perhaps. But, in spite of having frequently denounced rock and all its works, Buckley has yet to
intervene when any of the Starr stations turn to it to rescue them
from the financial jimjams induced by programming that has
drawn lower ratings and thus fewer advertisers. Hard rock and
even politically inflammatory talk have also been given thorough
testing when it has been supposed that they might rejuvenate interest in a Starr station; if they have proved useless, they have been

dropped again, but only for that reason. But Buckley has not scrupled to denounce the owners of periodicals for their refusals to protest the editors' policies, as he castigated Simon & Schuster for publishing Jerry Rubin's babble, *Do It!* One of Buckley's stations, WLOK in Memphis, uses broadcast editorials on Vietnam, poverty, censorship, and politics that, a member of its staff said, would strike Buckley dead if he ever heard them. Peter Starr, however, says Buckley knows what goes on in all the stations and has approved their respective policies and methods: "His beliefs have nothing to do with the service of a particular station to a particular market," Starr told the reporter, Richard Reingold. But Buckley refused categorically—and rather unwisely, one would think—to speak to him about Starr Broadcasting and its even-handedly profitable espousal of rock, pacifism, radicalism, "soul" —at least one black station has turned to Starr for advice on reaching blacks—and, in Dallas, the "Christian family," while the rest of Buckley is busily denouncing most of these.

Starr itself, in a sense, is part of that denunciation, since it is the sole owner of Arlhus Publishing Corp., which in turn is the sole owner of Arlington House, the only important publisher specialising in conservative books in the country, and of Nostalgia Book Club and Nostalgia Record Club. Nostalgia Book Club, like the Conservative Book Club, which Arlington House also owns, distributes Arlington House books, which are sold also in bookshops. Its titles are all non-fiction—about eighty per cent new, the rest being reprints. These are advertised almost exclusively in *National Review, Human Events*, and the other organs of the Right. One of Arlington House's most recent publications was the autobiography of Sir Oswald Mosley, the founder of the British Union of Fascists in the period between the wars. Another was Edith Efron's *The News Twisters*, about, of course, television. Describing itself in its advertisements as "Arlington House—Publishers for the Silent Majority," the firm listed for its 1971–72 list such relatively apolitical books as the reminiscences of an enthusiast of the swing-band era and a re-creation of *The Day the Market Crashed* in October, 1929, by a financial writer, Donald I. Rogers. There are nostalgic volumes about Hollywood, too. But then one comes to *Safe Places*, in which David and Holly Franke (in that order) list whatever parts of the United States are still havens from "drugs, riots, welfare burdens, crime, oversized taxes, pollution and noise." Boris Sokoloff's *The Permissive Society* examines "the cancer of permissiveness." The Dollar Growth Library consists of books on making money proliferate. The back list pushes Eugene Lyons' thirty-year-old scare effort, *The Red Decade*; Buckley's and Bozell's *McCarthy and His Enemies*; Gerhart Niemeyer's *Deceitful Peace: A New Look at the Soviet Threat*; a variety of books telling "the truth" about racism, atheism and "what really happened at Mylai"; Burnham's *Suicide of the West* and *The War We Are In,* which are amply described by their titles; *Freedom and Reality,* Enoch Powell's views on race, the welfare state, etc.; a number of titles by the patriarch of the Austrian school of free-market economists, Ludwig von Mises, to whom we shall return; *Enemies of the Permanent Things,* by Russell Kirk, who deserves better company; Victor Lasky's disgraceful *JFK: The Man and the Myth*; Aloïse Buckley Heath's one book, *Will Mrs. Major Go to Hell?*; her brother's *UP From Liberalism,* and David Franke's *Quotations from Chairman Bill: The Best of William F. Buckley Jr.* There are also books by and about Adam Smith and several exposures of Communist horrors here and there, as well as various special pleas for religion. Most of these titles are duplicated in the Conservative Book Club's list of its recent and older selections, plus such curios as Gen. Curtis LeMay's *America Is in Danger.*

The Conservative Book Club is minuscule in membership compared to those purely commercial organisations, the Book-of-the-Month Club or the Literary Guild. One does not often see Arlington House books on best-seller lists. But these facts should not be misinterpreted. The conservative firms do not have the money to engage in the mass hard-selling used by the big general firms, nor can they pretend to make the same kind of appeal. Membership in most general book clubs is constantly changing: people join to get a specific title at a bargain price and then defect; many others join in order to have the latest best-sellers visible to their guests, even if the books are rarely opened; but members of the Conservative Book Club, like buyers of Arlington House books, are steady repeat customers whose aim is not to get bargains or to impress but to be reinforced in their dogmas and, often, to be better armed for the conversion of the heathen. The process may be slow, and the printed word has long since lost its primacy in persuasion; but souls are being saved for conservatism at a steadily increasing rate, and even print is still a contributing factor.

XIX

Bill Buckley's inability to sit still is not merely literal. No matter how many things he is simultaneously engaged in, he seems almost always to be able—or, perhaps, to be driven—to take on more. During his Mayoral campaign in 1965 he was interested in the fight for freedom that Edgar H. Smith Jr. had begun seven years earlier after his conviction and sentence to death in New Jersey on a charge of murder. At the same time, Buckley was evolving what later became *Firing Line*; he was beginning a commentary on Ortega, *Revolt Against the Masses*, that aborted after twenty-five thousand words; he was actively editing *National Review*; he was regularly producing his column; he was lecturing and living out of a suitcase; he was writing for magazines of every kind, on a considerable variety of subjects, though always he came back to the fundamentals of his conservative creed. And he was active too in working for its furtherance—in the Conservative Party and in those curious organisations that he and Marvin Liebman loved so well, and that the Anti-Defamation League (no Christians need apply) watched as fiercely as they watched it—the sectarian sodalities against Communism, the defenders of such friends of man as Chiang Kai-shek and Moïse Tshombé. And Buckley was also listening to as much music as he could possibly manage (both his homes are constantly filled with it), sailing whenever he could, and somehow assuring his annual long ski vacation in Switzerland—though never very far from a telephone.

Since 1965 Buckley has published five books of his own, edited two others, and contributed to several more (*Violence in the Streets; The Beatles Book*—he likes the Beatles, very often; *Spectrum of Catholic Attitudes; Great Ideas Today*). Two of his own

269

books are reprints of pieces that he wrote for his column, for *National Review*, and for a variety of other magazines: *The Co-lumbia Teachers College Record, West Magazine, The Saturday Evening Post, The New York Times, Esquire, Book Week, TV Guide, Commonweal, The Atlantic Monthly, Life, Look, The New Guard* (the YAF organ), *Rudder*. He has written also for *Playboy*. The journalism has been reprinted in *The Jeweler's Eye, A Book of Irresistible Political Reflections*, which was a hard-cover Putnam's book in 1968 and appeared later in paperback; in *The Governor Listeth, A Book of Inspired Political Revelations*, published two years later by the same house and now out in paper-back, and in *Inveighing We Will Go*, which Putnam's brought out in September, 1972. *The Unmaking of a Mayor*, which Viking issued in 1966, is an exhaustive, informative, amusing, and de-pressingly accurate account of his Mayoral campaign—depressing above all in its documentation of the intellectual dishonesty and low level of competence of those who opposed him: not only were they no better than he; they were usually measurably worse, what-ever their professions of faith. In 1971 he published (again with Putnam's) *Cruising Speed, A Documentary*, which is the bewil-dering record of one week in his life (the week that began on 30 November 1970) and which his friend Harry Elmlark calls Buckley's nearest approach to printed introspection. Both the books edited by Buckley appeared also in 1970: *Odyssey of a Friend*, which consists of a selection of Whittaker Chambers' letters to him between 1954 and 1961, with notes explaining background, and a book with a dual title: in hard-cover, *Did You Ever See a Dream Walking?*; in the paperback American Heritage Series (the edition that Buckley calls "my textbook"), *American Conserva-tive Thought in the Twentieth Century*, which is an important anthology that ranks with Frank Meyer's similar 1964 book, *What Is Conservatism?* In this Buckley is represented by "Notes Toward an Empirical Definition of Conservatism," which also (under the *Dream* title) introduces his own anthology.

No easy labels apply when one has gone through all these things. Much of the journalism, it is true, represents a kind of simplifi-cation or vulgarisation (in the true sense: rendition into the Vul-gate) of the frequently byzantine abstractions of "my textbook" and the essays in Meyer's anthology; it is not difficult to trace the influence of Willmoore Kendall, of whom Arlington House published a bulky treasury in 1971 under the title *Willmoore*

Kendall Contra Mundum. (One-against-the-world is almost always immediately attractive, at least at first, even in those rare instances when the world may be right.) But there are many pieces that are not political or even polemic or bitchy, and that are also devoid of the family archness. Virtually everything that Buckley has written about Chambers is moving to any sensitive reader; and some of it is quite revealing of a rather admirable aspect of Buckley. Once, in a hotel lobby in Washington, he had abruptly to turn his back on a good friend in order to divert attention from Chambers, who was with him and to whom privacy was essential; Buckley could barely wait to make amends to the friend. His tributes to those he loved and admired are exemplars of English prose at its best; at such times he earns the praise that he gave to Adlai Stevenson: "Mr. Stevenson was devoted to a means of communicating his thought to the people, which, because it was based on the assumption of human intelligence, was, therefore, based on the assumption of human nobility." Or, again about Stevenson, as a Presidential candidate: "The kind of campaign Stevenson had waged was a paradigm—around which any candidate of the future should conjugate his own campaign." The eulogy to Frank Chodorov is beautiful and filled with kindness. That quality is totally absent from *Let the Rich Alone*, written less than a year later: "Nobody goes around talking about the excesses of the poor as a *political* problem, or, rather, nobody goes around saying the poor should be forbidden their excesses as a *political* matter (could you imagine a law forbidding ghetto dwellers from [*sic*] drinking whiskey or conceiving illegitimate children?)." Yet this is the same man who, for example, without a word to Professor Weiss endeavored to find a suitable post for Weiss's graduating son, the same man who in private wept at the Birmingham school massacre—he is man enough to be unashamed of tears.

It is possible, too, that he is truest to himself—or his multiple selves—in print rather than on the platform or the television screen. On the page he is least exposed to the contaminations of the crass, not the slightest of which is the temptation to amuse, and, if possible, to score at the same time. Here, too, he has time to consider substance and to flatter form—though there are times when he can lapse unbelievably. Perhaps one might be charitable, as in this illustration from *The Governor Listeth*, and blame the low assay of the subject: "Namath's complaint rises up from the shambles of questionably legal tapped telephone contents illegally passed on to *Newsweek* magazine which questionably legally publishes them, whereupon identifying the nefarious activities of questionably illegal men who are, after all, out of jail." Or, in spite of a more worthy subject, this: "I sat next to a most beautiful and lively young Catholic girl the other day at a public function who spoke to me of Catholicism at Vassar, which she attends." The author of that sentence would be the first to mince it if he saw it over some other prosateur's name.

In his brief introduction to *The Governor Listeth*, the title of which comes from The General Epistle of James in the King James Version, Buckley tells us that his tongue and pen are "at the service of people and ideas I venerate; that I do not understand myself, most of the time, to be at play, but rather, hoping to effect events and to affect people . . . this governor does greatly desire to influence, along the lines he most ardently listeth. There is no other reason for living by the word." The final sentence is arguable, but certainly supportable. Why, then, one must ask, waste time, energy, ink, and paper on annals of backchat with the likes of masters of ceremonies of television shows, or rehearsals of personal feuds such as Buckley's with that man of ever less beautiful letters, Gore Vidal? No one over the age of four takes television vaudevilles seriously or believes them to be even as spontaneous as professional wrestling matches, and it is difficult to conceive who would be excited by disclosures of the truth about their creaking machinery and machinists. Yet fifty pages of *The Governor Listeth* detailed this dreary business. The man who was to prove capable of writing *Myra Breckenridge* was outraged because "there's no humanity" in Buckley (does it, perhaps, take one to spot one?), and because not only Bill but at least two of his sisters, Aloïse and Patricia, had said all kinds of terrible and untrue things about Pope John XXIII, *America*, President Truman, Yale, Smith, and Vassar. But the untrue things that Vidal said they said turned out to have been said uniquely by himself in his attributions. In a way the vendetta that was to rage for years afterward was a seesaw of poetic irony, since its antagonists were constantly giving each other lessons in the same specialties.

In the first engagement, in 1962, Buckley probably struck the lower blow (though one would need calipers to make certain): he ordered his office to send to Jack Paar, the stage manager of the brawl, a telegram that was at once unpardonable and yet craftsmanlike in the nice aptness of its allusion to a past scandal in the literary world: "Please inform Gore Vidal that neither I nor my family is disposed to receive lessons in morality from a pink queer. If he wishes to challenge that designation, inform him that I shall fight by the laws of the Marquis of Queensberry. He will know what I mean." Buckley was dissuaded from dispatching the message, over which he must have toiled with considerable care; his refutation of Vidal's nonsense was read over the air, and for some time the embers were merely blown upon occasionally in one or another sideshow. Six years later, however, some genius at the American Broadcasting Co. conceived the idea of having Vidal and Buckley comment live on each night's doings of the 1968 Republican and Democratic National Conventions.* Buckley's guardian angel worked hard at talking him out of the deal, but he paid no attention, even though he knew his own feelings about Vidal well enough and every television critic in the country had observed the intensity of personal enmity that had marked all their appearances together. Somehow the angel got Buckley through Miami and the Republicans—the back-yard cat-fight dialogue is set down in all its juvenility in Buckley's book: at least he has the grace occasionally to beat his breast—and he and Vidal settled in in Chicago for the Democrats. Now there can be no question that almost everything that happened at that charade was certain to inflame Buckley; what was more, he had broken his shoulder in a boating accident, and his temper was even shorter than his norm. Vidal was as agitated as Buckley, if only by Buckley's being Buckley: and neither said anything calculated to make things easier. In a welter of words, if not facts, over the behavior of the demonstrators in the streets and parks, Vidal sudenly said: "As far as I am concerned, the only crypto Nazi I can think of is yourself." Howard Smith, ABC's moderator, attempted to do his job, but Buckley retorted to Vidal: "Now listen, you queer. Stop calling me a crypto Nazi or I'll sock you in your goddamn face [the same threat that Buckley had made to Chomsky on *Firing Line*] and you'll stay plastered." Finally someone had the wit to cut the program off the air.

The entire exchange was virtually an illustration of what Buck-

---

* In 1972, more prudently, the National Broadcasting Co. retained Buckley and his old skiing friend and intellectual sparring partner, John Kenneth Galbraith, to do a similar act during each day of the Democratic and Republican Conventions on an early-morning television exercise. It was at least reasonably dignified, and gratifying to both egos and pocketbooks.—C.L.M.

ley had said in a debate with Steve Allen in November, 1963: "There is at work against us an assault on the meaning of words, those instruments of civilisation by which we communicate with one another and correspond with our governors. Would that we could have a treaty suspending the abuse of rhetoric. The worst enemy of America is the debauchery of language." And he was probably quite honest when he said essentially the same thing in late 1971 by way of explaining the five-hundred-thousand-dollar libel suit that he filed against Vidal after Vidal went farther in *Esquire* for September, 1969, and said of Buckley that "in a larger sense his views are very much those of the founders of the Third Reich who regarded blacks as inferiors, undeclared war as legitimate foreign policy and the Jews as sympathetic to international Communism." Vidal also sued Buckley, but that action was thrown out; Buckley expected to win his, and in September of 1972 he did, when *Esquire* agreed to pay him one hundred fifteen thousand dollars and publish a suitable retraction in its November issue; Buckley thereupon dropped his action against Vidal with the observation that Vidal's estimated expenditure of seventy-five thousand dollars in legal fees might "teach him to observe the laws of libel." One's zeal for the First Amendment in no way lessens one's feeling of satisfaction that for once intellectual incontinence got what it deserved.

Vidal's counter-suit had long since been thrown out of court. He had claimed a million dollars on the ground that Buckley had defamed him by calling him, in print, a pornographer and a producer of perverted prose; but Judge Richard Levet in the Southern District of New York held that one who had written *Myra Breckenridge* (a singularly cruel and insensitive juvenility) had exposed himself to such criticism even if no reasonable man would agree that the criticism was warranted; and the proposition should be self-evident, or there could be no freedom for critics in any of the arts.

Buckley's explanation of the motive for his litigation is deserving of some attention, even though the defendant be worthy of none: "The philosophy behind the libel action is to make some minor historical contribution to the sanctity of the language. If anybody can call anybody a Communist or a Nazi, then the mint of social intercourse is so debased that distinctions are lost. If there's no difference between Adolf Hitler and Joe McCarthy, then Adolf Hitler wasn't that bad. It isn't simply a matter of Joe McCarthy absorbing the evil in Hitler, but also Hitler absorbs that which was non-Hitlerian in McCarthy, and eventually everybody is everything and you lose that sharp edge of distinction. The people who ought to be most grateful to me are the people who want to keep august the evil of Adolf Hitler."

The sharp edge of distinction is indeed as important as Buckley says it is; one could wish that he had thought of that always when he wrote or spoke, and that he would think of it still. It was in *The Governor Listeth*—which contains nothing to match his superb memorial, "The Last Years of Whittaker Chambers," in *Rumbles Left and Right*—that he announced that "in New York City one half of the chronically poor are disorganized poor who cannot be persuaded even to flush their own toilets." And it was in the same book that he wrote that the ordinary soldier who could commit murder at Mylai "is most likely a twenty-year-old whose ethical equilibrium was unbalanced well before he came to Vietnam. Unbalanced by a . . . society deprived of the strength of religious sanctions, a society hugely devoted to hedonism, to permissive egalitarianism, to irresponsibility, to an indifference to authority and the law. Such a society as—dare we say it—produced the kids who are attracted to the iconoclast of the day." Not even a blurred edge is now left to distinction. But it is this kind of translation of conservative thought into the vernacular in which Buckley excels and firmly believes: it is a major part of his mission. For the doctrine itself one must go rather to his "textbook" and to Frank Meyer's anthology, as beginnings; the real sources are Adam Smith, Burke, Augustine, St. Paul, Plato. For the world that the Buckleys and their followers would like to restore (if indeed it ever existed), one has only to go to Francis Russell's review of Frances Stevenson's account of her life with Lloyd George. The year that Russell has in mind, writing in *National Review* for 17 March 1972, is 1914:

"If Belgium had acceded to the Germans, if England had not come in, if France had been defeated after a six weeks' war in the 1870 manner and with the traditional indemnities, if the Russians had seen the handwriting on the wall in time; what a different and happier world we might have lived through in the last half century."

Let no innocent reader, however, be deceived: the Right in the United States in the last third of the twentieth century is quite as sectarian as ever the Left was in the years between the two wars; and, while all the Right may indeed sigh a pious *amen* to Russell's invocation, there would be no unanimity as to the best road back to Eden. Among all the apostles, to quote Leonard Levy, the general editor of the American Heritage Series, in his foreword to Buckley's anthology, "Mr. Buckley is the foremost expositor of rational, humanistic conservative thought in America today . . . he is also an enormously learned man and a serious thinker. . . . Mr. Buckley's conservatism shares nothing in common with the conservatism of Big Business or of the self-appointed super-patriots, bigots, and xenophobes. . . . He variously describes conservatism as a position, an attitude, and an ideology. . . . Mr. Buckley's conservatism is vigorously individualistic, in favor of ordered liberty, hostile to promiscuous equalitarianism, and pronouncedly tolerant . . . it has a deep streak of romantic utopianism . . . he finds the twentieth century to be a hideously science-centered age with a passion for equality that subverts the ideal society."

With most of Levy's assessment one must perforce agree, though one may raise an eyebrow at Levy's vision of ideological lacunae between Buckley and Big Business, or Buckley and the super-patriots: those are, rather, straits, and often they dry up. And there are clear and hardly broad limits to the tolerance. On the other hand, it becomes increasingly impossible to quarrel with Buckley's passionate revulsion at a technocentricity that has long since overcome national and ideological barriers. It is not with pejorative intent that one emphasises that in his own introduction to the anthology, which is a somewhat revised version of his essay in Meyer's earlier collection, Buckley has fused his thought and his sentiment on the whole problem of life in his time and the rightness of conservatism into what amounts to a credo. The body of the book is selected from the texts on which he has based his credo: they are as inconsistent one with another, at times, as he is with himself—which is to say, as any thinking man is with himself, for (in spite of what Buckley and his exemplars would wish) truth is not always or even necessarily knowable, or static. For those who have not the time or the disposition to give to the sources the study that Buckley has obviously devoted, this collection is an invaluable index to the basic thought from which he distills (and sometimes dilutes) the gospels that he would offer and interpret in the vulgar tongue.

The sharp edge of distinction is always present in this expansion of "Notes Toward an Empirical Definition of Conservatism," though one may wonder at the end precisely how much farther toward the definition one has moved. Buckley quotes from the letter that Chambers wrote when he felt that he must resign as an editor of *National Review* (the text used here is that of pp. 227ff. of *Odyssey of a Friend*—the letter is dated "Christmas Eve, 1958" —rather than what appears on pp. xviii–xix of Buckley's introduction to *American Conservative Thought*): "You . . . stand within, or, at any rate, are elaborating, a political orthodoxy. I stand within no political orthodoxy. You mean to be a conservative, and I know no one who seems to me to have a better right to the term. I am not a conservative. Sometimes I have used the term loosely, especially when I was first called on publicly to classify myself. I have since been as circumspect as possible in using the term about myself. I say: I am a man of the Right." Here Buckley stopped.

But it is most important that we go on, with Chambers: "I am a man of the Right because I mean to uphold capitalism in its American version. But I claim that capitalism is not, and by its essential nature cannot conceivably be, conservative. . . . Hence the native effort to rest in the past always makes us a little uneasy, seems merely nostalgic, antiquarian, futile and slightly fraudulent . . . Conservatism is alien to the very nature of capitalism, whose love of life and growth is perpetual change . . . conservatism and capitalism are mutually exclusive manifestations, and antipathetic. Capitalism, whenever it seeks to become conservative in any quarter, at once settles into mere reaction—that is, a mere brake on the wheel, a brake that does not hold because the logic of the wheel is to turn."

Buckley quotes none of this extremely provocative passage, the whole import of which, in other writings before and since, he has always violently contradicted without actually analysing it. Instead, he continues to claim Chambers, regardless of label, for the conservatives, though largely on the basis of Chambers's excommunication of Ayn Rand and her Objectivists in his criticism of her novel *Atlas Shrugged* in *National Review* in 1957. Chambers attacked Miss Rand and her disciples because of their "materialism of technocracy, of the relentless self-server who lives for himself and absolutely no one else, whose concern for others is explainable merely as an intellectualized recognition of the relationship between helping others and helping oneself. Religion is the first enemy of the Objectivist and, after religion, the state—respectively, 'the mysticism of the mind' and 'the mysticism of the muscle.' 'Randian Man,' wrote Chambers, 'like Marxian Man, is made the center of a godless world.' " This philosophy, Buckley declares, is definitively incompatible "with the conservative's emphasis on transcendence, intellectual and moral; but also there is the incongruity of tone, that hard, schematic, implacable, unyielding dogmatism that is in itself intrinsically objectionable, whether it comes from the mouth of Ehrenburg, or Savonarola, or Ayn Rand." Or, he might have added, Buckley.

He is compelled to concede the possibility of some virtue in the state, which "sometimes is the necessary instrument of our proximate deliverance." But, though he has learned that it is at least pragmatically possible for an atheist to be a conservative, he cannot really accept any belief short of his own, that "the struggle for the world is a struggle, essentially, by those who mean to unseat Him"—Him being God, and Buckley's insistence having cost him the collaboration of Max Eastman on the board of editors of *National Review*. Conservatism, Buckley states, is "a movement in which religion plays a vital role." It is with this continually in mind that he goes farther: "A conservative is properly concerned simultaneously with two things, the first being the shape of the visionary or paradigmatic society toward which we should labor; the second, the speed with which it is thinkable to advance toward that ideal society with the foreknowledge that any advance upon it is asymptotic; that is, we cannot hope for ideological home runs and definitive victories." But one thing remains certain: the state is still essentially an evil, though a necessary one, to be watched as suspiciously as any radical might eye its police or its military: its potential for good is in direct and exclusive proportion to its interventions in behalf of classical Manchester freedoms. As the authors represented in this book interpret intervention by the state for the sake of freedom, at least half the Bill of Rights and the later amendments in furtherance of its principles would be vitiated: for protection of such rights as freedom of expression and assembly, or of secularity in the schools, or of privacy of communication, is in this view a governmental infringement of the freedom of those who would limit speech and assembly, enforce religion in the schools, or abolish the protections against arbitrary arrest, search, seizure, and confinement.

Edmund Burke is the sun round which almost all these authors revolve, as he is the source of energy for Buckley's own kind of conservatism: "the Christian and classical idea of distributive justice," as Kirk calls it in his essay here, in which he decries the notion that it is unjust that some have more wealth or more leisure or more education or more opportunity than others, and in which, further, he invokes divine principle for these (to him) seeming inequities. Burke was frightened by the French Revolution, and his spiritual posterity even unto the seventh generation is still a little addled by it. So Jeffrey Hart, Dartmouth professor of literature, *National Review* editor, and syndicated columnist to the lesser Right, can praise Burke because "he did not make that grotesque but familiar distinction between property rights and human rights but viewed property as a human right." The magic of words becomes the magic of words (and thoughts) elided, and that sharp edge of distinction so cherished of Buckleyan conservatives is thus blunted by the implication that all human rights are the same and that property, being one of them, is necessarily the peer of all. To Burke as interpreted by Kirk and Hart one must add the convoluted mysticisms of Eric Herman Wilhelm Voegelin, late of Köln, Berlin, and Vienna, of Harvard, Yale, and the Sorbonne, driven out by the Nazis, now at the Hoover Institution of Stanford University—a philosopher of politics fixated at the perils of that very ancient heresy, Gnosticism, which, though it is almost two thousand years old, Buckley denounces as "the perennial heresy of the West." In what is probably the only clear sentence in his entire *oeuvre*, Voegelin wrote here that "the death of the spirit is the price of progress," and he did not bother to define his terms. The modernists merely perpetuate the Gnostic heresy of the attainability of earthly perfection: unceasingly they perpetrate "the Gnostic murder" of God, they "sacrifice God to civilization." Voegelin, whom Buckley delights in citing in any context, knows how it all must end: "Totalitarianism, defined as the existential rule of Gnostic activists, is the end form of progressive civilization."

Not all of Buckley's "textbook" is quite so rigid as Burke and Hart, so Calvinist as Kirk, so apocalyptic as Voegelin (who persists in the memory like Dr. Caligari). There is a great deal of tough sanity in many of these expressions of conservatism, emancipated from—better, never tainted by—the patois of what are so amusingly called the social scientists. (In *UP From Liberalism*, Buckley had earlier put forth what to every cultivated person has always been a truism but nonetheless requires regularly to be restated for an increasingly quantified and quantifying intelligentsia: "A successful novelist can do more to identify a national social tendency, or syndrome, than a dozen technicians.") What is often disturbing is what is intended, or aspired to, on the basis of sound premisses. One cannot quarrel with Kirk when he says that "the mass-mind, juke-box culture penetrates to every corner of the western world, and the man of superior natural talents is ashamed of being different," or that "the magazine-rack of any drug-store in America would suffice to drive Robert Lowe or Horace Mann to distraction," or that "there is no injustice or deprivation in the fact that one man is skilled with his hands, and another with his head, or that one man enjoys baseball and another chamber music." But on this truism he seeks to justify disparities in wealth and privilege, a priori: as part of the Christian order of things, in which no form of suffering is evil (but woes may indeed be advantageous to the soul) and the state must not eliminate the opportunity to give charity to the needy "for good unto the *giver* [his italics]."

Meyer, who is perhaps the most lucid spokesman in this collection, is often indistinguishable from Buckley. Both conceive democracy, with deliberate technicality, as being no more than "a mode or means of government which implies that what is morally right is what fifty per cent plus one think is right." Thus clothed, the idea is almost irresistible: of course one must scorn so quantitative a philosophy. "Conservative thought is shot through with concern for the person," Meyer says and Buckley often reiterates. "It is deeply suspicious of theories and policies based upon the collectivities that are the political reference points of Liberalism— 'minorities,' 'labor,' 'the people.' . . . [Conservatism] rejects absolutely the idea that society or men generally are perfectible. . . . It therefore rejects the entire Liberal mystique of 'planning,' which, no matter how humanitarian the motives of the planners, perforce treats human beings as faceless units to be arranged and disposed according to a design conceived by the planner. Rather, the conservative puts his confidence in the free functioning of the energies of free persons, individually and in voluntary cooperation." The state, according to this view, must be invoked by Liberalism at every stage "for effective control of the lives of individual human beings." To bolster his position, Meyer cites the 1964 Statement of Principles of the American Conservative Union.

This document proclaims the endowment of all men ("by their Creator") with inalienable rights, though it does not specify these. The concept is certainly unexceptionable, however: as much a part of the common political heritage of the West as the further reminders that governments are meant to serve men but have an inherent tendency to tyranny. With all this, as with the concern with individuals and their freedom, one must automatically agree. It is from these perfectly acceptable points of departure that the conservative forces led by Buckley and his associates go on to twist their conclusions in such a way as to legitimatise the destruction of many men's inalienable rights. The free-market principle is exalted to theological dogma and invoked to sanctify the destruction of the rights of the vast majority of individual persons—those who lack the means, the luck and/or the flexibility of scruple to claw their way to the top of the endlessly contesting heap. The rejection of certain "collectivities"—racial, political, religious—is also the rejection of the individual persons of whom they are composed; the "free functioning of the energies of free persons" can reach its apogee in their enslavement of millions of others whose freedom they have destroyed. Collectivities form spontaneously in any society, on the basis of common interests: the ruling class too (managers, owners, commissars, people's ministers, colonels— it makes no difference) is a collectivity, intent like any other on the protection of its own interests and quite as ready to employ the state that it rules to this end. Collectivity itself—whatever its social, political, economic philosophy—is by its nature the enemy of the individual: a truism that the conservative, concerned with his own collectivity, prefers to suppress. Here is the deceptiveness of his gospel of the individual, at least in its application: it is as much a doctrine of election and reprobation as the most fanatic Calvinism.

It is from this congeries of inherently contradictory ideas—each of which, in a vacuum, might be more or less a truth: but the *polis*, as Buckley, after Voegelin, is fond of calling it, is no vacuum —that the body of conservative doctrine represented by these people is able to derive its rationalisations. Brent Bozell contends that it is neither possible nor desirable to fix very much of policy in a Constitution, and therefore we have not only a fixed, written one but also a fluid, unwritten one, and that what is written may be merely, as in the case of the protections set forth in the First Amendment, symbolic: there was never any intent to protect total freedom of expression because it is dangerous, or to keep the sacred wholly out of the secular, because the Founding Fathers were believers. To seek through a Constitution to enforce the rights of members of a minority is to infringe individual freedom, he argues, by thrusting the government into men's private relations. Jaffa

reinforces the argument against absolute freedom of expression
as a theoretical good, though he advocates it "prudentially" until
a danger point becomes discernible: but he denounces the very
theory of a free market in ideas, and by name. Kendall, the most
abstruse of all except Voegelin, though Kendall makes no plunges
into mysticism, takes for his Bible *The Federalist*, and from these
sacred texts he evolves his theory of "the two majorities": the
Congressional, which the Founding Fathers intended, and the
Presidential, a later graft that they did not intend. (He contends
too that they did not intend, and ought not to have intended, any
of the guaranties that lesser minds than his are accustomed to
ascribe to the First Amendment.) The Congressional majority, as
expressed in the vote for both houses, assures government by
the "deliberate sense" or consensus of the people, through their
elected representatives, whereas the majority expressed every four
years in a Presidential election is the voice of direct majority and
equality, with which, he says, it is fatal to equate justice. The
tension between the executive and the legislative, in Kendall's view,
is a necessary epitome of that between the conservatives, who are
the legislators, and the liberals, who are the executive and the
appointed bureaucracy: the people can be trusted only to know
their neighbors and hence to vote intelligently and honestly only
for their immediate representatives, who will then know what is
best; whereas plebiscitary democracy, as Kendall calls it, would
give the majority "the power to make substantive policy decisions." Kendall, like Burke, would have the legislators, when they
consult at all with those whom they "represent," consult rather
"bank presidents than plumbers, bishops than deacons, editors
than rank-and-file newspaper readers, school superintendents than
schoolmarms."

American Conservative Thought in the Twentieth Century is
predominantly thus dogmatic and exclusivist; one wonders what
in its editor made him open the book with Garry Wills's provocative essay on "The Convenient State." (Today Buckley regards
Wills as a turncoat.) "The conservative," Wills says, "is typically
moderate, skeptical, critical. He forms a permanent opposition
to that permanent new theory or new regime that promises escape
from the hard human realities." Wills, going back to numerous
and diverse sources, declares for Calhoun's notion of a constitutional government as "that government in which all the free forms
and forces of society—or as many as possible—retain their life

and 'concur' in a political area of peaceful cooperation and compromise. . . . A constitutional regime gives both *life* and *limit* to government; it maintains a system that rules even society's rulers. . . . The art of constructing a just state consists in finding how to sacrifice the thinnest possible slices of individual 'sovereignty,' and the most uniform, so that all these contribute to the central storehouse of national sovereignty. . . . It will seek 'the common good,' not as some ideal scheme of order, or quantitative accumulation of individual goods, but as the real life of the 'commonalty,' of community in all its mutually enriching forms." And thus he reaches the significance of the title of his essay: ". . . 'convenience,' in its older English usage, meant consonance, especially the correspondence of things with thought. The convenient state has constant reference to man, and is adjusted to his real endeavors. It is the meeting of political institutions with the mystery and activity of man, a standing-together (constitution) of political discipline and the individual discipline of exercised freedom." This is indeed a conservatism that is "moderate, skeptical, critical": it has nothing in common with the conservatism that the Buckley group—which is by now the leader group in the American Right—has evolved.

Indeed, that conservatism has much more in common not only with the eternal dogmas of a Burke but with the ultra-materialism of an economic perspective as devoid of the "spiritual" as anything in Marx and Engels: less spiritual, indeed, than Marx's vision of ultimate freedom for all, even the weak. Buckley consecrates seventy pages of his "textbook" to three essays on economics, by Henry Hazlitt, Max Eastman, and the high priest of Chicago, Milton Friedman (Roepke, von Mises, and Hayek could not be included because the book was to gather the work only of American conservatives). What is said in all those pages comes down to the platitudes that were already tired when the second Roosevelt demonstrated their bankruptcy by salvaging the system that they had helped to precipitate into the abyss. Hazlitt is merely Adam Smith revisited, though the times and the circumstances have changed rather markedly and one can only wonder what so astute a thinker as the late Smith would have to say of a totally different economic world. Of course he—like Hazlitt after him—was right in inveighing against subsidies direct or indirect, against the imposition of obstacles to the free flow of goods and currencies and persons across borders; but these are not enough to solve the problems that the classical economists could not foresee: the human waste and social ferment created by the application of their theories *à outrance* and the dehumanisation of societies by the new superstition compounded of possession-power and machines.

Eastman, for whom it might be argued that exposure to Stalinism had purged him of his early Communism, is nevertheless, in his essay here reprinted, typical of all the opponents of any kind of economic planning: the tragic costs of the economic anarchy that has led to oligarchy under capitalism are not mentioned, not even alluded to; it is set out as an article of faith that a managed economy—under whatever name—means, automatically, an enveloping dictatorship. Writing as an admitted non-economist, Eastman repeats the Austrians' theory that free-market economics is the sole foundation of social and political freedom; he implies that, because there is no freedom in Soviet-dominated countries, there can be none as a result of the economic system; and he cites John Dos Passos on the abridgments of liberty that are alleged to have occurred in "Socialist" Britain. It is quite true that the Soviet Union allows no freedoms worthy of mention; the same was true of the Czarist government, which certainly imposed no curbs on free enterprise but rather, in its latter years, encouraged the growth of capitalism. It is totally untrue, however, that any liberties have been abridged in Britain under the Labour government. Curiously, the conservative enemies of regulated or mixed economies avoid any observations on the status of freedom in Sweden: the worst they can say of that "Socialised" country is that it is, by their lights, immoral; but that sad situation is hardly to be correlated with its economics.

Hard evidence in behalf of his thesis is equally avoided by Friedman, who can only marshal a series of pronouncements to the effect that nothing undertaken by government in the domain of economics has succeeded. To argue, as he does, that the railroads have pre-empted regulation by government and turned it into an instrument to throttle competition is to indict capitalism and its morals, not government intervention. Friedman blames the Federal Reserve System and international monetary authorities for the 1929 depression—and leaves us to take this on faith. In the same cavalier fashion he tells his conservative acolytes that public housing programs have created crime and blight, labor unions have practiced extortion and blackmail, social-security payments have not prevented the growth of the welfare rolls (under the law, of course, they cannot do so), control of communications has failed—he himself abandons the catalogue. What is sardonically interesting is his insistence that these failures arise solely from the fact that the activities were initiated by government "to force people to act against their own immediate interests in order to promote a supposedly general interest"; whereas Hazlitt's essay points out, in his italics throughout: *"The art of economics consists in looking not merely at the immediate but at the longer effects of any act or policy; it consists in tracing the consequences of that policy not merely for one group but for all groups."* It is Friedman's thesis that government's activity must be restricted to military defense and that the nation's health depends exclusively on "one of the strongest and most creative forces known to man —the attempt by millions of individuals to promote their own interests, to live their lives by their own values." One can hardly believe it is mere naïveté that ignores the possibility of some millions of conflicting interests and the havoc that must result from such economic anarchy. But apparently such questions are of no moment to Friedman or to the other extreme libertarians who would do away even with the public health services. These are curiously crippled men: one wonders whether they would even understand what Meyer wrote in his essay on "Freedom, Tradition, Conservatism": ". . . the only possible basis of respect for the integrity of the individual person and for the overriding value of his freedom is belief in an organic moral order. Without such a belief, no doctrine of political and economic liberty can stand."

Buckley's "textbook," of course, includes the requisite warning by James Burnham that Armageddon is at hand and the Beast of Communism is poised to fall upon us. Writing well before American capitulation to the facts of life, Burnham quite correctly pointed out that troubles between the mother country and the ideological colonies must not be exaggerated: whatever the Russians' quarrels with the Chinese or the Cubans or others of the "Socialist" countries, they would all make common cause, when the occasion arose, against the United States and, even in the midst of their domestic squabbles, they were all still joined by their shared commitment to the undoing of the capitalist colossus. In what the members of the conservative camp love to call Aesopian language when their enemies use it, Burnham makes plain his own and Buckley's firm belief in total military defeat of every revolution everywhere: on this, he would have us believe, the security of the United States depends. (As we shall observe, this same theme

was more vehemently developed by Buckley after his return from
China, to which he had gone as a member of the press accredited
to Nixon.)

Two of the essays included in the anthology cross all ideological
lines. Jane Jacobs on the need for diversity in cities and the blight-
ing hand of uniformity-minded planning commissions seems quite
out of place in this congregation of doctrinaires. So does Mortimer
Smith, who attacks the planned mediocrity of American educationists and the deliberate degradation of education to mere training in elementary survival skills. In their dealings with matters of
vital concern in which political or ideological divisions become
irrelevant, they are neither angry nor frightened; if they are hor-
tatory, it is in a most civilised fashion.

Buckleys have always insisted on their freedom from racial
prejudices, and in the "textbook" the problem is dealt with by
Ernest van den Haag, the "social scientist" and lay psychoanalyst
who teaches at New York University and the New School and
frequently contributes to *National Review*. What he says here
(which is sometimes at considerable variance with his testimony,
and its effects, in a 1963 school-segregation lawsuit in a Federal
Court in Georgia—*Stell et al. v. Savannah-Chatham County Board
of Education et al.*) seems to be designed to avoid any substantive
judgments on questions of "racial differences" but rather to illustrate a "conservative" approach to procedural problems of legitimate and illegitimate discrimination and demands, restrictions, and
rights. Consequently there is much negative and indirect address
to the problems, by way of justified condemnations of reverse
discrimination—that is, the special debasement of standards or
establishment of quotas to assure specific representation of blacks
in given schools or occupations or other areas without regard to
the general criteria usually imposed—and of the hypocrisies of
white liberals whose practices do not quite match their precepts.
Now all this is sound enough, as even some of the educationists
and "counter-culture" spokesmen are beginning to recognise: one
does not undo the damage of the ghetto by "educating" its children exclusively in its dialect and values. But what van den Haag
seems intent on conveying—and he treads most carefully: Buckley
himself is rarely so circumspect—is the notion that, again, the
problem of illegitimate racial discrimination—that is, discrimination based not on the individual's capacities but on his racial origins
—must be resolved through some analogy of the principle of

the free market and with the minimum government intervention possible.

The question is one to which Buckley himself refers fairly often in *Cruising Speed*, and with considerably less peevishness than in earlier discussions of the subject. One cannot help concluding that he does not yet believe altogether that there is anything more than spotty racial discrimination; he seems convinced that the main problem has nothing to do with race or color but is a matter simply of the same kind of characterological defect that keeps poor whites poor. There is not much about the poor in *Cruising Speed*; there is not much about anything in any serious vein. Yet the book ought to be read by anyone who is interested in the phenomenon of William F. Buckley Jr., if only because of the pervasive grace with which he performs the always difficult feat of writing about oneself without being either pompous or 'umble. It tells little about how he feels and thinks, or why; it does leave one amazed that he should be able to search his soul at all and find the time to put the results into words. His is a schedule of constant activity, so that one begins to search for a phrase that would be apt, the precise contrary of Whitman's "I loaf and invite my soul." For Buckley appears to do neither: with breakfast he has *The Times*, in the car he has his correspondence, his tapes, his files, his notes for lectures; hardly a meal, even with his wife, is free of one or another aspect of business or of business guests; wherever he arrives, the messages from his secretary are waiting. John Kenneth Galbraith, his economist friend, he tells us at the end of the book, urged him to give it all up for the academy and the writing of books: only books count, Galbraith told him. Briefly he sets down the reply that he did not give Galbraith: he cannot improve on his masters, but he can and does "advertise their profundity."

"What do you want?" I asked him in November of 1971: a nasty question, granted, to hurl at anyone without warning. "What is all this activity for?" (Obviously it is not for money.) There was a silence.

"Essentially, I think," he said, more slowly than usual, "people have to decide to what extent they are going to participate in public enterprises. Now, as you move in civilisation towards a world in which more and more the public enterprise overshadows the private enterprise, it becomes less and less difficult to understand why people feel that their stake in the public enterprise is absolutely essential in order to protect themselves privately. Now, if we lived in a world in which it just plain didn't matter what happened in Washington or Geneva, then I should think that the luxury of being totally private would be something that more of us could indulge ourselves in. But, as we live in an age in which the least tremor in Washington is likely to affect the price of beans in Monterey, you have got, as a matter of self-defense, to engage. And this is the nature of my own interest in the thing. Now, I say, recognising that after a while your temperament gets honed to a particular mode, I say: 'Wouldn't it be wonderful if the whole public problem were to disappear?' Whether, that having happened, I could retire to my poetry-reading and my sailing, I don't know. I simply don't know, because people develop certain nervous habits."

Pressed for a more private motive beyond that of preserving an order—though he boggled at that word—in which he believes, he added: "My attachment to the American way is a manifold attachment. In part I like parts of it because I like them." This was rather like his responses to questions about his esthetic preferences: "I like what I like: I like my friends"—who range from Trollope and Evelyn Waugh to Disney. "In part I like them because I see no likely prospect of their radical improvement in short order. In part I like the freedom that I am vouchsafed to indulge my own eccentricities, whether esthetic, athletic, or whatever. And in part I am dismayed by the quality of the arguments that are used to disparage them."

Specifics are difficult to come by. Urged to elaborate, he paused again; when he replied, it was with much reflection. "I consider myself a radical conservative, and I would like a whole lot of things to have developed differently. The paradigm of the society I would like to see is not one either toward which we are moving or one toward which it is likely that we can move. This doesn't mean that an energetic polemic in behalf of that kind of society isn't in order, but it must be understood as being primarily paradigmatic and functional." Beyond this he would not explore; he would say only (and, unfortunately, all too accurately): "We're moving toward statism. Toward statism where the collectivity is everything."

In this sense he contends that the Right has been losing ground, even though to an observer on a different hill the exact contrary would seem to be the case: no doubt it is a question whose collectivity one is fighting. "To the extent that you get an enlargement of the public sector you lose ground," he elaborated; "to the extent that you have an intellectual class that is so given to relativism that substantial numbers of it cannot distinguish between the liberties we enjoy and the liberties that are vouchsafed to a Soviet citizen, you lose ground. To the extent that society is pressed to answer the question *Shall we survive? Shall we resist revolutionary secret movements?* and it answers in the affirmative, then you are galvanising conservative impulses within the society."

One is more than a little shocked to find someone of Buckley's intelligence and sophistication seriously believing that "substantial numbers" cannot distinguish between life in the United States and life in a complete police state, or that there is so much secrecy left to revolutionary movements. Yet he does believe these things, and the quality of his belief helps to convince others. He denies any contacts with the Right in other countries, except for his two or three meetings a year with Otto von Habsburg in the very private society ("a sort of *institut des hautes études*") that he mentions in *Cruising Speed*; he is emphatic in stating that he has no contacts with the new Italian Fascist *Movimento sociale italiano* or with any of the German Right; but *National Review* has now begun trying to convey the impression that the MSI is not Fascist (though without categorically saying so: that would be, in view of the evidence so readily available, quite foolish). Through Lejeune, of course, he is in contact with the British Right, and in the winter of 1972 he conferred with its leaders on his way home from the Antarctic, Vietnam, India, and Israel.

The trip to the Antarctic, he said on the eve of departure, would be in part at least a vacation: he was to accompany his Senatorial brother, who is fascinated by wilderness of all kinds. But, ostensibly, their missions would be separate thereafter: James Buckley would be touring Southeast Asia for purposes connected with his business as a Senator and Bill would go on to Saigon, New Delhi, Jerusalem to film *Firing Line* programs (as, indeed, he did).

For all the charm and the apparent openness, however, one is left with a decided impression of an underlying disingenuousness —as befits, one would suppose, those who know not where the conspirator lurks.

XX

BUCKLEY CONSERVATISM gained recognition as a political force in New York State—and, since that is the least conservative of states, in the nation—in the Senatorial election of 1968, in which James Buckley, with his brother Bill as chairman of his campaign, polled more than a million votes. This represented somewhat less than seventeen per cent of the total cast for himself, Javits (who ran as a Republican and a Liberal), and Paul O'Dwyer, a reasonably Left Democrat. Henry Paolucci, the 1964 Conservative candidate for the Senate, had polled only a few more than two hundred thousand votes. In four years the Conservative Party, though the Buckleys had no more expectation of victory for James in 1968 than they had had for Bill in 1965, had quintupled its electorate in the state. In 1970 James Buckley was to be elected to the Senate with just under twice the number of votes that he accumulated in 1968.

What James Buckley calls his "quixotic" 1968 campaign was predicated on the certainty of defeat. "If there had been a risk of my winning, which there clearly wasn't," he explained, "then I couldn't, as a responsible man, have entered the race in the first place." His purpose, however, like his brother's three years earlier, he said, was to ascertain "the plausibility of a leverage party, namely the Conservative Party, its purpose having been that of reform: specifically, to re-establish a kind of two-party dialogue of choices. If it's a game plan [one is shocked to hear the Nixonian cliché from a man of intellectual substance], it's the Liberal Party's game plan: if the two national parties in this state cannot nominate somebody whom you can endorse, then, in order to be able to yield a measurement as to how desirable your endorsement would have been, you have to run somebody in opposition so that you can measure that latent support. This is what Bill referred to as jury-duty: he did jury-duty in '65 with the clear understanding that there was absolutely no freakish chance of his ever winning."

Yet James Buckley, like Bill, would be opposed to a demarcation between the two major parties as sharp as that in Britain between the Conservatives and Labour. "If you believe," he said, "that the two-party system is a prudent way of having our politics organised, and I do, then you have to recognise that you can't have that clear compartmentalisation you're talking about. There's bound to be overlapping. Basically it seems to me that each party ought to represent the responsible alternative within the scope of current acceptable American politics, and you're going to have to have within those alternatives a large spectrum of graduation. So I think that, to have an effective two-party system, there ought to be two points of view, and I think in American politics we do have them. But, if you so overlap as to destroy the ability to identify one party with one point of view in a given state or in a given community, then you have destroyed what makes two-party politics meaningful. It then becomes competing ball teams, and old affections or individuals mean everything, and then comes the glamorisation of candidates. . . . The party that's out of power ought to be the loyal opposition trying to argue its case responsibly and effectively enough to persuade enough people to make it the party in power." This kind of opposition, he believes, has not ceased to exist in the nation at large, though its atrophy in New York was what led to the creation of the Conservative Party there.

His 1968 campaign was based essentially on the party's original statement of principles and objectives, and it was addressed to those elements in the community that could not or would not understand the opposition to the Vietnam war, the inherent immorality of their own bigotries, and the responsibilities of every man to every other. This is not to say that any of these descriptives was applicable to their candidate, James Buckley, however strongly he favored the successful and more vigorous prosecution of the war, the preservation of a social and economic order of which he was a major beneficiary, and the traditional exclusion of the state from every possible aspect of life in reliance on the magic of the free-market philosophy as the nostrum for everything: what cannot be resolved by free-market methods must obviously be insoluble and therefore accepted. One may be quite certain that it was never his conscious intention to play on prejudice, as one may be equally certain that he never concerned himself with combatting it—or recognised what fantasies his followers were projecting on him. His own positions were reached with a maximum of intellection and a minimum of affect—a perceptible minimum, true, hardly likely to be attenuated by obvious self-interest. But this self-interest must not be exaggerated: there was no taint of dishonesty or even disingenuousness, as there was none of self-aggrandisement, in the concern that led him into active politics: he was no more (and no less) culpable in conceiving the interests of the nation to be identical with those of traditional free enterprise than, let us say, a factory worker equally convinced that there can be no differentiation between the interests of mankind as a whole and those of the industrial proletariat.

As Buckley's 1968 vote showed, there were by then more Conservatives than there had been before; but there were not yet enough. Nor were all conservatives convinced that the Republican Party was no longer where they belonged; many of the 2.8 million who elected Javits on the Republican ticket—plus four hundred thousand Liberals; O'Dwyer received slightly more than two million votes—did not especially like him, but they were afraid that a vote for a fourth-party man was wasted. Conservatives still thought that Nixon was different from Humphrey, and desirably so, and in voting for Nixon they allowed party loyalty to align them behind the rest of his ticket. And initially it did indeed seem that the basic tie was between Nixon and conservatism: everything that he did then was predicated on the greater good of those who had been his law firm's clients and their comrades and confederates in command of industry, finance, and labor, to say nothing of the military. Professor Paul Weiss observed that one of Bill Buckley's vulnerabilities was his assumption that everyone always acts on reasoned, ideological bases, and perhaps most of us share this assumption: certainly most conservatives believed it of Nixon even when they were uncomfortable over what they regarded as dangerous dalliances on the Left. Conservatives, including the Buckleys, were the last, almost, to abandon this construction of Nixon's behavior, whereas the man's whole record was there for anyone to have seen at once, from the day he entered politics, that he could be moved only by two things: advantage and, in opposite circumstances, desperation. I do not pretend to know beyond cavil why finally conservatives began to turn away from Nixon, any more than I can pretend to know why conservative and reactionary strength in the nation and the world at large has been increasing at an ever growing rate since at least the mid-1960's; but the two facts are undeniable, and in the case of the former the clear answer is the bankruptcy of the man the conservatives trusted and of the improvisations he foisted off on them as policies.

Yet he gave a formidable advantage to his future opponents on the Right—whose opposition is still at least as sorrowful as it is angry—when he made Buckley's friend and his own campaign television aide, Frank Shakespeare of Columbia Broadcasting System, director of the United States Information Agency. Shakespeare appointed as his assistant director for public information William F. Gavin, who had long been a contributor to *National Review* and who in April, 1972, traded his USIA post for a job as speech-writer to Senator Buckley; and he recommended that Nixon appoint William F. Buckley Jr. to the United States Advisory Commission on Information. Under the statute that constitutes the USIA's charter, members of this commission, who represent the public interest, "shall be selected from a cross-section of professional, business and public-service backgrounds." They are appointed by the President, and he selects, Gavin said, "Americans who have outstanding reputations in the field of communications." The other members, appointed by Lyndon Johnson, were Dr. Frank Stanton, chairman of the commission and president of CBS—though initially Shakespeare wanted to make Buckley chairman, and Stanton was perturbed by his own and Shakespeare's common CBS bond, Nixon was adamant; Palmer Hoyt, publisher of *The Denver Post*; Thomas Vail, publisher of *The Cleveland Plain Dealer*, and Morris Novik, who had for a long time been the guiding genius of WNYC, the radio and television station owned and operated by New York City. Buckley was appointed to succeed the aging Sigurd S. Larmon, long an executive of Young & Rubicam, an advertising agency with branches throughout Europe as well as the United States.

The Advisory Commission's members, according to Gavin, "make recommendations to the President, the Congress and the Director of the USIA on the policies and programs that govern the overseas information program. From time to time the Commission performs appraisals of the Agency programs and of their effectiveness." Its members are unpaid consultants, except for transportation and twenty-five dollars *per diem* when they travel on official business. Buckley made three extensive journeys for the agency, in 1969, 1970, and 1971; but he claimed no *per diem* for the 1971 trip. From the start, however, he made it known that he would write about the USIA whenever he wished, and the wish has not come seldom. He has also had Shakespeare as a friendly guest on *Firing Line*. Whenever Buckley writes about Shakespeare or the agency, he speaks no evil of either; indeed, there are those who have found it not quite right for a member of the USIA's ostensibly objective Advisory Commission, which is supposed to assay its worth and effectiveness, to serve as its voluntary press agent in newspapers and magazines here and in other countries. Some critics said that he should not use taxpayers' money to voyage over the world in praise of the man whose work he is supposed to appraise, whereupon Buckley offered full reimbursement; but this was ignored.

Buckley made it his business, in his travels, to inspect the contents of USIA libraries in foreign countries and to attempt to see to it that books and periodicals that he found politically offensive were replaced with others of more pleasing tendency. It is not easy to play holier-than-he on such matters: whatever high-minded purposes the USIA may tell the taxpayers it has, its job is to disseminate propaganda favorable to the United States, and the relation between propaganda and truth or fairness is at best tenuous. What was much more important was the fact of Buckley's membership in the Advisory Commission and his close ties with the man who ran the agency. Shakespeare, like Buckley, was fiercely anti-Communist, and together they could and did exert a powerful influence on the tone and intensity and substance of USIA activities; they were, further, in a position to carry out an effective propaganda campaign at home on behalf of the USIA without violating the statutory prohibition—the short-sighted unwisdom of which seems blatant—against the distribution of any USIA material within the United States. Senator Buckley, however, did use a USIA film on his monthly television "report." Shakespeare told Buckley, and Buckley told the rest of us, that the USIA was doing an excellent job (and this might even have been true); but where was the documentation? It was interesting (if one may anticipate for a moment) that, in spite of Bill Buckley's very public suspension of support for Nixon in the summer of 1971 and his propulsion of John Ashbrook into the 1972 Republican Presidential primaries, he was reappointed to the Advisory Commission without the slightest difficulty, regardless of an inspired rumor briefly floated by a news syndicate; and it was even more interesting that in mid-March Nixon was compelled to announce that Buckley had slapped his face by refusing the reappointment.

Even before his appointment to the Commission, Buckley had more than once been the President's guest, and their contacts before Nixon's election had long been close, though unpublicised until Buckley was ready to break with Nixon. This close relation, and Buckley's invitations to the White House, which in those days were never refused, wherever the White House might at the moment have been transplanted, were certainly useful to James Buckley in his 1970 Senatorial campaign. But what Bill Buckley's appraisals of and recommendations for the USIA actually were in the three years of his tenure cannot be divined, since all such texts are submitted formally by the commission as a body.

While Bill Buckley was traveling on behalf of the USIA, James, having returned to the family businesses after his 1968 blooding, was once more averaging fifty thousand miles of foreign travel a year. As a principal and at the same time a lawyer, he was, so to speak, "two skills, two positions in one packet." Most of this time was spent in investigating new areas of operation and deciding where to try to negotiate for concessions, and he was in constant contact with lawyers of other nations. From Thanksgiving of 1969 until the spring of 1970 he was out of the country, but his thoughts were still concerned with "the extent that the United States was concentrating power in Washington, because (a) this was destructive of the mobility of the United States and (b) it's antithetical to freedom. I think that we've seen evidences of a moral erosion in the country in terms of individual fiber and self-reliance." But during his stay in Indonesia, Australia, and the Philippines he "was pretty well insulated from the things that were happening. There was tremendous turmoil then, and I came home and suddenly this sort of thing overwhelmed me in terms of what you might call a naked visible deterioration in the fiber of American life. Now I'd seen how a number of Americans had gone to Australia to get away from the United States. It seemed to me that either you believe fundamentally in the country and don't want to emigrate, and therefore you do something about it, or you emigrate. Obviously, I had strong feelings about how the structure of the federal government ought to be ordered, and as a result of the quixotic exposure to politics in '68 I persuaded myself that, if I seriously felt that I could make a contribution by going into the Senate, I had a reasonable enough chance of succeeding to make the effort worth-while."

To hear him say these things in the privacy of his New York office, after he had been a year in the Senate, was to recognise that he was being quite genuinely modest. He had not expected to win, and one feels that at times he is not quite certain that he is really a Senator. The speculation by James Wechsler and others that James Buckley wanted to be nominated for the Vice Presidency in 1972 could be dismissed, even though there were undoubtedly many forces in both the Republican and the Conservative Parties that would strive to have him nominated, for reasons both interested and disinterested: disinterested in the same sense in which one is compelled to believe that he himself is disinterested: he may enjoy some aspects of being a Senator (and no doubt it has its pleasures), but his real motivation in seeking election, one is convinced, is precisely what he has said it was: to serve a cause in the prime importance of which he whole-heartedly believes.

He was not really optimistic when he began his campaign. Only a few months earlier Ralph de Toledano, who was a resident of New York in the same sense in which James Buckley is or the late Robert Kennedy was, had announced his own candidacy for the Senate as a Republican and asked Bill Buckley, who was in Switzerland, to be his campaign chairman. When Buckley objected that he had little time to give, de Toledano said that what he really wanted was Buckley's name and endorsement; but then, when James Buckley decided to run and the Conservative Party embraced him at once, de Toledano naturally released Bill from any commitment to him and then abandoned his own candidacy. De Toledano says, too, that William Rusher and other influential Conservatives were against him, partly because of clashes of temperament. He adds that they "were able to twist Jimmy Buckley's arm: he had sworn he would never run, and in fact that's why he took himself out of the state, so he could say: 'I'm not a resident.' Bill learned about Jim's decision to run after he'd made it."

The internal situation in the Republican Party in 1970, de Toledano added, was such that the Conservatives thought that there was a chance of victory provided the candidate was attractive enough. Governor Nelson Rockefeller's choice, the incumbent, Charles Goodell, was much disliked within the party, and his enemies, according to de Toledano, included his senior colleague, Jacob Javits. Richard Ottinger, the Democrat, was not considered a serious contender in himself. The Conservatives, then, having long nursed resentment at Rockefeller's cavalier dismissal of them, and regarding Goodell as a turncoat Republican who was becoming indistinguishable (in his policies and his votes; not in his personal character, which commands respect) from Robert Kennedy, sensed the rightness of the time: it was clear, from past elections and from day-to-day events such as the mounting verbal and often physical reaction in the streets to demonstrations for "liberal" and radical causes, that popular sentiment was moving toward conservatism. Every police car and every fire engine sported a flag; flag decals were numerous on private cars, taxis, trucks, city-owned vehicles; "patriotic" bumper stickers were increasing; anti-black propaganda and action were more visible; narcotics use was growing; the panders to prurience were spreading everywhere and prospering exceedingly (and to a considerable degree from those who were the loudest in condemnation of them): the swelling lower middle class was frightened and therefore angry, resentful of the increase in crime and the (exaggerated) scandals of growing welfare rolls, baffled by the interminable war that could not be won but was still taking lives. Republicans, Democrats, and the schizophrenic Liberal Party had demonstrated their incompetence: the people who read *The News* when they read anything at all "knew" where the trouble lay and where the cure was to be found: in a return to the old days (which, of course, most of them could not remember). Their incarnation, Nixon, was sedulously avoiding any endorsement of Goodell; Buckley was saying that he was the true Republican and that that was in fact why he had to run on the Conservative ticket: because the Republicans had been robbed of their own party: he was the real, the Nixon Republican, and, if he were elected, his votes in the Senate would prove it. Finally he obtained Nixon's tacit and Vice President Agnew's flamboyant endorsement, which further endeared him to the so-called silent majority.

His campaign was actually managed by the man who had persuaded him of the possibility of winning: F. Clifton White, the principal manager of Goldwater's 1964 Presidential campaign. White commissioned a poll and obtained a showing that sixty per cent of the electorate regarded itself as conservative or moderate

—enough, White reckoned, to stage an effective rebellion against liberalism in either major party. Moreover, Nixon made it clear that financial contributions for Buckley's Conservative campaign could be sought from affluent donors to the 1968 Republican Presidential fund. The essence of the appeal was what Buckley called the "shock of non-recognition" of what the country had come to as a result of dissent, violence, "smut," drugs. His peroration was always virtually the same: "There is nothing wrong with America or her values or her basic institutions which we cannot handle, if we substitute order and intelligence for the present drift. . . . Above all we must restore stability. . . . This is the job I want to do. I ask you to join me in the March for America. Thank you, and God bless you all."

That the public temper was turning Right was obvious. But the selection of White to run Buckley's campaign was very possibly the prime factor in the successful exploitation of the change. White, a public-relations practitioner who had been a significantly active figure in New York State and national Republican politics since 1948 (and who is still a practicing political consultant with an office in Manhattan), had worked closely with William Rusher, publisher of *National Review*, in launching the draft of Goldwater; and one of their closest collaborators was Ashbrook, later to be the anti-Nixon primary candidate of the conservatives. A former teacher of government at Cornell and at Ithaca College, White had been both Commissioner and Deputy Commissioner of Motor Vehicles for New York State under both Republican and Democratic administrations. He was and is a director of the Public Affairs Council, and on occasion had been retained to brief Peace Corps volunteers about American politics before they went off to serve abroad. A Mason, a Son of the American Revolution, and a Presbyterian elder, White presented the ultimate in credentials of respectability, which he offered Buckley in combination with the lessons of his three years of endeavor on behalf of Goldwater. In 1964 White was ahead of his market; in 1970 the market was ready to be opened.

James Buckley, however, was not White's creation, nor was he much, if at all, made over: he remained his own man. Since earliest childhood he had loved nature and spent every possible minute in the outdoors. He neither hunted nor fished, but he loved to hike, he was a dedicated bird watcher, and he knew everything that grew. As a child he loved canoe trips with the Coleys. Only re-

cently he had gone to the far north to join an expedition studying the life of the musk ox. He was a conservationist from childhood, quite prepared to vote against his party if the welfare of
the natural environment were in issue. A real Adam Smith conservative, he was firmly opposed to government subsidies to corporations as well as to the poor, the ill, or the farmers.

And he was gentle. One has only to meet him to know that
clearly those who know him best are right when they tell how in-
flexible he can be; but he is not cruel, he does not try to score
at the expense of others, and at times his shyness, suddenly emerg-
ing, reminds one of his sister Priscilla. He gives the impression of
somewhat greater sophistication than does his brother John; and
James is tall and lean, whereas John is much shorter and inclined
to stoutness. Goodell, his opponent and frequent platform competitor, was impressed with his gentleness and his evident sincerity;
and with his intelligence. James Buckley, though he speaks well
always, lacks Bill's delight in words for words' sake, and one suspects he is less inclined than Bill to intellectual games and antics;
his sense of humor is quieter, too, and his wit is softer and less
frequent. Many of those who are enjoyably dazzled by Bill are
also a little frightened by him, and a little distrustful of him because he is so different even if so persuasive; but such people are
thoroughly reassured by Jim, in whom there is no pretense, no
upsetting trace of the unfamiliar. He knows *The American Heritage Songbook* better than he knows the baroque. It is almost as
if the brothers had divided the market: the sophisticated conservatives for Bill, the stodgier, less imaginative for Jim. Which is not
to say that he impresses one as being devoid of imagination. How
closely they collaborate politically is a matter for speculation: they
are close personally, but James says there is "very little conscious
collaboration." He never joined Bill's withdrawal of support from
Nixon and, indeed, publicly dissociated himself from it and asserted his own continuing allegiance to the President, until March
of 1972, when, after Nixon's return from China, James Buckley
said that he would support Nixon for re-election but did not know
then whether he would campaign for him. Five months later
Buckley announced a crowded schedule of campaign speeches,
not only for Nixon but for other conservative Republicans in
many states, chiefly Southern.

Goodell, whom Buckley defeated in 1970, has appraised him
rather well, though Goodell believes that his own and Ottinger's

great mistake was to campaign exclusively against each other and to ignore Buckley as a serious factor until almost the end of the campaign, so that by then Buckley could have beaten either of them alone; whereas, Goodell says, that would not have been possible earlier. He was aware, too, that some of the regular Republican organisation people in various parts of the state, in spite of Rockefeller's friendship for Goodell, were working with the Conservative organisation on behalf of Buckley: upstate New York, after all, has always tended toward the Right, and one remembers how many Wallace emblems one saw there in 1968. (That Wallace did not always get the votes of those who liked him has consistently been misconstrued: those who feared that he could not be elected under his own name merely voted for him as Nixon, not altogether mistakenly believing Nixon to be the next best thing.)

The two most prominent Buckleys are very different from each other, in Goodell's estimation. "In a public debate or discussion or panel program or something of that nature," he said, "Bill will be acid. He will satirise, he will drip at times with sarcasm—master of the quick sharp thrust that draws blood. Jim doesn't do that kind of thing. And Jim, who is a very gracious, agreeable man, has a sense of humor: he can tease and be teased. I think the Buckleys are a force that is certainly to be taken seriously politically. Bill, for example, is a rational human being, who will (from my viewpoint) start from a false premise, but then he tries to be consistent by that premise and its application. This has led him at various times to take exception to the far Right—as a matter of fact, a certain number of the really fringe ones think he is a Socialist himself. The Buckleys are a definite force not only in themselves but with their associates—*National Review*, Rusher, some of the bright, practical technicians in politics.

"One of the things about Jim Buckley—a major factor in his campaign—was that he is a very bland and gracious and agreeable sort. Had he been strident, like most of the people who agree with him politically, he never would have won. He is moderate at the same time as very, very Right-Wing: he came through rather unscathed in this situation because he just stood up there and was grand and mannerly and made no harsh accusations, no extreme statements that alienated people. He came through as a person of whom a hard-hat could say: 'I'll vote for him. He's against the labor laws, he's against all the things we believe in, but he's for safety in the street and for patriotism.' And he was able to get away with it."

But Goodell believes (in a way rather reminiscent of the not very realistic Center and Left of the 1930's) that success would undo conservatism. "To the degree they get power," he said, "there will be less of a growth factor because it's one thing to be sniping from outside and it's another when you are in office and have responsibility and your program does absolutely nothing for the people to solve the major problems of this country. It just may be that by electing Jim Buckley, a Conservative, people will then see what he fails to do as a Senator more than what he does, and it will reverse this trend that has set in—without any question—and that I think still continues in the country toward a blind reactionary emotionalism, hostilities and negative feelings. They didn't create it: they rode the wave, which is not limited to the Right Wing." This observation was made against the background of sporadic violence on the Left and James Buckley's appalling espousal of the middle- and lower-middle-class Jewish bigots of Forest Hills in their resolve to keep public housing for the black poor out of the area from which fifty years earlier they themselves had been barred.

"Take Jim Buckley's program for solving the problems that were so very frustrating to the people in 1970: they were emotionally lashing out at different groups to try to find the fall guys, and Jim Buckley said: 'We need a new attitude of toughness' with reference to law and order, the crime problem. That struck a chord with people in New York who were more and more frequently being mugged or hearing of others being mugged in the neighborhood. Buckley's program for this was 'leave it to the local government.' To the extent drugs contributed to crime, he was against any federal drug program except saying we ought to get tough with France and Turkey, which has never worked. He was against a gun-control law. He was against the federal government being involved in trying to find a solution, including even giving money under the Law Enforcement System Act to train the local police: again, it ought to be handled at the local level—with the general rhetoric that, if we didn't send all that money to Washington, where they took out all the administrative costs, we'd get more out of it here if we raised and spent it ourselves. All of which is a very persuasive-sounding form of nonsense. If Jim Buckley were President of the United States for a year or two and carried through his basic philosophy of what he's for and what he's against and had the power to do it—had a Congress that would do it—it would reverse the trend toward conservatism or destroy this country in very fast order."

This has been the comforter of "liberals" for years, especially since the apparent fall of Fascism and Naziism. But what is conveniently overlooked is the somber warning emphasised by Karl Dietrich Bracher of the University of Bonn in his important book, *The German Dictatorship*: neither Fascism nor Naziism "fell" for internal reasons: each was overthrown by military defeat from without, but in Italy and Germany the doctrines persist and are once more gaining adherents and influence. There is no reason to suppose that conservatism or reactionism necessarily implies its own suicide, and that is precisely why the Buckleys, who are its extremely talented and attractive leaders, are to be taken with the utmost seriousness. "All this very persuasive-sounding form of nonsense" (which is not nonsense but menace in many respects) is persuading more and more people.

His "nonsense" and his personal warmth and naturalness had a great deal to do with overcoming the technical objection to James Buckley's nomination and election that arose out of his effective domicile in Sharon with his family—the same objection that was raised with equal validity against Robert Kennedy when the boy Attorney General decided to transform himself into the boy Senator of "the people." Since 1953 Buckley had maintained a small co-operative apartment in New York, where, when he was not traveling, he spent half his week, returning to Sharon and his family for the other half. Of course he had voted and otherwise behaved as a Connecticut resident in fact, just as Kennedy, until he decided to seek the New York Senatorial seat, had comported himself similarly in Massachusetts; indeed, Kennedy had not had even a *pied-à-terre* in New York but had hastily to buy a co-operative apartment in one of the newer and uglier East Side examples of assembly-line architecture. Neither is more or less defensible than the other, of course; and in each case the opposition seized on the fact for maximum exploitation, exaggerating it until it burst and its original importance was totally lost.

But it led to a local Sharon controversy that showed a number of Buckleys in a light that was the more revealing in its lack of flattery. In its first issue (5 November) after the 1970 election, *The Lakeville Journal* did not mention James Buckley's victory in New York, and his sister Jane Smith wrote a little note to the editor that is worth reprinting:

> "Curiouser and curiouser!
>
> "He was brought up in this community. His family lives here. He week-ends here.
>
> "He ran a political race which brought national attention. His victory was bannered on the front page of *The New York Times*.
>
> "All of which you wouldn't learn if you read only *The Lakeville Journal*."

Other letters to the paper said essentially the same thing. In the next issue an editorial note explained that the pressure of deadlines was responsible for the inadvertent omission.

But on the same page there was a letter from Robert H. Yoakum, who recalled Priscilla's and Bill's attacks on Robert Kennedy in *National Review* in 1968, when they called him a carpetbagger, and who attacked Mrs. Smith for her criticism of the paper's editorial judgment. "Once again," Yoakum wrote, "the older Buckleys like to have it both ways. In theory they are against carpetbagging, but in practice they indulge in it. In theory they are for free speech, but in practice they prosecute or deride it. In theory they are against corruption in government, but in practice (e.g., Senators Joe McCarthy and Tom Dodd) they support it. In theory they are for fairness, but in practice they assault their victims with charges of disloyalty and imputations of subversion." Yoakum's friend Judson Philips had been attacked for having called James Buckley a resident of Sharon and a carpetbagger, but *The Journal* was now being "reprimanded," Bethia S. Currie wrote, "for not remembering that the Senator-elect was brought up in Sharon, where his family all live and where some of us used to think he maintained a residence."

Mrs. Smith and John Buckley replied in separate letters. Mrs. Smith accused Yoakum of McCarthyism and questioned each of his charges against the Buckleys, concluding: "If he could be taken seriously one might sue for libel, but I think a slap on the wrist is more appropriate." John, more rashly, challenged Yoakum to cite examples in support of his charges; otherwise "he brands himself a fool or a scoundrel, and, in any event, a McCarthyite (Joseph)." Mrs. DeLancey Ferguson, so often John's adversary in private correspondence, wrote in the same issue that she was "a peace vigil-er on Sharon Green who has never believed that a Buckley in any office would be anything but a distressing event to anyone with a viewpoint to the left of the late Senator Taft," but she was ignored. So were Some Concerned Citizens of the Community, who asked in their letter whether "a thoroughly pleasant man of Senator Buckley's background and upbringing, who has 'the happy faculty for not antagonising people,'" was qualified to champion programs for the abolition of private fortunes, changes in the relations among social classes, and, itemised, a broadly Left social and economic scheme for the assurance of the decencies of life to everyone.

Yoakum proceeded to document his charges. He cited at least one issue in which *National Review* called Kennedy a carpet-bagger. He recalled John Buckley's 1967 threat to sue the writer of a letter to the local paper for libel, saying: "It wasn't the first time a Buckley tried to intimidate the paper with the prospect of a lawsuit—an exercise the Buckleys could afford and the *Journal* couldn't" (and this was an observation that one frequently heard in the Sharon-Lakeville area in the summer and autumn of 1971). Yoakum also described Bill Buckley's suit against Artie Shaw. He cited *National Review*'s praise for Franco's repressions in Spain and Bill's comment to the effect that riots like that in Watts, California, were "very much likelier to happen again so long as the nation coddles the anarchic teachings of . . . the Martin Luther Kings and their disciples." Bill Buckley's defenses of McCarthy and Dodd were particularised; so were *National Review*'s efforts to eliminate from Congress all those members who strove to abolish special tax privileges and to impose a genuine code of ethics on holders of both elective and appointive office. The use of accusations of subversiveness was documented with quotations from *National Review*, the example of Professor Harper's successful libel action, and James Buckley's statement during his campaign that Ottinger's record in the House of Representatives "could suggest" that he had "sought to condone violence preached by such groups as the Black Panthers and Students for a Democratic Society," that he "condones draft evasion," and that he was "insensitive to the threat posed by such groups as the Young Lords and the Ku Klux Klan." Yoakum quoted Priscilla Buckley's 1962 letter to *The Lakeville Journal* that emphasised the fact that a Communist paper had praised a peace movement complimented also by *The Journal*. Nor did Yoakum omit to remind people of Bill's singular delight in attacking his opponents on sexual grounds, of which we have already seen examples; Yoakum added the 1965 quotation about the "mincing ranks" of anti-war demonstrators who "strut their epicene resentment." He quoted, too, Buckley's 1968 column on the assassination of King: "Most likely the cretin who leveled his rifle on the head of Martin Luther King may have absorbed the talk, so freely available, about the supremacy of the individual conscience, such talk as Martin Luther King, God rest his troubled soul, had so widely, and so indiscriminately, made." Yoakum also recalled *National Review*'s innuendo-charged obituary of Edward R. Murrow in 1965.

Priscilla attempted to refute the "carpetbagger" charge by ascribing the use of the word to W. H. von Dreele, whom she rather amazingly described as a professional humorist; but Yoakum produced three other instances in the unsigned front section of the magazine that is the exclusive province of its editor-in-chief and his delegates. John Buckley, once Yoakum's bill of particulars was in print, was reduced to observing, also in print, that "I am now convinced that he is not a scoundrel." A grace note ended the whole display, however, when one Alfred Thompson of Sheffield, Massachusetts, who signed himself "a Sheffield scoundrel," wrote to recall the commandment to Christians not to judge but to tolerate their fellows, and to inquire: "Is John not a Christian? Or is he a Buckley Christian exempted from the admonitions of Christ?"

James, of course, took no part in any of this, nor did Bill. But neither of them disavowed any of the acts engaged in by way of defense. It seems legitimate to suppose that Jim, at least, though one senses in him a capacity to coil and spring in some circumstances, was pained by at least some of what came out. Sensibly, however, he ignored it and went about the business of taking his seat in the Senate, where from the start he comported himself with typical good manners—typical, that is, of Buckleys, not of Senators. His view of his position in relation to Bill was, in sum, this, as described a year later: "He and I occupy different functional slots, which is something that he and I mutually understand. He's in the job of delineating ultimate goals, ideals, ideas, of analysing, and so on. I happen to be in the spot which is the purely political instrumentality through which one has to work to achieve these things, but I have to view things within the restrictions of the immediate political options, so that, whereas Bill can say:

'That is where we want to be,' I've got to say: 'In order to get there, where, first of all, we can't get to immediately, maybe we have to move two or three yards in this direction and then zigzag all over the place, always keeping the goal in mind.' " While Bill and Jim "agree as to what the objectives are and we operate in the same wave-lengths, so that normally our views coincide," there is occasional fundamental division of opinion; one instance was to occur when the question of Ashbrook's primary campaign arose.

Listed in the *Congressional Directory* as "Conservative-Republican," James Buckley is a member of five Senate bodies: the Committees on Aeronautical and Space Sciences, on the District of Columbia, on Interior and Insular Affairs, and on Public Works, and a subcommittee on air and water pollution, a subject in which he is intensely interested. For the greater part he has voted with the regular Republicans in the Senate, though he threatened to rebel at the party line that favored funds for a supersonic transport plane, a subsidy to the bankrupt Lockheed Aircraft Corp., and a family-assistance plan with a guaranteed annual income; and he broke out of the Republican ranks over the admission of China to the United Nations, Nixon's visit to Peking, his ironically named New Economic Policy (the American NEP ostensibly controlled the economy whereas fifty years earlier Lenin's had—briefly—emancipated it), and strategic-arms limitation. Buckley's first important Senate vote was cast in February, 1971, in favor of sustaining the existing rule requiring a two-thirds majority in order to cut off filibusters.

He had pledged himself to constructive work for the protection of the environment—largely through a tax-incentive plan to encourage industry to reduce pollution—and this was the basis for his opposition to the SST project. "The one thing I want to prove in six years," he had told *The New York Times*, "is that a man can call himself a conservative and care about the people in the ghetto." This he proposed to demonstrate by helping to develop federally financed "self-help and retraining programs" for residents of slums—not by attacking the slum problem. His "brain trust," he had said after his election, was the board of editors of *National Review*, though he hoped to enjoy the counsel of such incumbent Republican Senators as John Tower of Texas, Hugh Scott of Pennsylvania, and Margaret Chase Smith of Maine. The men were among the most conservative Republicans in the Senate, and Mrs. Smith was hardly less so. Buckley hoped too, he said before taking his seat, that the New York Republican Party would ultimately absorb the Conservative Party: at least that was how he phrased it then; at other times he was wont to say that it was the Conservative Party that was offering the Republicans the chance to survive.

He was characteristically discreet in his entrance into his career in the Senate. He paid the requisite courtesy calls on his seniors and putative superiors, and he maintained almost friendly relations for a while with his New York colleague, Jacob Javits. (In *New York* magazine, a sports writer described the normal behavior of James Buckley and his family as "their ridiculous civility to each other"—which tells one all one needs to know about the state of America today.) Coolness between the two Senators set in rapidly, however, as they voted on opposing sides of an increasing number of measures, Buckley opposing, for example, legislation that would compel federal safety standards in automobile manufacture, or (more surprisingly) supporting a measure that would reduce the powers of the Environmental Protection Agency.

Outside the Senate the interest in Buckley was rising swiftly. More than fifteen hundred speaking invitations poured in from schools and colleges and from business, professional, and patriotic organisations in virtually all the states; until he had established himself in the routine of office, he refused almost all of them: indeed, he has never quite resigned himself to the encroachments on his working time and energy made by what amount to command invitations to official celebrations, patriotic and religious observances, and similar rites. He did lead a St. Patrick's Day Parade in Buffalo but reporters who were present could not help noting how uncomfortable this kind of thing made him. Unlike so many of his eminent colleagues, he was extremely sparing in the issuance of press releases and the convocation of press conferences. Later he did begin distributing a bi-monthly newsletter to political leaders, contributors, and volunteer workers in New York State; and once a month he appeared in a question-and-answer television program, syndicated to stations in the state, that ran a similar monthly interview with each of three other public officials.

He was reticent, too, in introducing legislation, though he often sponsored bills jointly with other Republicans. He had been in office three months before he offered his first proposal, for a joint resolution demanding the termination of all American economic aid to countries that did not act to end the narcotics trade. In the meantime he had made a number of floor speeches on behalf of more vigorous prosecution of the war in Vietnam, and he had written a newspaper article calling for higher pay for draftees. His speech at the second annual Conservative Awards dinner— its sponsors were the American Conservative Union, YAF, *National Review*, and *Human Events*—was inserted into the *Congressional Record* by John Ashbrook: in it Buckley had described his own election as the result not of fear but of hope, citing forty-two per cent of the blue-collar vote and nine hundred thousand Democrats who had crossed the line to support him (one is always mystified by the assurance of such pronouncements, whoever makes them) in their determination to stamp out "the seemingly uncontrollable rise in crime rates and welfare rolls; the noisy disruptions of trials; the explosion of pornography; the flight from reality manifested both by the Woodstock phenomenon and the peace-at-any-price movement." It was precisely this kind of careful hodgepodge—the worse because, undoubtedly, he believed what he was saying—that had got him and other reactionaries elected and that is bound to have growing appeal in the foreseeable future precisely because of the fact that some of it is true: crime and welfare are increasing, pornography (whatever that is; but let us follow the common acceptance, for convenience) is everywhere; trials are being disrupted; drugs and rock are indeed taking the place of reality (and of political action), but they have nothing in common with the peace movement that is in no sense a peace-at-any-price movement; and the solution is not to turn backward, or even to stand still, but to attack the diseases and not the symptoms or the patients, always bearing in mind the citizen's—one had almost said the subject's—inalienable right to choose other things if he does not like pornography, drugs, and rock. What is worth some speculation, however, is the considerable advantage that enures to the established order in the continuation of this version of bread and circuses both as a distraction for those who might otherwise think and act and, at the same time, as a conveniently perennial object of righteous public objurgation.

It was April before Buckley first spoke from the floor of the Senate, to attack Nixon's broad plans for sharing federal revenues with the states and to introduce a complicated bill of his own for "revenue shifting," in which the government would have no discretion but would merely do a mechanical job, which would deprive it of any influence in local affairs. He had finally voted, to the dismay of many of his supporters, to build an experimental SST, on the ground that only a working model could resolve the pollution question; but he was to stand firm against the Lockheed subsidy. Two months after his maiden speech he introduced a bill that would compel the federal courts to discipline "unruly" lawyers, the obvious symbol of this evil being (in his view) William Kunstler, whom Bill Buckley was soon to skewer so mercilessly on television. Jim Buckley memorialised the Kent State murders by reading into the *Congressional Record* an anonymous student's tribute to the National Guard of Ohio and his condemnation of the "radicals" who had "sought" that confrontation.

And the Senator discovered the Zionists. His father had discovered Israel in a costly lesson many years before, and the Buckley companies were well out of that country by 1971. Senator Buckley addressed a celebration of the "rebirth twenty-three years ago of the State of Israel," and from it he purported to draw a very different lesson for his compatriots: the lesson of "patriotism" and self-sacrifice for a nation, of appeasement's snare and isolationism's delusion, of the inevitability of "a great deal of trouble, pain, problems, sweat, sorrows, frustrations along with the joys and happiness you may be lucky enough to harvest." All these things he commended to the attention of the New Left that emphasised "only . . . 'creativity,' 'love,' 'brotherhood,' 'self-expression.' " In sum, he committed himself to Israel and to the endeavor to commit the United States to Israel.

It is difficult to write dispassionately of this. If Bill Buckley had done nothing else admirable, he would deserve lasting credit for having reminded the politicians of the fact that their constituents are Americans and should be appealed to as Americans without hyphens; Bill Buckley himself disdained to eat pizzas or blintzes or "soul" food for votes, or to pander to those who did. It is of course unpardonable that Zionists—not a few of them on government salaries—have for years encouraged the ignorant and the opportunist to believe that Zionists and Jews are identical in their persons and in their interests; it is even worse that non-Jewish politicians should inject into domestic concerns the irrelevancies and the sentimentalities of putative external loyalties in order to curry electoral favor in a supposed bloc. This ought to be as repugnant to James Buckley as it has been to his brother, who was rightly insulted when it was suggested that Irish Catholics ought *ipso facto* to vote for the Kennedys; and there is more than one Jewish Conservative whose vote James Buckley lost by addressing the voter not as an American Conservative but as a Jewish Conservative. Yet Buckley was to repeat the offense in even more scandalous circumstances when he carried to the President of the United States the fight of the Forest Hills Jews to keep out the poor and the black. He has always said that the basis for his action was the unwarranted encroachment of government on the individual, the protection of the right of free association, and probably he believes what he says; one is tempted in fact to half-believe it, given the philosophical roots of his political action. It is nonetheless a great pity that he did not find some less questionable constituents than these bigots whose local spokesman is a real-estate trader who has grown rich by furthering on the West Side of Manhattan the very integration of housing that he opposes in his own residential district because "it's okay for Columbus Avenue but not for Forest Hills." I quite believe that James Buckley is not in the least anti-Semitic; but the choices he has made in his political dealings with Jews have been of invaluable worth to anti-Semitism in New York and the United States.

The rest of his activity as a Senator has been almost invariably consonant with positions throughout the Right Wing, though at times *Human Events* has been frightened by traces of deviationism undiscernible by others. Buckley has been and is active on behalf of the so-called voucher system, "which," as he told the Senate in May, 1971, "would introduce the principles of the market economy and competition into governmental financing of education." As elaborated in a study by Yale Brozen and Roman Weil of the Graduate School of Business of the University of Chicago, at the expense of the American Conservative Union, this program would provide for the issuance of a voucher by the local governmental unit to each recipient of schooling (or, if he is a minor, to his parents). The voucher would be worth the cost of a year's schooling in that jurisdiction. If the recipient elected to go to the public schools, he would pay with the voucher; if he elected to attend a private school, he would present it there and the school would redeem the voucher at its face value. It has always been implicit in all such efforts to subsidise non-public schools that the principal beneficiaries will be Catholic parochial schools; since 1954 it has been equally implicit that the second most important beneficiaries would be the private schools hastily set up as a means of circumventing the Supreme Court's desegregation decision; and in Virginia a similar system is already in operation. Buckley and the Conservatives, opposed as they are to big central government, would have Washington mandate the system for the nation.

He has opposed legislation for amnesty to draft resistants as he has opposed bills to send only volunteers for the assignment to Vietnam. And of course he resisted legislation for the mandatory termination of that war by the end of 1971. In the debate over the extension of the draft law, he offered an amendment reducing the effective period by four months, but his real objective, as he pointed out, was to attempt to win the Senate to the concept of an all-volunteer military—one of the few proposals on which, though some conservatives oppose it, he has the approval of most of those who are normally his adversaries. Otherwise, in matters military, they are most vigorously against him: for Buckley, admittedly inspired by *National Review*, stands for the constant augmentation of the nation's military position (one says in current jargon, I believe, "posture") and for its active deployment in as many areas as possible by way of protection for American clients (he has named only Israel) and deterrent to aggression by the Soviet Union. In spite of their opposition to him in this domain, Young Americans for Freedom, as we have seen, have in fact become even more enthusiastic about him.

In large part this derived from his refusal to endorse Nixon's reversal of position with respect to China, which overshadowed Buckley's effort, defeated in the Senate, to add forty-two million dollars for the improvement of missiles to the already huge arms budget. Claiming the backing of twenty other Senators, he demanded that Washington reduce its contributions to the United Nations if Taiwan, under the dictatorship of Chiang Kai-shek, should be expelled as the condition of China's admission. James Buckley had not joined his brother in withdrawing support for the President because of his policies on China and the domestic economy, but he was unambiguous in his opposition to both.

At the same time, however, he maintained his ties with the Administration by his vigorous cooperation in the unsuccessful efforts to defeat the proposal—which Nixon ultimately vetoed—for federally financed day-care centers for the children of working mothers. Trumpeting the destruction of the family, *Human Events* started the major opposition, and Buckley said that the program "threatens the very foundation of personal liberty," while

others in the ranks talked of "Sovietization" of children, and
John Buckley saw them being made into "moppets in uniform."
And there was a further demonstration of continuing ties when
the USIA decided not only to increase the broadcasting of special
Jewish programs to Russia by the Voice of America but also to
make the announcement through James Buckley, who was directly authorised by Shakespeare to disclose the decision at a
Westchester Jewish rally. Buckley's appeals for such action had
been paralleled by similar pleas from Goldwater and a clutch of
Democratic Senators. Buckley, moreover, announced that he had
asked Nixon to place the question of Russian Jews high on the
agenda for his visit to Moscow in 1972.

Late in 1971 the Buckleys extended their grip to the National
Endowment for the Humanities. Nixon was prepared to ask the
Senate to confirm Stephen Hess as the chairman of this federal
source of millions of dollars in grants to historians and other
scholars engaged in research. Hess was a liberal Republican, as
the phrase is used, who headed the White House Conference on
Children and Youth, which had turned out a set of recommendations for social services and increased personal freedom, educational opportunity, and academic advances that had made conservatives' blood run backward. Hess, a close associate of the
Ripon Society, which consists of what might be called the Left
in the Republican Party, had also campaigned vigorously for
the frightening Family Assistance Plan. Conservatives could not
stomach the prospect of his heading the humanities program: they
wanted it to develop, in the words of *Human Events*, "a new
generation of responsible scholars."

Frank Meyer thereupon suggested Professor Ronald Berman,
a forty-year-old *National Review* contributor who has a Yale
doctorate and who has taught at Columbia, Kenyon College, and
the University of California at San Diego. Berman is much esteemed by Reagan and by such academic conservatives as Seymour
Martin Lipset. Thus Berman was the ideal paymaster for the
thirty million dollars annually distributed to kept intellectuals, and
James Buckley made a major effort to see that he got the job. When
some qualified persons to the left of Lipset also joined the attack
on Hess on the ground that he was academically unequipped for
the post, the White House at first wanted as Right-Wing an activist as it could find, but it was soon apparent that this would
be folly. Backed by the Buckley group, Berman was then put

forward as the perfect compromise: Nixon accepted him and the Senate confirmed him.

At the end of Buckley's first year as a Senator he insisted that he wanted no higher political office but would like to remain in the Senate for several terms. This is quite standard utterance, but it was certain that he did not consider himself sufficiently seasoned yet for further progress. Unquestionably he had been and would be subjected to considerable pressure to allow his candidacy for the Vice Presidential nomination to be advanced if Nixon should dump Agnew; but Buckley himself, predicting Nixon's re-election, insisted that Agnew's renomination would be a "definite asset" toward that end. He simply ignored—until August of 1972, when he did not disavow it—gossip to the effect that he might have his eye on the Governorship of New York, or that others might want it for him. Conservatism, he felt, had made considerable gains in the state and the nation, in spite of the NEP and the reversal on China; and there were signs of strain between Buckley and the Conservative Party in its criticisms of Nixon's "liberal" appointees to the federal bench. Buckley said nothing when the party formally suspended its support of the President, thus aligning itself with his brother and the *National Review* group. Nor had Senator Buckley endorsed any Conservative candidates for local and state offices, and in this the pundits professed to see a new reconciliation between Conservatives and Republicans. The impression was diluted when Buckley announced his approval of a state bond issue—ostensibly for public transport, though much of the proceeds, had the referendum approved it, would have gone for highways and bridges—that the party, like many far to its left, opposed. And even before 1972 had begun, the state Republicans had begun to invite him to various speechifications and he was accepting. Further rapprochement could be scented.

At the beginning of January he set out for Antarctica and "Southeast Asia—the first part is essentially self-indulgence (at my own expense, I might add). I'm going to Antarctica because of my long-term interest in matters polar." Southeast Asia, he explained, meant "New Zealand, the Philippines, Thailand, probably Cambodia, South Vietnam, Taiwan, and Japan"; and the purpose was "kind of upgrading, updating rather, such information as I find." A few days later his office said that he was in Antarctica on a Navy mission and that he would be "largely" paying his own expenses for the rest of the journey, to which South Korea was added. From New York to Antarctica and Manila he was accompanied by Bill, for whom this leg of the journey seemed, from the tone of his entertaining but inconsequential columns filed from polar regions, to be principally a relaxation. As James Buckley progressed through the various countries on his itinerary, quotations from him appeared in the American press, and the tenor was always the same. The "Free Chinese," as he and his brother and their circle call Chiang's supporters and subjects, had been cruelly betrayed and were to be commended for their courage in not yielding to despair; indeed, American capitulation to China—as it was viewed by conservatives—had betrayed all our Asian allies and posed the threat of their imminent absorption by the Communists. A *New York Times* report from Tokyo said that Buckley had "called on President Nixon to issue a statement after the Peking meeting saying: 'I didn't do any of you in.' "

Almost immediately after his return to this country, Buckley entered the abortion controversy, demanding that state laws that had been liberalised be repealed. The major threats to society, he said, are drug abuse, pornography, and "the barbaric slaughter of the innocents" made possible by the new abortion legislation in many states. He has also asserted, in an article that he wrote for *The New York Times*, that the United States is in danger of being undone in Indochina by reason of its excess of good will and its deficiency in aggressivity.

And the way in which he says such things—which he certainly believes—can be extremely persuasive, especially to a nation in which the rate of growth is greatest in the production of bewilderment.

XXI

"BUCKLEY IS a gifted polemicist; a philosopher he is not," *Time* said, in its 13 November 1967 issue, about William F. Jr.—the hostility of which was worthy of remark, since the publication was the property of his good friends Clare and Henry Luce. The article added that Buckley's friend and *National Review* collaborator, M. Stanton Evans, editor of *The Indianapolis News*, believed that Buckley could be a philosopher if he set himself to it: Russell Kirk has said the same thing in conversation, and it is a plausible assessment. "But," Evans added, according to *Time*, "he has left the metaphysics to others. He has concentrated instead on a high-level conservative journalism, acting as a broker and analyst of ideas rather than as an originator of them."

In the eighteen years of its existence the brokerage house of *National Review* has lost or fired a fairly low proportion of its customers' men and has steadily increased its client list and even occasionally taken a flier of experimentation in the issues it has handled, inviting independents like Murray Kempton and even eminent radicals like Professor Eugene Genovese to state their positions for serious consideration. Some of the major changes in personnel have been mentioned, but it might be worth-while to rehearse the list even at the risk of repetition.

Ayn Rand and Buckley pronounced simultaneous anathemas on each other when *National Review* published Whittaker Chambers' dissection of her monstrously egocentric philosophy as put forth in her novel *Atlas Shrugged*. Max Eastman left in protest against the magazine's and the movement's theocracy. Brent Bozell was driven out by their enslavement to this world. Chambers, after the long and arduous courtship by which Buckley had brought him into the magazine, left after little more than a year because he could not really share the ideology of the movement or endure the inner disputes of its apostles. William Schlamm departed because he was too bloodthirsty a *revanchiste* for anyone but Chancellor Adenauer's Christian Democrats, Franz Josef Strauss's Christian Social Union, and the neo-Nazi NPD. John Chamberlain and Suzanne La Follette left because of their differences with Buckley on the kind of material to be run in the magazine. Revilo P. Oliver's disaffection was *sui generis*, as we have seen. And it was Richard Nixon who said: "Buckley's articles cost the Birchers their respectability with conservatives. I couldn't have accomplished that. Liberals couldn't have, either."

But the most important schism—though it was never really total —was that between *National Review* and Buckley's old guru/disciple from Yale, Willmoore Kendall, the only conservative polemicist as skillful, as arrogant, and as consistently peevish in tone as Buckley, and alone in being sometimes more—much more— turgid. Buckley, indeed, is still much under his influence, and often cites him. It was generally believed that during his brief term on the board of editors of *National Review* Kendall was never on speaking terms with more than one colleague at a time, and there was never any way of knowing when that man would be replaced. Much later Kendall professed to see within the ruling class of *National Review* a pronounced bias against everyone born white, Anglo-Saxon, and Protestant—the only persons, in his view, who ought to constitute the ruling class anywhere, whether in *National Review* or in the nation or, for that matter, in the world:* he was too anti-democratic even for his colleagues, whom in his later years he liked to describe as "self-styled" or "socalled" or "misled" conservatives, especially since not all of them shared his passionate conviction that such decisions as "whether Christendom or Communism shall inherit the earth are *always* arbitraments by force, that is, by war. They *have* to be, because arbitrament by discussion between conflicting world-views is out of the question [his italics]." (Yet Kendall could be at odds with James Burnham, who believed that the Third World War had indeed already, and rightly, begun between just those forces.)

Russell Kirk—one of Kendall's "three sages of conservatism"; the others were the late Clinton P. Rossiter of Cornell (a "part-

* See *Willmoore Kendall Contra Mundum* (New York: Arlington House, 1971), *passim*, but especially p. 394, n. 23, and pp. 590–91.

time" sage) and Frank Meyer, who is largely supposed to have been much more libertarian than Kendall—has pointed out that Kendall had evolved into a "conservative of sorts" from an initial position of Rousseauistic majoritarianism. What Kirk has had to say of Kendall may be of some value in understanding Buckley, who was so close to him for so long and who may be temperamentally not unlike him in some respects.

"Kendall," Kirk explained, "was a man who loved to quarrel with people and essentially to take the losing side. He always wanted to be in the opposition, and I suppose it may well have been a liberal element in his character, or even a radical element. But since the conservatives tended to be the losing side, he determined to join them. At the same time he had a desire to dominate whatever side he was on, but, because of his curious push toward alienating people, of course he could never succeed in dominating. Since he wasn't stronger than they and couldn't command them, he was always certain to be in an even more forlorn minority." Kirk, who has known Buckley since the publication of *God and Man at Yale* in 1951, was impressed by Professor Paul Weiss's observation that it was Buckley, not Kendall, who had the better mind and the stronger personality. "I think Buckley did have the better character, probably the stronger character, and the better mind potentially," Kirk continued, "but one was a much better educated man at the time and the other had far less experience in the world."

A strong bond between Kendall and the Buckley circle, of which Kirk is an intimate and eminent member, was always the shared disgust expressed by Kendall at most contemporary conservative writing in America: he said it was "shot through and through with a fundamental, though gracefully concealed, anti-intellectualism." But there were times when Kendall suspected that the taint had spread to at least some members of the group, and he himself might well have been accused of a touch of that leprosy when, for instance, he inveighed, like Buckley, against academic freedom and warned the university that "it can either go back willingly to its proper business of communicating American beliefs, American traditions, to the nation's youth, or someone will have to *make* [his italics] it go back to it. And remember: the ultimate weapon—refusing to deliver the groceries—is always in the hands of the people the American university is trying to bluff." This was the logical conclusion to be drawn from his earlier judgment: "Buckley, in this speaker's view, carried his battle to the wrong people, that is, the intellectuals, where his few converts were always easily outflanked by the Liberals. But Conservatives now know, from McCarthy's example, who are the right people to carry battles to." Kendall noted with satisfaction that "McCarthyism has accomplished much, remains strong in America." He was perfectly correct, and it is still strong. What is interesting is that two British conservative authors whom Buckley greatly admires, Evelyn Waugh and T. S. Eliot, were equally dismayed at his relations with McCarthyism.

Kendall was, by relatively late conversion, a devout Catholic—so devout that he applied, successfully, to the Rota for two simultaneous annulments of prior marriages in order to be able to enter upon a third within Holy Mother Church—but never the fanatic that Brent Bozell became. His, Kirk says, is "what Paul Elmer More called 'the demon of the absolute.' . . . Brent is always saying that most deviate from the truth, whether religious or political; they don't adhere to the dogmas, and we must purge ourselves of them, narrow our band, and march on: eventually, because of the truth, we shall prevail. He looks for a dogma in all things."

One of the most important members of the *National Review* group—not least because of his rôle as an editor of *National Review* for so many years, which, though he never left Woodstock, kept him in much closer and more constant contact than, say, Kirk—was Frank Meyer. My only communication with him was by letter and telephone, and it was sparse: his reasons for virtual silence command respect, for he firmly believed (though Buckley disagreed with him: like everyone else, he consulted Buckley when I informed him that I should want to talk to him for the purposes of this book) that one ought not to write books about the living; and he said that he would find himself unable to talk freely. Consequently, he told me little; much of what can be authoritatively learned about him and his views has had, of necessity, to come from secondary (though sound) sources.

Meyer was probably the most libertarian member of the *National Review* group. Buckley calls himself a libertarian and rejected the adjective "qualified" in spite of the bounds that he himself sets to his libertarianism. Meyer, who regarded himself as a radical libertarian, viewed Buckley as having somewhat retreated from an earlier libertarianism. Of himself, he said that it would be inaccurate to suppose that, as others might have done, he had moved from Communism to the Right because of a need for an authority to which to submit: "I fretted for a dozen years in the Communist Party because I hated its repressiveness: I went Right for release from authoritarianism." Burnham is equally emphatic to the same effect. But others regard Meyer as similar to Bozell in that "he's again looking for political dogmas years after having been a member of the CP. He discovers that this is a God that failed and therefore he shifts to the opposite side. On the opposite side he still desires a sort of Communist Party formation in which there should be discipline, there should be organisation. Again he's always looking about for deviationists to expel—in part because he does believe that they are dangerous and in part because it's a matter of habit." This came from a fellow-Conservative but it recalled Wechsler's description of Meyer's rôle in the Communist Party as detector of heretics and formulator of theory. The second function is one that he largely fulfilled in *National Review* as well: he had a department called "Principles and Heresies." Another member of the group insisted that "Meyer has always fought Buckley at *National Review*. Frank has never ceased being a conspirator, and he considers himself the theoretician of American conservatism."

Ralph de Toledano, who claims to have brought Meyer and Buckley together, believes that Meyer, as intelligent and articulate as he was, "owes Bill one hell of a lot. Bill has given him a free hand, built him up. His reputation in the Right-Wing conservative movement derives from his column in *National Review*." De Toledano is no more dogmatic than anyone else in attempting to answer the natural but extremely difficult question: Why do so many older men of such acknowledged accomplishment in their own areas gather round Buckley? Meyer's own answer is as good as any, and perhaps better: basically, he said, the key is Buckley's ability to keep very different people working together and reasonably happy. (*Time* said Buckley "made it his business to keep the fractious conservatives from splitting"—the example it chose was Kirk, the traditionalist, against Meyer, the libertarian.) Buckley, Meyer added, possesses "charm, but of a deep kind"; and one is constrained to agree. Besides, Meyer concluded of Buckleyism and *National Review*, "this is the only game in town." He agreed, however, that it need not be.

According to other sources, one of the deepest quarrels between Meyer and Buckley flared in 1971, when, after *The New*

York Times published the Pentagon documents, Buckley insisted
on confecting a new set, some from the genuine source and some
very skillfully contrived, and passing it off in *National Review*
as genuine. The job was so well done that virtually everyone of
every complexion was thoroughly gulled, until Buckley confessed
the hoax. His reasons for its perpetration were partly serious—
to embarrass *The Times* and emphasise the heinousness and the
frightful peril of what it had done—and partly no more than mis-
chievous. But Meyer is supposed to have held angrily aloof from
the enterprise and to have regarded it as a typical Buckley prank.

The most that Meyer would say publicly was that his own view
of Bill Buckley was not uncritical, and this seems to be common
knowledge, though no reliable particulars are available from any
source. Meyer himself was on terms of warm, close friendship with
a number of people who had split with Buckley but with none of
whom Meyer himself agreed: Bozell, Rothbard, Wills. Wills believes that there are very few conservatives in the American Right,
with which he has always disagreed on the war in Vietnam, on
the conservatism imputed to Nixon, and, above all, on what he
calls the emulative ethic, which he loathes but which Meyer upheld with a zeal reminiscent of that of another convert, Bozell, for
another creed.

Meyer and Burnham were the most important figures at *National Review* itself, next to Buckley, until Meyer's death in April,
1972; there is no sign of a successor. Their traditionalism (despite
Meyer's disclaimer) was at least as strong as his; but their primary
strength was in political and, to a lesser degree, economic ideology.
To the extent to which there is a philosopher practicing in the
Buckley movement, he is Kirk, a man whose culture is staggering
and whose personal warmth and humanity belie the austerity of
his beliefs. Like Buckley himself, Kirk has a lively imagination
and a taste for play, which in his case takes the form of literary
fantasy never wholly divorced from social criticism: in fact he is
far more the social than the political critic and philosopher, and his
roots are solidly founded in literature and in the American tradition—for such a thing does exist. He is not rich; he has never
suffered poverty. His father was a union man, "a locomotive
engineer, an engine driver who during the Hoover years would
utter some vaguely radical slogans but otherwise had been a pretty
thoroughly conservative fellow all his life—went as far as sixth
grade in school. He's attached to his society, though he was a farm

boy and his family was driven off the farm by industry, and he doesn't like that. Still he doesn't dissent from the general pattern of society; he believes in the Constitution and the political institutions he knows. He thinks we are better off here, probably, than anywhere else. Any radical he looks upon with deep suspicion. I suppose his attitude is pretty typical of the average American's. That, I think, is the large reservoir of sentiment to which one can appeal."

In this Kirk is unquestionably correct. And indeed it is probably true, as one tends to learn on the always unsettling road of expatriation, that this country is, at the moment, still less bad than any other. The average American portrayed by Kirk, moreover, is probably much more amenable than one might suppose to the kind of society that the traditionalist conservatives would like to rejuvenate (for it has not disappeared): in a word, an orthodox society implying the promise of the immutable. Kirk's endorsement of such a society is no contradiction of his deep scholarship or of his appreciation for the radical innovators of literature who were either apolitical, like Joyce and Proust, or politically the opposites of their artistic selves, like Eliot and Pound. Kirk's view of society, as his recent study of Eliot evidences, is wholly orthodox; he might object to some of the tone but he would certainly subscribe to the substance of Kendall's summary of the conservative position with its espousal of orthodoxy and religion, its express declaration against liberty: the conservative "finds in the First Amendment no mention of a right to think and say whatever one pleases, or of a duty on the part of American citizens to tolerate and live with and interminably discuss any and every opinion that their neighbors may take into their heads. And he holds that if the First Amendment *does* [Kendall's italics] recognize such a right and such a duty, then the moment is coming when the First Amendment will itself have to be brought into line with Conservative principles regarding the character of the good society. . . . The Conservative views with horror the thesis of Mill's essay 'On Liberty,' according to which a man can hold and publicly defend any opinion, however repugnant to morality, and still be regarded as a good—or even acceptable—citizen." Kirk, I think, is too civilised to view with horror; some of the Buckleys may be. And Kirk is too good a scholar to betray the ideal of true academic freedom. But essentially what Kendall has said here is the basic tenet of the social and political action of the Buckleyan conservatives, who are by now the unchallenged leaders of the Right.

William Rusher, the publisher of the *National Review*, is a less-known figure but an important one; and his weekly appearances with *The Advocates* on the educational television network are making him more familiar across the country. I have briefly described the program's format. His own participation may be worth some attention. Eminently personable, if undramatic, in aspect, he is well dressed and well spoken, but essentially so colorless as to allay any suspicion that he may be "different." Hence what he does is made more acceptable. In a presentation of the case for public support of religious schools, for instance, he calls to witness four parents: a friendly neighborhood WASP doctor, an Aunt Jemima on whom most blacks would turn their backs, a rabbi never shown without his Israeli flag in his hand, and a Chinese lady. His trump card is "Professor John Vandenberg of Calvin College"; but one has to send for *Barron's College Guide* to learn that Calvin College is a church college and hence the good professor can hardly be called a disinterested witness. Rusher's technique in cross-examination of hostile witnesses is aptly described in Aryeh Neier's analysis of Buckley's *Firing Line* technique. The result is bound to please because, whatever the ethics of the thing, it is good "show-business."

All these people ride the lecture circuit, most of them under the management of M. Catherine Babcock, Inc., of Virginia Beach, on behalf of the conservative cause. Most are in their forties or older; but there are younger members of the *National Review* group who also mount the platform at colleges all over the country, and almost all these are teachers in universities, from Harvard on down. Like Kirk, Peter Witonski, who is not yet thirty, has an earned degree from St. Andrews in Scotland (B. Phil.; Kirk's is a doctorate in letters); Witonski also has the same degree from Oxford. He writes correspondence for *The Spectator* of London and speeches for James Buckley, to say nothing of his own four-volume *Wisdom of Conservatism*, and a book on education for Knopf. D. Keith Mano, a respectable novelist born in 1942, was a fellow of Clare College, Cambridge. David Brudnoy, a young product of Yale, Harvard, and Brandeis, teaches in a New England college. *National Review* is always grooming new young men (one sees few young women in its pages) from the colleges to spread the conservative word among their co-evals; and the high proportion of young persons on the volunteer staffs of both campaigning Buckleys was visible evidence of the growing appeal of their doctrines to at least a large number of what Bill Buckley likes to call "the kids."

The all but canonised ideologists of the Buckley movement are not such safely dead philosophers as Burke, though such mentors are reverenced, but living economists: Frederick Hayek (in spite of the break between him and Bill Buckley, his ideas are still respected), Ludwig von Mises, and Milton Friedman. All are firm exponents of the free-market philosophy, and all carry it over from economics to the philosophy of society and politics. But Hayek is essentially a nineteenth-century classic Liberal who cannot stomach the American conservatives' bigotries any more than he can tolerate any other kind of vulgarity: he is above all a humanist in the best sense of the term, and his dread of the welfare state as the threshold to inevitable serfdom has never blunted his sensibilities to human suffering. When Hayek places the individual above the state, he does not mean only this individual and not that. Von Mises, who was born in Lwow when it was called Lemberg and was part of Austria-Hungary, is known by now even to the readers of the strident *Human Events*, which hailed him on his ninetieth birthday in 1971 for his contributions to the free-market philosophy and the marginal-utility, subjective-value theory developed by Carl Menger and, later, Eugen von Boehm-Bawerk. The essence of the theory is that all market values and processes depend on the interaction of the personal values of innumerable individuals: to oversimplify, the consumer is the sovereign of the market and of production. According to von Mises, such things as business cycles and depressions and inflations are the work not of wicked business men or wicked labor leaders but of meddling governments and their monetary manipulations: the functions of government should be limited to the protection of every citizen's life, property, and equal rights and to the adjudication of disputes. Conceding human fallibility, von Mises emphasises the need for unflagging vigilance to prevent or rectify error: once established and properly set in motion, the true free market will end social and economic injustice and assure world peace.

Milton Friedman, who personifies the so-called Chicago school, is not essentially different, except that his presentation is often less scholarly and more entertaining than Hayek's or von Mises's. His son calls him a libertarian anarchist; others call him a free-market fanatic. He is generally credited with the paternity of the school-voucher program, as part of his dogmatic attachment to personal freedom as the *summum bonum* in every area, whatever the practical difficulties of putting it into practice or the antagonisms that he evokes. Thus he would get rid of the stock exchange and the draft, as well as the governmental post office and the public schools. Basically he is an abstractionist working in the vacuum of pure ideas; but he is articulate and showmanlike: his debates and lectures are richly leavened with wit. *Time* said of him a few years ago that "he is the rare theorist whose influence is best measured not by the devotion of his followers—though that can be extreme—but by the extent to which his ideas have altered the thinking of his opponents." His brilliance and his unorthodoxy, as well as his wit, would naturally have appealed to Buckley, whose admiration for him is great.

All the leaders of this conservative group—and a few of those who have left it, voluntarily or otherwise—have been gaining audiences far outside their own territory: on television, in magazines, even in what they regard with sullen anger as the shrine of "liberalism," *The New York Times*. It has frequently invited Bill, James, and Reid Buckley to write essays for its page of opinion opposite the editorials, where too it has published Friedman, Burnham, Meyer, Kirk: all the faithful, plus such rebels as Karl Hess, Murray Rothbard, and Jerome Tuccille, the author of *Radical Libertarianism*, who teaches a course on anarchism at the New School. Tuccille was especially exercised in the winter of 1970–71, after Hess's and Rothbard's defections had led *The New York Times Magazine* to run two articles on the new schism in the Right and Buckley, he said, had become "hysterical" because he had "hoped to keep [the rupture] under cover, referring to it, whenever he did, as a family squabble rather than the permanent breach it has become." Tuccille ridiculed Buckley's fear lest the libertarians become "the Birchers of the seventies," and he sounded a warning that is the more impressive for its provenance, even though perhaps it be less than accurate in its low appraisal of the state of Buckley support as a result of the libertarians' escape; for it has since become clear that the division has not only eliminated a certain ambivalence within conservatism but also made its ranks much more attractive to many who hesitated in fear of what they viewed as its continuing tolerance of "permissiveness."

But Tuccille was quite correct in his observation that the Buckleyan conservatives had blended "Agnewism so carefully with Robert Welchism that the remaining differences are scarcely noticeable. A case can be made that the conservatism of Buckley is even more dangerous than that of George Wallace and Robert Welch since Buckley manages to spout the same hair-raising political philosophy in polysyllabic rhetoric. He makes it sound more respectable, so to speak. . . .

"[Buckley's] chief contribution to conservatism has been to upgrade the quality of its style. He has managed to cloak his Roman authoritarianism under heavy layers of convoluted verbiage. Because he is so opaque, so adroit at sidestepping issues, he is a greater potential threat than his 'plain-spoken' Right-Wing colleagues."[*]

It was quite true that Hess, Rothbard, Tuccille himself, and many other real libertarians were far more concerned with true freedom and the end of United States imperialism than they were with the Buckleyans' "Unholy Crusade to rid the world of Communists." But the real libertarians whether of Left or Right or Center, even if assembled in a single Congressional District, could not elect one representative; and the jehad against Communism had never lost any of its glamor or its sanctity for the outback— which, psychologically and culturally, is everywhere in the majority. It was for the more moneyed members of it that *National Review* began in 1968 to issue its twenty-four-dollar-a-year semi-monthly newsletter—mimeographed—about all the goings-on on the Left, *Combat*. This publication frequently annoyed the Anti-Defamation League, whose sensibilities are always rather erratic; but in the main it seemed a harmless enough exercise in hysteria, real or simulated, in the interest of bringing in a more or less honest buck. For a while Eugene Lyons, the former Communist who wrote *The Red Decade*, a best-seller, and then took De Witt Wallace's gold piece, was listed as editorial adviser. The publishing corporation was Communications Distribution, Inc., an older spawn of the expatriate Liebman: it had a post-office box as its address after Liebman left Madison Avenue for Chepstow Villas. Subtitled

* *The New York Times*, 28 January 1971, p. 35, cols. 6–8.

"The Newsletter that keeps you informed about the revolutionary struggle in America today," it offered such vital and otherwise unavailable intelligence as this (the headlines of a mid-1971 issue):

ANTIWAR GROUPS DIVIDE UP RALLY DATES • ACTIVISTS WAGE SLOGAN BATTLE • FIST-FIGHTS MAR OPENING OF PEACE CONFAB • PANTHERS JERK PLATFORM FOR REWRITE • GARRY SAYS NEWTON WAS A MORON • CBS GIVES U.S. AUDIENCE TO VIET CONG • REVEAL RED LINKS TO BACON ATTORNEYS

In addition to these main stories, the final section, labeled "Briefly," contained items such as this: "The Gore Vidal-Benjamin Spock New Party held its convention secretly in Albuquerque this month." Secrecy was so important that all the major newspapers, wire services, and broadcasters were invited to, and did, cover the convention in the normal course of business. One would not have expected anything quite so tawdry from "A National Review, Inc., Publication," unless one had been reading *National Review* fairly regularly. *Combat* died quietly, of malnutrition, in June, 1972.

Charitably looking the other way, however, and contemplating the finer side of Bill Buckley, *The New York Times* frequently invited him to write for its Sunday *Book Review*, and some of his pieces were excellent, especially when the book at issue was not political or otherwise tendentious. The same paper published his dissertation on Emile de Antonio's *Millhouse*, a documentary film anthology about the Nixons that left them flayed, and in this piece one could hardly recognise the Buckley who had launched into public castigation of the President whose pre-Presidential career he was so angrily defending against the unembellished truths presented by de Antonio. This was less important than the implication, in the very publication of the piece, that Buckley was by now the recognised voice of American conservatism.

The prestige of that recognition was immeasurably enhanced by *The New York Times Magazine*'s publication of Buckley's detailed recapitulation of what he considered to be Nixon's betrayal of his constituents and the conservatives—who had theretofore been largely equated—just five days after the nation-wide announcement that the cream of the conservative hierarchy had "resolved to suspend our support of the Administration." The declaration, issued in New York on 26 July 1971—Buckley's *Times* piece appeared in the issue of 1 August—was signed by twelve men, who gave their names, with their affiliations, in alphabetical order so that none could be assumed to have precedence. This is the text of their statement:

During the first two and one-half years of the Administration of President Nixon, we hoped that substantial headway would be made to reorient the country's policies, foreign and domestic.

We touch only lightly on the failures of Mr. Nixon's Administration domestically. It is a fact that we continue to have inflation and unemployment, excessive taxation and inordinate welfarism. It is also a fact that, notwithstanding the reforms he has proposed, and the excellent public servants whose aid he has enlisted, we continue to have an intolerable crime rate, an apathetic court system, and a Supreme Court given in certain matters to ideological abstraction.

These domestic considerations, important as they are, pale into insignificance alongside the tendencies of the Administration in foreign policy. Applauding though we do the President's steadfastness in resisting the great pressures upon him to desert Southeast Asia, we note:

1. His failure to respond to the rapid advance of the Soviet Union into the Mediterranean basin.

2. His failure to warn against the implications of the current policies of the West German government.

3. His overtures to Red China, done in the absence of any public concessions by Red China to American and Western causes.

4. *And above all*, his failure to call public attention to the deteriorated American military position, in conventional and strategic arms, which deterioration, in the absence of immediate and heroic countermeasures, can lead to the loss of our deterrent capability, the satellization of friendly governments near and far, and all that this implies.

In consideration of this record, the undersigned, who

have heretofore generally supported the Nixon Administration, have resolved to suspend our support of the Administration.

We will seek out others who share our misgivings, in order to consult together [Buckley should have deleted this redundancy] on the means by which we can most effectively register our protests.

We do not plan at the moment to encourage formal political opposition to President Nixon in the forthcoming primaries, but we propose to keep all options open in the light of political developments in the next months.

We reaffirm our personal admiration and—in the case of those of us who are his friends or who have been befriended by him—our affection for Richard Nixon, and our wholehearted identification with the purposes he has over the years espoused as his own and the Republic's. We consider that our defection is an act of loyalty to the Nixon we supported in 1968.

Jeffrey Bell, Capitol Hill Director, American Conservative Union

William F. Buckley Jr., Editor, *National Review*

James Burnham, Editor, *National Review*

Anthony Harrigan, Executive Vice-President, Southern States Industrial Council

John L. Jones, Executive Director, American Conservative Union

J. Daniel Mahoney, Chairman, New York Conservative Party

Neil McCaffery, President, Conservative Book Club [and Arlington House]

Frank S. Meyer, Editor, *National Review*

William A. Rusher, Publisher, *National Review*

Allan H. Ryskind, Associate Editor, *Human Events*

Randal C. Teague, Executive Director, Young Americans for Freedom

Thomas S. Winter, Editor, *Human Events*

None of these signers flinched in his brave resolve, nor did any of the organisations represented by the individuals. None would have ever had a good word to say for Woodrow Wilson, and all were branded by this document with the clear stigma of Wilsonism. To these chieftains of conservatism, clearly, it was their country's mission to carry the faith by fire and sword whithersoever the need beckoned, and to guide the errant foreigners back to the road of righteousness. It was an article of faith that the Mediterranean should be an American or, at most, a NATO lake, as the Indian and Pacific Oceans must be SEATO seas and the Atlantic belonged, with the Arctic and Antarctic, to NATO. It was equally an article of faith that other governments that were or wished to be our clients had no right to shape their own policies or in any way to lessen the international tensions that were being so diligently maintained by the two major powers. Thus the Social Democratic government of West Germany was guilty of betrayal in its efforts to arrive at a peaceable *modus vivendi* with East Germany, the other Soviet satellites, and the Soviet Union itself, with all of which it was seeking maximum freedom of intercourse within the community of nations. As for "the deteriorated American military position," that cumbersome hoax had been exposed repeatedly inside and outside Congress: every available reliable piece of evidence made it clear that the peace-loving United States, in spite of its record-breaking expenditures of weapons and explosives in its concern for peaceful enjoyment of freedom under its kindly Indochinese dictator, was still far ahead of every other nation in the world in its capacity for immediate and protracted further peace-keeping.

Buckley's own exegesis of "A Declaration" in his article for *The Times*, which, of course, obtained far wider circulation than his own *National Review* could have given it (the circulation ratio is about ten to one), eminently deserves consideration. Well into the body of the piece he quotes from an open letter by his brother-in-law Brent Bozell to American conservatives, and at no time does he speak ill of it. "Historians will differ," Bozell had written, "as to the moment when the movement you lead ceased to be an important political force in America. But there will be no one to dispute that it was all over by November, 1968, with Nixon's victory. This is because (1) Nixon in 1968 was your man, and (2) Nixon in 1968 had repudiated you." What Bozell meant, Buckley said, was that Nixon had rejected every distinctive feature of conservatism and yet the conservatives had knowingly supported him and thus become "powerless to affect his future course." Contemporary American conservatism, Bozell and Buckley said, had "four historical attitudes: anti-statism (as represented by Hoover and Taft); nationalism (as suggested by the name of

General MacArthur); anti-Communism, and constitutionalism, 'which [here Buckley was quoting Bozell] has never had a single champion of the stature of the others, but which may be recalled by thinking of Bricker, or more recently, Thurmond.* . . . On every front where your program has confronted secular liberal-ism's, you have been beaten. Consider your campaigns against big government, against Keynesian economics, against compulsory welfare; your defense of states' rights and the constitutional pre-rogatives of Congress; your struggle for a vigorous anti-Soviet foreign policy; your once-passionate stand for the country's flag and her honor.' " (This was the same Bozell who wrote two months later in *The Times* that advocates of population control "believe that the poor, helpless, despised and rejected should not have been allowed to be"; that the proof of their cruelty is the fact that "there is a little fellow in Bombay," whose "stomach is swollen" and who lives in wretched squalor: "the demographic mind eyes him and observes it would be better had his father been sterilized, or his mother aborted him—or, better still, had he never been conceived. He disagrees"—Bozell knows this, as he knows that the boy "was wanted by his maker, and probably by his parents, and now he wants himself." So it may seem to the rich parents of ten children whom they can afford to send across the ocean to study.)

What perturbs Buckley even more than the high misdemeanors listed by Bozell is "Supreme Court decisions that transfer [*sic*] the First Amendment into an antireligious instrument of Bolshevik ruthlessness" and "the mysterious added difficulty of doing busi-ness." To judge by the contents of both the general and the financial press since 20 January 1969, every effort has been made by the Administration—and on the whole quite successfully—to maintain the solid reservoir of unemployment that is so often supposed to be good for the country, to prevent any rise in wages and salaries commensurate with rises in prices, to squelch impudent "consumerism," to assure steady increases in the cost of utilities,

---

* Senator John Bricker of Ohio, a Republican, had fought against every effort to involve government in any furtherance of the common good or restriction of economic oligarchy, and to largely negate the effectiveness of the United Na-tions and its conventions, charters, and treaties. Senator J. Strom Thurmond of South Carolina, the Democratic twin of Bricker and a vigorous white-suprem-acist, had formed the Dixiecrat Party in protest against evidence of common decency among the Democrats, and had then become a Republican and delivered the nominating speech for Nixon at the 1968 convention.—C.L.M.

to vitiate any movement toward expensive or even inconvenient measures for reducing pollution, and to see to it that the Justice Department does not interfere with monopolies, cartels, segregation, or any other aspect of the status quo whose desirability is notified to it by the business community. As for the sorcery ascribed to the Supreme Court's decisions, Buckley does not say and no living seer can guess what these may be.

Buckley exhumes a bit of pre-1968 history by way of grounding what he is about. For instance, in a car in Central Park in 1967 Nixon told Buckley: "Barry Goldwater found out you can't win an important election with only the Right Wing behind you. But I found out in 1962 that you can't win an election without the Right Wing." Earlier, in his home in New York—in December, 1966—Nixon had told Buckley and other, unnamed friends that Ronald Reagan was a serious contender for the nomination; but "the American Right, almost all of it, never anticipating a serious bid by Reagan, agreed to go with Nixon until he lost a primary." Thus Nixon arrived at Miami backed by "John Tower, Strom Thurmond, Barry Goldwater, *National Review* and *Human Events*," against which combination Reagan could not successfully appeal to conservatives, who, obviously, dominated the convention. "There are those," Buckley said, however, "who believe that with the defeat of Reagan in Miami Beach, the American Right changed permanently. And that, sensing this, Richard Nixon went busily to work undermining the structural positions of the Right."

To the philosophic mind all things are possible, even the supposition of substance in Richard Nixon; even the imputation of a certain fetal Machiavellianism, if only for the sake of speculative entertainment. Buckley, however, and many more like and unlike him believe that neither Nixon nor any other man in his station ever acts otherwise than on the promptings of reason and ideology; but they do not offer their theory as to the reason and ideology that instigated and justified this great betrayal that they profess to discern. They are consistent, to a degree, though, because they propose, in a kind of tabloid Skinnerism, to offer—as Buckley does in his *New York Times* homily—some such persuasion (or warning) for the President should he seek re-election. Buckley pointed out that "the pressures mount against him by the same Right Wing whose backing only a few years ago Mr. Nixon acknowledged as indispensable."

To American conservatives, it is the responsibility of the United

States "to intervene where necessary to prevent a crucial aggrandizement (here and there there would be differences on whether
the aggrandizement was crucial or merely incremental) in the
power of realistic potential aggressors: in brief, the Soviet Union
and China. . . . The question now is truly planted: is what we
Americans have so markedly superior to what the Soviet Union
has as to warrant (1) the expenditure of $80 billion per year on
the military, and (2) a foreign policy based on an explicit preference for the risk of nuclear war, over against submission?" Buckley's answer to both parts is *Yes,* and Nixon's had better be: "If
Mr. Nixon comes forward saying, bluntly, that his program for
—if you like—American rearmament could mean the difference
between life and death for America itself, could mean the difference between the continued independence of the Middle East and
of Western Europe, and their satellization by the Communist
powers, he will have the American Right. The whole of it." The
Right, Buckley implies, can be persuaded to forgive its fallen
angel most of his domestic ineptitudes, "provided there is no suspicion—none at all would be tolerated—that Mr. Nixon has been
taken in by the other side's reveries," which Buckley alleges to be
based on the notion that the Communists have been morally redeemed: a superstition that must be collapsed by Richard Nixon
(one falls unconsciously at times into Buckley's rhetoric) "if the
suspicion widens, as it is now doing, that he indulges it; and the
tactical question is, how long can he postpone doing so, before
the American Right comes to the conclusion that he is not one
of us?"

Nothing is easier than to disagree with almost everything that
Buckley has said, and especially with all that he has left unspoken,
in this essay. But one *must* be happy that he wrote it and that *The
Times* published it. Some of the cards, at least, had been played;
one could begin to surmise what might still be in the hand. One
could know how sympathetically, six months later, Buckley would
read what his monarchist friend, Erik v. Kuehnelt-Leddihn, was
to write in *National Review* about West Germany and the West
in general: "The churches were once sources of authority. Army
and church traditionally worked together. The church, like the
army, had a tradition of service, sacrifice, altruism and *obedience*
[emphasis added]. Officers, priests and ministers often came from
the same families. Today the churches have become sources of
subversion, falsifying the message of the Gospel."

Buckleyan conservatism is prepared to set that right. It has every right to make such pretensions: a Buckley has at least as much entitlement as a Kennedy or a Lindsay, or, for that matter, as sorry a figure as a Humphrey—or any demagogue, black or white—to offer his ideas, if not himself, for his nation's leadership. And that is precisely what the Buckleys, with the assistance of the best of circumstances, are at last in a position to do, as they have so long wanted and believed themselves endowed and ordained to do. And, being conservatives, they initiated their activist phase in a conservative fashion, addressing themselves to the duly constituted authorities. Thus too did the Founding Fathers before they made their war of national liberation, because they too were conservatives.

XXII

EARLY IN DECEMBER, 1971, there were reports in the newspapers that Representative John Ashbrook of Ohio, who had been a Republican Congressman for more than ten years, might enter some of the early primaries in 1972 as a candidate against Nixon for the party's Presidential nomination. In the middle of the month Nixon vetoed the "wildly radical" child-development bill; subsequently there were reluctant avowals that the Ashbrook rumors had been instrumental in the President's action. At the end of the month—on 29 December—Ashbrook formally announced his entry into the New Hampshire and Florida primaries, scheduled, respectively, for 7 and 14 March. At the same time he indicated that, though his was a serious candidacy, he might renounce it provided that Nixon took four steps that would show his amenability to the conservatives: an early assurance that he would not dump Agnew, the relegation of the Family Assistance Plan to some legislative limbo, an increase in funds for arms development and in Presidential pressure on Congress for it, and a journey to Taipei, after Peking, for the purpose of reassuring Taiwan, or Formosa, that the United States had not deserted her. Ashbrook also ruled out an independent candidacy in the event of Nixon's renomination.

Almost three weeks earlier, on 9 December, J. Daniel Mahoney announced, in his capacity as its chairman, that the Conservative Party of New York, which had endorsed Nixon in 1968, was withdrawing its support, making clear "its over-all disappointment with the Nixon performance" and encouraging Ashbrook to enter the race. Mahoney and the other signers of Buckley's original personal suspension of support wanted Ashbrook to run as a

conservatives have done in the past." And the past, as Burke and his disciples had long since taught, was in all things superior to the present and the future and even the possible.

Mrs. Luce touched the core of the problem when she said that it was "sophomoric" of her "conservative friends" to expect any President to be able to fulfill all his promises. Presidents, she said, take over their defeated rivals' best issues. She was "amazed" that Nixon "has stuck as well as he has" to conservatism. What she did not say—what may or may not have occurred to her; perhaps she thought it impolitic to state at that time and in that situation —was that it was precisely this "sophomoric" purism of her "conservative friends" that was perilous. There were those who found sophomoric naïveté in the ideas and the demands and the arguments and the methods out of which the October Revolution grew, and they might have been right, but it is convictions, after all, that are always the most dangerous of all weapons in politics.

In conversation not long after this broadcast, James Buckley was more forthcoming. His brother and the Manhattan Twelve, as the signers of the July declaration were by now being called, were not seeking to get rid of Nixon, the Senator stressed: "A suspension of support is quite different from an active effort to defeat. I think it's an effort to dramatize the size and importance of the conservative constituency and the size of its concern so that the President will not be tempted to appeal to one group to the exclusion of another." But he was manifestly troubled by the distance to which the suspension of support had gone: "I have heard the proposal that somebody be entered in the New Hampshire primary described not again as a McCloskey-type operation, not an effort to destroy but rather a way of really dramatizing that there is serious concern." Asked whether, then, a sizable vote for Ashbrook would be presented to Nixon as a warning of conservatives' restiveness, he replied: "That is, I'm sure, the intention, but there are tremendous problems, which are why I personally am not in favor of this method of demonstrating. First, you may end up insufficiently demonstrating the size of that support because people will be saying: 'Obviously Nixon is not going to be deprived of the nomination, and we don't want him to appear weak when the alternative might be to elect [Senator George] McGovern. So the New Hampshire primary might accomplish quite the opposite of what it is intended to accomplish. Second, once you launch something like this, it's apt to get out of hand. You can't turn on or off something of this sort. It's apt to excite national attention."

James Buckley emphasised that he was speaking as "primarily a conservative—with a small c, a small c. I don't consider myself as part of any party apparatus." On an issue-by-issue basis, he said, he believed the majority of the country was composed of lower-case conservatives; if the Presidential election were held that January day in 1972, "a lower-case conservative candidate and platform would be more likely to win if the man and the issue were given proper ventilation. I think that Nixon is going to have an excellent chance of winning to the extent that he is able to telegraph the basic conservative values." This is corroborated by Burnham's assessment: "I think that it's possible that there is a kind of innate conservatism in the majority of the American people, though inchoate and not in a very conscious way, . . . but as an organized, conscious movement, no: conservatism is a minority view." There is no basis for any rational challenge to this analysis, which can probably be extended to any society: what we know and what we remember (or what we like to think we remember) are almost invariably to be preferred to what we can only surmise.

Though John Buckley was not a signer of the July declaration, he is emphatic in his adherence to it and in his view of Ashbrook as a lever with which to push Nixon back to where he belongs. He was careful in appraising the possible consequences of a refusal by Nixon to bow to the apparent lesson of a significant Ashbrook showing. In his view, such a refusal could damage Nixon in the election only if the Democrats had nominated a candidate who could be regarded as conservative, such as Senator Henry Jackson. John Buckley wants—and one finds this eminently reasonable—to see a new alignment of parties: a Left and a Right, as in Britain. But to him all radicals are of the Left by virtue of their radicalism: he would instance both Hitler and George Wallace. "The conservative element in this country," he said, "feels that it has been used and abused, by Nixon: used, to get him into the White House, and, once he was there, he went one hundred eighty degrees from his '68 program. People are sore, they're upset, they're confused." And the sentiments of the majority, he is convinced, are conservative.

The Buckleys and their friends are important enough in the

conservative sector—majority or minority—to have frightened Nixon and the run-of-the-mill hacks whose only concern is electoral success. Their reactions were typical of their trade: angry White House telephone calls expressed baffled resentment at Bill Buckley's sponsorship of Ashbrook: after all, the President's staff had appointed Buckley friends to important posts, and the President had himself moved to help James Buckley win election. Anthony R. Dolan, once a member of Senator Buckley's press staff, pointed out in *The New York Times* early in March of 1972 the extremely important fact that Nixon and people like him could not grasp, largely because it has become so rare in any aspect of American life from politics to publishing: the Buckley conservatives are concerned with beliefs, with principles, with—if the word is not too dirty—morality, for all their condescension to tactics of which, according to John Buckley, Bill Buckley's own wife at times disapproves. The conservatives have not compromised their integrity by exercising discretion in their rhetoric and their actions; but men like Nixon and John Mitchell cannot conceive integrity: their highest good is the deal that wins. The Buckleys are not only principled but stiff-necked, and the people whom they have attracted to their rather gallant venture for a cause that to others is repellent are of their own kind: they do not need success because their concern is ideas and principles, and for these they are quite willing to take great risks. Treated by wheeler-dealers as wheeler-dealers, they can only—and justly—be insulted. Dolan is right, then, when he warns the merchants of politics that "the opposition could grow from its present embryonic stage to full-scale revolt—a revolt far beyond the ability of Ashbrook or Buckley to control. If they really do seek to prevent this, Mr. Nixon and his advisers must realize that the origin of the growing conservative opposition is a principled one; it can be controlled only with reversals in Administration policy and not with the purely political threats or enticements one uses with a maverick precinct captain."

Ashbrook, forty-three years old at the time of his announcement of candidacy, had served six terms in the House of Representatives. He had been chairman of the American Conservative Union, a prominent figure in the Goldwater draft, and a militant in the conservative wing of the Young Republicans. He and Buckley were old friends. He had written for *National Review, Human Events, New Guard*, and similar publications, and he was artic-

ulate and thoughtful. Among the thirty-one thousand members of
the Conservative Book Club his popularity was exceeded only by
that of Goldwater, Reagan, Tower, and Bill Buckley; among what
for convenience one must call liberals he was regarded as one
of the most effective and intelligent men on the Right: but he
objected to their usually calling him ultra-conservative. Having
started at Harvard as a conservative, he said, he found his convictions immeasurably reinforced by his exposure to Schlesinger,
Galbraith, and Bundy; he took his law degree at Ohio State. In
1956, when he was twenty-eight, he won his first public office—
the legislative seat once held by his father—a year after he had
been elected, without opposition and through the cooperation of
two close friends from Harvard, to the chairmanship of the Young
Republican National Federation. The two Harvard friends were
Rusher and White, with whom he later cooperated in the Goldwater draft and the founding of the American Conservative Union.
Ashbrook is an active member of the Advisory Board of Young
Americans for Freedom and of the Executive Committee of Buckley's and Liebman's Committee of One Million Against the Admission of Communist China to the United Nations—a brand
name that is bound to make one laugh, but what is in that package
is rather less risible.

The conservatives had given Ashbrook a rating of ninety-eight
per cent for his votes in the House, where he was the author of
an amendment to an education bill that would have barred the
use of federal funds for the busing of school children. The importance of this is not his opposition to busing—which has been
very validly attacked on a number of grounds from a number
of points of view, by no means all of them Right-Wing—but his
desire to prevent school districts receiving federal funds from
exercising that local option for which as a general rule conservatives have taken to beating their drums. One is a little shaken
to learn that, when he is asked what is really happening in Washington, he quite seriously urges his inquirers to read *Human
Events*; but then Buckley too has allowed his name to be used
in its advertisements. Ashbrook, apparently, like Buckley, really
believed that Nixon would base his actions as President on the
principles that he had put forward as the basis for his election,
and consequently his disillusion was sharp—and quick: it set in
and began to be made public as early as March of 1969, because
of "the President's failure, so far, to clean out the State Depart-

ment." Foreign policy and domestic economics completed Ashbrook's disaffection (yet, even after he had been entered in primaries, he indicated that he might ultimately back Nixon for re-election).

The candidacy frightened Nixon and his friends, who made desperate *démarches* to Buckley, Rusher, and Ashbrook himself, and even promised "concessions"; but Ashbrook had already said: "I do not believe his [Nixon's] statements" in the broad areas of government policy in general and economics in particular. Buckley said in his column that "Mr. Ashbrook's entry into the race is the expression of an *élan vital* in the conservative movement, which has been strangely muted during the past several years in Congress." *The Washington Post*, which is anything but conservative, viewed Ashbrook's challenge as an intelligent means of achieving the conservatives' objectives and exerting pressure on Nixon to do more than make, if one may be permitted the redundancy, empty promises. Ashbrook hardly expected to be nominated, let alone elected; but he did expect to be re-elected to Congress. He was.

In the first two primaries he did not make any sensation. It was important to his backers that, as a Republican opponent of Nixon, he should do substantially better than McCloskey, and indeed he did, by as much as two-thirds. Still, in both New Hampshire and Florida, Nixon was decisively the winner—his eighty-seven per cent in Florida was reminiscent of our creature's ninety per cent in Vietnam, or the kind of endorsement that Hitler and Stalin used to manage. Ashbrook was sufficiently heartened, however, by his own ten per cent in New Hampshire and nine per cent in Florida to continue his candidacy through June, concentrating most of his effort and expenditure on Indiana, on 2 May, and California, on 6 June; his name was on the ballot in other states as well. But nowhere did he do better than in New Hampshire. Though Ashbrook's Florida vote was more than twice McCloskey's, it was well below the fifteen per cent that the conservatives had hoped to accumulate in the Republican primary.

Ashbrook was quite right when he said, the day after the Florida primary, that "the Florida vote, taking Democrats and Republicans together, proved my point that the electorate is more conservative than generally believed." Inasmuch as Wallace had got forty-two per cent—the largest single share—of the Democratic vote and Ashbrook and Nixon (who, it is true, is not a conservative—he is a *Luftmensch*—but who is nothing else either) together took ninety-six per cent of the Republicans, the conclusion is hardly startling. It remained to be seen, the year being still young, how many of those Wallace admirers who had voted for Nixon in 1968 as a *pis aller* would return to him in 1972 throughout the country, and how many new converts he could make. It was indeed ironic that, as Ashbrook also remarked, "the people voted for the issues I've been talking about—busing and school prayer—but somehow this was translated into votes for Mr. Nixon and not me." One major reason, of course, might well have been the fact that Ashbrook's total campaign expenditure in Florida was about eight thousand dollars, whereas the President will not say how much he spent in Florida and New Hampshire or where the money came from. It is generally assumed that a single Nixon mailing in Florida accounted in itself for more than fifty thousand dollars.

On the day after the Florida primary Bill Buckley provided what seemed—but was not—definitive evidence of rupture with Nixon: he refused reappointment to the Advisory Commission of the USIA. "Taking all factors into account," he wrote, he could not serve three years more; he felt that he had already given the USIA as much counsel "as I have to give it." Indeed, one had long wondered whether and how he would have been able to do otherwise, given his own sharp sense of fitness and the consistently harsh criticism that he had been directing against the President for six months, with waspishness that intensified during Buckley's presence on Nixon's visit to China and that grew steadily nastier after his return to the United States. But he has never lost sight of his cause, which is paramount and for which he can cheerfully dispense with scrupulosity: barely two weeks after the release of his letter to Nixon and the conventional "Dear Bill" reply, subscribers to *National Review* found their magazine mailing labels being used by the Finance Committee for the Re-Election of the President. The arguments put forward by Nixon's first Secretary of Commerce, Maurice H. Stans, who was chairman of the committee, emphasised that the President "has brought us out of a devastating war and set us on the path to peace"—only a few days after Nixon had ordered the indefinite suspension of the Paris peace talks—because "he has helped bring back law and order to America" and because "he has halted the runaway inflation he inherited from the Democrats, and has helped return America to a sound fiscal economy, which will mean better living for all."

It is most interesting that Buckley's letter of refusal was sent to Washington from his vacation home in Switzerland. **According to** *The New York Times,* he was unavailable for comment, though one had thought *The Times* was rather well staffed in Geneva, which is not far from where the Buckleys ski. Nor did *The Times* note the label coincidence. One day, perhaps, the "liberals" may understand how stupid it is to give so little notice to what one does not like.

It remained questionable, however, just how much good it had done the man of principle in the White House among conservatives—always titillated by such as Wallace—to start moving, even before the first primary, from sanctimonious mealy-mouthing to the kind of action that represented at least something of a victory for the Buckley group. First there was Nixon's veto of the child-development legislation; then there was his re-endorsement of Agnew—which was aptly described in a political column as further evidence of Nixon's "habit of making calculating gestures of appeasement to the Republican Right when it grows restive." As of mid-March, however, Agnew told journalists that Nixon had not yet invited him to join the 1972 ticket; nor was he mentioned in Stans's appeal, though it hailed the President's Supreme Court appointees by name because they "can be expected . . . to protect the interests of the average, law-abiding American." Suddenly, too, Nixon took new interest in augmenting appropriations for what he and the rest of the politicians still have the gall to call "defense." Among the most significant appeasements of the Buckleyan conservatives was Nixon's designation of one of the most unsavory of the paladins of the Right, Richard Kleindienst, to be Attorney General when Mitchell resigned to manage the 1972 Presidential campaign. Kleindienst had long been marked by overt racism (in act if not in word), an affection for large corporations (especially those that contributed generously to his party) that was not quite platonic, and a cavalier contempt for civil liberties.

But probably the most important evidence of the power of the conservatives was Nixon's characteristically sneaky attempt in late March to destroy school busing of every kind under the pretense and pretext of not doing so. One need be neither a black nationalist nor a white supremacist to recognise the multiple valid arguments against busing, the best of which is that busing is typical of the short-sightedly self-serving superficiality that—like Agnew's preference for punishing the arrested rather than "agonising over the causes of crime"—attacks symptoms and allows diseases to flourish. But it has always been manifest that the conservatives' opposition to compulsory busing was not exclusively thus grounded and that the blue-collar hard-hats hated busing because of a prejudice against blacks and Latin Americans quite as vicious as the more urbane conservatives' prejudice against poverty: their concern for the possible psychological dislocations to be suffered by the ghetto children was not quite so great as their preoccupation with the inviolability of their own compounds, nor was their great philosophical principle of central as against local determination of social issues. It is more manifest still that Nixon was not even aware of any issues at all except that of re-election: he could hear the howls and see the people flocking to the man who speaks his secret self, George Wallace. So he threw another sop with his disingenuous plan for a legislative moratorium on busing while plans were elaborated to extirpate it altogether without a constitutional amendment to that effect. There was, after all, more than one argument against amendment: the best, from the conservatives' point of view, was not their philosophical objection to bigger government but simply the length of time that would be required for the amendment process to be completed.

The New York Conservative Party had formally announced support for Ashbrook's candidacy. Speaking for the unanimous executive committee, Mahoney made complete sense: "The Ashbrook candidacy is the only effective protest against the wayward policies of the Nixon Administration on national defense, Red China and Taiwan, runaway spending and deficits, wage-price controls and welfare." What Mahoney did not mention was what the Buckleys and the other conservative leaders had long demanded: that the President and Congress, or at least the President, act to hamstring the judiciary.

The Buckleys were pleased by this interference with any judicial enforcement of unwelcome laws—so much for pious talk about governments of laws rather than of men; but they at once attacked Nixon's corollary proposal of an Equal Education Opportunities Act that would provide funds for the improvement of inferior—in practice, all-black—schools. *The New York Times* opposed this too, but on a much better ground: that virtually everything in this new proposal already existed in the Elementary and Secondary Education Act of 1965, which required merely to be enforced.

The Buckley conservatives attacked Nixon's proposal on the automatic basis of states' rights, of course. But what they objected to fundamentally, as Bill Buckley has written consistently over the years, was the whole concept of equal opportunity, to say nothing of equality. The notion that all men are born equal has always been an object of their ridicule; and, interpreted literally, it is indeed pitiably vulnerable to every verbal caricature. But as Buckley and his growing army know quite well, it was never so meant: it meant and means that every man has the same rights —not privileges—as every other man. It is this principle that the Buckley conservatives contest, on the ground that the more diligent, the more talented, the more God-fearing, and the more fortunate have on that account rights that do not enure to the commonalty. This deliberate refusal to distinguish between rights and privileges is coupled with the refusal to concede the dangers inherent in a society based on privilege, which is by definition exclusivist.

Always hopeful though not always sanguine of success in their determination to force Nixon back to the Right, the Buckleys had to face simultaneously the extinction of Ashbrook's candidacy leverage and the sudden (and, as the Buckleys had loudly assured themselves, impossible) surge of McGovern's on the other side. The day after the California primary in June, Ashbrook announced that he would no longer seek convention delegates— he had acquired none; instead, he would take to the convention platform committee in August his fight for "the principles that made our party great . . . these survival issues. . . ." One day after that James Buckley announced that he would campaign for Nixon's re-election, and he bade his followers to do likewise, whether as Republicans or as Conservatives. The Conservative Party did not at once signify its fealty; but at the end of August (after the Republican Convention), the Conservatives formally adopted the Republicans' candidates and electors. But Buckley, noting that Nixon had lost New York State in 1960 and 1968, predicted that, with the Conservatives' backing, Nixon would win the state in 1972. Buckley's only real objections to the President were his so-called economic controls and the agreements on strategic-arms limitations.

Bill Buckley, ten days later, analysed Ashbrook's campaign in his column and found that, while it had incited no great rebellion on the Right against Nixon, it had shown Nixon the danger of a crystalisation of public opinion against him if he did not stop improvising and adopt Ashbrook's positions. That Ashbrook does represent a force stronger than the votes for him would indicate is indeed probable, but one may wonder whether Buckley was right in predicting that, without Ashbrook's help, "Mr. Nixon has had it." All things considered, the Buckleys would of course have to embrace Nixon again, however gingerly, if the Democrats chose McGovern; and the Conservatives' frantic effort to prevail on the Democrats to nominate anyone but McGovern would lead one to believe that they would have been relieved by such an eventuality because they could then in good conscience have seen no possibility of a lesser evil in November.

National Review was so frightened of McGovern (the Conservatives always overestimate the electorate) that it devoted an entire section to violent attacks on him by various hands, rejoicing in such unprincipled compromises as he began to accept in order to succeed and ridiculing what idealism he seemed to be preserving. In the opinion of *National Review,* McGovern's nomination threatened economic collapse, military defeat, and spiritual and sexual degeneration almost immediately; it was all the more important, the magazine made plain, to force Nixon back to Ashbrook's "four major survival issues": "failure to restore military superiority," the appeasement of the Communist bloc, the federal budget deficits, and Nixon's proposal for a guaranteed annual income, which, Ashbrook and Buckley believed (or anyway said), would add twelve to fifteen million people to the welfare rolls and "reinforces the concept that welfare is a way of life." McGovern, as Buckley wrote in his column after the Democratic Convention, was the choice of "a convention that sometimes seemed to be saying that the most you can do for your country is evade the draft, smoke pot, abort your babies, have a homosexual affair, and receive, in return for nothing at all, a thousand dollars a year from your fellow-citizens." Nixon was bad enough, but, "if McGovernism triumphs, nobody will ever be off the public payroll." Apparently the Democrats had not seen the handwriting on the full-page advertisements across the country the day before their convention opened. In these expensive broadsides forty-five signers, led by Bill Buckley, his *National Review* colleagues, and Mahoney, warned that the nation must elect only a man who subscribed to rugged individualism, as it used to be called, a forever free economy, curbs on the courts, and more and better mass-murder machines.

James Buckley's name was not listed. Ten days after this advertisement's appearance, he and the Conservative Party demanded in the most urgent terms that Nixon keep Agnew for another term; the party, indeed, announced that otherwise it could not support the President. No one suggested an acceptable alternative; those who envisaged James Buckley in the post seemed prepared to wait four years. The Senator himself proclaimed Agnew "something of a folk hero to millions of middle Americans"— and, tragically, he was completely correct. Meanwhile, in another of those delightful illustrations of high political principle, Governor Rockefeller agreed to be the chairman for Nixon's New York State campaign; he gave his blessing to an alliance between Republicans and Conservatives, and he named that other maculate tribune of the people, Jacob Javits, one of his two vice-chairmen: the second was James Buckley. Javits had suggested that Agnew be dumped, but he had done so just strongly enough to be able to get it on the record for display to his "liberal" constituents: he would not, he said, actively oppose Agnew. Of course not: he knew James Buckley was right about the man's standing with the rednecks; *National Review* was even more enthusiastic; and Javits was a loyal servant of his party, at any rate. He was quite ready to lend himself to the detestable bloc appeals: "Mr. Javits," to quote *The New York Times*, "presumably could be useful in the Nixon campaign's effort to woo liberal Republican and Jewish votes in the larger cities." Buckley was already the darling of those blocs that have historically been least wavering in the ranks of the Mugwumps—one does not like the fact of this bloc/Mugwump concatenation, but one can hardly pretend it out of existence. Nonetheless one must point out that Buckley had always avoided any deliberate ethnic or religious theme except in his rival pitch for Israel as a touchstone for eligibility to public office in the United States. In spite of his normal aversion to public appearances—an aversion that has no doubt been inevitably eroded to some degree by circumstance—he crammed his autumn schedule with speeches on behalf of the President and his re-anointed Vice President. Agnew, Buckley said, must be elected President in 1976.

In the closing weeks of August, 1972, the two dominant Buckley brothers, with whatever apprehensions, conjured their big and little conservatives to keep Nixon and Agnew: the palace revolt was hardly a memory, trotted out as the Republican Convention opened so that there might not be a second defection by the prodigal. On the first day of this questionable spectacular, it was announced that "the Administration" had selected Senator Buckley to make the seconding speech after Governor Rockefeller had placed Nixon's name in nomination. That same day, *National Review* subscribers received the issue of 1 September, with an editorial of a curious cast and a seven-page anthology of "real" Republican statements culled from Nixon speeches and party platforms of other years, such as Nixon's vow never to allow "Red" China to enter the United Nations. The editorial itself said that the magazine's "editors prefer the re-election of Richard Nixon and Spiro Agnew next November." Then it asked itself: *"Faute de mieux?"* and answered itself: "This is not the season to be churlish." Clearly, the Buckley conservatives, like the majority of Americans, were so badly frightened by George McGovern (as indeed everyone ought to be, though for far different reasons) that almost anything would do, even their unreliable whilom knight. At least he could be relied on to see that for four more years there would be no risk of power to the people if they were foolish enough to keep him on the public payroll.

Late in September of 1972 rather detailed word about another facet of the Buckleys' precautionary crusade against McGovern got out. Youth Against McGovern was formed in Washington, with an address that was also a mail drop for YAF—which supplied about half the initial membership of Youth Against McGovern, according to its executive director, Ken Tobin. He did not give figures. But he did claim credit for many anti-McGovern demonstrations at airports. What is especially interesting, moreover, is the fact that the chairman of this new group, which said it had already raised twenty-five thousand dollars and was hoping to triple or quadruple the amount, was Christopher T. Buckley, whose father is William F. Buckley Jr. Francis Donahue need not have worried about the young man, who was just starting his second year at Yale: the dynasty was in no danger of extinction.

Privilege and exclusivism are what Buckleyan conservatism is principally about. Like almost all such bodies of political/social thought, it has the magic quality of making everyone who is attracted to it feel that it is not he who is excluded: there is a note here or a note there in it that will give it appeal to everyone, and it is indescribably easy to believe that it is oneself who is that better, more desirable person who is being exhorted to protect himself against the unworthy horde, whether one is a new millionnaire or a crew-cut dock-worker with a two-family house in Queens. The solidity of identity achieved and established, rooted in millennia, is what is by implication offered to the new majority, the white non-Anglo-Saxon conglomerate that has begun to find a voice and a leader corps that offers it, in those leaders' own term, a new order, the security of an absolute, remarkably reminiscent of that other new order that was seemingly defeated in war a generation ago and is resurgent where it flourished before and where in the past it had never taken root—especially in France and Britain and the United States. In all these countries these new leaders have the same common cause and present the same common danger.

What, then, is to be done about these dangerous men? Morally, only one course is possible (though to expect Americans to understand, let alone care, what morality is is naïve): to give them every opportunity to express their views. If my enemy has less right than I to be heard, then neither he nor I has any rights.

And it is the "practical" side of that proposition that must be urged on Americans, since that is all that they understand: let the enemy be heard. That enemy to the contrary, truth, or what is taken for truth (there being, that enemy to the contrary again, no absolutes), will prevail: not all the lions of Rome were able to save the world from what is called Christianity, and not all the napalm—or even all the *Trinkgeld*—of Washington will be able to save anything from what is called Communism. Even the most cynical of observers—and, by definition, this is supposed to exclude the conservatives, and in especial the Buckleys—cannot seriously contend that ideas can be overcome other than by ideas, that logic can be altered, or justice be done, or men be redeemed, by repression. Men can be exterminated, perhaps; but not the Thousand-Year Reich, the dictatorship of the proletariat, or even the Holy Inquisition has been able, for example, to affect the quality of heterodoxy. Heretics can be wiped out; heresies are immortal.

Bigotry, exploitation, fear, and greed are equally invulnerable

Principal Bibliographical References

FERGUS REID BUCKLEY, *Eye of the Hurricane* (New York, 1967).

PRISCILLA L. BUCKLEY AND WILLIAM F. BUCKLEY JR., editors, *W.F.B.—An Appreciation* (New York, 1959); *Maureen Buckley O'Reilly: 1933–1964* (New York, 1968).

WILLIAM F. BUCKLEY JR., *God and Man at Yale* (Chicago, 1951); *UP From Liberalism* (New York, 1959); *Rumbles Left and Right* (New York, 1963); *The Unmaking of a Mayor* (New York, 1966); *The Jeweler's Eye* (New York, 1968); *The Governor Listeth* (New York, 1970); *Cruising Speed* (New York, 1971); *Inveighing We Will Go* (New York, 1972).

———, editor, *The Committee and Its Critics* (New York, 1962); *Odyssey of a Friend* (New York, 1970); *Did You Ever See a Dream Walking?* (*American Conservative Thought in the Twentieth Century*), New York, 1970.

WILLIAM F. BUCKLEY JR. AND L. BRENT BOZELL, *McCarthy and His Enemies* (Chicago, 1954).

Dialogues in Americanism (Chicago, 1964).

BENJAMIN R. EPSTEIN AND ARNOLD FORSTER, *The Radical Right* (New York, 1966).

ARNOLD FORSTER AND BENJAMIN R. EPSTEIN, *Danger on the Right* (New York, 1964).

DAVID FRANKE, editor, *Quotations from Chairman Bill* (New Rochelle, 1970).

ALOISE BUCKLEY HEATH, *Will Mrs. Major Go to Hell?* (New Rochelle, 1969).

NELLIE D. KENDALL, editor, *Willmoore Kendall Contra Mundum* (New Rochelle, 1971).

FERDINAND LUNDBERG, *The Rich and the Super-Rich* (New York, 1968).

J. DANIEL MAHONEY, *Actions Speak Louder* (New Rochelle, 1968).

FRANK S. MEYER, editor, *What Is Conservatism?* (New York, 1965).

RICHARD M. ROVERE, *Senator Joe McCarthy* (New York, 1959).

SENATE FOREIGN RELATIONS COMMITTEE HEARINGS, *Investigation of Mexican Affairs* (Washington, D.C., 1920).

STEPHEN SHADEGG, *What Happened to Goldwater* (New York, 1965).

MARK SHERWIN, *The Extremists* (New York, 1962).
LOUISE TANNER, *Here Today* . . . (New York, 1959).
EDWARD BENNETT WILLIAMS, *One Man's Freedom* (New York, 1962).

And the files of *The Freeman, Human Events, National Review, National Review Bulletin, Combat, New Guard, Triumph; Catholic World, Commonweal, America; Group Research Report, The New York Times,* etc.

INDEX

Abortion issue, 144–145, 146, 148, 176, 257, 314
Academic freedom, Buckleys and, 67–68, 76–77, 79–80, 83–84, 94–95, 101. See also *God and Man at Yale*
Actions Speak Louder (Mahoney), 203, 228
Adenauer, Konrad, 124, 316
Adler, Larry, 82
Advocates, The, 129, 322
AFTRA, 194–197
Age of Suspicion (Wechsler), 118
Agnew, Spiro, 4, 7, 169, 172, 205, 297, 334, 347
Allen, Steve, 155, 274
Almirante, Giorgio, 5, 6
America, 102, 191, 205
America First, 27, 88, 138
America Is in Danger (LeMay), 268
American Association of Mexico, The, 15, 18
American Civil Liberties Union, 81, 106, 115–116, 128, 140, 170, 193–196, 197, 221, 248
American Conservative Thought in the Twentieth Century (W. F. Buckley Jr.), 270, 275–286
American Conservative Union, 135, 175, 199, 280–281, 308, 310, 340
American Conservatives Confront 1972, 336
American Federation of Television and Radio Actors, see AFTRA
American Mercury, The, 88, 91, 97, 120, 126, 223
American Nazi Party, 248, 252
American Opinion, 105, 126, 199, 236
American Stock Exchange, 38–40
American Veterans Committee, 78, 81–82
Amnesty International, 214–215
Anderson, Alan S., 41
Anderson, Tom, 236

Anti-Communism: of American and European conservatives, 6; and Brent Bozell, 66; of Buckleys, 3, 67, 100–101, 120, 139, 141–142, 160–161, 216, 220; and conservatism, 185, 325; of John Birch Society, 236
Anti-Semitism, 27, 59, 120, 241, 310
Arlington House, 104–105, 143, 157, 158, 267–268
Ashbrook, John M., 171, 173, 294–295, 298, 306, 308, 334–336, 337, 338, 339–342, 344–346
Atkinson, Ti-Grace, 73, 146
Atlantic Monthly, The, 91, 96, 270
Atlas Shrugged (Rand), 277, 315

Baldwin, James, 241, 246
Baldwin, Roger, 129, 144, 193, 214, 215
Baroody, William Sr., 222, 223
Beame, Abraham, 229, 235, 239, 241, 247
Beatles Book, The, 269
Bell, Jeffrey, 328
Bellow, Saul, 91
Benenson, Mark, 214–215
Benson, George Stuart, 125
Bentley, Elizabeth, 36
Berman, Ronald, 312–313
Black, Algernon D., 248
Blacks, William F. Buckley Jr.'s attitude toward, 54–55, 80, 189, 212, 230, 233, 246–247, 253–254, 256
Blanding, Sarah Gibson, 67–68, 79
Blue Book (Welch), 236
Boehm-Bawerk, Eugen von, 323
Bolan, Thomas A., 151
Borghese, Marchese Valerio, 5, 6
Borland, Hal, 119
Bouchex, Jeanne, 52
Boyd, James, 262–263
Bozell, L. Brent, 87, 113, 118, 123, 124, 126, 144, 145, 146, 148, 154, 157, 185, 186, 199, 268, 318, 319, 320, 329, 330;

Bozell, L. Brent (*Cont.*)
  Barry Goldwater and, 222–223; career of, 143–148; on conservatism, 319–320; on Constitution, 281–282; as debater, 59–60; influence on William F. Buckley Jr., 61–62; John Buckley on, 143; leaves *National Review*, 315; and *McCarthy and His Enemies*, 102, 106; as *National Review* writer, 128; at Yale, 54, 62, 65–67
Bozell, Leo B. Jr., see Bozell, L. Brent
Bozell, Patricia Buckley, 49, 87, 123; on American Catholics, 147; attack on Vassar, 100–101; career of, 143–148; personality of, 152; religious and political views of, 145–147; and Sarah Gibson Blanding, 67–68; and Ti-Grace Atkinson, 146. See also Buckley, Patricia
Bracher, Karl Dietrich, 302
Bricker, John, 330
Bronson, Frances, 208–209
Browder, Earl, 103
Brown, Marion, 41
Brozen, Yale, 310
Brudnoy, David, 322
Buckley, Aloïse Steiner, 20, 23, 24, 27, 28, 65, 140, 154; description of, 20, 22, 29; influence on her children, 29–30; politcal views of, 50; and publication of *God and Man at Yale*, 96–97; and religion, 25; and YAF, 170, 175
Buckley, Aloïse, 20, 21, 24, 45, 49, 87; education of, 53, 54; and *National Review*, 129–130; writings of, 138–139. See also Heath, Aloïse Buckley
Buckley, Ann (Mrs. James Buckley), 140, 154
Buckley, Ann (Mrs. John Buckley), 140, 154
Buckley, Betsey Howell (Mrs. F. Reid Buckley), 99, 151, 154
Buckley, Carol, 20, 29, 45–46, 87, 153–154. See also Learsy, Carol Buckley
Buckley, Christopher Taylor, 7, 71, 348
Buckley, Claude, 12
Buckley, Edmund, 12
Buckley, F. Reid, 10, 20, 45, 49, 70, 154, 217; career of, 99–100, 151–153; in childhood, 44, 47, 52; as debater, 59; Francis Donahue on, 71–72; on his father, 23; letters to *Yale Daily News*, 75, 83; marries Betsey Howell, 86–87; and *National Review*, 130; Rollin G. Osterweis on, 87; at Yale, 44, 56, 65, 66, 80, 87–88, 99
Buckley, (William) Hunt, 136

Buckley, James, 1, 20, 70, 82, 86, 87, 117, 141, 199, 229, 231, 263, 289, 322; on anti-Semitism, 27; and Catawba Corp., 31, 42; Charles Goodell on, 299–302; in childhood, 24, 43, 47, 52; description of, 137, 298–299; early career of, 35; elected to Senate, 1, 2, 204, 212, 247, 302–305; and family business interests, 100, 137; first Senatorial campaign, 265; and Forest Hills housing fight, 310; goals of, 6–8; and National Endowment for the Humanities, 312–313; personality of, 8, 236; political ambitions of, 313–314; political views of, 295–296, 314; and 1972 Presidential election, 299, 335, 337–338, 345, 347, 348; and radio broadcasts to Soviet Jews, 312; Richard Nixon and, 299, 311, 314; and Richard Ottinger, 304; Senate record of, 306–312; Senatorial campaigns of, 142, 215, 290–292, 296–298; trip to Southeast Asia, 313–314; on William F. Buckley Jr., 305–306; and YAF, 169, 171, 172–173; at Yale, 53, 56, 65
Buckley, Jane, 20, 46, 51, 87, 139–140, 149. See also Smith, Jane Buckley
Buckley, John (grandfather), 10–11
Buckley, John W., 20, 28, 31, 49, 61, 86, 168, 231, 303–304, 305, 339; and Catawba Corp., 37; in childhood, 47, 52; education of, 53; and family business interests, 35, 41, 42; on federally financed day-care centers, 312; marries Ann Harding, 66; personality of, 140–143; on Second World War, 50
Buckley, Maureen, 20, 45, 49, 52, 87, 129, 139, 151, 153. See also O'Reilly, Maureen Buckley
Buckley, Patricia, 20, 24, 46, 51; and Brent Bozell, 54, 66–67; on Patricia Taylor, 86; at Vassar, 54, 73. See also Bozell, Patricia Buckley
Buckley, Patricia Taylor (Mrs. William F. Buckley Jr.), 86, 88, 154, 339
Buckley, Priscilla (sister of William F. Buckley Sr.), 11
Buckley, Priscilla, 14, 20, 24, 42, 49, 51, 87, 100, 129, 140, 166, 303, 304, 305; as managing editor of *National Review*, 128, 133, 134, 136–137; personality of, 139; and William F. Buckley Jr.'s Mayoralty campaign, 228
Buckley, William F. Jr., 20, 24, 46–47, 48, 49, 148, 149, 205, 303, 314, 340; on abortion issue, 144; and academic freedom, 68, 76–77, 79–80, 94–95; and Adam Powell and Thomas Dodd

cases, 150–151; American Civil Liberties Union and, 193–197; on American Nazi Party, 252–253; and Amnesty International, 214–215; on assassination of Martin Luther King Jr., 305; and Barry Goldwater's Presidential campaign, 220, 221, 222–223; and Brent Bozell, 66–67; and boating, 50, 117, 167; as candidate for post in Yale Corporation, 264; as chairman of *Yale Daily News*, 69–85; in childhood, 43–44, 46, 52; choice of protégés, 4, 261; and commercial broadcasting interests, 265–267; compared with James Buckley, 299, 300; compared with Willmoore Kendall, 317; as debater, 59–61, 63–65, 72, 114–117, 155–156, 253–254, 258–260; and 1972 Democratic Party Convention, 346; and Edgar H. Smith Jr., 213–214; on education, 54, 76 ff., 168; education of, 22 ff., 46; and equal opportunity concept, 345; and ethnic vote, 234, 309–310; family creed and, 1–2; father's influence on, 49; on First Amendment, 106; and Francis Donahue, 70–72; and Frank Meyer, 183, 319–320; and Frederick A. Hayek, 90, 132–133, 323; and *Firing Line*, 249–257; goals of, 6–8, 287–289; and Gore Vidal, 51, 146, 272–275; graduates from Yale, 84–85; and guaranteed annual income proposal, 346; and Harry Elmlark, 207–212; impact of mass media on, 155–156, 207, 256–259; on impact of 1965 Mayoralty campaign, 247–248; and inception of Conservative Party, 202; and start of newspaper column, 207–213; on internal fights of Conservative Party, 324–325; on Irish Catholic background, 10; James Buckley on, 305–306; and James Buckley's Senatorial campaign, 290; James A. Wechsler on, 119–121; on John Ashbrook's campaign, 346; and John Birch Society, ix, 199, 236–237; Karl Hess and, 223–224; on "liberal Establishment," 226; libel suit against Artie Shaw, 231–234, 304; and McCarthyism, 103–107; marries Patricia Taylor, 86; on mass values, 225; "maturing" of, 120; Mayoralty campaign of, 142, 180, 212, 215, 225–247; Michael Harrington on, 188–189; moral character of, 198–199; Murray Kempton on, 117–118; and Murray Rothbard, 183–185; and *National Review*, 110–113, 123–137,

315–325; as *New York Times* writer, 326–330; and "On the Right," 213–218; and Otto von Habsburg, 185; and Pentagon hoax, 320; personality of, 8–9, 46, 65, 101–102, 211, 271, 288; political development of, 55–56; political viewpoint of, 3, 219–220, 275–283, 288–289, 291–292; and 1972 Presidential election, 336, 348, and see also Ashbrook, John M.; as public figure, 98–99, 205–206, 231; and publication of *God and Man at Yale*, 88–95; and publication of *McCarthy and His Enemies*, 104–106; publishing interests of, 267–268; and racial discrimination, 83, 167 ff., 211, 232–233, 287; and Reid Buckley, 44, 82–83; and Revilo P. Oliver, 148, 199–200; and Richard Nixon, 3, 4, 108, 173, 213, 220–221, 292–295, 311, 334–335, 348; Robert Yoakum on, 304–305; on rock music, 266; Rollin G. Osterweis on, 59–60; and Roman Catholic encyclicals, 182–192; Ronald Hamowy on, 205; and Roy M. Cohn, 4, 108–109; schedule of, 211, 269, 287; and scholarships for blacks, 54–55, 80; on segregation, 167–168; speech at Holy Name Society breakfast, 229–231; suit against AFTRA, 194–197; supporters of, 180, 225; on Supreme Court decisions, 330–331; and Thomas Dodd, 261–263; and Thomas Emerson, 62–64, 96, 140; threatens suit against Gordon Hall, 121–122; and U.S. Advisory Commission on Information, 3, 265, 293–295, 342–343; and *UP From Liberalism*, 156–165; on Vietnam war protesters, 247, 305; and Whittaker Chambers, 107–108, 109–113, 271, 315–316; and William F. Rickenbacker, 181–182; William Rusher and, 129; and Willmoore Kendall (q.v.), 56–58, 61, 62, 74; writes for *American Mercury*, 88–120; writing career of, 165–166, 216–220, 269–272; and YAF, 171–172, 178–181; at Yale, 54–56, 58–63, 72–73, 75–76, 79–85

Buckley, William Frank Sr., 10, 88; background, 10–11; business career of, 31–42; Douglas Reed on, 35–36; early career in Texas and Mexico, 11–12; early years in Sharon, Conn., 20, 21; and education, 28–29; expelled from Mexico, 13, 18–19; and *God and Man at Yale*, 96–97; influence on family, 100–101; and Juan Vicente Gomez, 32; and Lend-Lease, 50; and

Buckley, William Frank Sr. (*Cont.*)
Mexican politics, 12–19; marries Aloïse Steiner, 20; and Maureen Buckley, 149; and *National Review*, 112; proposes private school, 28–29; real-estate ventures of, 14–15; rejects military governorship of Vera Cruz, 14; relations with his children, 22–26, 47–49; as student, 11; testimony before Senate subcommittee, 15, 16–19; wealth of, 19; and Second World War, 27–28

Buckley family: ambitions of, 6–8; American beginnings of, 10–19; and anti-Communism, 3, 141–142; attitudes toward public office, 53; attitudes of Sharon residents toward, 26–28; and Barry Goldwater's Presidential campaign, 220; and China policy, 314; combativeness of, 138 ff.; compared with Kennedy family, ix–x, 4, 23, 53, 118; and Conservative Party, 5, 142–143; creed of, 1–2; danger of, x, 6, 53, 219, 348–350; education of children in, 21–24, 101; family loyalty of, 2, 25, 43, 45; financial status of, 31–42; and *Grelmschatka*, 49–50; influence on William F. Buckley Jr., 82–83; Karl Hess on 223–224; as leaders of American conservatism, ix; and local Sharon activities, 140; and lower-middle-class supporters, 4–5; and Marvin Liebman, 201; Michael Harrington on, 188; Murray Rothbard on, 187; and *National Review*, 124–137; and *New York Times*, 324; reasons for public support of, 7–9; relations among members of, 45–48, 51–52, 154; William B. Coley on, 21–22, 23–24; and Second World War, 50–51; and YAF, 168–174, 175, 177, 178, 180–181

Buckleyan conservatives, see Conservatism; Conservatives

Bundy, McGeorge, 91, 96, 340

Burke, Edmund, 9, 112, 143, 186, 278–279, 282, 283, 323

Burnham, James, 5, 57, 68, 73, 91, 98, 105, 110, 111, 113, 124, 128, 132, 133, 157, 176, 185, 187, 197, 226, 237, 242, 268, 316, 319, 320, 324; on Communist threat, 285–286; on Greek régime, 214; on John Birch Society, 237; and *National Review*, 131–132

Burnham, Philip, 128

Caldwell, Taylor, 171

Calles, Plutarco Elías, 19

Canada Southern Petroleum, Ltd., 34, 40

Canso Natural Gas, Ltd., 34, 35

Canso Oil Producers, Ltd., 34, 35

Capouya, Emile, 259

Capp, Al, 4

Caribbean Enterprises, Inc., 167

Carlin, William J. C., 72, 76, 77

Catawba Corporation, 28, 31, 36–38, 39, 41

Catholic Worker, The, 188, 189

Catholic World, The, 102, 105, 190–192, 205

Central Intelligence Agency, 49, 87, 100, 197

Chagrin et la pitié, Le (Ophuls), 350

Chamberlain, John, 90, 91, 97, 100, 110, 111, 124, 128, 157, 166, 171, 183, 186, 316

Chamberlin, William Henry, 226

Chambers, Whittaker, 36, 107–108, 109–113, 116, 120, 157, 261, 270, 315; on Ayn Rand's philosophy, 277–278; on civil liberties, 169–170; on Joseph McCarthy, 107; and *National Review*, 110–113, 277, 315–316; William F. Buckley Jr. on, 271

Charlton, Thomas J., 154

Cherne, Leo, 252, 253

Chiang Kai-shek, 269, 314

China, Richard Nixon's policy on, 3, 111, 168, 342

Chodorov, Frank, 99, 124, 183, 202, 271

Chomsky, Noam, 231, 253, 254, 273

Chou En-lai, 213, 221

Christian Anti-Communist Crusade, 104, 250

Christian Commonwealth Institute, 145, 146–147

Churchill, Winston, 168, 202, 208

Civil liberties, conservatives on, 169–170, 181, 184–185, 252–253

Civilian Review Board issue, 248

Clancy, William, 189

Clark, John Abbot, 99, 124

Clark, Mark W., 171

Clark, Ramsay, 212–213

Coastal Caribbean Oils, Ltd., 34, 40

Coffin, Henry Sloane, 97

Coffin, William Sloane Jr., 58, 60, 73, 97, 120, 172, 253, 257

Coffin, Mrs. William Sloane Sr., 58, 59

Cohn, Roy, 4, 108, 119, 151, 261

Coley, Peter, 22, 44, 52, 298

Coley, William B., 21, 46, 52, 64, 117, 298

Colley, Nathaniel S., 74

Combat, 325–326

Commager, Henry Steele, 127
Commentary, 158, 196
Committee and Its Critics, The (W. F. Buckley Jr.), 197–198
Committee of One Million Against the Admission of Communist China to the United Nations, 104, 202, 340
Commonweal, 102, 128, 185, 189, 205, 230, 270
Communist Party, 79, 103, 109, 183, 198, 319
Conscience of a Conservative, The (Goldwater), 222
Conservatism, 275–283; atheism and, 278–281; Buckleys as leaders of, ix, 127–128; and European Right, 5–6; future of, 348–350; growth of, 5–9; Jerome Tuccille on, 325; Murray Rothbard on, 185–187; philosophers of, 323–325; religion and, 205; rise of, 2–3; and Russell Kirk, 320–321; Whittaker Chambers on, 111–112; William F. Buckley Jr. on, 219–220. See also Conservative Party; Conservatives
Conservative Book Club, 143, 268, 328, 340
Conservative Mind, The (Kirk), 98–99
Conservative Party of New York State, 6, 108–109, 175, 188, 199, 328; and Buckley family, 5, 142–143, 306–307; Declaration of Principles of, 203–204; and electoral politics, 225–229, 236, 242–247, 265, 334–350; growth and perspectives of, 204–205; origins of, 200–203; relations with James Buckley, 313
Conservatives: attitudes toward Nixon, 173; attitudes toward YAF, 177–178; and civil liberties, 184–185; on foreign policy, 332–333; and George McGovern, 346–348; increased communication among, 175; Jewish, 135, 310; on liberalism, 157–158; power of, 343–344; and 1972 Presidential election, 334–348; and referendum on Civilian Review Board, 248; and Richard Nixon's trip to China, 111; ruptures among, 324–325; and two-party system, 292; and William F. Buckley Jr.'s withdrawal of support for Nixon, 327–329. See also Conservatism; Conservative Party
"Convenient State, The" (Wills), 282–283
Cooley, Ann, 100. See also Buckley, Ann Cooley
Corrigan, Kevin, 88–90, 190–191

Corporation for Public Broadcasting, 129, 209, 250–251
Costello, Timothy, 240
Coudert, Frederic R. Jr., 238
Coudert Brothers, 32, 41
Crime in America (Clark), 212–213
Crocker, George N., 197, 198
Cross and the Flag, The (Smith), 204
Cruising Speed, A Documentary (W. F. Buckley Jr.), 133, 144–145, 148, 165, 200, 207, 209, 270, 287, 289
Cultural and Scientific Conference for World Peace, 67–68

Davis, Angela, 13
Davis, Clyde Brion, 118
Day the Market Crashed, The (Rogers), 267
Deceitful Peace: A New Look at the Soviet Threat (Niemeyer), 268
Dellums, Ronald V., 211, 255, 258
Denny, George V. Jr., 118
Dewey, John, 93, 226
Dewey, Thomas E., 63, 75
Did You Ever See a Dream Walking? (W. F. Buckley Jr.), 270
Dimes, Edwin K., 234
Do It! (Rubin), 267
Dodd, Thomas, 4, 66, 150, 151, 253, 261–264, 303, 304
Doheny, Edward L., 16
Dollar Growth Library, 268
Donahue, Francis, 70–72, 348
Dos Passos, John, 157, 284
Draper, Paul, 82
Dreele, W. H. von, 134–135, 177–178, 305
Drug problem, 176, 246, 301
DuBois, L. Clayton, 29, 154, 175
Duggan, Lawrence, 36

Eastman, Max, 57–58, 91, 97, 98, 110, 124, 130, 278, 283, 284, 315
Edison, Charles, 175
Education: of Buckleys, 21–24, 28–29; Buckleys on, 83–84, 152, 168; conservatives on, 286–287
Efron, Edith, 267
Eisenhower, Dwight D., 29, 84, 107, 111, 113, 149, 163, 164, 179, 184, 257
Eliot, Charles Luke, 76
Eliot, T. S., 220, 230, 321
Ellsberg, Daniel, 213
Elmlark, Harry, 207–212, 216, 270
Emerson, Thomas I., 62–64, 65, 79, 81, 95, 96, 140
Enemies of the Permanent Things (Kirk), 268

Equal Education Opportunities Act, 344–345

Esquire, 167, 233, 270, 274

Ethel Walker School, 46, 47

Ethnic vote, 238–239, 309–310, 347

European Right, 5–6, 289

Evans, Medford, 124

Evans, M. Stanton, 124, 175, 197, 315

Eye of the Hurricane (R. Buckley), 99, 152–153, 252

Facts Forum, 120, 130

Family Assistance Plan, 312, 334

Federal Bureau of Investigation, 79, 82, 212

Federal revenue sharing, 308–309

Fellows, Harold E., 256

Ferguson, Mrs. DeLancey, 140, 141, 303–304

Ferman, Irving, 197, 198

Fernandez, Ramon, 225

Firing Line, 7, 107, 178, 189, 209, 269, 273, 289, 294; financing of, 250; guests on, 258–260; inception of, 249–251; and National Review, Inc., 125; organization of, 251–252; reasons for popularity of, 256–257

Forest Hills issue, ix, 301, 310

Fourth House, The (Rickenbacker), 182

Franco, Francisco, 80, 168, 185, 219, 304

Franke, David, 267, 268

Franke, Holly, 267

Frawley, Patrick, 250

Freedom and Reality (Powell), 268

Freeman, Neal, 209, 238

Freeman, The, 67, 97, 100, 111, 166

Friedan, Betty, 257

Friedman, Milton, 130, 283–285, 323–324

Fulbright, J. William, 175

Fullman, Christopher E., 102–103

Furtwängler, Wilhelm, 76

Galbraith, John Kenneth, 116, 117, 273n, 287, 340

Gavin, William F., 293–294

Genovese, Eugene, 315

German Dictatorship, The (Bracher), 302

Gieseking, Walter, 76

"God and Man at *National Review,*" (Corrigan), 190–191

God and Man at Yale (W. F. Buckley Jr.), 49, 56, 64, 78, 86, 87, 88–95, 99, 101, 102, 108, 114, 120, 121, 123, 141, 161, 264, 317

Goldbloom, Maurice, 214, 215

Goldwater, Barry, 21, 106n, 141, 157, 171, 179, 201, 220, 222–223, 226, 236, 297, 298, 312, 331, 340

Goldwater, Barry Jr., 171

Gomez, Juan Vicente, 32, 36

Goodell, Charles, 297, 299–302

Goodman, Paul, 242

Governor Listeth, The (W. F. Buckley Jr.), 216, 270, 271–272, 275

Graham, Billy, 257

Great Ideas Today, 269

Great South Bay (R. Buckley), 152

Greenfield, Jeff, 210–211, 252, 253–254

Grelmschatka, 49–50

Gresham, William Lindsay, 206

Guinzburg, Thomas H., 59, 73

Gun-control issue, 142, 301

Gunning, Rosemary, 238

Haag, Ernest van den, 142, 286–287

Habsburg, Otto von, ix, 185, 289

Hall, Gordon, 121–122

Hammarskjöld, Dag, 132, 132n, 167, 176

Hamowy, Ronald, 205

Harding, Ann, 66. See also Buckley, Ann Harding

Harper, Fowler, 64, 82, 231, 304

Harrigan, Anthony, 328

Harrington, Michael, 4–5, 155, 188–189

Hart, Jeffrey, 112, 133, 279

Hart, Merwin K., 88

Harvard Crimson, 82, 114, 121–122

Hayek, Frederick A., 89, 90, 130, 132–133, 141, 176, 283, 323, 324

Hazelton, Nika, 134

Hazlitt, Henry, 91, 283, 285

Heath, Aloïse Buckley, 11, 48–49, 52, 128, 138–139. See also Buckley, Aloïse

Heath, Benjamin W., 37, 41, 42, 154

Heath, Edward, 136

Heath, James, 46

Hefner, Hugh, 254, 258

Henry Regnery Co., 88, 90, 104, 107, 197

Hentoff, Nat, 195

Herberg, Will, 135, 186

Hess, Karl, 88, 124, 128, 130, 175, 187, 197, 223–224, 324, 325

Hess, Stephen, 312

Himes, Joseph H., 32, 34

Hiss, Alger, 107, 109, 213

Hitler, Adolf, 50, 93, 146, 242, 274–275

Holmes, Oliver Wendell, 106, 226

Holy Name Society, 229–231, 232, 234

Hook, Sidney, 7, 186

Hoover, Herbert, 95, 329

Hoover, J. Edgar, 79, 82

Horowitz, William, 264
House Un-American Activities Committee, 66, 104, 131. See also *Committee and Its Critics*
Howell, Betsey, 86–87. See also Buckley, Betsey Howell
HUAC, see *Committee and Its Critics*; House Un-American Activities Committee
Huerta, Victoriano, 13, 15
Human Events, 108, 126, 135, 175, 199, 219, 308, 311, 312, 323, 328, 331, 340
Humanae Vitae (Pope Paul), 190
Humphrey, Hubert, 159, 292, 333
Hunt, H. L., 120, 130
Hutchins, Robert Maynard, 160, 219
Hutchinson, Ward, 50–51
Huxley, Elspeth, 135

Income and Employment (Morgan), 96
Intercollegiate Society of Individualists, 124, 183–184, 202, 205
Inveighing We Will Go (W. F. Buckley Jr.), 182, 216, 270

Jackson, David Sidney, 38–39
Jackson, Jesse, 256
Jaffa, Harry V., 106, 106n
Javits, Jacob, 200, 202, 203, 240, 290, 292, 297, 307, 347
Jeweler's Eye, The, A Book of Irresistible Political Reflections (W. F. Buckley Jr.), 216, 221, 270
Jews: definition of, 10; of Forest Hills, ix, 301, 310; and *National Review*, 183
JFK: The Man and the Myth (Lasky), 268
John Birch Society, ix, 7, 104, 105, 124, 125, 147, 171, 197, 199, 200, 201, 237, 248; Barry Goldwater and, 222; *National Review* and, 199, 236–237; on poverty, 236; and William F. Buckley Jr., 316
John XXIII, Pope, 144, 189, 190, 192, 272
Johnson, Hewlett, 75
Johnson, Lyndon B., 21, 201, 211, 264, 293
Johnson, Sam, 211
Jones, John L., 328
Jones, Sam, 128
Jordan, K. Ross, 42

Kamschatka, 28, 29, 52
Kearful, Francis J., 16–18
Keating, Kenneth, 227
Keller, James A., 149

Kelley, Dr. Charles, 222
Kempton, Murray, 116, 117–118, 121, 158–159, 168, 215–216, 234, 245, 258, 315
Kendall, Willmoore, 56–58, 61, 62, 64, 74, 82, 87, 98, 102, 105, 106, 107, 110, 112, 126, 128, 157, 183, 197, 198, 226, 270–271, 282, 316–318
Kennedy, John F., 21, 108, 199–200, 333
Kennedy, Joseph P., 27
Kennedy, Raymond, 76–78, 92
Kennedy, Robert, 2, 108, 227, 252, 296, 297, 302
Kennedy family, 6, 178, 179; compared with Buckley family, ix–x, 4, 23, 53, 86, 118
Kent State, 121, 309
Khruschchev, Nikita, 145, 184, 201
Kilpatrick, James Jackson, 135
King, Dr. Martin Luther Jr., 230, 304, 305
Kirk, Russell, ix, 7, 68, 91, 98–99, 110, 112, 124, 128, 153, 163, 171, 199, 220, 268, 279, 280, 315, 316, 317, 320–321, 322, 324
Kitchel, Denison, 222, 223
Klein, Julius, 262
Kleindienst, Richard, 343
Kline, Robert, 249–250, 251
Kneller, Dr. George F., 59
Knowland, William F., 128, 171
Kohlberg, Alfred, 104, 125
Kohler, Herbert Sr., 175
Kolko, Gabriel, 186
Ku Klux Klan, 26, 304
Kuehnelt–Leddihn, Erik v., 124, 135, 332
Kuhn, Irene Corbally, 29–30, 139, 171
Kunstler, William, 253, 255, 309

La Follette, Suzanne, 110, 124, 128, 166, 316
Lakeville Journal, The, 28, 49, 50, 118, 119, 138, 139, 141, 142, 302–305
Lakeville Journal Opinions Unlimited, 118
Larmon, Sigurd S., 293
Lasky, Victor, 108, 268
Learsy, Carol Buckley, 45, 136. See also Buckley, Carol
Learsy, Ray, 154
Lejeune, Anthony, 135–136, 201, 289
LeMay, Curtis, 268
Lend-Lease, 27–28, 50
Leo, John, 230–231
Leo XIII, Pope, 103, 190
Lequerica, José Felix, 79–80
Lerner, Max, 258

"Let the Rich Alone" (W. F. Buckley Jr.), 221, 271
Levet, Richard, 274
Levy, Leonard, 276
Lewin, Dr. Ralph A., 59
Libel litigation, Buckleys and, 114, 121–122, 141, 231–234, 274–275, 304
"Liberal Establishment," 115, 226
Liberal Party, 200, 247, 297
Liberalism: Its Meaning and History (Schapiro), 162–163
Libertarianism, 184, 187, 325
Liberty or Democracy (Kuehnelt-Leddihn), 135
Liebman, Marvin, 103–104, 168, 169, 171, 175, 200–202, 238, 250, 269, 325
Life, 1, 90, 91, 270
Lindbergh, Anne Morrow, 50, 242
Lindsay, David, 229
Lindsay, John V., 53, 108, 227–229, 235, 236, 240–241, 247, 248, 252, 264, 333
Loeb, William, 171
Loyalty in Government Employees (Emerson), 140
Luce, Clare Boothe, 148, 247, 253, 258, 315, 336, 337
Luce, Henry, 90, 315
Lundberg, Ferdinand, 19
Lynd, Staughton, 257, 258
Lyons, Eugene, 88, 124, 135, 268, 325

MacArthur, Douglas, 90, 130
McCaffery, Neil, 328
McCall's, 45, 153–154
McCarthy, Joseph, 4, 76, 90, 97, 102, 104, 107, 108, 111, 114, 116, 125, 128, 151, 160, 166, 185, 197, 210, 261, 263, 274–275, 303, 304. See also *McCarthy and His Enemies*; McCarthyism
McCarthy, Mary, 100, 255
McCarthy and His Enemies (W. F. Buckley Jr. and Bozell), 104–106, 114, 118–119, 141, 143, 268
McCarthyism: and William F. Buckley Jr., 103–107; Willmoore Kendall on, 318; and *Yale Daily News*, 76. See also McCarthy, Joseph
McCloskey, Paul, 335, 341
McCormick, Edward, 31, 39
McCullough, Hester, 82
Macdonald, Dwight, 116, 117, 258
McFadden, James, 149
McGovern, George, 337, 345, 346–348
Mackenzie, Ross D., 197, 198
McMahon, Francis E., 191
McMillan, Miles, 216
Maguire, Russell, 120, 223

Mahoney, J. Daniel, 200–201, 202, 203, 228, 237, 248, 328, 334–336, 344, 346–347
Mailer, Norman, 153, 155, 206
Manion, Clarence, 171
Mano, D. Keith, 322
Mao Tse-tung, 213, 221
Marrecco, Anthony, 254
Martin, William McChesney, 264
Marx, Groucho, 258
Marx, Karl, 93, 143, 159, 283
Mater et Magistra (Pope John), 190, 192, 205
Matthews, Rev. Dr. J. B., 131, 160
Mencken, H. L., 15, 88, 149, 182, 186, 257
Meng, John, 193
Mexico, 11–19
Meyer, Frank S., 110, 113, 124, 128, 133, 152, 157, 183, 184, 185, 201, 226, 237, 266, 270, 275, 280–281, 285, 312, 318–319, 324, 328; Conservative Party and, 201, 203–204; and Pentagon hoax, 320; on own rôle in Communist Party, 319; William F. Buckley and, 319–320
Mill, John Stuart, 198, 321
Millhouse (de Antonio), 326
Mises, Ludwig von, 130, 268, 283, 323, 324
Mitchell, John, 4, 343
Mitchell, Jonathan, 124
Montgomery, George S. Jr., 32, 33, 34, 37–38
Morgan, Theodore, 96
Morris, Robert, 129
Movimento sociale italiano, 5, 6, 289
Mosley, Sir Oswald, 242, 267
Moynihan, Daniel Patrick, 186
Mundt, Karl, 171
Murrow, Edward R., 159, 305
Myra Breckenridge (Vidal), 272, 274

Nathan, George Jean, 88
National Endowment for the Humanities, 312–313
National Renaissance Party, 248
National Review, 5, 14, 35, 50, 58, 78, 90, 99, 105, 120, 121, 142, 153, 155, 165, 175, 180, 189, 197, 199, 208, 209, 217, 219, 221, 228, 231, 241, 269, 275, 277, 279, 293, 300, 304, 306, 308, 311, 312, 328, 329, 332, 342, 347; and abortion issue, 148; and ACLU, 193; and Adam Powell and Thomas Dodd cases, 150–151; advertisements for, 253; beginnings of, 110–113; and

Brent Bozell, 143, 144; Buckleys as writers for, 129–130, 138–139; business operations of, 133–137; and Catholics, 148, 192; on China policy, 168; and *Combat*, 325–326; Conservative Party candidates and, 226; credo of, 123, 127; and Dag Hammarskjöld's death, 132–133; early associates of, 130–131; editorials on Spain, 168; and Ernest van den Haag, 142, 286; on European Right, 289; fifteenth-anniversary party, 70; financing of, 125–126; and *Firing Line*, 125, 250, 251; first issue of, 128; influence of, 2, 179; initial staff of, 124; and John Birch Society, 199, 236–237; Karl Hess and, 223–224; lectures by staff of, 322–323; libel suits against, 231; premises of, 167; and Maureen Buckley, 149 ff.; Max Eastman and, 278; Murray Rothbard and, 184–187; ownership and control of, 124–126; and "Pentagon Papers hoax," 216, 320; personnel changes at, 315–323; and 1972 Presidential campaign, 173, 346–348; Publisher's Statement, 124–125, 127; and radio station KOWH, 265; Revilo P. Oliver and, 200; Richard Nixon and, 331; Robert Yoakum on, 303–305; staff of, 166, 183; subscribers to, 335; supporters of, 166; and Thomas Dodd, 263; Whittaker Chambers's resignation from, 277; William F. Rickenbacker and, 181–182; William Rusher and, 128–129; and YAF, 171, 176

National Review Bulletin, 131, 132, 142, 165, 167

National Review, Inc., 125, 216

National Stock Exchange, 31–32, 40

National Weekly, The, 110

Neier, Aryeh, 194–195, 196, 258, 322

New Class, The (Djilas), 113

New Guard, The, 174, 176, 270

New York Daily News, 91, 200, 225, 238, 241, 297

New York Herald Tribune, 230–231, 335

New York magazine, 195, 266, 307

New York Post, 116, 120, 159, 160, 209, 230, 258

New York Review of Books, The, 225, 242

New York Times, The, 19, 37, 90, 119, 127, 141, 151, 153, 154, 159, 175, 185, 195, 214, 223, 230, 238, 264, 270, 287, 314, 319–320, 324, 325n, 330, 343, 347

New York Times Magazine, The, 29, 175, 326–332

News Twisters, The, (Efron), 267

Newsweek, 108, 272

Nichols, Louis, 82

Niemeyer, Gerhart, 124, 268

Nixon, Richard M., 4, 6, 97, 121, 128, 133, 169, 178, 179, 197, 200, 201, 209, 258; China policy of, 213, 311, 314; conservatism and, 292–293, 320, 331, 343–344; on electoral rôle of Right Wing, 331; James Buckley and, 297–298, 299, 306, 308–309, 312; John Ashbrook on, 340–341; and John Ashbrook's campaign, 171, 346; on John Birch Society, 316; and McCarthyism, 104; Marvin Liebman and, 201; and 1972 Presidential election, 334–348; and William F. Buckley Jr., 2–3, 108, 220–221, 293, 295; William F. Buckley Jr. on, 326–330; and YAF, 172, 173–174

Nock, Albert Jay, 61, 149, 156, 166, 182, 186, 257

"Notes Toward an Empirical Definition of Conservatism," (W. F. Buckley Jr.), 270, 276–277

Novik, Morris, 293

Objectivism, 130, 277

Obregón, Alvaro, 12, 15–19

O'Doherty, Kieran, 200–201, 202, 227, 335

O'Dwyer, Paul, 290, 292

Odyssey of a Friend (W. F. Buckley Jr.), 270, 277

O'Hair, Madalyn Murray, 257

Oliver, Revilo P., 130, 148, 199–200, 236, 316

"On the Right," 335; content of, 213–218; origins of, 207–213; reaction to, 215–216

Ophuls, Marcel, 350

O'Reilly, Gerald, 129, 149, 154

O'Reilly, Maureen Buckley, 148–152. See also Buckley, Maureen

Ortega y Gasset, José, 68, 101, 106, 156, 157, 165, 224, 225, 259, 269

Osborn, Robert, 50, 141, 142

Osterweis, Rollin G., 59–60, 87, 95

Ottinger, Richard, 297, 299–300, 304

Paar, Jack, 220, 272–273

Paige, D. D., 12

Pancoastal Oil, 34, 40

Pan-Israel Oil Co., 34

Pantepec Oil Co., 19, 32–34, 38–40

Paolucci, Henry, 226, 227, 290

Paul VI, Pope, 189, 190
Pauling, Dr. Linus, 64, 231, 233
Pelaez, Manuel, 15, 16–17, 18
Pentagon documents, 320
Perez, Leander, 130, 253, 260
Permissive Society, The (Sokoloff), 267–268
Perry, Frank, 176
Philips, Judson, 140, 142, 303
Pierce, E. A., 32, 34
Pius XI, Pope, 103, 190
Playboy, 199, 254, 256
Police, conservatives on, 186–187, 230, 248
Poling, Rev. Daniel, 159
Pollution, conservatives on, 245–246
Ponce Pilate (Caillois), 221–222
Populorum Progressio (Pope Paul), 190
Powell, Adam Clayton, 150–151
Powell, Enoch, 135, 268
Powell, Lewis, 335
Progressive Party, 63, 67

Quadragesimo Anno (Pope Pius XI), 190
Quotations from Chairman Bill: The Best of William F. Buckley Jr. (Franke), 268

Racism, Buckleys and, 3, 12, 18, 210–211, 286–287
Rahv, Philip, 225
Ramparts, 184, 185
Rand, Ayn, 130, 177, 180, 182, 261, 277, 278, 315
Reader's Digest, 48, 57, 262
Reagan, Ronald, 133, 171, 172–173, 181, 182, 201, 312, 331, 340
Reasoner, Dean, 37, 41
Red Decade, The (Lyons), 268, 325
Reed, Douglas, 14, 19, 35–38, 88
Regnery, Henry, 88–89. See also Henry Regnery Co.
Rehnquist, William, 335
Reid, Fergus, 32, 34
Religion: Buckleys and, 3–4, 11, 25, 75 ff., 102–103, 145–147, 190–191; conservatism and, 205, 278–281; and YAF members, 176, 181
Republican Party, Conservative Party and, 200, 202, 292–293, 296–298, 306–307
Rerum Novarum (Leo XIII), 190
Revolt Against the Masses (W. F. Buckley Jr.), 269
Revolt of the Masses (Ortega), 165, 225

Rich and the Super-Rich, The (Lundberg), 19
Rickenbacker, William F., 181–182, 197, 198
Robinson, Carol Rhoades, 24–26
Rockefeller, Nelson, 200, 202, 203, 296–297, 347, 348
Rockwell, George Lincoln, 248, 252–253
Rodell, Fred, 64–65, 81, 82, 91–92, 96, 97, 123, 233
Roepke, Wilhelm, 124, 283
Rogers, Donald I., 267
Roosevelt, Eleanor, 159, 208
Roosevelt, Franklin D., 27, 28, 29, 60, 63, 101, 188, 283
Roosevelt, Theodore, 29
Roosevelt's Road to Russia (Crocker), 197
Rossiter, Clinton P., 316–317
Rothbard, Murray, 130, 175, 183–187, 223, 320, 324, 325
Rousselot, John, 171
Rovere, Richard M., 106, 143, 159, 226
Rubin, Jerry, 267
Rumbles Left and Right (W. F. Buckley Jr.), 216, 219–220, 275
Rusher, William A., 125, 128, 129, 133, 194, 296, 298, 300, 322, 340, 341; and *Advocates*, 129, 194, 322; and Barry Goldwater campaign, 223; and *National Review*, 125–126, 128–129; and William F. Buckley Jr.'s Mayoralty campaign, 228
Russell, Earl, 258
Russell, Francis, 275–276
Ryskind, Allan H., 328
Ryskind, Morris, 124, 128, 130

Safe Places (Franke and Franke), 267
Schapiro, J. Salwyn, 162–163
Schlamm, William S., 105, 110, 111, 112, 113, 124, 128, 130, 149, 236, 316
Schlesinger, Arthur Jr., 4, 116, 117, 127, 159, 340
Schoenman, Ralph, 258
Scott, Hugh, 306
Second World War, Buckleys and, 27–28, 50
Seeds of Treason (Lasky and de Toledano), 108
Senator Joe McCarthy (Rovere), 106
Servants and Their Masters (R. Buckley), 153
Sewall, Richard, 87–88
Seymour, Charles, 84
Seymour, Whitney North Sr., 170, 220
Shadegg, Stephen, 222–223

Shakespeare, Frank, 3, 293, 294, 312
Shapley, Harlow, 96
Sharon, Connecticut, 20–21, 26–28, 29, 43, 51, 140, 168, 302–305
Sharon Statement, 169–170, 175
Shaw, Artie, 231–234, 304
Sheehan, Susan, 45, 153–154
Shostakovitch, Dmitri, 67, 76, 79
Smith, Adam, 92, 143, 192, 226, 283, 299
Smith, Edgar H. Jr., 156, 213–214, 261, 269
Smith, Jane Buckley, 136, 141, 303. See also Buckley, Jane
Smith, Margaret Chase, 306
Smith, William F., 87, 136, 154
Social Security, conservatives on, 163–164, 204
Socialist Party, 4, 155, 188
Sokoloff, Boris, 267–268
Spock, Dr. Benjamin, 139, 201, 253, 258, 326
Stans, Maurice H., 342
Stanton, Dr. Frank, 293
Starr, Peter, 265
Starr Broadcasting Groups, Inc., 157, 167, 265–267
Steibel, Warren, 250, 251
Stevenson, Adlai, 159, 271
Steiner, Aloïse, 20. See also Buckley, Aloïse Steiner
Stone, George Norton, 25, 142
Strauss, Franz Josef, 316
Suicide of the West (Burnham), 268
Supreme Court, 166, 311, 330–331, 335, 343
Susskind, David, 250

Tablet, The, 102, 192
Taft, Senator Robert A., 84, 97, 329
Taylor, Patricia, 86. See also Buckley, Patricia Taylor
Teague, Randal Cornell, 147, 171–178, 211, 328
Thadden, Adolf von, 5, 6
Thomas, J. Parnell, 66, 263
Thomas, Norman, 155, 258, 260
Thurmond, J. Strom, 171, 182, 330, 331
Time, 28–29, 91, 109, 139, 186, 233, 257, 315
Time and Tide (Rhondda), 135
Toledano, Ralph de, 88, 105, 107, 108, 109, 110, 186, 197, 202, 219, 223, 296, 297, 319
Tower, John, 306, 331, 340
Triumph, 99, 124, 144, 145, 146, 148, 205
Truman, Harry S., 29, 63, 272
Tuccille, Jerome, 187, 324–325

Two-party system, 235, 291
Tynan, Kenneth, 131, 199

United Canso Oil & Gas, Ltd., 35, 40, 41
United States Information Agency, 2–3, 211, 293, 312; Advisory Commission on Information of, 293–294, 335, 342–343
United World Federalists, 54, 66
Unmaking of a Mayor, The (W. F. Buckley Jr.), 165, 216, 228, 241, 242, 270
UP From Liberalism (W. F. Buckley Jr.), 2, 156–165, 268, 279
Utley, Freda, 124, 128

Valenti, Jack, 201
Vance, Cyrus R., 264
Vassar College, 54, 100, 143
Vater, Edward, 126–127
Vecchione, Pasquale, 66
Vidal, Gore, 4, 51, 96, 131, 146, 172, 211, 272–275
Vietnam war, 3, 139, 186, 215, 237, 239, 291, 305, 308
Village Voice, The, 155, 195
Violence in the Streets (W. F. Buckley Jr.), 269
Voegelin, Eric, 145, 242, 279, 281, 282
Volkart, Edmund H., 77
Voucher system, 310–311, 324

Wagner, Robert F., 227
Wakefield, Dan, 167
Wall Street Journal, The, 1, 90, 196, 242
Wallace, De Witt, 325
Wallace, George, ix, 143, 181, 260, 300, 325, 335, 341, 342, 343, 344
Wallace, Henry, 56, 63, 67, 74, 140
Wallace, Lois, 218
Wallace, Tom, 218–219
War We Are In, The (Burnham), 268
Warren, Earl, 143, 166, 260
"Warren Court," 66, 156, 213
Warren Revolution, The (Bozell), 143, 147
Washington Post, 159, 335, 341
Washington Star Syndicate, 135, 207
Waugh, Alec, 135
Waugh, Auberon, 135
Waugh, Evelyn, 288
Wave of the Future, A Confession of Faith, The (Lindbergh), 50, 242
Weaver, Richard, 124, 182
Wechsler, James A., 116–117, 118–121, 127–128, 159, 193, 296, 319

Wechsler, Mrs. James, 120
Weil, Roman, 310
Weiss, Paul, 58, 72–73, 74, 81, 95, 99, 116, 120, 172, 210–211, 257, 258, 271, 292, 317
Weiss, Victoria, 58, 73
Welch, Robert, 125, 143, 199, 200, 236, 325
West, Rebecca, 258
W.F.B.—An Appreciation, 32, 47
What Happened to Goldwater (Shadegg), 222–223
What Is Conservatism? (Meyer), 270
White, F. Clifton, 297–298, 340
Wicker, Tom, 195
Wiggin & Dana, 35, 82, 86, 100
Will Mrs. Major Go to Hell? (Heath), 268
Wilhelmsen, Frederick, 145, 146
Williams, C. Dickerman, 128, 197–198, 233, 252
Williams, William B., 232
Willmoore Kendall Contra Mundum (Kendall), 270–271, 316n
Willoughby, Charles A., 130
Wills, Garry, 94, 130, 260, 282–283, 320
Wilson, Woodrow, 12–13, 328
Winchell, Walter, 38, 39
Winter, Thomas S., 328
Wisdom of Conservatism (Witonski), 322

Witonski, Peter, 322

YAF, *see* Young Americans for Freedom
Yale, 53–56, 58–66, 69 ff., 92
Yale Corporation, 97, 264
Yale Daily News, 44, 54, 56, 66, 68–85, 90, 96, 165, 197, 212, 218
Yoakum, Robert H., 140, 141, 142, 263, 263n, 303, 304–305
Young Americans for Freedom, 6, 95, 143, 147, 205, 308, 328; differences within, 175–176, 181; influence of, 5; James Buckley and, 7, 169, 171, 172–173, 311; and John Birch Society, 199; Marvin Liebman and, 168, 202; National Advisory Board of, 170–171, 340; and older conservatives, 177–178; organization and finances of, 174–175; and Richard Nixon's Presidential candidacy, 173–174; Sharon Statement of, 169–170; and William F. Buckley Jr., 7, 168–169, 171–172, 175, 178–181; and Youth Against McGovern, 348
Young Communist League, 103, 118, 169
Youth Against McGovern, 7, 348

Zhukov, Marshal, 163, 164
Zionists, 309–310